Classics of
Administrative Ethics

ASPA Classics

Conceived and sponsored by the American Society for Public Administration (ASPA), the ASPA Classics series will publish volumes on topics that have been, and continue to be, central to the contemporary development of public administration. The ASPA Classics are intended for classroom use and may be quite suitable for libraries and general reference collections. Drawing from the Public Administration Review and other journals related to the ASPA sections, each volume in the series is edited by a scholar who is charged with presenting a thorough and balanced perspective on an enduring issue. These journals now represent some six decades of collective wisdom. Yet, many of the writings collected in the ASPA Classics might not otherwise easily come to the attention of future public managers. Given the explosion in research and writing on all aspects of public administration in recent decades, these ASPA Classics anthologies should point readers to definitive or groundbreaking authors whose voices should not be lost in the cacophony of the newest administrative technique or invention.

Public servants carry out their responsibilities in a complex, multidimensional environment. The mission of ASPA Classics is to provide the reader with a historical and firsthand view of the development of the topic at hand. As such, each ASPA Classics volume presents the most enduring scholarship, often in complete, or nearly complete, original form on the given topic. Each volume will be devoted to a specific continuing concern to the administration of all public sector programs. Early volumes in the series address public sector performance, public service as commitment and diversity and affirmative action in public service. Newer volumes include equally important dialogues on reinventing government and public service ethics.

The volume editors are to be commended for volunteering for the substantial task of compiling and editing these unique collections of articles that might not otherwise be readily available to scholars, teachers, and students.

Books in This Series

Classics of Administrative Ethics

Edited by Willa Bruce
University of Illinois at Springfield

Westview
PRESS
A Member of the Perseus Books Group

Copyright © 2001 by Westview Press, A Member of the Perseus Books Group

Published in 2001 in the United States of America by Westview Press, 5500 Central Avenue, Boulder, Colorado 80301-2877, and in the United Kingdom by Westview Press, 12 Hid's Copse Road, Cumnor Hill, Oxford OX2 9JJ

Find us on the World Wide Web at www.westviewpress.com

Library of Congress Cataloging-in-Publication Data
A CIP catalog record for this book is available from the Library of Congress
ISBN 0-8133-9811-8 (pbk.)

The paper used in this publication meets the requirements of the American National Standard for Permanence of Paper for Printed Library Materials Z39.48-1984.

10   9   8   7   6   5   4   3   2   1

CONTENTS

ILLUSTRATIONS

INTRODUCTION

This book is a collection of classic articles about administrative ethics that have been printed in journals sponsored by the American Society for Public Administration (ASPA). Because their source is only ASPA, they do not represent every important article in the field. They do, however, represent the generative ideas that have guided thinking about ethics in public administration since the beginning of the first ASPA-sponsored journal—*Public Administration Review (PAR)*—in 1940 and present the work of the important scholars writing about administrative ethics, most of whom published in *PAR*.

To frame the book and its contents, it is necessary to define the terms "administrative," "ethics," and "classics," as used here. "Administrative" refers to those persons in positions of authority who carry on the business of government at the federal, state, local, or nonprofit level. They may be appointed or elected. They may be street-level bureaucrats, or they may be top-level executives. "Ethics" is the study of the nature of morals and moral choices and the rules governing a profession that define professional conduct. A "classic" is a publication that has stood the test of time and practice and is as relevant for today's world as it was for the time it was written.

The works in this volume are seminal to thinking about ethics in public administration. They form the basis for the development of thought and contain many of the original ideas from which current thinking about administrative ethics has developed. They span the years 1941–1985, those forty-four years being the time it took from publication of the first article about administrative ethics in an ASPA-sponsored journal to the completion of the first ASPA Code of Ethics and its implementation guidelines.

To be included in this volume, an article had to be about administrative ethics and meet both the definition of a "classic" and the following criteria: (1) it had to relate to administrators and not be about philosophical or political ethics, citizenship, policy, or government agencies per se; (2) it had to be important to the development of current thinking about administrative ethics; (3) it had to be about a topic that students of administrative ethics in the twenty-first century will need to know about and consider; and (4) it had to have been published between 1940 and 1985. In this book, articles are arranged according to the theme they represent. Within those book parts, they are arranged chronologically to give readers a perspective on the development of thinking on a particular ethical concern.

The perennial themes in administrative ethics that are represented by classic articles in ASPA-sponsored journals are organized in parts, as follows:

1. Administrative Responsibility
2. Solving Ethical Dilemmas
3. Corruption
4. Codes of Ethics
5. Enforcing Ethical Behavior
6. Ethics Education
7. Professionalism
8. Ethics in the Twenty-First Century

Each part begins with an introduction and brief discussion of the theme in administrative ethics that it represents. These sections contain the classic articles that represent the work of the finest thinkers in the field of administrative ethics. Although early ASPA publications contain several articles written by women about public administration, only two women published in the field of administrative ethics in an ASPA journal before 1985. Their work is included in this volume. Not surprisingly, archaic language permeates many of the articles, and the reader concerned with "political correctness" will be required to forgive several of the authors.

The period of 1940 to 1943 introduced the importance of including ethics in the canon of public administration. Prior to World War II, efficiency and technical competence were the guiding values of public administration—this was, after all, the time when the politics-administration dichotomy had lulled us into believing that public administrators were separate and apart from political decisions and their ramifications.

During the war years, we began to see how shallow and ineffective these kinds of values are. We had only to look at the atrocities committed by government employees in wartime Germany to realize that morality must enter into any decision calculus. Yet ASPA publications are surprisingly silent about issues of values and morals in the years during and immediately following World War II. It never occurred to the public administration community to question the purpose of the war or how it was conducted. This was true of Korea and Vietnam as well. Even though a vast bureaucracy was needed to carry on defense efforts, the war was like the elephant in the parlor—those who published in ASPA journals seem to have pretended it didn't exist and went about business as usual.

From 1943 until 1951, no one in an ASPA publication wrote about, reported on, or in any way acknowledged that ethics exist or should exist. During 1946, two Acts of Congress addressed improving the organization of government. The Administrative Procedures Act standardized many federal government managerial practices, and the Employment Act created the Council of Economic Advisors and declared full employment to be a part of federal government policy. In 1947, President Truman created the Hoover Commission to study and improve government operations, which was the impetus for passing the Budgeting and Accounting Procedures Act. Also in 1947, President Truman issued an executive order to establish a program to find and deal with subversives in the federal bureaucracy, and by the 1950s, Senator Joseph McCarthy had embarked on a crusade to find and eliminate "Communists" employed in government. People who wrote for ASPA seem to have been preoccupied with basic management rationality in government that left ethics aside until people outside of government began to talk about the "managerial mess"[1] in Washington.

The years 1952 through 1955 produced three articles and a book review about ethics in ASPA-sponsored journals. Herbert Emmerich, in 1952, informed ASPA about the corruption in government service. In 1953, Phillip Monypenny described himself as skeptical about congressional action on ethical standards that suggest the need for a code of ethics. In 1955, Robert C. Wood viewed ethics as a problem of executive management, not of the ordinary bureaucrat. Another eleven years passed before anyone talked about ethics in government service. That person was Stephen K. Bailey, in his oft-cited 1964 *PAR* article, "Ethics and the Public Service." In 1967, the American Political Science Association developed its Code of Ethics, which Dwight Waldo, as editor, put in *PAR*. In 1967, Todd R. La Porte warned of the dangers of too much emphasis on technology and too little emphasis on ethics. Apparently no scholar publishing in ASPA-sponsored journals heeded his warnings until after Watergate, when, according to James L. Sundquist, the public administration community felt guilty and wondered how it could have let Watergate happen. Sundquist's answer is that we gave too much power to the president.

When one considers the dearth of publications about ethics throughout the 1950s and most of the 1960s, one has to wonder why. Perhaps the answer lies in the times, when big issues were swirling around us and government was assuming a much bigger place in American life than it had ever possessed. We had jobs to do, and we had learned the values of efficiency and responsibility. The complex interrelationship of the government and the private sector had expanded. There was no time for ethical research and reflection.

Perhaps regime values[2] constrained questioning larger issues. Regime values in the United States are reflected in the Constitution and are a part of our culture, our laws, and Supreme Court decisions. Administrative ethics as a field of study, research, and theory development is supportive of the regime, for it represents the fundamental political order. Administrative ethics focuses on improving the practices of a regime.

Because of American confidence in the Constitution and the way of life it has fostered, public administrators have traditionally supported the fundamental right of political officials to act on our behalf while we focus on carrying out legislative mandates and policy directives. The concern of administrative ethics had been with issues of technical rationality and efficiency. Those publishing in ASPA journals in the 1950s, 1960s, and early 1970s appear to have seen no need to change that. In 1974, the National Academy of Public Administration report prepared at the request of the Senate Select Committee on Presidential Campaign Activities devoted only four pages to ethics. Public administration scholars and practitioners appear to have become complacent. Watergate in 1974 was unexpected.

One suspects that in this period, discussions about ethics in public administration occurred but simply rehashed the old Friedrich-Finer dichotomy and thus appeared not worth publishing. Public administration scholars and practitioners, like others in this country, were caught by surprise when the Watergate scandal came to light. Not that public administrators had been involved in the scandal, but as visible government employees, ASPA members seemed to share the blame. Indeed, Watergate had as much negative impact on appointed government employees as it did on elected officials. We were all embarrassed.

The congressional response to the declining faith in government was the Ethics in Government Act of 1978.[3] Even Watergate, however, took a while to influence publications about administrative ethics in ASPA-sponsored journals. Ultimately, Watergate led to passage of the Ethics in Government Act of 1978 as amended by public laws 96-19 and 96-28. With this legislation, financial disclosure obligations were instituted, and the Office of Government Ethics and the Office of Senate Legal Counsel were created. Ultimately, also, Watergate raised the consciousness of the public administration community about the necessity for firm ethical principles and thorough consideration of the values of morality, integrity, and honesty.

The numbers and variety of publications about administrative ethics mushroomed, with different groups of scholars concentrating on different dimensions of the field. This proliferation of topics within the field of administrative ethics is reflected in the chapters in this collection.

It is hoped that readers of this volume will have their own thinking about ethics in government awakened and stimulated. The complexity of ethical concerns raised by the writers included here still challenge the thinking and action of the best minds in both scholarship and practice. The desire for more ethical action and accountability than was evidenced in the 1940s is still relevant. The challenges are as great, and their resolution is as urgent.

The following people were indispensable in the preparation of this book: J. Walton Blackburn, Marsha Branson, and Randall Miller. I am also indebted to Genie Stowers and the ASPA Publications Committee for conceiving the idea of the ASPA Classics series, and to Marc Holzer of Rutgers University, who refined and implemented the concept, making it a reality.

Willa Bruce
University of Illinois at Springfield

Notes

1. U.S. Senate Subcommittee of the Committee on Labor and Public Welfare (1951), *Ethical Standards in Government*. Washington, D.C.: U.S. Government Printing Office.

2. See John A. Rohr, "Bureaucratic Morality in the United States," *International Political Science Review* 9, no. 3 (1988):167–178.

3. Ethics in Government Act of 1978, PubL 95-521, 92 Stat 1824–1867.

CREDITS

Original publication information about the articles compiled herein is given below, arranged according to order of appearance in this volume.

Part 1: Administrative Responsibility

Chapter 1: Finer, Herman. (1941). Administrative responsibility in democratic government. *Public Administration Review.* Summer 1941, Volume 3, pp. 335–350.

Chapter 2: Leys, Wayne A. R. (1943). Ethics and administrative discretion. *Public Administration Review.* Winter 1943, Volume 3, Number 1, pp. 10–23.

Chapter 3: Sayre, Wallace S. (1951). Trends of a decade in administrative values. *Public Administration Review.* Winter 1951, Volume 7, pp. 1–9.

Chapter 4: Bailey, Stephen K. (1964). Ethics and the public service. *Public Administration Review.* December 1964, Volume 24, Number 4, pp. 234–243.

Chapter 5: Thompson, Dennis F. (1985). The possibility of administrative ethics. *Public Administration Review.* September/October 1985, Volume 45, Number 5, pp. 555–561.

Part 2: Solving Ethical Dilemmas

Chapter 6: Graham, George A. (1974). Ethical guidelines for public administrators: Observations on rules of the game. *Public Administration Review.* January/February 1974, Volume 34, pp. 90–92.

Chapter 7: Wachs, Martin. (1982). Ethical dilemmas in forecasting for public policy. *Public Administration Review.* November/December 1982, Volume 42, Number 6, pp. 562–567.

Chapter 8: Willbern, York. (1984). Types and levels of public morality. *Public Administration Review.* March/April 1984, Volume 44, Number 2, pp. 102–108.

Chapter 9: Stewart, Debra W. (1984). Managing competing claims: An ethical framework for human resource decision making. *Public Administration Review.* January/February 1984, Volume 44, Number 1, pp. 14–22.

Part 3: Corruption

Chapter 10: Emmerich, Herbert. (1952). A scandal in utopia. *Public Administration Review*. Winter 1952, Volume 12, pp. 1–9.

Chapter 11: Sundquist, James L. (1974). Reflections on Watergate: Lessons for public administration. *Public Administration Review*. September/October 1974, Volume 34, pp. 453–461.

Chapter 12: Caiden, Gerald E., and Naomi J. Caiden. (1977). Administrative corruption. *Public Administration Review*. May/June 1977, Volume 37, Number 3, pp. 301–309.

Chapter 13: Werner, Simcha B. (1983). New directions in the study of administrative corruption. *Public Administration Review*. March/April 1983, Volume 43, pp. 146–154.

Part 4: Codes of Ethics

Chapter 14: Monypenny, Phillip. (1953). A code of ethics as a means of controlling administrative conduct. *Public Administration Review*. Summer 1953, Volume 13, Number 3, pp. 184–187.

Chapter 15: Zimmerman, Joseph F. (1982). Ethics in the public service. *State and Local Government Review*. September 1982, Volume 14, Number 3, pp. 98–106.

Chapter 16: Chandler, Ralph Clark. (1983). The problem of moral reasoning in American public administration: The case for a code of ethics. *Public Administration Review*. January/February 1983, Volume 43, pp. 32–39.

Part 5: Enforcing Ethical Behavior

Chapter 17: Wood, Robert C. (1955). Ethics in government as a problem in executive management. *Public Administration Review*. Winter 1955, Volume 15, Number 1, pp. 1–7.

Chapter 18: Bowman, James S. (1980). Whistle-blowing in the public service: An overview of the issues. *Review of Public Personnel Administration*. Fall 1980, Volume 1, Number 1, pp. 15–27.

Chapter 19: Dempsey, Charles L. (1985). The inspector general concept: Where it's been, where it's going. *Public Budgeting and Finance*. Summer 1985, Volume 5, Number 2, pp. 39–51.

Part 6: Ethics Education

Chapter 20: Rohr, John A. (1976). The study of ethics in the P.A. curriculum. *Public Administration Review*. Winter 1976, Volume 36, Number 4, pp. 398–406.

Chapter 21: Heffernan, William C. (1982). Two approaches to police ethics. *Criminal Justice Review.* Spring 1982, Volume 7, Number 1, pp. 28–35.

Chapter 22: Mayer, Richard T., and Michael M. Harmon. (1982). Teaching moral education in public administration. *Southern Review of Public Administration.* Summer 1982, Volume 6, Number 2, pp. 217–226.

Part 7: Professionalism

Chapter 23: Brown, David S. (1983). The managerial ethic and productivity improvement. *Public Productivity and Management Review.* September 1983, Volume 7, Number 3, pp. 223–250.

Chapter 24: Cooper, Terry L. (1984). Citizenship and professionalism in public administration. *Public Administration Review.* March 1984, Volume 44, pp. 143–149.

Chapter 25: Frederickson, H. George, and David K. Hart. (1985). The public service and the patriotism of benevolence. *Public Administration Review.* September/October 1985, Volume 45, pp. 547–553.

Chapter 26: Rohr, John A. (1985). Professionalism, legitimacy, and the constitution. *Public Administration Quarterly.* Winter 1985, Volume 8, pp. 401–418.

Part 8: Ethics in the Twenty-First Century

Chapter 27: La Porte, Todd R. (1967). Politics and "inventing the future": Perspectives in science and government. *Public Administration Review.* June 1967, Volume 27, pp. 117–127.

Chapter 28: Scott, William G., and David K. Hart. (1973). Administrative crisis: The neglect of metaphysical speculation. *Public Administration Review.* September/October 1973, Volume 33, pp. 415–422.

Chapter 29: Gawthrop, Louis C. (1984). Civis, Civitas, and Civilitas: A new focus for the year 2000. *Public Administration Review.* March 1984, Volume 44, pp. 101–107.

Part ONE

Administrative Responsibility

The beginning discussion about public administration ethics in the United States is known as the "Friedrich-Finer debate." This debate began our search for understanding about what it means to be ethical in the public service, and it begins this collection of classics. The first argument in the debate was constructed by Professor Carl J. Friedrich, who believed that government needs moral and upstanding public servants who can be trusted to demonstrate responsibility because of their own conscience and personal moral codes. For Friedrich, the public employee should be responsible to the standards of the profession, should feel a sense of duty to the public, and should adhere to the technology of the job needing to be done. Herman Finer is appalled by this philosophy and rails against it. He does not trust public servants to be independently responsible and calls for strict laws to govern administrative behavior and provide a code of correction and punishment for those who deviate from legislated standards.

Friedrich first published his position on administrative responsibility in a book he coauthored,[1] and later in the journal *Public Policy*.[2] Finer's first rejoinder was in the 1936 *Political Science Quarterly*. Neither of these publications are related to ASPA at all, so the first round of the debate is not included in this book. Fortunately, Herman Finer chose *Public Administration Review* as the vehicle for his most comprehensive argument, and that article, which was published in 1941, begins this volume with Chapter 1. Fortunately, also, as a part of his rebuttal, Finer summarizes Friedrich's main points. Thus, readers of "Administrative Responsibility in Democratic Government" are able to capture the essence of the debate.

1

Those who know the history of public administration as a field of study will remember that the period of the 1930s and 1940s was a time of public administration orthodoxy in the United States. People in this country had survived the Great Depression, and Franklin Roosevelt was embroiled in a reorganization that forever elevated the role and responsibility of government in the lives of citizens. The Friedrich-Finer debate was a part of the discussion about the right and proper role of government and the role played by those employed to administer it. In light of the massive increase in payroll and services, it was critical to consider the importance of administrative responsibility and ascertain how it could be encouraged. Surprisingly, the Brownlow Commission, appointed by Roosevelt in 1937 to assess and advise on the government's reorganization, did not address the issue of administrative responsibility, per se. Rather, the commission report focused on issues of structure, budget, and personnel management. It was left to the scholars who did not officially serve the president to consider the issues of administrative responsibility. Their concerns and solutions are as timely now as they were then. Now, more than fifty years after Carl Friedrich and Herman Finer debated how to achieve administrative responsibility, we still do not know, and our ideas still cluster around the two poles they represent.

Chapter 2, "Ethics and Administrative Discretion," was published in *PAR* in 1943 in the midst of World War II. Its author, Wayne A. R. Leys, argues that "the art of war cannot by itself save us from . . . tyranny. Improvements in the art of government are necessary, too." For Leys, the art of government requires understanding administrative discretion and practicing ethics, which he describes as "the art . . . of making wise choices." Leys clarifies the difference between philosophical ethics and administrative discretion, which is what we now call "applied ethics," and he calls for administrators to understand and rely on traditional ethical schools of thought. His arguments bridge the opposing arguments of Friedrich and Finer. For Leys, "both/and" is a better approach than "either/or."

The decade of the 1940s forever shaped our thinking about public administration in general and administrative ethics in particular. In his *PAR* article, "Trends of a Decade in Administrative Values" (Chapter 3 here), Wallace Sayre assesses the 1940s and concludes that the most powerful value to emerge was efficiency. He bemoans the emerging attempt to separate facts from values and the discussions that imply that ethics is not a legitimate part of administration. He also notes with satisfaction that "the construction of a system of administrative responsibility . . . has thus been the subject of a many sided debate" and concludes that the 1940s saw an increase in the importance of values in public administration.

What values were important was yet to be articulated. Whether emphasis should be upon normative institutional arrangements or upon responsible administrators had still not been agreed upon. The essence of the Friedrich-Finer debate was not resolved, and others took it up in one form or another.

The next frequently cited ASPA-sponsored article on the subject was Stephen K. Bailey's "Ethics and the Public Service" (*PAR*, 1964; Chapter 4 here). This article was originally written as a tribute to Paul Appleby. It refutes the argument that morality is influenced by a government system of hierarchy and rules. It offers, instead, a theory of personal ethics for the public service by suggesting that certain moral qualities and mental attitudes are necessary for responsible government administration. The three moral qualities are courage, optimism, and fairness tempered by charity. The three mental attitudes are a recognition of: the moral ambiguity of all persons, the contextual forces that condition moral priorities, and the paradoxes of procedures. The public administrator who has these qualities will be the one able to meet Friedrich's and Leys's high standards for administrative responsibility and discretion.

Bailey's article not only brings together the founding notions of administrative responsibility, but it lays the foundation for the developing trends in virtue ethics, integrity, and citizenship ethics. It, however, does not resolve the debate initiated by Friedrich and Finer.

Chapter 5, also first published in *PAR*, is Dennis Thompson's "The Possibility of Administrative Ethics," which demonstrates that a means for ensuring administrative responsibility was still being sought in the 1980s. In this version of the debate, Thompson views administrative ethics as individual moral actions that he defines as "the application of moral principles to the conduct of officials in organizations." He sees administrative ethics in the public sector as a type of political ethics, then affirms that disagreement still exists over whether morality in organizations is possible. He describes the 1980s "obstacles to administrative ethics," which are by then construed as the "ethic of neutrality" and "the ethic of structure." Arguing that these are not compelling reasons to negate the possibility of developing and using moral judgment, Thompson concludes that administrative ethics are possible. He leaves it to the next wave of scholars to identify ideas about how to operationalize that possibility.

So ends Part 1. It has provided the beginning framework for understanding the competing claims about how to identify and ensure administrative responsibility in public organizations. It has also identified the nascent themes in administrative ethics that have become permanent fixtures in the study of ethics in public administration.

Throughout this book, the reader will note that each chapter ends with a piece dated between 1982 and 1985. The year 1984 was a watershed for public administration ethics. This was the year of the first public administration conference about ethics, the same year that ASPA developed its first code of ethics. The early 1980s were the years after the crisis of Watergate, when administrative ethics came into its own as a field of study deserving of rigorous and dedicated pursuit. This was the period when the earliest voices were crystallized into concrete areas of concern. This was when the themes identified for organizing this book were solidified.

Notes

1. Carl Friedrich and others (1935), *Problems of the American Public Service.* New York: McGraw Hill.

2. Carl Friedrich (1940), "Public Policy and the Nature of Administrative Responsibility," *Public Policy*, pp. 3–24.

1

ADMINISTRATIVE RESPONSIBILITY IN DEMOCRATIC GOVERNMENT

Herman Finer
University of London

Administrative responsibility is not less important to democratic government than administrative efficiency; it is even a contributor to efficiency in
the long run. Indeed, it is tempting to argue that the first requisite is responsibility, and if that is properly instituted efficiency will follow. Elaboration of this point should be unnecessary in the era and under the stress of
the events which now make up our days.

To the subject of administrative responsibility, Professor Carl J.
Friedrich has made several interesting and sagacious contributions,[1] and
he deserves our gratitude for having reintroduced its discussion among
primary problems. Yet these contributions have by no means said the last
word on the subject. Indeed, he has put forward a number of propositions
which must arouse earnest dissent. In answer to an earlier contribution of
his I said,

> It is most important clearly to distinguish a "sense of duty" or a "sense of re-
> sponsibility" from the fact of responsibility, that is, effective answerability. I
> am anxious to emphasize once again that the notion of *subjective* responsibil-
> ity (in my definition of it), whether as intellectual integrity or general loyalty
> to the spirit and purpose of one's function, is of very great importance in
> maintaining the level of efficiency. It is stimulating and sustaining, like the will

5

to believe. But we must first of all be perfectly clear about its nature in order that we may not burke the question of whether or not such responsibility is sufficient to keep a civil service wholesome and zealous, and how far, in its own nature, it is likely to break down so that political responsibility must be introduced as the adamant monitor of the public services. For the first commandment is, Subservience.[2]

My chief difference with Professor Friedrich was and is my insistence upon distinguishing responsibility as an arrangement of correction and punishment even up to dismissal both of politicians and officials, while he believed and believes in reliance upon responsibility as a sense of responsibility, largely unsanctioned, except by deference or loyalty to professional standards. I still maintain my belief while in a more recent article[3] Professor Friedrich still maintains his, so far as I am able to follow his argument. I propose therefore to treat the subject in two divisions, first, a more extended version of my own beliefs and, second, a critical examination of his article.

I

Most of the things I have to say are extremely elementary, but since it has been possible for a writer of eminence to discount their significance I may be forgiven for reaffirming them. The modern state is concerned with a vast sphere of services of a mixed nature. They are repressive, controlling, remedial, and go as far as the actual conduct of industrial, commercial, and agricultural operations. The state, which used to be negative— that is to say which was concerned to abolish its own earlier interventions and reduce such controls as ancient and medieval polity had caused it to undertake—has for some decades now abandoned laissez faire and can be called ministrant. Its work ranges over practically every sector of modern individual and social interest, from sheer police work, in the sense of apprehending and punishing assaults on person, peace, and property, to the actual ownership and management of utilities. I need not dwell on this point further, nor upon the range and detailed intensity of the state's operation, nor the large percentage of men and women among the gainfully occupied population it employs in the strategic positions in society. The weight and immensity and domination of this behemoth, for our good as well as for our control, are well known to all of us. But academic persons are less subject to the power of the colossus than the worker, the economic entrepreneur, the sick and the needy of all kinds. The academic person is therefore likely to regard the weight of the administrator's hand as not needing to be stayed or directed by the public custodian.

Are the servants of the public to decide their own course, or is their course of action to be decided by a body outside themselves? My answer is that the servants of the public are not to decide their own course; they are to be responsible to the elected representatives of the public, and these are to determine the course of action of the public servants to the most minute degree that is technically feasible. Both of these propositions are important: the main proposition of responsibility, as well as the limitation and auxiliary institutions implied in the phrase, "that is technically feasible." This kind of responsibility is what democracy means; and though there may be other devices which provide "good" government, I cannot yield on the cardinal issue of democratic government. In the ensuing discussion I have in mind that there is the dual problem of securing the responsibility of officials, (a) through the courts and disciplinary controls within the hierarchy of the administrative departments, and also (b) through the authority exercised over officials by responsible ministers based on sanctions exercised by the representative assembly. In one way or another this dual control obtains in all the democratic countries, though naturally its purposes and procedures vary from country to country.

What are we to mean by responsibility? There are two definitions. First, responsibility may mean that X is accountable for Y *to* Z. Second, responsibility may mean an inward personal sense of moral obligation. In the first definition the essence is the externality of the agency or persons to whom an account is to be rendered, and it can mean very little without that agency having authority over X, determining the lines of X's obligation and the terms of its continuance or revocation. The second definition puts the emphasis on the conscience of the agent, and it follows from the definition that if he commits an error it is an error only when recognized by his own conscience, and that the punishment of the agent will be merely the twinges thereof. The one implies public execution; the other hara-kiri. While reliance on an official's conscience may be reliance on an official's accomplice, in democratic administration all parties, official, public, and Parliament, will breathe more freely if a censor is in the offing. To convince himself of this the student needs to scrutinize once again the rather uncomfortable relationship between Sir John Reith of the B.B.C. and the public and Parliament[4] (Sir John was a man of moral hauteur), the deep shelter policy of Sir John Anderson's technical experts and parliamentary opinion thereof, and Sir John's Defence Regulations in draft and Parliament's attitude thereto.[5]

Democratic systems are chiefly embodiments of the first mentioned notion of responsibility, and dictatorial systems chiefly of the second. The leading textbooks by Germans on the Nazi system of government explain the essence of the Nazi system by a slavish dressing up of Hitler's dictum that all authority proceeds from above downward, and all responsibility from below upward. But when responsibility gets to Hitler, where does it go then? Mussolini's essay on fascism is nothing but an exercise revolving around the central thesis that since One Man can at times represent the people more validly than any other arrangement, that One Man owes no responsibility outside himself. The Stalinite doctrine is "democratic centralism," which simply means that after a period of discussion the central authority, that is to say Stalin and a few self-chosen friends, decides the course of policy and bears no responsibility to an agency outside himself.

In the democratic system, however, there is either a direct declaration in the constitution of the primacy of the people over officeholders, whether politicians or employees, or else in authoritative documents or popular proverbs the constitutional omission is made good. Thus, in the Weimar Constitution, Article I declared the issuance of sovereignty from the people. Thus, the Committee on Indian Reforms of 1934 said, "so there arise two familiar British conceptions; that good government is not an acceptable substitute for self government, and that the only form of self government worthy of the name is government through ministers responsible to an elective legislature." And thus, we are all familiar with the essential meaning of the American dictum, "where annual election ends tyranny begins."

Democratic governments, in attempting to secure the responsibility of politicians and officeholders to the people, have founded themselves broadly upon the recognition of three doctrines. First, the mastership of the public, in the sense that politicians and employees are working not for the good of the public in the sense of what the public *needs,* but of the *wants* of the public as expressed by the public. Second, recognition that this mastership needs institutions, and particularly the centrality of an elected organ, for its expression and the exertion of its authority. More important than these two is the third notion, namely, that the function of the public and of its elected institutions is not merely the exhibition of its mastership by informing governments and officials of what it wants, but the authority and power to exercise an effect upon the course which the latter are to pursue, the power to exact obedience to orders. The Soviet government claimed (in the years when the claim seemed profitable to it internationally) that it was a democratic government; but its claim was supported by two arguments only, that the government worked for the good of the people, their economic well-being, and that the people were allowed to inform the government of their will through a multitude of institutions. The Soviet government never sought to employ with any cogency the third and really vital argument that it could be made to conform to the people's will by the people and against its own will. This last alone is responsibility in democratic government.

Democratic government proceeded upon the lines mentioned because the political and administrative history of all ages, the benevolent as well as the tyrannical, the theological as well as the secular, has demonstrated without the shadow of a doubt that sooner or later there is an abuse of power when external punitive controls are lacking. This abuse of power has shown itself roughly in three ways. Governments and officials have been guilty of nonfeasance,[6] that is to say, they have not done what law or custom required them to do owing to laziness, ignorance, or want of care for their charges, or corrupt influence. Again there may be malfeasance, where a duty is carried out, but is carried out with waste and damage because of ignorance, negligence, and technical incompetence. Third, there is what may be called *over*feasance, where a duty is undertaken beyond what law and custom oblige or empower; overfeasance may result from dictatorial temper, the vanity and ambition of the jack in office, or genuine, sincere, public-spirited zeal. As a matter of fact, the doctrine of the separation of powers as developed by Montesquieu was as much concerned with the aberrations of public-spirited zeal on the part of the executive as with the other classes of the abuse of power. Indeed, his phrase deserves to be put into the center of every modern discussion of administrative responsibility, *virtue itself hath need of limits.* We in public administration must beware of the too good man as well as the too bad; each in his own way may give the public what it doesn't want. If we wish the public to want things that are better in our estimation, there is a stronger case for teaching the public than for the imposition of our zealotry. A system which gives the "good" man freedom of action, in the expectation of benefiting from all the "good" he has in him, must sooner or later (since no man is without faults) cause his faults to be loaded on to the public also.

As a consequence of bitter experience and sad reflection, democratic governments have gradually devised the responsible executive and an elected assembly which enacts the responsibility. Within the system, there has been a particular concentration on the subservience of the officials to the legislature, ultimately through ministers and cabinet in a cabinet system, and through the chief executive where the separation of powers is the essential form of the organization of authority. Where officials have been or are spoilsmen, the need for holding them to subservience is particularly acute, since the spoilsman has not even a professional preparation to act as a support and guide and guarantee of capacity. With career men, the capacity may be present. What is needed, however, is not technical capacity per se, but technical capacity in the service of the public welfare as defined by the public and its authorized representatives.

Legislatures and public have realized that officials are monopolist no less than the grand men of business who have arrogated to themselves the exclusive control of the manufacture or sale of a commodity and therewith the domination, without appeal by the victim, of an entire sector of national life. The philosophy and experience of the Sherman Anti-Trust Act have significant applications to administrative procedures in public administration. The official participates in the monopoly of a service to society so outstanding that it has been taken over from a potential private monopolist by the government. This monopoly is exercisable through a sovereign agency armed with all the force of society and subject to no appeal outside the institutions which the government itself creates. This is to be subject to a potentially grievous servitude.

How grievous can be surmised in one or both of two ways. One can reflect on the merits of competitive industry which satisfies the consumers best as to price and quality and variety while it remains competitive, so that the consumer can cast a more than daily vote most effectively for the producer he prefers by buying his goods or services, and expel the others from office by *not* buying from them. One can notice, too, how producers, on the plea of "service before self" and the like, attempt to escape consumer's control; and memories are stirred of Adam Smith's dig at traders who affect to trade "for the public good." Or, second, one can have experience at first hand, not merely of the coercive side of public monopolies, say the contract powers of a municipal electricity undertaking, but of its administration of charitable undertakings, say in the feeding of school children or hospital management. The conceit of Caesar making concessions *ex gratia* to "subjects" can be noticed too palpably.

To overcome the potential evils flowing from public monopoly, democratic governments have set up various controls. It is these controls, and especially their modern deficiencies, which seem to have worried Professor Friedrich into a position where he practically throws the baby out with the bath. He feels that there is need of some elasticity in the power of the official, some discretion, some space for the "inner check," and he sees also that existent controls (either intentionally or by the accident of their own institutional deficiencies) do actually leave some latitude to the official. He argues therefore that heavy and, indeed, primary reliance in the making of public policy and its execution should be placed on *moral* responsibility, and he pooh-poohs the efficacy of and need for political responsibility. He gives the impression of stepping over the dead body of political responsibility to grasp the promissory incandescence of the moral variety.

Let us review the chief controls exercised over politicians and officials in democratic government, and their deficiencies and the remedy of these deficiencies. In traversing their inadequacies I am dealing with those loopholes for administrative discretion or the policy-making power of officials which have given Professor Friedrich so much concern. First, the legislative definition of the duties and powers of officials may not be precise because the legislators were not very clear about what they wanted. It is doubtful, for example, whether the planning clauses in the T.V.A. statute represented any clarity of purpose in the legislative mind. Legislative draftsmanship may be slipshod. Or the statute may be simply misunderstood, thus offering latitude to officials. If all the items of administrative determination arising out of the elbowroom allowed by these causes were gathered together they would no doubt be considerable. Since this latitude exists, it calls for one or both of the available remedies the continuing control of the representative and judicial agencies over the official and an omnipresent sense of duty *to the public* on the part of the official. But the remedy is not, as Professor Friedrich suggests, the institution of specific legislative policies which may please the heart of the technical expert or the technocrat. I again insist upon subservience, for I still am of the belief with Rousseau that the people can be unwise but cannot be wrong. The devices for securing the continuing responsiveness of the official are, of course, the law courts, the procedure of criticism, question, debate, and fact-finding, and parliamentary control of the purse within the assembly, and, in the U.S.A., the election of executive or administrative officials and their recall.

It has been suggested by Professor Laski that to overcome judicial bias in the interpretation of social legislation a preamble might be set at the head of every statute so that the intention of it should be rendered less mistakable.[7] Such a device might serve the purpose of making the official amenable to the legislature, except that I have grave doubts whether the legislature can express its intention any better in a preamble than it does in the particulars of the whole statute.

Next, the enormous congestion of modern legislative assemblies and the heritage of antiquated procedure mean that a sufficiently frequent review of legislation and its administrative outcrops cannot be secured to remedy, or to punish, or to act by power of anticipation on the official mind. But these are not insuperable problems and there is no need for us, seeing contemporary deficiencies, to jettison political responsibility prematurely.

Third, there may be a want of understanding by members of Parliament and congressmen of technical issues involved in the law and the administration, and this shortcoming has meant a leaning upon the supply of these things available in public employees. But the growth of advisory bodies, formal and informal, in the major governments of our own time has tremendously limited the need to rely wholly upon official initiative. Attention to the further development of advisory bodies is the line of progress here, not surely the handing over of our fate to officials who, by the way, are themselves only too grateful for instruction by such bodies.[8]

It is true, further, that the exercise of the power of control by the legislature, such for example as Congress' detailed attention to and itemization of financial appropriations, may destroy movement, flexibility, and the like, on the part of the administration. This point is stressed by Professor

Friedrich; queerly enough, he does not deduce from this criticism that a more rational parliamentary procedure is required, but that there is need of more administrative discretion. He even goes to the inexplicable extreme of proposing that some action is better than none, whatever the action is!

In short, these various drawbacks of political control can be remedied. They can be highly improved, and it is therefore unnecessary to proceed along the line definitely approved by Professor Friedrich of more administrative policy making. As a democrat, I should incline to the belief that the remedying of these drawbacks is precisely our task for the future. The legitimate conclusion from the analysis of the relationship between Parliament and administration is not that the administration should be given its head, but on the contrary that legislative bodies should be improved. Conceding the growing power of officials we may discover the remedy in the improvement of the quality of political parties and elections, if our minds are ready to explore.

Even then I am willing to admit an external agency could not attend to every administrative particular without introducing an element of coercion and fear into administration which might damage originality, joy in work, the capacity for creative suggestion, and day-by-day flexibility. No external agency could do this; and none that we know would want to. But because some latitude must be given—both owing to the technical impossibility of complete political coverage, and the wise recognition that the permitted latitude can be used for technically good policy which though not immediately acclaimed or wanted may become so in a short while upon demonstration to the public—there is no need to overstress the auxiliaries to political control. Such auxiliaries as approved by Professor Friedrich are: referenda by government departments, public relations offices, consultation of academic colleagues in order to temper "partisan extravagance," "education and promotional functions," the administrative scrutiny of a congressman's mail. These are harmless enough.

But when Professor Friedrich advocates the official's responsibility to "the fellowship of science," the discard of official anonymity, the entry of the official into the political arena as an advocate of policy and teacher of fact versus "partisan extravagance," the result to be feared is the enhancement of official conceit and what has come to be known as "the new despotism." It seems to me that in the article in *Public Policy* a theoretical aberration regarding the value of devices for eliciting public opinion, auxiliary to the medium of the legislative assembly, has led to pushing these auxiliaries into the principal place. Where the external, propelling, remedial, and punitive power of legislative bodies and administrative superiors acting after the administrative event, and upon the imagination of the official before it (and therefore relying upon fear), is weak, other techniques can be and have been added.

For example, statesmen have invited the expression of public opinion through letters, and the departments are deluged with complaints and, let us hope, occasional praise. The rise of the public relations officer has led to the education of public opinion and the evocation of that public opinion other than through Parliament. (But beware lest he become a tout!) The British Broadcasting Corporation, for instance, has set up various councils of listeners, and it seeks their advice—and no doubt at the same time explains to them why it is not really so bad as the public thinks it is. There is the inspectorial contact of the central government with the local authorities. A few months ago the Ministry of Information began to avail itself of the services of a number of people formerly employed in the Market Research Bureau to take samples of public opinion, and they came to be known as "Duff Cooper's Snoopers." Members of Parliament challenged the need for these, seeing that they themselves are channels of public opinion.

All these devices have their value, but let it be remembered that they do not and cannot commit and compel the official to change his course. Officials may, in spite of them, still think that what they are doing is for the good of the public, although the public is too ignorant to recognize what is for its good. However, the more the official knows of public reactions the better. My qualm is that the official is very likely to give himself the benefit of the doubt where the information he elicits admits of doubt, whereas when the legislative assembly asserts an opinion it also asserts a command. This is the very essence of the *Report of the Committee on Ministers' Powers*—upon this, you may say, hang all the laws and the prophets. It said:

> It is unfair to impose on a practical administrator the duty of adjudicating in any matter in which it could fairly be argued that his impartiality would be in inverse ratio to his strength and ability as a Minister. An easy going and cynical Minister, rather bored with his office and sceptical of the value of his Department, would find it far easier to apply a judicial mind to purely judicial problems connected with the Department's administration than a Minister whose head and heart were in his work. *It is for these reasons and not because we entertain the slightest suspicion of the good faith or the intellectual honesty of Ministers and their advisers* that we are of opinion that Parliament should be chary of imposing on Ministers the ungrateful task of giving judicial decisions in matters in which *their very zeal for the public service can scarcely fail to bias them unconsciously.*[9]

Besides these arrangements the official may be kept responsive to the will of the legislative assembly by all the devices of legal responsibility. This point need not be adumbrated in any detail as it has been the subject of so many recent analyses and proposals for reform in the standard works of administrative law. I need only refer to works like Port's *Administrative*

Law and John Dickinson's *Administrative Justice and the Supremacy of the Law.* In addition, there is the regular intradepartmental discipline resting upon the professional prospects and career, the salary, the retirement pay, and the chances of promotion, transfer, distinction, and honors, or vice versa, of the civil servant, going right up the hierarchy to those who are in direct contact with the secretaries of departments and the chief executive in the United States and the permanent secretaries and the ministers in Great Britain.

Even when the best has been accomplished with all this mechanism and the rewards, punishments, and incentives by which it functions, there may be still a gap between the controls and those official actions which would give the greatest public satisfaction. We should do all we can to reduce this gap to its minimum. Where our powers reach an impasse we will be obliged to rely upon two ways out: the education of the official and the influence of his professional organizations.

As for education—which should be part of the official's training before entry and then should be continued in various ways after entry[10]—besides the purpose of technical excellence, it should be shaped to make the official aware of the basic importance of his responsibility to the parliamentary assembly, and the errors into which he will be liable to fall unless he makes this his criterion. He should realize the dangers in the belief that he has a mission to act for the good of the public outside the declared or clearly deducible intention of the representative assembly. No one in his right mind would deny the importance of suggestions persuasively presented by the expert; but there is a world of difference between acknowledging the value of such suggestions and following the path of increasing administrative independence simply because there is *faute de mieux* already some independence.

Again, my own studies in the field of the professional organizations of local and central government officials in Great Britain have taught me what a great power for the good can be exercised by them.[11] Besides keeping members up to the mark and up-to-date in the exercise of their profession, they do embody a sense of responsibility in the second sense in which we use that term, as devotion to the highest standards of a craft or to a special body of people in the community—such as the consumers of electricity or passengers on petrol or trolley buses, or the frequenters of public baths, or the payers of income tax. They engender and develop this sense of responsibility, and it is a valuable product. But even with this we must require principally and austerely the subservience of the public official. Without this requirement, we shall gradually slip into a new version of taxation without representation. There will result the development of a profession or corporate spirit, and bodies which at first are beneficial in their freshness become what Rousseau and Hobbes have called "worms in the entrails of the body politic." We shall become subject to what has, in a short time, almost always been to the detriment of the public welfare—producer's control of the products, the services, the commodities which the producer thinks are good for the consumer and therefore ought to be produced at the consumer's expense, though the consumer does not want the services or commodities in question and strongly prefers something else.

II

In the article in *Public Policy* to which reference has been made, Professor Friedrich takes a position radically different from my own as hitherto stated, though most of the facts to which both of us refer are common ground. Before turning to a detailed criticism of his thesis, it is useful to state his position in general. He argues (a) that the responsibility of the official that of any moment to us today is not political responsibility but moral responsibility; (b) that the quality of administration and policy making depends almost entirely (and justifiably so) upon the official's sense of responsibility to the standards of his profession, a sense of duty to the public that is entirely inward, and an adherence to the technological basis of his particular job or the branch of the service in which he works; (c) that the public and the political assemblies do not understand the issues of policy well enough to give him socially beneficial commands in terms of a policy; (d) that, in fact, legislatures and the public have been obliged to allow or positively to organize more and more latitude for official policy making; (e) that there are satisfactory substitutes for the direction of officials and information as to the state of public opinion through the electorate and the legislature in the form of administratively conducted referenda public relations contacts, etc.; and, therefore, (f) that political responsibility, i.e., the responsibility of the administrative officials to the legislature and the public, is and should only be considered as a minor term in the mechanism of democratic government, so much so, indeed, that officials may rightly state and urge policies in public to counteract those advocated by the members of the elected legislatures.

Let us commence the critical discussion with a passage of Professor Friedrich's on Goodnow's *Politics and Administration*. In 1900 Professor F. J. Goodnow's work, one of the pioneer incursions into a fairly untilled field, made the following distinction between politics and administration. "There are then, in all governmental systems, two primary or ultimate functions of government, viz. the expression of the will of the state and the execution of that will. There are also in all states separate organs, each of which is mainly busied with the discharge of one of these functions." Professor Friedrich imputes to Goodnow "an almost absolute distinction" in this functional difference. As a matter of fact, Goodnow uses the term "*mainly* busied with the discharge of one of these functions," and deserves credit for the broad distinction.

The distinction in the present writer's mind is this. By the "political" phase of government we mean all that part which is concerned with eliciting the will and winning the authority of the people. The process is carried on differently in democratic and dictatorial states. The elements of coercion and persuasion differ in magnitude and kind, and the place of the electorate, parties, parliaments, and ministers differs. This process ends with a law; with the approval (by positive ratification or by lapse of time for rejection) of administrative rules based on the original statute; and with control of the application of the law. The distinctive mark of this political part of the governmental process is that its agencies are practically unfettered in their authority over the making of policy and its execution. Where a written constitution and judicial review are absent, these political agencies are bounded only by the hopes and fears arising out of the electoral process. What of the administrative side? Administration begins where the legislature says it shall begin. It begins where the administrator begins, and the legislature decides that. Administration may include the making of rules and policy, which *looks* like legislation or politics. But its essence is that the administrator, elected or appointed (and most usually in modern states the latter), cannot himself determine the range or object of that policy. He has authority, but it is a conditioned, derived authority.

Thus, in the governmental process in general, there are agencies which are concerned with making and executing policy, and there is a descending narrowing latitude of discretion in the making of policy. The latitude is greatest where electorate meets legislature; it then tapers down through a descending line of the administrative hierarchy until the discretion left to the messenger and the charwoman and the minor manipulative grades is almost nil. There have been polities where there was an almost complete fusion of these functions, e.g., at some stages of Athenian democracy. But modern states are obliged at some point convenient to each in a different degree to distinguish them, with the first as authority and master over the second.

Professor Friedrich calls this distinction of Goodnow's (shared by all other authorities I can recall) "misleading," a "fetish," a "stereotype," in the minds of theorists and practitioners alike. Are we then to be permitted to offer worship only to fallacies? He produces the queerest explanation for this alleged "absolute antithesis" of Goodnow's. It is this:

> That it is built upon the metaphysical, if not abstruse, idea of a will of the state. This neo-hegelian (and Fascist) notion is purely speculative. Even if the concept "state" is retained—and I personally see no good ground for it—the idea that this state has a will immediately entangles one in all the difficulties of assuming a group personality or something akin to it (p. 6).[12]

This explanation is surely very fanciful. Later on, Professor Friedrich is constrained to admit: "Politics and administration play a continuous role in both formation and execution [of policy], though there is probably more politics in the formation of policy, more administration in the execution of it." "More" is a delicious understatement. But the understatement is not intended; it is part of a thesis that the amount of policy made by modern officials is of very great magnitude, in terms of proposing and later executing with latitude of interpretation. But this is only a play on the words "making" and "policy." What important "policy" does any federal official "make"? Has any federal official more authority than to propose? Certainly we expect those who are paid by the public to think and propound solutions to do their job well. But this is nothing new. By misusing the word "make" to suggest instituting and carrying into the law of the land, and only by this torsion of meaning, can Professor Friedrich's thesis at all come into court—that administrative responsibility to the legislature, the real policy-forming body of the nation, is in modern conditions impossible or unnecessary.

Professor Friedrich then reiterates an earlier statement of his: "Nor has the political responsibility based upon the election of legislatures and chief executives succeeded in permeating a highly technical, differentiated government service any more than the religious responsibility of well-intentioned kings." He then says, "An offended commentator from the British Isles [who appears to be the present writer] exclaimed that if I imagined that to be true of England I was 'simply wrong.'" Yes! that the power of the House of Commons in permeating the British civil service, right down to its local offices, and making it responsive to the House as the master delegate of the electorate, is most effective, is true, is demonstrably true, and ought not be denied. Nor can it be compared in delicateness or constancy with the "religious responsibility of well-intentioned kings," which appears to be an enthusiasm of Professor Friedrich's, for he undertakes to defend it by history, though he does not do so. Does it hold good of the Tudors, Stuarts, and Hanoverians? If so, why has British history been one long resolute struggle for the supremacy of Parliament and the reduction of the monarch to a dignified cipher?

Professor Friedrich begins his article in *Public Policy* with some remarks on the Munich Pact, with the intention presumably of showing that administrative responsibility to Parliament is ineffective. He offers it as evidence that "pious myth-makers" have no right to accept the claim that the formal dependence of the Cabinet upon the confidence of the House of Commons effectively insures responsible conduct of public affairs by officials, high and low. (He reverts to this example later also.) As a matter of fact, this example proves the exact converse of Professor Friedrich's intention. The Munich Pact only too well carried out the will of Parliament. Mr. Harold Nicolson, M.P., now Under Secretary to the Ministry of Information, even jeopardized his career by denouncing the hysteria with which the invitation to Munich and peace was received by Parliament. It is true that thereafter, as the consequences came to light, Parliament and people felt that the Government had been wrong—but they too were completely implicated. The revulsion of feeling caused the Government, under parliamentary pressure, to give up its appeasement policy and push on with civil defense preparations and rearmament.

Professor Friedrich argues that "even under the best arrangements a considerable margin of irresponsible conduct of administrative activities is inevitable." He is sanguine enough to continue (p. 4): "Too often it is taken for granted that as long as we can keep the government from doing wrong we have made it responsible. What is more important is to ensure effective action of any sort." Of any sort! This surely is exactly the doctrine to stimulate a swelling of the official head. Though I am not inclined to argue by *reductio ad absurdum,* such a phrase, if taken seriously, must encourage public employees to undertake actions which would very soon arouse the cry of Bureaucracy! and New Despotism! Friedrich himself tones down his own objurgation shortly afterward, but does not discard it.

Professor Friedrich has somehow come to believe that "parliamentary responsibility is largely inoperative and certainly ineffectual" (p. 10). Is he referring to the policy-making powers of administrators, or the acts of the Cabinet? His criticism seems to apply to the Cabinet, and not to the subject of his essay, viz., the responsibility of *officials,* for, citing the case of Munich and "the last few years," he seems to be concerned mainly with a foreign policy of which he did not approve but of which a large majority of his "ineffectual" Parliament emphatically did. And then he claims the benefit of this demonstration, I suppose, for the thesis that in England the civil service is out of hand?

On this point there are two records which might be summed up as follows. On questions of foreign policy, the Government, misguided as it may have been (in my view as well as Professor Friedrich's), was steadily supported by a large majority in Parliament, and I should guess a large one in the country. As for control over the administration, has Professor Friedrich heard of Parliament's actions on the Unemployment Regulations of 1934, the reform of the Post Office, the reform of the constitution of the B.B.C., the special areas, the preparation of the scheme of civil defense, the partial success in getting a Minister for the Coordination of Defense, the overthrow of Sir Samuel Hoare, the speeding up of arms production? And, during the war, the successful pressure of Parliament for the removal of certain ministers, e.g., from the Ministry of Information, for more reasonable use of the powers of interning refugees, its control over government contract methods, over appointments in the civil service, over the Defence Regulations proposed by the Home Secretary, over economic and fiscal, policies and administration, and, finally, over the very existence of the Chamberlain Government itself? I have listed only a few of the outstanding successes of Parliament in controlling (a) the government in general, and (b) the proposals of administrators and their parliamentary chiefs before they were "made" into policy by Parliament.

The conclusion of this section of the essay (p. 7) reads: "Admittedly, many commentators have dwelt at length upon the frequently irresponsible conduct of public affairs in Great Britain and elsewhere." This is of course true; they have; and they have been right. But that does not mean that the examples are many, important, or long continuing. Nor would any person claim perfection for any system. You do not prove the value of your enthusiasm by showing that there are some flaws in existing political arrangements. Rather is political science a comparative weighing of the imperfections of alternative consequences. Even so, this should hardly lead the author to the conclusion that runs like a scarlet thread throughout the entire treatment, that if political responsibility is imperfect it is to be cast out in favor of a sense of responsibility in the bosom of the official: "a sense of duty, a desire to be approved by his fellow officials, and a tendency to subordinate one's own judgment as a matter of course" (p. 8), a point that Friedrich cites with evident approval from shaky evidence given to him orally by a Swiss official. Without the existence of the Federal Assembly, for how long does Professor Friedrich think the Swiss civil service would remain in tune with the humor of the people and responsive to its wants?

Professor Friedrich then turns to that agitation against the civil service which was summed up in Lord Hewart's book, *The New Despotism*. Alas, for the thesis of the author! *The Report of the Committee on Ministers' Powers*, while showing that, certainly, our civil service was very useful, showed that only in a few respects, and those not very important or deepseated, were its members escaping control. He seems to harbor an objection to the power which the parliamentary majority would have over the rule-making authority of the administrator though submitted to a committee of the House for sanction (p. 12). What is wrong with this? Even if a special scrutinizing committee is organized, why should not the majority views of the whole House prevail? What is wrong with the majority? As for "the Henry VIII clause" (i.e., the power given by statute to the Minister heading a department to "remove difficulties" which are obstacles to the putting of the act into effect), this sounds very gruesome; but a glance at Mr. Willis' book on the *Legislative Powers of Government Departments* will show how trivial were the uses of it.[13] And Sir Cecil Carr has more recently shown that the hullabaloo was about very little indeed.[14] In the light of these authors and the distinguished membership of the committee, is not the suggestion that the Committee on Ministers' Powers "soft-pedals the real trouble" somewhat daring?

In the effort not to let reconsideration correct his first misconception of
"responsibility," Professor Friedrich finds himself compelled to adopt quite
an undemocratic view of government, and to throw scorn upon the popular will. I do not think for a moment that he really is antidemocratic, but
his line of argument presses him to enunciate views which might lead to
this suspicion. The error in his conception leads to an error in the consequence; and the error in the consequence is precisely what officials (not
constrained by principle and institutions to the dictates of political responsibility) would begin to use as an argument to justify their irresponsibility:
conceit of themselves and scorn of the popular will. Thus (p. 12)

> The pious formulas about the will of the people are all very well, but when it
> comes to these issues of social maladjustment the popular will has little con-
> tent, except the desire to see such maladjustments removed. A solution which
> fails in this regard, or which causes new and perhaps great maladjustments, is
> bad; we have a right to call such a policy irresponsible if it can be shown that
> it was adopted without proper regard to the existing sum of human knowl-
> edge concerning the technical issues involved; we also have a right to call it ir-
> responsible if it can be shown that it was adopted without proper regard for
> existing preferences in the community, and more particularly its prevailing
> majority.

The answer to this argument is this. It is demonstrable that the will of
the people *has* content, not only about what it desires, but how maladjust-
ments can be remedied, and some of its ideas are quite wise. The popular
will may not be learned, but nevertheless the public's own experience
teaches it something, the press of all kinds teaches it more, and political
parties and the more instructed members of the community play quite a
part. "The people" consists of many kinds of minds and degrees of talent,
not of undifferentiated ignorance and empty-mindedness. Legislative assemblies created by election, in which political parties play a vital part,
also exist; and they are not so dumb. Their sagacity is not to be ignored or
derided. Second, a policy which is based upon an incomplete or faulty
grasp of technical knowledge *is not* an irresponsible policy, for to use the
word "irresponsible" here is to pervert it by substituting it for the words
"incomplete" or "faulty" or "unwise." It is surely wisest to say that the
full grasp of knowledge is to be used by the official within the terms of the
obligation and policy established for him by the legislature or his departmental superior; otherwise it looks as though an independent position
were being claimed for the official. Nor is it wise to make responsibility to
"the community" an addendum to a "proper regard to the existing sum of
human knowledge, etc., etc." And, by the way, the state seems to have
cropped up again in the word community!

"Consequently," continues Professor Friedrich, "the responsible administrator is one who is responsible to these two dominant factors: technical knowledge and popular sentiment. Any policy which violates either standard, or which fails to crystallize in spite of their urgent imperatives, renders the official responsible for it liable to the charge of irresponsible conduct." But just as surely there is no responsibility unless there is an obligation to someone else; no one is interested in a question of responsibility as a relationship between a man and a science, but as it involves a problem of duty—and the problem of duty is an interpersonal, not a personal, matter. Responsibility in the sense of an interpersonal, externally sanctioned duty is, then, the dominant consideration for public administration; and it includes and does not merely stand by the side of responsibility to the standards of one's craft in the dubious position of a Cinderella. If the community does not command, there is no call for the technical knowledge whatever; and, however magnificent the grasp of technical knowledge and the desire to use it, it must be declared irresponsible whenever it becomes operative except under a direct or implied obligation. Many a burglar has been positively hated for his technical skill.

There is another consequence of his thesis which Professor Friedrich would not like, I feel certain, if he had developed its implications. He declares: "Administrative officials seeking to apply scientific 'standards' have to account for their action in terms of a somewhat rationalized and previously established set of hypotheses. Any deviation from these hypotheses will be subjected to thorough scrutiny by their colleagues in what is known as the 'fellowship of science.'" What is the force of the phrase "have to account for their action?" Exactly to whom? By what compulsion? Does this phrase mean only that there is left to the official the vague, tenuous reaching out of his qualms in view of the known or possible public opinions of the men with whom he studied or those who are the present leaders of the profession? Suppose he despises their grasp of knowledge and scorns their judgment—is he therefore irresponsible? Suppose that they are conservative, while he is one of a minority of progressive practitioners? When is he responsible and when irresponsible? When he follows the ancients or marches with, perhaps even leads, the pioneers?

This question takes us directly into the history of these professional organizations of colleagues, "the fellowship of science," the associations, the guilds, of medical men, engineers, accountants, lawyers, and others. Even if such fellowship were fully organized to implement Professor Friedrich's wish, whom could the ordinary man trust for a better deal, the great osteopath, Mr. (later Sir as a mark of popular gratitude) Herbert Barker, or the elders of the British Medical Association, the organization which banned him; Whistler, Charles Ricketts, or the Royal Academy; an Epstein or the stone chippers favored by the Society of Sculptors? I do not err, I believe, in thinking that there are analogous instances in American experience, which Professor Friedrich could supply better than I can. But there is before us the judgment of the District Court of the District of Columbia regarding the American Medical Association's action against medical practitioners—their expulsion because they participated in a group medicine clinic. Which criterion: groupist or anti-groupist?

I do not deny all value to such guild organization; I affirm and applaud some of these organizations. Yet, appraised from the very angle of the theory which I am here opposing, they must be seen as broken reeds in a long-run view of governmental devices to keep men in the van of social progress, technically defined, and still less to satisfy progress as the populace, the consumer, asks for it. Professor J. M. Gaus, who is quoted in support of the claim that responsibility is professional, is by no means so zealous in the service of the notion as Professor Friedrich who quotes him, for he says: "The responsibility of the civil servant to the standards of his profession, *in so far as those standards make for the public interest,* may be given official recognition." I have italicized the proviso, and it is essential, I am sure, to Professor Gaus's view. Who would define the public interest—who could define it? Only the public, I believe or its deputies.

Professor Friedrich seems to be so obsessed by modern technology, and the important part which the knowledge of it must play in the establishment of policy, that he seems to forget how old this problem is, and what the answer of the ages has been to the very problem he poses. Does he think there was no question of "technical needs" three hundred years or three thousand years ago, or of the relationship of those who provided the knowledge and service to those members of the public who were its consumers? Governments owned warships, weapons, sewers, baths, roads, and irrigation works, and even had mines and forests to administer, and domestic and foreign trade to regulate. The relationship of the public to the mysteries of religion and ecclesiastical procedures—a very important technique in the context of good living—was for centuries one of the most critical problems in the history of political responsibility. "The creative solutions for our crying technical needs," as Professor Friedrich calls them, have for centuries been offered by the experts of various kinds, and the verdict of mankind has been that they need the expert on tap and not on top. All important questions are begged by throwing in the word "creative." It is no news to tell us, as we are told here, that nature will have her revenge if her laws are not understood and followed in any particular piece of administration. Of course that is so. But there is a wider concept of nature than that which relates to interest in the "technical"; there is also the nature of man as a political animal. We are entitled to believe, from the reading of his millennial administrative history, that *his* nature, as well as physical nature, is thwarted where the primacy of public responsibility is challenged by blurred interpretations, theoretical and practical, of the term responsibility.

Nor is there any novelty in the fact that political responsibility (the importance of which Professor Friedrich admits in a scanty oasis of one paragraph in twenty-four pages) acts by its power on the official mind in anticipation of action by the sanctioning organs of popular control. In pursuance of his denigration of the British system of political responsibility he rather misinterprets the function of questions in the House of Commons. Their principal function is not to inform ministers of public reaction to policy, but to discipline administration. Ministers know already through other procedures. Questions are a *force*. Only ask the officials who prepare the information for the ministers whether they are not in an anxious sweat until the House is appeased!

Why, this is almost the ideal instrument for exercising that power of anticipation over the officials' mind, and therefore upon his sense of obligation to the community, which indirectly implies an obligation to the expertness he commands. I say this with diffidence, since the article seems a little severe on British experience. Nor am I an idolator of every item of parliamentary technique as it now operates. It should certainly be improved; but it ought not to be scouted.

There are occasions when Professor Friedrich seems to admit the fundamentality of political responsibility, but the relapse certainly and fatally follows. Thus he says (pp. 19, 20): "The whole range of activities involving constant direct contact of the administrator with the public and its problems shows that our conception of administrative responsibility is undergoing profound change. The emphasis is shifting; instead of subserviency to arbitrary will we require responsiveness to commonly felt needs and wants." Whose is the arbitrary will? The parliamentary assembly's emanating from popular election? Let us beware in this age lest we destroy our treasure altogether because it is not the purest of pure gold.

I come now to the last matter in which I care to take issue with Professor Friedrich, the relationship between administrative responsibility and the doctrine of official anonymity.

Professor Friedrich believes:

It must seriously be doubted whether technical responsibility, which, as we have shown, is coming to play an ever more important role in our time, can be effectively secured without granting responsible officials considerable leeway and making it possible for them to submit their views to outside criticism. The issue is a very complex one. Opinions vary widely. People try to escape facing these difficulties by drawing facile distinctions, such as that officials might discuss facts but not policy. It might cogently be objected that facts and policies cannot be separated (p. 22).

The rejoinder to this statement in the first place is that it is possible in some cases at any rate to distinguish facts and policy quite clearly. For example, the government or the representative assembly in seeking a policy to deal with rural water supplies might properly expect to receive from an official a description of the existing situation, in terms of the total water resources of the country, the supplies and the sources of supply in various rural vicinities, what those supplies cost per thousand gallons, whether the nearest supplies beyond the jurisdiction of each unit need pumping stations or whether the water will come down by being piped, what are the costs of pumping and distribution in various other areas, and so on. What the assembly shall do about it, once these facts are before it, is a matter of policy. A wise civil servant, careful to preserve his own usefulness and that of his colleagues, and not reckless in the face of the always imminent cry of bureaucracy and despotism, would not urge a policy upon it. Still less would he use public advocacy to spur on his political chief or connive with reformist groups having a purposeful policy. He would rather confine himself to frank private demonstration of the alternatives and their advantages and disadvantages, to his political chief, or where the political system requires, to the committee of the assembly at their request.

That, however, is not all. If Professor Friedrich really believes that the severance of fact and policy is impossible, then a fortiori the civil servant should preserve his anonymity, on pain of bringing himself and his colleagues into partisan contempt. And Professor Friedrich does really seem to contemplate a war of all against all. He seems to approve of the fact that six reporters proceeded to a federal department whose head had ruled that his subordinates were not to give interviews and violated the chief's rule by getting six different stories. Is this the way to promote official responsibility to the chief? To the technical standards? To the "fellowship of science"? Does Professor Friedrich approve of this piece of press impudence? Has he ever investigated what such impudence cost the T.V.A. in prestige, morale, and administrative efficiency in the old days? Nor can I view with equanimity the grave consequences of such proposals as this: "In matters of vital importance the general public is entitled to the views of its permanent servants. Such views may often provide a salutary check on partisan extravagances. Such views should be available not only to the executive but to the legislature and the public as well" (p. 23).

This doctrine surely is to set up the official against the political parties, to make the official the instrument of conflict between the "general public" (which I thought had already been thrown out of court earlier in Friedrich's article) and the legislature. He would set the official, I suppose, against the chief executive also, for he has been elected by the general public, and may utter as many "partisan extravagances" as he pleases in the course of a four-year term. It is not clear whether Professor Friedrich thinks that the civil servant shall pursue moral responsibility as far as a crown of thorns, whether once he has embroiled parties and public and legislature he must resign. As matters are, he would certainly be kicked out by the legislature or chief executive, and it would serve him right. For democracy is ill served by and justifiably abhors those who, appointed to be its servants, assume the status and demeanor of masters.

III

The foregoing critical analysis of Professor Friedrich's view on administrative responsibility as stated in *Public Policy* shows, I think, its untenability both in its main drift and in most of its particular secondary though related aspects. The analysis reveals the following propositions as cogent and justifiable, in contradiction to Professor Friedrich's contentions.

Never was the political responsibility of officials so momentous a necessity as in our own era. Moral responsibility is likely to operate in direct proportion to the strictness and efficiency of political responsibility, and to fall away into all sorts of perversions when the latter is weakly enforced. While professional standards, duty to the public, and pursuit of technological efficiency are factors in sound administrative operation, they are but ingredients, and not continuously motivating factors, of sound policy, and they require public and political control and direction.

The public and the political assemblies are adequately sagacious to direct policy—they know not only where the shoe pinches, but have a shrewd idea as to the last and leather of their footwear: and where they lack technical knowledge their officials are appointed to offer it to them for their guidance, and not to secure official domination; and within these limits the practice of giving administrative latitude to officials is sound.

Contemporary devices to secure closer cooperation of officials with public and legislatures are properly auxiliaries to and not substitutes for political control of public officials through exertion of the sovereign authority of the public. Thus, political responsibility is the major concern of those who work for healthy relationships between the officials and the public, and moral responsibility, although a valuable conception and institutional form, is minor and subsidiary.

Notes

1. "Responsible Government Service Under the American Constitution," in Friedrich and others, *Problems of the American Public Service* (McGraw-Hill, 1935).
2. 51 *Political Science Quarterly* 582 (1936).

3. "Public Policy and the Nature of Administrative Responsibility," in *Public Policy, 1940* (Harvard, 1940), pp. 3–24.

4. Cf. Finer, "Personnel of Public Corporations," in *The British Civil Servant* (Allen and Unwin, 1937).

5. Cf. Finer, "British Cabinet and Commons in War Time," 56 *Political Science Quarterly* (September, 1941).

6. I use the terms nonfeasance and malfeasance in a common sense, not a legal sense—they are convenient.

7. Committee on Ministers' Powers, *Report, 1932, Addendum*.

8. Cf. R. V. Vernon and N. Mansergh, *Advisory Bodies* (Allen and Unwin, 1941).

9. Pp. 78, 79. The italics are mine.

10. Cf. Finer, *The British Civil Service* (The Fabian Society, and Allen and Unwin, 1937), pp. 243 *et seq.*

11. Cf. *Municipal Trading* (Allen and Unwin, 1941), especially the last two chapters, for a development of this point.

12. Page references are to *Public Policy, 1940*.

13. Cf. also Finer, *British Civil Service*, pp. 217–280.

14. *Concerning English Administrative Law* (Columbia University Press, 1941).

2

Ethics and
Administrative Discretion

Wayne A. R. Leys
Central Y.M.C.A. College, Chicago

During a time when men are risking their lives to defeat the dictators, some of us should be willing to face certain questions about administrative discretion. Dictatorship is limitless discretion which is restrained neither by public law nor by conscience. The art of war cannot by itself save us from such tyranny. Improvements in the art of government are necessary, too. Under the complex conditions of an industrial society those who enforce the laws must make at least part of the laws which they enforce. We can no longer pretend that executives merely fill gaps that have inadvertently been left in statute and constitution. Legislators admit that they can do little more with such subjects as factory sanitation, international relations, and public education than to lay down a general public policy within which administrators will make detailed rules and plans of action. More and more discretionary powers must be delegated to those who are charged with the regulatory and service functions of government. Wisdom in the exercise of those powers, therefore, is one of the safeguards that stands between us and a tyrannical or disorderly handling of our most vital interests.

Despite the growing importance of administrative discretion, it is a subject which is usually approached negatively, i.e., from the standpoint of the lawyer or judge who is interested in the *limits* of discretion. We have a large literature dealing with legislative restraint and judicial review. Much of this literature may be as necessary in the development of good administration as the negative criticism of rule-making and planning which greeted popular legislatures in the eighteenth century, when it was feared that those bodies would use their new powers tyrannically or foolishly. But we cannot expect administrators to act wisely if their only guides are statements of what they must *not* do. Those who are given discretionary powers must ask how the quality of discretion may be improved. Yet, as recently as 1939, Professor Leonard D. White, in his *Introduction to the Study of Public Administration,* remarked that the study of administrative discretion had never been undertaken from the administrative point of view.

As an addict of philosophy I cannot lay claim to the administrative point of view. Notwithstanding this handicap or advantage, I want to open the discussion. In view of the fact that ethics is the art (some say, science) of making wise choices, it would seem to be relevant to the problem of increasing the wisdom of administrative choices. Plato, Aristotle, Cicero, Bentham, and Kant, among others, tried to articulate moral principles for the guidance of legislators. Cardozo wrote an intelligible treatise on moral principles for judges who find that they have considerable discretion in certain cases. Why shouldn't ethics, the age-old quest for standards of conduct, help the administrator? The administrator is also looking for standards.

Some Unpromising Approaches

Executives in government probably feel that they could use some suggestions for the development of good standards and good judgment; but, influenced perhaps by none-too-enthusiastic memories of certain courses in college, they may doubt that ethics has any practical suggestions. If I take issue with this doubt, it is not that I regard everything that is called ethics as particularly relevant to the problems of administrative discretion.

I am not going to undertake a critical discussion of professional codes of ethics, such as the code adopted by the International City Managers' Association in 1924. Excellent as these precepts are for some purposes, they throw little light on the question of what to buy with the playground fund. There may be fifty ways of spending the money that are, all of them, compatible with the admonition to be diligent, above-board, free from avarice, and loyal to superiors. Professional codes of ethics do not contain the principles that we are looking for, because they prescribe standards for the administrator's *own* conduct. When we ask how his discretionary powers may be used wisely, we are asking about the standards which an administrator ought to prescribe for *other people*—citizens, departments, corporations, subordinates.

Another kind of ethics which is relatively unimportant for our problem is moralizing about the power of sin. Any observer of government must regret certain actions which have been, in his opinion, victories of selfishness and stupidity over the public interest. But where such conflicts are clearly recognized, the damage has already been done. We have been outvoted, or our own desires have prevailed over our conscience and we have had to act before we could resolve a mental conflict. Of course, we may ask what we ought to do next in such an imperfect situation; but that is quite a different topic from the contemplation of what might have been.

> If, of all sad words of tongue or pen
> The saddest are, "It might have been,"
> More sad are these we daily see:
> "It is, but hadn't ought to be."

The kind of ethical analysis which is profitable relates not to such closed questions but to the open questions, the as-yet-undecided questions of policy. I refer to the questions in which it is not yet clear what course of action will be both successful and in the public interest. The commissioners who are still puzzled as to what freight rates are fair, the directors who have not yet determined the standard by which milk shall be judged pure, the executives who have not yet decided which location for a public enterprise is in the public interest or what favors are legitimate public services: these men are confronted by the live kind of options which the great moral philosophers faced when they asked. *What* is good? It so happens that the philosophers spent part of their time discussing another question, viz., How great is the power of good will when we know what is good but are restrained by impulses and old habits? In answering this latter question the philosophers usually sermonized. Unfortunately the sermons are better known than the philosophers' analyses of the problem of setting up standards. The sort of ethics which may improve administrative decisions is concerned with the discovery of standards for right action rather than with the exhortation to do what has been already declared right.

Have the famous Occidental philosophers agreed upon anything concerning the standards for wise action? If I say, "Yes," it may seem that I am trying to speak for a roomful of prima donnas, for nearly every philosopher has started out by "refuting" his predecessors. The contentious aspect of the philosophical tradition is emphasized by the current academic custom in my field of carrying the student "through a hypercritical maze of ethical theories in order, finally, to convince him of the author's own particular theory as to the ultimate end of conduct" (I use the words of Professor Roland Warren). Philosophers are an argumentative lot, but their disputes often turn on "fine points." When we compare the philosophers with the lawyers, the merchants, the priests, and the politicians, we find the philosophers usually standing together. They are distinguished from other groups by the questions with which they are preoccupied and, especially, by the way in which they formulate the questions. If "the technique or treatment of a problem begins with its first expression as a question," as Suzanne Langer remarked in her *Philosophy in a New Key,* and if philosophers are unique in their phrasing of questions, they may occasionally have some very practical suggestions for solving problems that are faced by the non-philosophical. Indeed, I believe that the history of philosophical ethics can be viewed as an exploration of insoluble problems, some of which, by rephrasing, have been transformed into answerable questions.

What have the philosophers to contribute toward the development of standards in those areas where the administrators are granted much latitude by the legislature? Their first (and perhaps their only) contribution is a criticism of the administrator's conception of his problem. In the section that follows I shall state and criticize the late Ernst Freund's view, which seems to be widely accepted among public administrators and legislators. According to Freund, the problem of the official endowed with discretionary powers is to increase the definiteness of legal standards. I shall try to show why the use of "definiteness" in formulating the task baffles those who ask how administrative sagacity may be increased. Then I shall restate the problem and indicate the sort of answers that may be expected with the help of the ethical disciplines.

Standards and Administrative Law

Political scientists and lawyers commonly treat administrative discretion as the consequence of indefinite terminology in legislation. The legislature is supposed to supply the public official with standards of conduct by which he can determine whether citizens are to be coerced, cajoled, or let alone. If the legislative standard is definite, the administrator has no discretionary power, but only the ministerial power of determining the facts in the case. If, on the other hand, the legislative standard is not precise, the administrator must use his own judgment in deciding exactly what rule the citizen is to obey, and, in some cases of violation, just what is to be done about the unruly person.

Professor Ernst Freund took this view of the situation and did much to popularize it in the United States.

> When we speak of administrative discretion, we mean that a determination may be reached, in part at least, upon the basis of considerations not entirely susceptible of proof or disproof. A statute confers discretion when it refers an official for the use of his power to beliefs, expectations or tendencies instead

of facts, or to such terms as "adequate," "advisable," "appropriate," "beneficial," "competent," "convenient," "detrimental," "expedient," "equitable,"
"fair," "fit," "necessary," "practicable," "proper," "reasonable," "reputable," "safe," "sufficient," "wholesome," or their opposites. These lack the
degree of certainty belonging even to such difficult concepts as fraud or discrimination or monopoly. They involve matter of degree or an appeal to judgment. The discretion enlarges as the element of future probability preponder-
ates over that of present conditions; it contracts where in certain types of cases
quality tends to become standardized, as in matters of safety.[1]

Freund tried to distinguish gradations in the freedom of administrative
discretion. Although he made the attempt several times, he was apparently
never quite satisfied with his results. In his article on "The Use of Indefinite
Terms in Statutes"[2] he describes three grades of indefiniteness:

It is possible to distinguish roughly three grades of certainty in the language of
statutes of general operation: precisely measured terms, abstractions of common certainty, and terms involving an appeal to judgment or a question of degree. The great majority of statutes operate with the middle grade of certainty.

He describes the middle grade as follows:

Abstractions of common certainty may be furnished by words of popular usage, by technical terms, or by circumscribing definitions. No general rule can
be laid down as to which of these serves statutory purposes best, although a
good deal might be said about the illusory certainty of some technical terms
and of cumulations and qualifications sanctioned by traditional practice.
Every common abstraction has its "marginal" ambiguity, which mere elaboration of definition cannot altogether remove.

A banking law which directs the banking commission to refuse a charter unless a new bank has a paid-in capital of at least $15,000 falls into the first
grade of certainty or definiteness: the standard has precisely measured terms.
The second grade of legislative definiteness may be illustrated by a law
which empowers the Bureau of Immigration to refuse admittance to a mentally defective person: "mentally defective person" is an abstraction of
common certainty.
The third grade is exemplified in a statute which empowers a commission to compel an employer to take "appropriate" measures to keep his
premises "reasonably safe and sanitary." The language calls for a judgment
and raises a question of degree.
In his later and more systematic treatise Freund recognized an even
greater freedom of choice that is conferred by statutes that are indefinite to

the extent of not mentioning the conditions on which an official shall act. Thus, a permit may be required for a parade, but the police are not told on what basis they shall determine whether a permit shall be issued. Occasionally a statute will emphasize the discretion of the official by saying. "He shall have absolute . . . (or free) . . . discretion, and there shall be no appeal."

James Hart distinguishes four grades of administrative discretion. He uses the names (1) discretionary, (2) judgment passing, (3) fact-finding, and (4) ministerial. This is a somewhat different classification, but the extremes of complete freedom of choice and no freedom are similar to Freund's version.

Freund based his generalizations upon grants of regulatory power. Whether he would have adopted a different analysis if he had studied the discretion conferred upon officials of government corporations and service departments, I do not know. But it is clear that his emphasis in dealing with discretion is upon the indefiniteness of legislative standards. Where the legislature has been indefinite, the administrator must somehow become definite. It is impossible to prove just what the legislature meant. A question of public policy has not been completely decided by the legislators, and the enforcer of public policy must complete the decision. It follows that if we want wise public policies, we must have wisdom in the executive as well as among those who are called lawmakers.

These are the terms in which a student of administrative law phrases the need for ethical acumen and sound judgment. The administrator, charged with discretionary responsibilities, has to make an indefinite standard of action precise and explicit. How can he develop a definite standard?

Now let us evaluate Freund's analysis. It would be unbecoming of an amateur to question the accuracy of Freund's vast knowledge of administrative law, and my remarks should be construed as a conflict between the philosophical and the legal points of view rather than as an attempt on the part of a legal novice to find fault with a legal master. To one who is accustomed to philosophical modes of thought Freund's three or four grades of definiteness in legislative standards do not seem to have improved greatly the organization of his knowledge. In particular, I question his conception of the administrator's task as that of arriving at a definite standard. It may be recalled that Freund even suggested that the normal process would be for the legislature to enact the standards which the administrator should succeed in defining. Administrative discretion would thus be the means of eliminating the need for administrative discretion in the future.

To say that definiteness or susceptibility of proof is an inadequate criterion of a good standard may be to state a trifling proposition. Let me say it. Of course, I do not believe that Freund meant to imply that definiteness is a *sufficient* test of good administrative standards; but his failure to specify other tests gives an undue emphasis to "definiteness," as witness such a statement as the following:

> It appears from the foregoing that the normal function of an administrative order is to make a generic statutory prohibition or requirement definite.

The entire tradition of philosophical ethics is against acceptance of definiteness as an adequate criterion of good judgment. While Socrates and Kant and Bentham were constantly engaged in the work of definition, the popular standards to which they were opposed had only too much definiteness. And the philosophical standards which the philosopher rejects are usually definite. But he considers them to be definitely bad. The doctrinaire man is definite. The shrewd villain is definite in his standards. Something other than definiteness is lacking.

The crucial philosophical criticism of Freund's analysis is that it gives a misleading appearance of simplicity to the concept of definiteness. Philosophical controversies have long since sensitized students of philosophy to the indefiniteness of "definiteness." "Indefinite" may mean (1) "vague," "without limits," or it may mean (2) "ambiguous," "capable of referring to several set limits but not certainly specifying any one limit."

The indefiniteness of definiteness accounts for the difficulty of using Freund's classification of standards. It is doubtful whether any two observers could agree in assigning a hundred miscellaneous statutes to the three pigeon holes which he suggests. Where, for example would you place an old Wisconsin statute which required "joints, knuckles, and jacks of tumbling rods of all threshing machines to be *securely* boxed"? To judge the exercise of administrative discretion merely by the definiteness which the administrator gives to an indefinite statute is to oversimplify the discretionary problem. Is the administrator confronted with a really vague and unexplored subject? Or is he faced with a choice which the legislature has been unable or unwilling to make, a choice between two or more definite standards?

Legislative bodies are indefinite in their language for more than one reason. At times their failure to be specific or clear is an oversight. Again, it may be a recognition of their own lack of skill and experience. It may indicate the existence of a subject which can never be dealt with in general rules. Sometimes, the legislators do not feel that they can afford to spend the time required to hit the nail on the head. In all of these cases "indefiniteness" is probably vagueness.

On the other hand, the legislature may beat around the bush because it cannot muster a majority in favor of a clear-cut standard. The indecisiveness of the language then indicates the existence of several standards about which there is no vagueness at all. The statute is passed either in the hope that an administrative agency can settle a quarrel or from a desire to evade the issue. Pendleton Herring makes it clear that the vague language of statutory instructions for the Tariff Commission and the Federal Trade Commission did not imply a lack of definite standards which might have been applied in these fields.

> Congress has to an increasing extent escaped the onus of directly settling group conflicts by establishing under vague legislative mandates independent regulatory boards. . . . Upon the shoulders of the bureaucrat has been placed in large part the burden of reconciling group differences and making effective and workable the economic and social compromises arrived at through the legislative process.[3]

Where the legislature passes the buck in this way the problem is not a merely technical question of making vague standards definite. If the administrator becomes definite before something else happens, his rulings will be regarded as more unsatisfactory than if he, too, remains indecisive and ambiguous. "Moral gesture" legislation amounts to an instruction to do nothing specific, but most "pass-the-buck" legislation is an instruction to resolve the conflict between groups who want definite but rival standards to be legalized.

From the standpoint of administrators and administrative law there are many other observations to be made concerning discretionary powers and the improvement of their exercise. For our purposes, however, the significant points are: (1) the emphasis upon indefinite statutory language as the means of conferring discretion, and (2) the judgment of administrative success by the definiteness of standards supplied in such cases. A preliminary criticism of this diagnosis has called attention to two meanings of "indefiniteness": (1) "vague" and (2) "ambiguous." Particularly where discretionary powers are granted by ambiguity, it is doubtful whether "definiteness" is an adequate criterion of discretion.

Standards and the Philosophical View

The philosophical analysis of the problems of choice differs from Freund's. Its fundamental distinction is not between definite and indefinite standards. The philosopher is mainly concerned with the distinction between general (or abstract) standards, on the one hand, and specific standards, on the other hand. He wants to know whether you act on a general principle or only on an immediate, concrete rule. Some people suppose that "definite" is equivalent to "particular" whereas "indefinite" means the same as "general" or "abstract." This is not true. "You must not make that stairway too steep" is not general, though it is indefinite. "Educational facilities for the two races shall be equal" is definite, though it is quite general.

Dewey and Tufts stated the philosophical distinction in their *Ethics* as follows:

> Rules are practical: they are habitual ways of doing things. But principles are intellectual; they are the final methods used in judging suggested courses of action. . . . The intuitionist . . . is on the outlook for rules which will of themselves tell agents just what course of action to pursue; whereas the object of moral principles is to supply standpoints and methods which will enable the individual to make for himself an analysis of the elements of good and evil in the particular situation in which he finds himself.

Freund recognized this distinction, but he was interested in general principles that should serve as standards in the work of the legislator. He made little use of the distinction between general principle and detailed rule in his study of the standards which the legislature provides for the administrator.

Rules of action, which tell you just what acts to commit or avoid, are illustrated by the Biblical commands: "Neither shalt thou commit adultery," "Thou shalt make no covenant with the Jebusites," "These are the beasts which ye shall eat: the ox . . . etc." The more general type of moral principles can also be found in the Bible: "Whatsoever ye would that men should do unto you, do ye even also unto them." The Golden Rule does not tell anyone *what* he should do, but only supplies a test which presumably should be applied to all plans of action.

In philosophical ethics the discussion often begins with the statement of detailed rules of action, but rather quickly moves to the level of general principles. Thus, Book One of Plato's *Republic* opens with the statement of several specific rules, such as, "Return borrowed property"; then Plato turns to the more general principles of justice: "Do good to your friends and Harm to your enemies," "Seek the happiness of the whole state," and "Let everyone do that for which he is best suited."

Of course, an ethics which supplies criteria of action rather than detailed rules of action runs the risk of mistaking a general criterion for a plan of action. The "visionary" moralist has decided that good will is the proper motive or that peace is the desirable result of conduct, and then he has forgotten that he still needs an institutional plan for carrying out his intention or achieving the result that he prizes.

The philosopher's interest in general principles does not imply a desire to live without detailed plans of action. Plato knew it was impossible to act-in-general. But general principles offer not only a bird's eye view of life but also the possibility of studying the wisdom of contemplated actions. Until deliberations reach the level of generality, alternative courses of action can be compared only in dogmatic fashion. Let A say, "Five dollars a day is a fair wage," while B contends that five dollars is not a fair wage. Unless A

and B agree to appeal to general principles, all that they can do is to oppose the authority of one rule of action to the authority of another. Or, to
put it another way, A can claim that his plan is endorsed by better men
than the men who endorse B's plan. A may admit that he is the better man
whose intuition gives authority to the five-dollar-plan. Or more modestly,
he may claim that his plan is approved by God, the prophet, the Pope, the
philosopher-king, or mother. In this case, the rule of action is right because
an expert says so. If the expert's qualifications are challenged, the debate
must degenerate into name-calling or an appeal to force.

This is an explanation why many philosophers have refused to believe
that any given act is either right or wrong in itself. If thought and talk
about conduct are to be more than dogmatic assertions, a plan or rule of
action cannot by itself be accepted as an ethical standard.

Criteria of Action as Standards

As soon as appeal is made to general principles to settle the wisdom of conduct, attention is directed to a statement that does not tell anyone what to
do. The general principle merely states a criterion by which to test detailed
rules of action.

Many criteria of conduct have been proposed in the course of the last
three thousand years. Usually they specify either a motive or a result which
an act must have in order to be acceptable. Some of the criteria have been
institutional, e.g., the requirement of loyalty to state, family, church, or
property, or the requirement that actions preserve and promote these institutions. Other criteria have not referred directly to institutions, and perhaps they are the best known ethical standards: the preservation of life,
peace, my pleasure, security, health, abundance of food and possessions,
aesthetic enjoyments, friendship, good will, harmony, equality, or freedom.

Many moral philosophers went no further than to articulate one of these
criteria. If they were asked, "Why should I seek my own pleasure?" or
"Why is equality worth striving for?" they could only answer, "I cannot
doubt it, and, begging your pardon, you are a fool to ask such a question."
One ethical criterion was their ultimate standard, and they usually claimed
that they were satisfied on the point by an indubitable intuition.

Although the philosophers all hoped to find a single acid test of sound
judgment, most of them recognized in one way or another that no one criterion of action is entirely adequate for testing the value of conduct. It is
quite possible to evaluate any action with, say, the standard of equality;
but action that stands the test of equality may be deficient from the standpoint of freedom or happiness or loyalty to the family. No doubt, every
well-known ethical criterion, when taken as an absolute, can be used to
justify bad conduct. Thus, "It is right to help a friend. Therefore, I did

right in overlooking Smith's donation of government property to his friend." Or, "It is a man's duty to support his family. Therefore, Jones did right in defrauding Miller, for the proceeds were used to buy shoes for the baby." Or, "It is a good thing to protect health. Therefore, the commissioner should prohibit all fairs and conventions, for they increase the probabilities of an epidemic."

Such sophistry ignores the qualifications attaching to the principles to which appeal is made; each principle is treated as absolute. Reasonable men, on the contrary, find a conflict between criteria. They say, "Health is good, *other things being equal*," knowing full well that other things are frequently not equal.

Methods of Ranking Criteria

Moralists who recognize the conflict of values try to find some method for deciding which is the higher value. Much work remains to be done before these analytical methods will be readily applicable to the complicated problems of government.

At the present time I am inclined to classify ethical methods accordingly as they look away from the immediate choice situation or not. When the disciples of Socrates or Jesus find themselves torn between loyalty to country and love of peace or between regard for health and love of excitement, they are apt to look beyond their immediate circumstance. They ask what they would prefer in other situations, and thus seek by generalization to determine the permanent and universal *ranking* of values. In my language, they try to determine which criterion should always and everywhere be the ultimate test of action, and in which order other tests should be applied. Critical questions are propounded to direct the mind away from obsession with the practical alternatives as they appear in the immediate situation:

A. What is always and everywhere good?
B. What could we do without?
C. What would I want if I were in the other fellow's shoes?
D. What do I usually prefer?
E. What will seem insignificant in a twelve-month or as soon as I am out of my present predicament?

Having assigned to values, ends, or criteria an order which seems permanent and universal, the moralist determines which of his immediate alternatives is consistent with this general value order. His motto is to put first things first, and not to treat ends as means. But this motto is meaningful only because he has previously engaged in an ethical generalization. He has looked away from his own conflict of the moment and decided what *in general* is most worthwhile.

The second method of comparing rival values may be called utilitarianism (although I include here not only Mill and Bentham, but also the pragmatists and part of Aristotle). The utilitarian does not attempt to assign permanent places in a general value series to health, life, country, home, etc. Rather he assumes that there is no point to saying once and for all that the enjoyment of food is more or less important than the enjoyment of friendship. He values both kinds of enjoyment and tries to secure both of them as far as possible in each choice situation. The question is, Which action will secure more of these goods and which will secure less in the present circumstance? He concentrates attention upon the immediate choice and its possible consequences. He asks such questions as these:

A. What are the pros and cons, the advantages and disadvantages, of the various alternative actions?
B. What are the pleasures and what are the pains consequent upon the alternatives, and how do they compare in number, duration, intensity and extent, certainty and propinquity?
C. Have I thought of all the consequences of the contemplated actions? Have I thought of everything that I value in this particular situation and its eventualities?
D. Which alternatives would I regard as extreme actions and which would seem to be the golden mean?

Having taken steps to apply all relevant tests to the contemplated choice, the utilitarian tries to pick the alternative that entails the most advantages and the fewest disadvantages. In my language, he prefers the conduct that satisfies the greatest number of criteria to the greatest degree. For this purpose he concentrates attention upon the immediate discretionary situation and its possible repercussions.

Utilitarianism is still a philosophical method of handling value-conflicts, although it fixes one's gaze upon the immediate situation rather than upon a universal hierarchy of values. It insists upon an analysis of the values involved in one's present decision, and applies a general value principle, i.e., that one should prefer the course of conduct which realizes the most values and the fewest disvalues.

Neither the Platonic type of ethics nor the utilitarian says that a particular act, such as raising the tariff, is always right or always wrong. The Platonist will say that some value like good will or harmony is more important than the personal profit of a few: then he will examine the immediate situation to discover whether raising the tariff is a rule of action by which personal profit would nullify good will or harmony. The utilitarian will ask *how much* benefit is conferred upon the protected industry, how much indirect benefit accrues to the nation, how much ill will is generated, how much loss is incurred by other industries, etc. Then he will adopt or reject the tariff rule according to its net benefit or detriment.

This brief restatement of ethics is incomplete, but it will bring to mind the differences between the philosophical approach and Freund's approach to the problem of standards.

Another Classification

The legal and the philosophical analyses of discretion may be juxtaposed by asking what kind of standards (from the standpoint of ethics) Freund was talking about. The "indefinite" legislative standards might be rules of action; again, they might be criteria for evaluating rules of action.

Obviously, the granting of discretionary power always involves some indefiniteness with respect to the rule of action. Even if the status and identity of the actor and the conditions under which he must act are completely specified, at least the description of what he is expected to do must be vague or ambiguous; otherwise, the administrator would have no choice to make. In order to arrive at a useful classification of discretionary powers, therefore, we must ask whether the criteria of action are indefinite; and, if indefinite, whether they are ambiguous or vague.

We shall distinguish three classes of discretionary powers: (1) technical discretion, which is freedom in prescribing the rule but not the criterion or end of action; (2) discretion in prescribing the rule of action and also in clarifying a *vague* criterion—this is the authorization of social planning; (3) discretion in prescribing the rule of action where the criterion of action is *ambiguous* because it is in dispute—this amounts to an instruction to the official to use his ingenuity in political mediation.

1. *No discretion as to criterion.* This class of discretion is, in ordinary language, merely the choice of means to an end which is not in question. The legislature leaves it to the experts to hit upon the kind of action that will obtain a desired result. How the result is obtained is, within limits, a master of indifference to the law-making body: it is the area of discretion for the administrator.

   Typical of this grade of discretion are many of the delegations of power to regulate the processing and sale of food products. The criterion is not in dispute: it is the health of the consumer as far as science and the arts can achieve it without making costs prohibitive. Sometimes the regulating officials not only prescribe the rule of action but actually invent the rule, as in the famous case where scientists in the employ of the government worked out a new method of cleaning and canning blueberries.

Discretion is also limited to choosing the means of reaching a predetermined result in the regulation of insurance companies. The criterion or end is the solvency of the companies and the protection of the policyholders. Other examples are the rule-making powers of industrial and mining commissions with respect to safety, and the licensing powers in such trades as those of barbers, dentists, keepers of foster homes, and warehousemen. Technical discretion is likewise illustrated in the governmental services, e.g., the freedom with which military administrators act is limited by the avowed purpose of national security and victory in war. The protests over the Eisenhower-Darlan agreement are an interesting evidence of the technical character of military discretion.

In the history of ethics when the rule of action is all that is in question, we find that appeal is made to the judgment of an expert. The expert sets the standard. Moral philosophers have usually identified some expert-in-general, such as God, the priest, or the philosopher. In public administration it is interesting to note that the expert is an expert-in-particular. If the administrator is not himself a man of specialized training or experience, he will very likely hold hearings or take the recommendations of the appropriate specialists: bacteriologists, social workers, actuaries, the American Standards Association, or the American Bankers Association. Of course, experts don't always agree. Many arts are far from perfection. When the criterion is not in question, the chief difficulty in adopting a wise administrative standard is that of finding an occupational or scientific group which has attained at least semiprofessional status. Insofar as health, safety in employment, solvency, etc. are definite and agreed-upon criteria, there may be *relatively* little trouble about standards in the sense of rules of action. It is not always possible to give an absolutely precise interpretation to the legislative formula, such as eventuated in the first Illinois mining law which required "a sufficient supply" of pure air in mines and which was translated into the prescription that air currents moving at a stated velocity follow a specified route. But such indefinite language as "reasonable diligence" and "reputable practices" will be capable of satisfactory definition if there is an organized art or trade, and *if* the criterion of action is not controverted. As we shall see presently, it is in situations where the criterion is not agreed upon that expert opinion loses its effectiveness and acceptability in setting standards (rules of action).

2. *Discretion regarding a vague criterion.* Legislative power is delegated in a few fields where the legislature and the public find themselves unable to define either the rule or the criterion of action. These are the subjects on which most of those in the community do not know even the results which they desire. For a time, at least, the administrator may be free not only to choose the means but also the end of action. The legislative standard is indefinite in the sense of being vague.

The most common example of this type is in public education. The wayfaring man is able to tell, quite roughly of course, whether his child is sick or well, prosperous or poverty-stricken, safe or injured; but when is his child well educated? Although the pursuit and encouragement of school work has become almost a religion in this country, most of the friends of education have had only vague notions of what they desired. The first constitution of Massachusetts enjoined legislatures and magistrates to "cherish the interests of literature and the sciences and all seminaries of them." The Nebraska Legislature enacted a bill in 1864 regulating the establishment of colleges and universities with an object "to promote the general educational interests and to qualify students to engage in the several pursuits and employments of society, and to discharge honorably and usefully the various duties of life." Other state school laws have been even vaguer as to the controlling purposes of the school system. If the criteria or objectives sound definite, the appearance of definiteness quickly disappears when we ask about the relative importance of literature and the sciences, or the relative merits of general and vocational education, or just what constitutes vocational success.

It is true that the Morrill Acts prescribed the curricula for the land grant colleges and that many state legislatures require or prohibit the teaching of certain subjects. Statutes declare the ages of compulsory school attendance and sometimes the minimum requirements for teacher certification. But it is doubtful whether the eighteen states that require the teaching of American history had a much clearer conception than the thirty states that do not require it of the precise and complete contribution of this study to the life of the child and the state. In any event, the teachers of history and their superintendents have had difficulty trying to decide what they should accomplish. The criterion being vague, the school boards, regents, and superintendents were often free to prescribe the governing objectives. This explains, in part, why educational literature is replete with discussions of the aims of education.

Of course, legislatures have occasionally set both a definite rule of action and a definite criterion in school legislation. Tennessee's legislature prohibited the teaching of evolution; nine states have laws directing instruction in the humane treatment of animals, and thirty-three states require the school officials to supply instruction concerning the effects of narcotics, stimulants, and alcohol. It should be observed that as the educational administrators define the aims of education they sometimes arouse a part of the community to the definition of opposite aims. But school administration is probably the best example of discretionary powers conferred by vagueness of the legislature as to criteria.

There are other administrators besides the school men who receive this type of discretionary power. Boards of censorship, heads of government enterprises like the TVA, city planning commissions, professional licensing authorities, and library boards may be mentioned in this connection. Where the legislative criterion is really vague, the official has the broadest kind of discretion, the discretion of an accredited social planner.

Faced with the necessity of choosing an objective, administrators may proceed in hit-or-miss fashion; they may seek the definition in ethical and political literature; or they may themselves use such methods of ethical generalization and specification as we described in an earlier section. Judging by the history of public education, I should say that the greatest danger faced by the official at this point is "professionalism" in the bad sense of the word. By that I mean a tendency to fall into the habit of judging proposals by their effect on departmental expansion and convenience, regardless of what is *said* to be the guiding principle. At least, the educational world is shaken periodically by charges that school officials, blinded by bureaucratic loyalties, fail to sense the emerging value possibilities of our civilization.

3. *Discretion limited by rival criteria.* The third brand of discretion is the kind which Herring discusses in his book on *Public Administration and the Public Interest.* The legislature directs the administrator to regulate or license in the "public interest" or to see that someone serves the "public necessity and convenience." The language is indefinite, but it does not stand for a vague criterion of action. Rather, the public or the legislature is divided in favor of two or more sharply defined objectives.

Illustrations of discretion under these conditions engaged most of Herring's attention. The Tariff Commission received indefinite standards because the importers and consumers judged tariffs by different criteria than did the domestic manufacturers. The Federal Radio Commission was not told to require the use of the radio primarily for education nor was it told to encourage the use of radio primarily for amusement and advertising, for the simple reason that both purposes had strong support. The Bureau of Home Economics got into trouble over Circular 296 because the Department of Agriculture was conceived by some as promoting the farmer's prosperity and by others as promoting the health of the community.

More recently, the President and the State Department have come in for heavy criticism on account of the agreements which they negotiated under the Reciprocal Trade Agreement Act. The Supreme Court has declared that the President must be allowed a greater degree of discretion in international affairs than in domestic matters, and the Act in question explicitly conferred the power to reduce tariffs "wherever he finds existing import restrictions are unduly burdening or restricting American foreign trade." Yet it is safe to say that whatever the President might or might not have done under the Act, he would have been charged with an unwise exercise of discretion. If the cattle men and the distillers had been satisfied, we may be sure that at least the editors of the *New Republic* would have been dissatisfied. The trouble here is not a vague standard expressed in vague language, but many definite standards unable to come to anything but a vague agreement, which is hardly any agreement at all.

Another example of recent difficulties with an ambiguous criterion is the work of the National Defense Mediation Board during 1941. As William M. Leiserson diagnosed the situation (as reported by the *United States News* of February 27, 1942), there were two antithetical ideals of labor relations, neither of which had a decisive adoption by Congress.

> But instead of dealing with the general policy problem of the Office of Production Management separately from the labor disputes problem, it was thought that, by permitting labor organizations to nominate their own representatives on this Board, labor controversies would be adequately handled, and nothing would have to be done about the dissatisfaction with the policies of the Office of Production Management ... The attempt to make decisions without guiding policies or principles leads employers and workers to conclude that an award in a particular case establishes a policy which the Board will apply in all its cases. Decisions, therefore, will appear and, in fact, are likely to be arbitrary and capricious.

The reason that arbitrariness was detected in the Mediation Board's awards was that the interested community contained several cocksure factions. By contrast, in areas where criteria remain vague, as in education, many inconsistent decisions can be made without a guiding policy, and hardly anyone will recognize the inconsistency.

The discretion of the administrator in the presence of two well-defined but hostile criteria is hardly more than authorization to do what he can to settle a conflict. The administrator guides or echoes or resists a political process in which there must eventually be some synthesis, victory, or compromise of divergent objectives. In so far as administration is subordinated to sheer political power there will be no opportunity for rational deliberation. Nevertheless, many of the policy decisions are determined at least partially by hearings and by public discussions. To that extent, the administrator can attempt to guide the deliberations of himself and interested parties in a rational manner. To that extent, he may be aided by the philosophers' methods of resolving the conflicts between antipathetic criteria. Because the administrator is meeting a problem of ends rather than a problem of means, the administrator who is merely a technical expert may be incompetent in this situation. Our analysis therefore supports the plea for general administration.

It is not always easy to identify the competing criteria. No group likes to admit that its criterion of right action is merely its own desire for pelf. I believe that Dexter Keezer was referring in part to this difficulty when he wrote:

> If the Administrator of the NRA could have appealed to a broad array of well-digested facts bearing upon the issues involved in the drafting of codes, this lack of balance between the powers of employers, wage-workers and consumers as pressure groups might not have been of major consequence.[4]

As I interpret the NRA conflicts, it was not merely the absence of well-digested facts that made it difficult for the administrator to lift the issues above the arbitrament of unadorned pressures: it was also the absence of a clear and honest statement of the criteria represented by the competing pressure groups. The problem was to give every value a hearing which, at the same time, should be a grilling. But some people were busy disguising the values.

After the issues have been clarified so as to reveal the rival objectives, the administrator who is fortunate enough to preside over a semirational deliberation will probably employ one of the calculating or ranking methods by which philosophers have sought to resolve the conflicts between values. He will probably try to get the partisans to appreciate the criteria urged by their opponents. If he can get either side to say, "There is something we didn't think of," he will have gone far toward the avoidance of a foolish decision. A study of the amendments and repeals of rulings by our wartime agencies reveals a number of cases where the administrator and the interested parties had simply failed to appreciate the magnitude of the interests adversely affected by the original rulings. I am thinking not merely of economic interests that were ignored, but also, in cases where decisions were inspired by economic considerations, of adverse effects upon the recreational and educational side of community life.

An acquaintance with the ethics of Sidgwick, of Aristotle, of Hartmann, or of Dewey is no guarantee of wisdom in administrative decisions, but the leading principles and methods of these philosophers are articulations of the ways in which uncongenial values may be recognized and given a preference that will stand the criticism of experience. Ethics can at least give the administrator an enlarged vocabulary with which to discuss the subtle elements in a conflict of values.

The law sometimes specifies methods of comparing antagonistic values. This is the root meaning of "due process of law," although courts were for a time inclined to give "due process" a narrow construction which meant little more than testing action by its effect on property rights, regardless of other criteria. Occasionally the courts are quite voluble in specifying the "considerations" that are to be weighed in arriving at an administrative decision. In *Smyth v. Ames* the Supreme Court listed certain "evidence" to "be considered" in valuations for rate-making purposes, perhaps unwisely limiting the considerations to various aspects of the public utility company's prosperity, and omitting criteria such as goods and services that would be made available or restricted in the community by a given rate. The legislature may mention such "considerations," too. The Wisconsin banking law of 1921 specified the constituent criteria of "public convenience and advantage." "And it also shall investigate the character and experience of the proposed officers, the adequacy of existing banking facilities, and the need of further banking capital; the outlook for the growth and development of the city, town or village in which it is to be located, and the surrounding territory from which patronage would be drawn; the methods and banking practices of existing bank or banks; the interest rate which they charge to borrowers; the character of the service which they render the community, and the prospects for the success of the proposed bank if efficiently managed." Although the criteria thus imposed upon the administrator are often vague, they are the most abstract type of legal principle and remind one of the terms in which philosophers talk about the problems of choice, i.e., they suggest a method for resolving the conflicts between rival criteria, which, in turn, are the basis for selecting detailed rules of action.

The discretion conferred by a deadlocked or timid legislature is much more limited than we usually suppose. Indefinite language that expresses an unreconciled contradiction between opposed criteria gives the administrator some freedom of action, but it is really a freedom to decide little more than by what procedures and proposals he will try to bring various factions into an agreement.

Conclusion

I have tried to bring the administrative and the philosophical points of view into a mutually beneficial juxtaposition. The task was difficult because of differences in occupational vocabularies. If I have taken liberties with both languages I hope that neither the philosophers nor the administrators will be outraged by my malapropisms, but will generously make efforts of their own to bridge the word-chasm that separates the two fields. Philosophers can certainly profit from a knowledge of administrative problems, and I have been told that administrators need some philosophical insights.

The philosophical criticism of current administrative and legal views of discretion is that the administrator puts too much stress on achieving definiteness of standards. My own first reaction to the problem of discretionary powers is that Freund's classification according to definiteness should be supplanted or complicated by some other distinctions. I have suggested a three-fold classification which distinguishes:

1. Merely technical discretion, where the legislature has stated or assumed that the administrator knew the results which it desired;
2. Discretion in social planning, where the legislature doesn't know exactly what it ultimately will want in the way of results; and
3. Discretion in the work of reconciliation, where the legislature has, in effect, asked the administrator to break a political deadlock.

These three types of discretionary grant are identified by the legislature's disposition respecting criteria. If the legislature specifies or assumes a criterion, the administrator plays the role of the technical expert. If the legislative criterion is vague, the administrator has authority not only to work out definite rules of action but also to propose goals for governmental activity: he is an accredited social planner. If, on the other hand, the legislature is sharply divided regarding the criterion of action, the administrator does not have either the freedom of the technician or the freedom of the planner, but only a certain leave to mediate and facilitate negotiations between warring pressure groups.

Freund was correct in taking indefinite terminology as a sign that the legislature has delegated discretionary power; but to understand the nature of the discretion thus granted, it is necessary to do more than classify the language according to its definiteness. In objecting to Freund's classification I do not pretend to refute it (classifications cannot be "refuted") or to deny that it is useful for some purposes. I merely suggest that the classification according to definiteness fails to emphasize vital differences in the kinds of choice which the administrator has to make.

I do not see how an official can proceed to a wise and democratic use of his discretion unless he first determines whether the criteria of action are settled, vague, or in dispute. If the statute itself does not make this clear, the official may have to inspect legislative debates or public opinion. Having clarified this matter, he should, I imagine, find the classical methods of ethics useful in (1) testing the compatibility of his technically defined rules with a settled criterion, (2) in articulating a vague criterion, and (3) in rationalizing debate where the criteria are in dispute.

Notes

1. *Administrative Powers over Persons and Property* (University of Chicago Press, 1928), p. 71.
2. 30 *Yale Law Journal* 437–55 (1921).
3. *Public Administration and the Public Interest* (McGraw-Hill Book Company, 1936), p. 7.
4. Quoted by Herring, op.cit, p. 245.

3

TRENDS OF A DECADE IN ADMINISTRATIVE VALUES

Wallace S. Sayre
The College of the City of New York

"The sense of the importance of values," wrote a thoughtful observer in 1950, "needs to pervade the study of administration." The prime reason for this imperative, he continued, is the large participation of the administrative agencies in giving purpose and content to modern government in the United States, a participation which seems increasingly "to transfer the search for the public interest to the administrator" and to expect recommendations from the administrative hierarchy which accord with its own concepts of the public interest.[1]

Measured in these terms a decade is a very brief period in which to identify with any certainty the significant landmarks which mark out the general directions in which our basic premises about public administration have moved. The perspective for reviewing the administrative values of the 1940's does not yet give the observer that 20-20 hindsight which Paul Porter has urged all administrators to transform into 20-20 foresight. But it is clear that we have been concerned with administrative values, although perhaps insufficiently concerned; and, as the decade closed, both the students and the practitioners of public administration had become more inquisitive about basic assumptions and preferences, more conscious of and less dogmatic about the questions which probed into long-accepted canons.

48

I

The dominant administrative values with which the decade began, it can be asserted at the risk of great oversimplification, were those concepts embodied in two profoundly influential documents: the *Report* of the President's Committee on Administrative Management; and the *Papers on the Science of Administration* by Gulick, Urwick, and others, a group of essays initially assembled for the use of the President's Committee. Although these documents were published in 1937, their preeminence continued well into the following decade. They gave to the students and practitioners of administration in 1940 a closely knit set of values, confidently and incisively presented. In magisterial tones the President's Committee proclaimed:

> Fortunately, the foundations of effective management in public affairs, no less than in private, are well known. They have emerged universally wherever men have worked together for some common purpose. . . . Stated in simple terms these canons of efficiency require the establishment of a responsible and effective chief executive as the center of energy, direction, and administrative management; the systematic organization of all activities in the hands of a qualified personnel under the direction of the chief executive; and to aid him in this, the establishment of appropriate managerial and staff agencies. There must also be provision for planning, a complete fiscal system, and means for holding the Executive accountable for his program. (p. 3)

These precepts were elaborated and buttressed by the Gulick and Urwick essays, especially in the justly famous "Notes on the Theory of Organization" by Gulick and in the persuasive essay on "Organization as a Technical Problem" by Urwick. In these documents, confident and experienced men wrote eloquently and with contagious conviction of a public administration which was nearing the stature of a science, a public administration in which it would be possible "to put values and ends to one side, or to assume them as constants, just as is done in the pure sciences," as Gulick hoped in his concluding essay, so significantly entitled "Science, Values and Administration." "In this way," he continued, "it may be possible to approximate more nearly the impersonal valueless world in which exact science has advanced with such success."

The decade did not, of course, begin with a note of unanimity upon such important matters. John Gaus, reviewing the Gulick-Urwick *Papers* in the *American Political Science Review,* stated with gentle emphasis the reservation which was a prophetic anticipation of the trends of the next decade. He questioned

> . . . the emphasis on separating out certain techniques of administration from the tasks which the state undertakes, and hence from the political forces

which are responsible for them. . . . There is, in these papers, inevitably a certain thinness. . . . [We do not] see administration as a "going concern," actual and tangible, the product of political forces and values and in turn creating new political forces and new values. Unless we explore the questions discussed in this volume, we cannot equip our states for their tasks. But unless we relate these questions . . . to our politics, we will not find what we may have to contribute used by those who need to use these contributions and have the power to do so.[2]

Still other values, more clearly identified now by the gift of hindsight, were being formulated at the opening of the decade but major attention to them was still deferred; notable among these were the broad and suggestive concepts to be found in Chester Barnard's *The Functions of the Executive;* in Pendleton Herring's *Public Administration and the Public Interest;* in Arthur Macmahon and John Millett's *Federal Administrators* and *The Administration of Federal Work Relief;* and in John Gaus and Leon Wolcott's *Public Administration and the United States Department of Agriculture.* And Schuyler C. Wallace was even then preparing his forceful statement of skepticism that "the type of administrative organization best suited to the needs of the country" would be based upon any simple formula.[3] In these, and in other sources, was to be found evidence that the values of public administration were not yet settled and finite.

II

The decade of the 1940's closed, we may say at less risk of oversimplification, with a more complex set of administrative values than that with which it began. No closely related set of documents now embody the accepted doctrines in such high degree as did the President's Committee *Report* and the Gulick-Urwick *Papers* in 1940. Heterodoxy, not orthodoxy, is the distinguishing characteristic of administrative values in 1950. Yet most observers would describe this circumstance as a sign of the growth of public administration toward maturity, toward a greater and more crucial significance in our society, toward a broader and enriched concept of the range of values involved.

It is difficult to name the landmarks which form the natural boundary for the end of the decade in the field of administrative values. Yet it is possible to identify some of the major sign posts which have directional significance for the decade of the 1950's.

Perhaps the most nearly dominant note for the emerging decade is set by Paul Appleby's *Policy and Administration* (1949), with its forthright declaration (p. 170) that

Public administration is policy-making. But it is not autonomous, exclusive or isolated policy-making. It is policy-making on a field where mighty forces contend, forces engendered in and by the society. It is policy-making subject to still other and various policy makers. Public administration is one of a number of basic political processes by which this people achieves and controls governance.

This complete rejection of the non-normative concept of public administration, unequivocal in its repudiation of the separation of politics from administration, is consistent with the earlier theme and substance of Appleby's *Big Democracy,* issued at mid-decade. Then Appleby had asserted: "It is the whole contribution of the executive branch I have in mind when I think of 'public administration.'"

In sharp contrast stands the new text by Simon, Smithburg, and Thompson, *Public Administration* (1950), which represents the first systematic exposition of public administration as a social process, and which aspires to construct, on new psychological and sociological foundations, a science of public administration which will be non-normative, free from values, desires, and prejudices, "a science in the sense of an objective understanding of the phenomena without confusion between facts and values."

Bearing witness to the continuity as well as to the diversity of values in public administration at mid-century, the Hoover Commission *Reports* (1949) restate the durable concepts of the President's Committee of 1937, especially those "canons of efficiency [which] require the establishment of a responsible and effective chief executive as the center of energy, direction, and administrative management." The Hoover Commission regards certain propositions as immutable:

> The President, and under him his chief lieutenants, the department heads, must be held responsible and accountable to the people and the Congress for the conduct of the executive branch. Responsibility and accountability are impossible without authority—the power to direct. The exercise of authority is impossible without a clear line of command from the top to the bottom, and a return line of responsibility and accountability from the bottom to the top. The wise exercise of authority is impossible without the aids which staff institutions can provide. . . .[4]

The commission does not appeal explicitly to science in administration, although its values clearly embrace the precepts of scientific management. It does not stress the separation of politics from administration; instead, although one searches in vain for an explicit statement of its position upon this dilemma, the commission is obviously enunciating a constitutional doctrine which is in its essence political.

The case studies of the Committee on Public Administration Cases (1949, 1950), now beginning to exert an influence as yet unpredictable in its proportions, provide still another landmark. The values most visible in these cases are those which relate administration to policy formation, to choices of means affecting goals, to the political process broadly conceived; the premises least evident, if not altogether absent, are those which would lead to a non-normative science of administration.

These somewhat arbitrarily chosen landmarks for the administrative values of 1950, selected from the great abundance of thoughtful inquiry into the foundations of public administration which has marked the past decade,[5] suggest at least the general contours of today's value systems in public administration. The debate about values, it is apparent, is not ended. The quest for a science of public administration divorced from all values (save the master value of objective science itself) continues to attract the energies of some students; others seek a theory of public administration in which values are seen as the indispensable essence.

No one has stated more inclusively, more concisely, or more wisely, the mood of pluralistic values and of wide-ranging hypotheses with which the new decade begins than has Arthur Macmahon in responding to Dwight Waldo's question as to whether there is a study of administration "as such":

> The reviewer ventures to sketch the beginnings of an answer. The endlessly special conditioning role of purpose is obvious. The unique political context of public administration in each country at any given time is the prime factor. The heaviest stress in training must rest here. Within the distinctive political frame, general to government and peculiar to the society in question, each program and each specific policy within it conditions structure and procedure. But there are universals; they arise from two sources. First, some elements of universal applicability come, like mathematics, from the logic of existence as the mind knows it. This logic presents categories of possibility, like area and function as bases of groupage. The concept called a principle appears characteristically as a rigid limitation of alternatives, not a choice. The essence of principle is relative in a double sense. The imperative of a limited choice channels attention to the factors, largely related to the purpose at hand, which indicate the preferable alternative. Second, some elements of general applicability flow from the fact that human beings are sufficiently alike to show common characteristics of behavior when they associate with each other in the same types of relationship in organizations for different purposes. Considerable predictability thus enters the art of living with others. But we must be cautious about regarding even the deepest traits as constants that are permanent. For, apart from individual variations, prevailing personality structures are conditioned by cultures and change with them. It is the highest privilege and duty of public administration to contribute wholesomely to this interaction.[6]

Here would seem to be the main values which will characterize the emerging decade: "the endlessly special conditioning role of purpose"; "the unique political context of public administration"; "each program and each specific policy within it conditions structure and procedure"; "some elements of universal applicability" come "from the logic of existence"; "the concept called a principle appears characteristically as a rigid limitation of alternatives, not a choice"; "some elements of general applicability flow from the fact that human beings are sufficiently alike to show common characteristics of behavior"; "but we must be cautious about regarding even the deepest traits as constants that are permanent." If the next decade is to bring to public administration the unity of a new synthesis of competing values, this is its most likely blueprint.

Perhaps the trends of the decade in administrative values may now be described in preliminary terms: there have been no sharp turns, no violent repudiations of the values with which we began the decade; instead, the stream of values has been widened—some earlier and narrower values have been relatively submerged, other and broader values have become more sharply visible, some new values have been added, but the elements of continuity are as evident, if not as emphatic, as those of change. The most striking difference between 1940 and 1950, in the realm of administrative values, is the growth in meaning—the value enrichment—of the phrase "public administration." This enlargement of values may be seen from various perspectives. The adjective *public* is now frequently, in effect, italicized. Our values, in one context, have moved from a stress upon the managerial techniques of organization and management to an emphasis upon the broad sweep of public policy—its formulation, its evolution, its execution, all either within or intimately related to the frame of administration. In another context, our values have moved away from the confining view of an "administrative man," responding mechanically to the imperatives of technological management, toward broader and deeper perspectives of human behavior in cooperative action.

III

The trend in administrative values is nowhere more sharply illuminated than in the changing interpretations placed upon the concept of the role of science in administration. At the beginning of the decade there was a confident aspiration toward a science of administration; indeed it was widely asserted that the canons of such a science were already known. At the end of the decade the exponents of a science of administration are still present, but they espouse a new set of canons and reject the earlier "principles" founded upon scientific management. The advocates of a "science" of public administration are most clearly represented in 1950 by Herbert Simon,

Donald Smithburg, and Victor Thompson in their text *Public Administration*. They say:

> The study of the behavior of persons in organizations can be non-normative—that is, it can be freed from the desires, values, and prejudices of the person making the investigation and can be made to rest upon an objective analysis of human interaction. . . . This book will largely be concerned with administration as a science—not science in the sense of the exactness that the physical sciences have achieved, but science in the sense of an objective understanding of the phenomena without confusion between facts and values.

But, they hasten to add,

> . . . This emphasis on the factual does not mean that we discount the importance of values. . . . No knowledge of administrative techniques [i.e., facts] . . . can relieve the administrator from the task of moral choice—choice as to organization goals and methods and choice as to his treatment of the other human beings in his organization. His code of ethics is as significant a part of his equipment as an administrator as is his knowledge of administrative behavior, and no amount of study of the "science" of administration will provide him with this code.[7]

This newer approach to the value of science in administration has performed successfully its skeptical function; it has placed on the defensive all the concepts of scientific management. Yet it has not won the field for itself. It has earned great influence for a new set of factors—primarily psychological and sociological—but its proposition that these new "facts" can be transmuted into a science of administration *sans* values has led one penetrating observer to comment that "one is left with the suspicion that the purer a science of administration, the less will it be socially relevant."[8]

Still another critic, Robert A. Dahl, has argued cogently that:

> . . . the student of public administration cannot avoid a concern with ends. . . . A non-normative science of public administration might rest on a basic hypothesis that removed ethical problems from the area covered by the science. . . . Can such a basic hypothesis be created? To this writer the problem appears loaded with enormous and perhaps insuperable difficulties. . . . We are a long way from a science of public administration. No science of public administration is possible unless: (1) the place of normative values is made clear; (2) the nature of man in the area of public administration is better understood and his conduct is more predictable; and (3) there is a body of comparative studies from which it may be possible to discover principles and generalities that transcend national boundaries and peculiar historical experiences.[9]

Dahl is seemingly skeptical that a science of public administration will be the fruit of this generation.

It is of course obvious that all those who see public administration as primarily a political process, or who stress the unique political context which controls the form and substance of public administration, must reject both the larger claims of the new "science" and its rigid separation of facts from values; indeed, they cannot escape describing the fact-value dichotomy as merely a new and subtle version of the earlier formulation of the separation of politics from administration.

IV

The changes and turns in the decade's debate over the basic hypothesis of public administration—that is, whether it shall strive to be primarily a non-normative science divorced from values, or whether it shall aspire toward a theory of governance which embraces the political and social values of a democratic society as well as the "facts" of administrative behavior—are especially revealed in the discussions of the responsibility and accountability of the agencies of administration. These discussions have a common concern: how to reconcile the great, unprecedented growth of administrative power with democratic government.

An important segment of the literature of public administration during the decade has been concerned with the relationship of the executive, especially the Presidency, to the system of administrative responsibility and accountability. Thus the President's Committee *Report* described its first canon of efficiency as "the establishment of a responsible and effective chief executive as the center of energy," a canon upheld by the committee's judgment that "the American Executive must be regarded as one of the very greatest contributions made by our Nation to the development of modern democracy—a unique institution." "The preservation of the principle of full accountability of the Executive to the Congress," the *Report* asserted, "is an essential part of our republican system." The essential instrument for the enforcement of this full responsibility was to be found in the recommendations of the committee for an integrated, hierarchical administrative organization responsive to the command of the President.

This prescription was underscored a decade later by the Hoover Commission with its even sharper emphasis upon the concept of a clear line of command from the top to the bottom and a return line of responsibility and accountability from the bottom to the top, with the President at the apex of an unbroken, fully integrated hierarchy. This doctrine of a symmetrical administrative structure under the almost exclusive direction of the President is made most explicit in the commission's draft of proposed implementing legislation, the General Executive Management bill of 1949, in which the direction of the administrative agencies seems to be merged with the constitutional realm of presidential power as a correlative of the principle of "centralized political responsibility" which the proposal describes as having been provided for in the Constitution. The proposed act declares:

> The executive agencies exist in order to enable the responsibility of the President, as set forth in Article H of the Constitution, to be discharged efficiently. . . . All such executive agencies, and the heads thereof, are merely representatives of and acting for the President; and whenever any function is vested by law in any such agency or in the head thereof, such function is so vested merely for convenience. Such function should be treated as a function actually vested in the President and being exercised by the executive agency concerned, or the head thereof, pursuant to authority so to do derived from delegations by the President. In connection with the exercise of any such function, the executive agency and the head thereof is (unless the function be quasi-judicial in nature) at all times subject, in respect of all matters relating to its exercise (including the time, manner, and extent of its exercise), to the direction and control of the President.

The same provision is then stated for subordinate executive agencies (bureaus, divisions, boards, administrations, authorities, agencies, etc., within principal agencies), and their actions also are made subject to the direction and control of "the head of the principal executive agency in which such subordinate executive agency exists or of which it is an organizational unit." There are but two reservations: functions in or under a principal executive agency may not be transferred under the terms of the bill, nor may functions be abolished.[10]

These are clearly value premises which exalt the power of the elected chief executive over a tightly knit hierarchy as the keystone in a system of administrative responsibility. As such, they reflect not only the deep-running and powerful currents of the Hamiltonian and Wilsonian concepts of presidential power; they are a logical, perhaps in large degree an inescapable, response to the facts of modern government.

But the stress upon these values of the executive has evoked, increasingly throughout the decade, a determination that other values related to responsibility and accountability shall not be overlooked or submerged. The most eloquent and unequivocal spokesman for one group of competing values, the doctrine of legislative supremacy, is Charles S. Hyneman in his *Bureaucracy in a Democracy* (1950). "Congress should specify in the statute," he believes, "every guide, every condition, every statement of principle, that it knows in advance it wants to have applied in the situations that are expected to arise. This rule derives from a concept of legislative supremacy." This practice he would modify only in terms of two controlling considerations: one, Congress should not spend so much time on one statute that it neglects other matters it regards as of greater importance; two, Congress should not impose detailed controls over administrative officials which will defeat congressional objectives. The general rule, "that Congress should have what it wants," Hyneman would extend to the creation and to the definition of the structure of the administrative organization that is to administer a governmental undertaking, but he would make stronger the modifying considerations. In all the other fields of administration where Congress has constitutional responsibilities—in providing the money, fixing standards of administrative conduct, reviewing the action of the bureaucracy, choosing the members of the bureaucracy— Hyneman places greater reliance upon the legislative institution as the guarantor of responsibility and accountability than do the reports of the President's Committee or of the Hoover Commission.[11]

Another emphasis on the theme of responsibility is also prominent at the close of the decade. This is the assertion that the administrative agencies themselves have a representative role in our governmental system. From this perspective it is argued that the system of responsibility must include a recognition of the representative function of the bureaucracy and make provisions for its responsible operation. Thus, for example, Norton Long has recently contended that

> ... the theory of administration has neglected the problem of the sources and adequacy of power. ... The bureaucracy under the American political system has a large share of responsibility for the public promotion of policy and even more in organizing the political basis for its survival and growth. ... The agencies ... have or develop a shrewd understanding of the politically feasible in the group structure within which they work. Above all, in the eyes of their supporters and their enemies they represent the institutionalized embodiment of policy, an enduring organization actually or potentially capable of mobilizing power behind policy.

Long concludes that "attempts to solve administrative problems in isolation from the structure of power and purpose in the polity are bound to prove illusory." The solution, he believes, must lie in the prior development of a responsible two party system; until then the efforts to reorganize the executive branch or the legislative branch may effect improvement but in a large sense must fail to provide an adequate system of responsibility.[12]

Not all the observers who emphasize the representative function of the administrative agencies carry their conclusions this far, even though they would agree that political parties are major institutions in a system of responsible government. They center their attention, instead, upon methods through which the representative role of the administrative agencies may be recognized, clarified, and improved within the administrative hierarchy itself. The most widespread application of this approach may be found in the growing practice of admitting citizen representatives and representatives of organized interest groups to participation in the administrative process. The use of local boards in agricultural policy-making and in the administration of price control and rationing are cases in point; so also are the advisory committees representing the most relevant interest groups, now an almost universal practice among administrative agencies.

The premise that administrative agencies are themselves representative institutions, engaged in a representative process comparable to, even if lesser than, the representative role of elected executives and legislatures is a concept which now engages the attention of many students.[13] The reconciliation of this premise with other elements in a responsible government, especially the accommodation of the premise to the competing concepts of executive supremacy or legislative supremacy, is an unresolved dilemma of major proportions. One approach to the resolution of these opposed values is to give emphasis to the total political process as the guardian of responsibility, a view expressed by Appleby in his conclusion that "all of the political processes are *together* important to popular government."[14] There are, he fears, some dangers implicit in administrative devices for citizen participation, especially the wish that reliance may be placed upon representatives not broadly enough representative. "We must remember," he emphasizes, "that *there is nothing so fully democratic as the totality of the political processes in a free society.*"[15]

There has been at least one other important focus for the decade's debate concerning the proper structure of a system of administrative responsibility. The decade began with a wide division of opinion upon the importance of the judicial process in administrative action. The question was centered less upon the role of the courts in the supervision of administration than upon the degree to which the judicial process should be introduced into the administrative process itself. The Walter-Logan bill, vetoed by President Roosevelt in 1940, expressed in strongest terms the views of those who sought a judicialization of many forms of administrative action; the *Report* of the Attorney General's Committee in 1941 took a more moderate view.[16] The war temporarily adjourned the debate, but in 1946 the Administrative Procedures Act reflected both the revival of the issue and the seeming triumph of the more extreme views. The act emphasizes the values of uniform procedures in administrative decisions affecting private rights and of procedures which conform so far as possible to the patterns of judicial action. At the end of the decade critics and proponents of the judicial process within the administrative process are still in disagreement, but the issue itself has lost prominence as an item of major concern in the continuing discussions about administrative responsibility.[17]

The construction of a system of administrative responsibility appropriate to the governmental tasks of a democratic society at the midpoint of the twentieth century has thus been the subject of a many sided debate throughout the decade. The elected chief executive with unadulterated responsibility for and control over an integrated administrative hierarchy, the institutions of legislative control over the objectives, structure, and methods of administrative agencies, the necessities of the representative functions of administrative agencies themselves, and the values of the judicial process within administration have each in turn been presented as the central institution for responsibility. And, at the end of the decade, there is emerging a more inclusive emphasis upon the values of the total political process of democratic constitutional government as the source and guarantee of responsibility, an emphasis which avoids invidious comparisons among its several institutions. But if this latter emphasis has the great virtue of restoring a balanced view of the whole, it also leaves unresolved the task of relating and differentiating the several parts in their expected contributions to responsible administration.[18]

V

The sense of the importance of values in public administration has increased significantly during the decade, and especially at its close. If it is true that much energy was expended in the search for a science of administration which would be neutral as to values, it is also true that the debate which this search evoked from its very beginning resulted eventually in a new and greater emphasis upon the role of values in public administration. The indispensable function of values in public administration is now conceded on all sides; the continuing debate on this score is about the relative importance of "facts" and "values," and about the usefulness of this distinction in the study and practice of administration.

The central concern about values in public administration in a democratic society turns around the arrangements for the responsibility and accountability of the administrative agencies for their policies and their programs of action. As students of public administration and administrators seek new perspectives on this fundamental problem they become increasingly aware of the continuum and of the important nuances of its differentiation. This suggests that the basic search in the study of administration is more for a theory of government than for a science of administration.

The inclusion of public administration within a theory of government brings into the range of emphasis other important values which cannot be more than suggested in this article. Among them the new emphasis upon purpose as the value which gives clearest meaning to the machinery of administration can hardly be exaggerated in its future significance. "A clear statement of purpose universally understood is the outstanding guarantee of effective administration," Luther Gulick concluded from his reflections upon the administration of World War II; "translation from purpose to program is the crucial step in administration."[19] No less central is the emerging emphasis upon the fuller values of democratic administration, that morale in administration depends upon a vital participation in the definition of purpose by those who are affected by it as citizens and as civil servants. This is an emphasis upon which exploration is only beginning in public administration; its growth depends upon the contributions of all the social sciences to the greater understanding of those forms and methods of administration which contribute vigorously to the health and growth of democratic society.[20] The values to be contributed to public administration by the other social sciences promise to be one of the brightest features of the coming decade; and, among these contributors, the parent, political science, should not be the least significant.

Notes

1. E. S. Redford, "The Value of the Hoover Commission Reports to the Educator," 44 *American Political Science Review,* 283–98 (June, 1950). This penetrating essay is rich in many value insights.

2. 32 *American Political Science Review* 132–34 (February, 1938). Two years earlier, in *The Frontiers of Public Administration* (University of Chicago Press, 1936), John M. Gaus, Leonard D. White, and Marshall E. Dimock had stressed the great involvement of public administration in social and political values.

3. *Federal Departmentalization: A Critique of Theories of Organization* (Columbia University Press, 1941).

4. *General Management of the Executive Branch,* p. 1.

5. The most useful brief bibliography, accompanied by comments of acute and suggestive insight, is to be found in John M. Gaus, "Trends in the Theory of Public Administration," 10 *Public Administration Review* 161–68 (Summer, 1950).

6. Arthur W. Macmahon, "The Administrative State," 8 *Public Administration Review* 211 (Summer, 1948).

7. *Public Administration* (Alfred A. Knopf, 1950), pp. 19–24.

8. Fritz Morstein Marx, reviewing Simon's *Administrative Behavior,* in 8 *Public Administration Review* 65 (Winter, 1948).

9. "The Science of Public Administration: Three Problems," 7 *Public Administration Review* 1–11 (Winter, 1947).

10. 81st Cong., 1st sess., S. 942, H.R. 2613. The bills were introduced in the two houses in February, 1949, read twice, and referred to the respective committees on Expenditures in the Executive Departments.

I am indebted to Nathan D. Grundstein, Wayne University, for his thoughtful and suggestive comments on this and related matters in an unpublished paper,

"Presidential Power, Administration and Administrative Law," read at the Michigan Academy of Arts and Sciences, March, 1950.

11. See especially his chapters 5–10. Elias Huzar, *The Purse and the Sword* (Cornell University Press, 1950); Robert A. Dahl, *Congress and Foreign Policy* (Harcourt, Brace, & Co., 1950); and A. W. Macmahon, "Congressional Oversight of Administration: The Power of the Purse," 58 *Political Science Quarterly* 160–90, 380–414 (1943), each emphasize in separate ways the values of legislative institutions in a system of administrative responsibility.

The views expressed by Hyneman in 1950 were also stated with great eloquence by Herman Finer in a wider context, "Administrative Responsibility in Democratic Government," 1 *Public Administration Review* 335–50 (Summer, 1941).

12. Norton E. Long, "Power and Administration," 9 *Public Administration Review* 257–64 (Autumn, 1949). At the beginning of the decade, E. S. Wengert had criticized the orthodox neglect of the representative and democratic values of administration. The public interest would be discovered, he felt, in the degree "the administrator can call upon those affected by his action to assist in shaping administrative policy." See his "The Study of Public Administration," 36 *American Political Science Review* 313–22 (1942).

13. For varying emphasis upon this matter, see Paul H. Appleby, *Policy and Administration* (University of Alabama Press, 1949); John M. Gaus, *Reflections on Public Administration* (University of Alabama Press, 1947); V. O. Key, *Politics, Parties and Pressure Groups*, 2d ed., 1947, chapter 23, "Administration as Politics," pp. 701–25; J. Donald Kingsley, *Representative Bureaucracy* (Antioch Press, 1944).

14. See *Policy and Administration*, p. 164.

15. "Toward Better Public Administration," 7 *Public Administration Review* 93–99 (Spring, 1947).

16. Attorney General's Committee on Administrative Procedure, *Final Report*, 1941; Robert M. Benjamin, *Administrative Adjudication in the State of New York* (Albany, 1942); James Hart, *An Introduction to Administrative Law*, 2d ed. (Appleton-Century-Crofts, 1950).

17. Vincent M. Barnett, Jr., "Judicialization of the Administrative Process," 8 *Public Administration Review*, 126–33 (Spring, 1948), and Frederick F. Blachly, "Sabotage of the Administrative Process," 6 *ibid.*, 213–27 (Summer, 1946), provide critical appraisals of the Act of 1946. Charles S. Hyneman, *Bureaucracy in a Democracy* (Harpers Brothers, 1950), gives a sympathetic evaluation; see especially chapters 8, 21.

18. Arthur A. Maass and Laurence I. Radway, "Gauging Administrative Responsibility," 9 *Public Administration Review* 182–93 (Summer, 1949), in a penetrating and provocative essay have presented criteria of administrative responsibility which are based upon the following generalizations: (1) "An administrative agency should be responsible for formulating as well as executing public policy." (2) "An administrative agency cannot and should not normally be held directly responsible to the people at large." (3) "An administrative agency should be responsible to pressure groups so far as necessary to equalize opportunities for safeguarding interests, to acquire specialized knowledge, and to secure consent for its own program." (4) "An administrative agency should be responsible to the legislature, but

only through the chief executive, and primarily for broad issues of public policy and general administrative performance." (5) "An administrative agency should be directly responsible for conforming to the general programs of the chief executive and for coordinating its activities with other agencies of the executive branch." (6) "An administrative agency cannot be held independently responsible to the organization or policies of political parties." (7) "An administrative agency should be responsible for maintaining, developing, and applying such professional standards as may be relevant to its activities."

19. Luther Gulick, *Administrative Reflections from World War II* (University of Alabama Press, 1948), pp. 77–8.

20. Wayne A. R. Leys, "Ethics and Administrative Discretion," 3 *Public Administration Review* 10–18, 1943; F. Morstein Marx, "Administrative Ethics and the Rule of Law," 43 *American Political Science Review* 1119–44 (1949); Wallace S. Sayre, "Morale and Discipline," in F. Morstein Marx (ed.), *Elements of Public Administration,* 1946), pp. 478–497, and "Organization as Social Process," 9 *Public Administration Review* 45–50 (1949).

In a study of *Administrative Loyalty,* to be published by the Louisiana University Press in 1951, Paul H. Appleby provides another of his important landmarks in the development of administrative values.

4

ETHICS AND THE PUBLIC SERVICE

Stephen K. Bailey
Syracuse University

When Dean Appleby was asked to deliver the Edward Douglass White lectures at Louisiana State University in the Spring of 1951, he chose as his topic, *Morality and Administration in Democratic Government.* He preferred the term "morality" because he did not wish to suggest his lectures were "either a treatment in the systematic terms of general philosophy or a 'code of administrative ethics'."[1]

His attempt instead was to cast the light of his uncommon wisdom upon what he considered to be the central ethical and moral issues of the American public service. These issues centered upon the felicitous interaction of moral institutional arrangements and morally ambiguous man.

In some ways *Morality and Administration* is a disconcerting book. The essays are discontinuous. Each one is chocked with insight, but in the collection viewed as a whole, theoretical coherence and structure emerge implicitly rather than explicitly. Some inherently ambiguous terms like "responsibility" are clarified only by context. The final chapter, "The Administrative Pattern," is not the logical fulfillment of the preceding chapters. It stands beside the other essays, not on top of them. Furthermore, in spite of the highly personal connotation of the word "morality," Dean Appleby spent most of his time discussing the effect of the governmental system upon official morality rather than vice versa. He saw in the American governmental system a series of political and organizational devices for promoting ethical choices. The most serious threats to the "good society" came, in his estimation, not from the venality of individuals but from imperfections in institutional arrangements.

A Normative Model for Personal Ethics

His normative model ran something as follows: politics and hierarchy force public servants to refer private and special interests to higher and broader public interests. Politics does this through the discipline of the majority ballot which forces both political executives and legislators to insert a majoritarian calculus into the consideration of private claims. Hierarchy does it by placing in the hands of top officials both the responsibility and the necessity of homogenizing and moralizing the special interests inevitably represented by and through the lower echelons of organizational pyramids.[2] Both politics and hierarchy are devices for assuring accountability to the public as a whole. The public makes its will known in a variety of ways and through a variety of channels, but its importance is largely in its potential rather than in its concrete expressions. "Its capacity to be, more than its being, is the crux of democratic reality."[3] Politics and hierarchy induce the public servant to search imaginatively for a public-will-to-be. In this search, the public servant is often a leader in the creation of a new public will, so he is in part accountable to what he in part creates. But in any case the basic morality of the system is in its forcing of unitary claims into the mill of pluralistic considerations.

The enemies of this normative model, then, are obvious: they are whatever disrupts politics and hierarchy. For whatever disrupts politics and hierarchy permits the settlement of public issues at too low a level of organization—at too private a level, at too specialized a level. As Madison saw in *Federalist* #10, bigness is the friend of freedom. But Appleby saw more clearly than Madison that bigness is freedom's friend only if administrative as well as legislative devices exist to insure that policy decisions emerge out of the *complexity* of bigness rather than out of the simplicity of its constituent parts. The scatteration of power in the Congress, the virtual autonomy of certain bureaus and even lesser units in the executive branch, an undue encroachment of legal and other professional norms upon administrative discretion, the substitution of the expert for the generalist at the higher levels of general government, the awarding of statutory power at the bureau rather than at the department level, the atomized character of our political parties—these, according to Dean Appleby, are the effective enemies of morality in the governmental system. They are the symptoms of political pathology. "Our poorest governmental performances, both technically and morally," he wrote, "are generally associated with conditions in which a few citizens have very disproportionate influence."[4] ". . . the degradation of democracy is in the failure to organize or in actual disintegration of political responsibility, yielding public interest to special influence."[5]

Here, then, is the grand design. Government is moral insofar as it induces public servants to relate the specific to the general, the private to the public, the precise interest to the inchoate moral judgment. Within this context, a moral public decision becomes one in which

> the action conforms to the processes and symbols thus far developed for the general protection of political freedom as the agent of more general freedom; ... leaves open the way for modification or reversal by public determination; ... is taken within a hierarchy of controls in which responsibility for action may be readily identified by the public; ... and embodies as contributions of leadership the concrete structuring of response to popularly felt needs, and not merely responses to the private and personal needs of leaders.[6]

It is no disparagement of Dean Appleby's contributions to a normative theory of democratic governance to point out that he dealt only intermittently and unsystematically with the moral problems of the individual public servant. The moral system intrigued him far more consistently than the moral actor. All of his books and essays contain brilliant flashes of insight into the moral dilemmas of individual executives, administrators, and legislators, but there emerges no *gestalt* of personal ethics in government. One can only wish that he had addressed himself to a systematic elaboration of the personal as well as the institutional aspects of public ethics. For the richness of his administrative experience and the sensitivity of his insight might have illuminated uniquely the continuing moral problems of those whose business it is to preserve and improve the American public service.

Perhaps, without undue pretension, this memorial essay can attempt to fashion a prolegomena [*sic*] to a normative theory of personal ethics in the public service—building upon and elaborating some of the fragments which Dean Appleby scattered throughout his writings and teaching.

Dean Appleby's fragments suggest that personal ethics in the public service is compounded of mental attitudes and moral qualities. Both ingredients are essential. Virtue without understanding can be quite as disastrous as understanding without virtue.

The three essential mental attitudes are: (1) a recognition of the moral ambiguity of all men and of all public policies; (2) a recognition of the contextual forces which condition moral priorities in the public service; and (3) a recognition of the paradoxes of procedures.

The essential moral qualities of the ethical public servant are: optimism; courage; and fairness tempered by charity.

These mental attitudes and moral qualities are relevant to all public servants in every branch and at every level of government. They are as germane to judges and legislators as they are to executives and administrators. They are as essential to line officers as to staff officers. They apply to state and local officials as well as to national and international officials. They are needed in military, foreign, and other specialized services quite as much as they are needed in the career civil service and among political executives. They, of course, assume the virtue of probity and the institutional checks upon venality which Dean Appleby has so brilliantly elaborated. They are the generic attitudes and qualities without which big democracy cannot meaningfully survive.

Mental Attitudes

The Moral Ambiguity of Men and Measures

The moral public servant must be aware of the moral ambiguity of all men (including himself) and of all public policies (including those recommended by him). Reinhold Neibuhr once stated this imperative in the following terms: "Man's capacity for justice makes democracy possible, but man's inclination to injustice makes democracy necessary."[7] American public ethics finds its historic roots in the superficially incompatible streams of Calvinism and Deism. The former emphasized a depravity which must be contained; the latter emphasized a goodness which must be discovered and released. The relevance of this moral dualism to modern governance is patent. Any law or any act of administrative discretion based upon the assumption that most men will not seek to maximize their own economic advantage when reporting assets for income tax purposes would be quite unworkable. But so would any law or any act of administrative discretion which assumed that most men would use any and every ruse to avoid paying taxes at all. Similarly, any administrative decision threatening the chances of re-election of a powerfully placed Congressman almost inevitably invokes counter forces which may be serious both for the decision maker and for the program he or his agency espouses. But administrative decisions fashioned totally out of deference to private ambitions and personal interests can negate the very purposes of general government and can induce the righteous reaction of a voting public.

The fact is that there is no way of avoiding the introduction of personal and private interests into the calculus of public decisions. As James Harvey Robinson once wrote,

> In all governmental policy there have been overwhelming elements of personal favoritism and private gain, which were not suitable for publication. This is owing to the fact that all governments are managed by human beings, who remain human beings even if they are called kings, diplomats, ministers, secretaries, or judges, or hold seats in august legislative bodies. No process has

been discovered by which promotion to a position of public responsibility will do away with a man's interest in his own welfare, his partialities, race, and prejudices. Yet most books on government neglect these conditions; hence their unreality and futility.[8]

The most frequently hidden agenda in the deliberations of public servants is the effect of substantive or procedural decisions upon the personal lives and fortunes of those deliberating. And yet the very call to serve a larger public often evokes a degree of selflessness and nobility on the part of public servants beyond the capacity of cynics to recognize or to believe. Man's feet may wallow in the bog of self-interest, but his eyes and ears are strangely attuned to calls from the mountain top. As moral philosophy has insistently claimed, there is a fundamental moral distinction between the propositions "I want this because it serves my interest," and "I want this because it is right."

The fact that man is as much a rationalizing as a rational animal makes the problem of either proving or disproving disinterestedness a tricky and knotty business. "I support the decision before us because it is good for the public," may emerge as a rationalization of the less elevated but more highly motivational proposition: "I support the decision before us because it will help re-elect me, or help in my chances for promotion, recognition, or increased status." But the latter may have emerged, in turn, from a superordinate proposition: "Only if I am re-elected (or promoted) can I maximize my powers in the interests of the general citizenry." Unfortunately, no calipers exist for measuring the moral purity of human motivations.

But, in any case, few would deny the widespread moral hunger to justify actions on a wider and higher ground than personal self-interest. In fact, the paradox is that man's self-respect is in large part determined by his capacity to make himself and others believe that self is an inadequate referent for decisional morality. This capacity of man to transcend, to sublimate, and to transform narrowly vested compulsions is at the heart of all civilized morality. That this capacity is exercised imperfectly and intermittently is less astounding than the fact that it is exercised at all. A man's capacity for benevolent and disinterested behavior is both a wonder and a challenge to those who work below, beside, and above him. It is in recognition of this moral reality that Dean Appleby wrote in one of his most eloquent statements,

the manner and means of supporting one's own convictions, including inventiveness in perceiving how high ground may be held, are one measure of skill in the administrative process.[9]

But appeal to high morality is usually insufficient. It is in appreciating the reality of self-interest that public servants find some of the strongest forces for motivating behavior—public and private. Normally speaking, if a public interest is to be orbited, it must have as a part of its propulsive fuel a number of special and particular interests. A large part of the art of public service is in the capacity to harness private and personal interests to public interest causes. Those who will not traffic in personal and private interests (if such interests are themselves within the law) to the point of engaging their support on behalf of causes in which both public and private interests are served are, in terms of moral temperament, unfit for public responsibility.

But there is a necessary moral corollary: a recognition of the morally-ambivalent effect of all public policies. There is no public decision whose moral effect can be gauged in terms of what game theorists refer to as a "zero-sum" result: a total victory for the right and a total defeat for the wrong. This ineluctable fact is not only because "right" and "wrong" are incapable of universally-accepted definition. It is because an adequate response to any social evil contains the seeds of both predictable and unpredictable pathologies. One can, in the framing of laws or decisions, attempt to anticipate and partly to mitigate the predictable pathologies (although this is rarely possible in any complete sense). But one mark of moral maturity is in the appreciation of the inevitability of untoward and often malignant effects of benign moral choices. An Egyptian once commented that the two most devastating things to have happened to modern Egypt were the Rockefeller Foundation and the Aswan Dam. By enhancing public health, the Rockefeller Foundation had upset the balance of nature with horrendous consequences for the relationship of population to food supplies; by slowing the Nile, the Aswan Dam had promoted the development of enervating parasites in the river. The consequence of the two factors was that more people lived longer in more misery.

The bittersweet character of all public policy needs little further elaboration: welfare policies may mitigate hunger but promote parasitic dependence; vacationing in forests open for public recreation may destroy fish, wild life, and through carelessness in the handling of fire, the forests themselves. Unilateral international action may achieve immediate results at the cost of weakening international instruments of conflict resolution. Half a loaf *may* be worse than no loaf at all. It also may be better in the long run but worse in the short run—and vice versa.

Awareness of these dilemmas and paradoxes can immobilize the sensitive policy maker. That is one of the reasons why both optimism and courage are imperative moral qualities in the public service. At best, however, awareness or moral ambiguity creates a spirit of humility in the decision maker and a willingness to defer to the views of others through compromise. Humility and a willingness to compromise are priceless attributes in the life-style of the generality of public servants in a free society. For they are the preconditions of those fruitful accommodations which resolve conflict and which allow the new to live tolerably with the old. Humility, however, must not be equated with obsequiousness, nor willingness to compromise with a weak affability. As Harold Nicolson once wrote,

> It would be interesting to analyze how many false decisions, how many fatal misunderstandings have arisen from such pleasant qualities as shyness, consideration, affability or ordinary good manners. It would be a mistake . . . to concentrate too exclusively upon those weaknesses of human nature which impede the intelligent conduct of discussion. The difficulties of precise negotiation arise with almost equal frequency from the more amiable qualities of the human heart.[10]

Men and measures, then, are morally ambiguous. Even if this were not a basic truth about the human condition, however, moral judgments in the public service would be made difficult by the shifting sands of context. An awareness of the contextual conditions which affect the arranging of moral priorities is an essential mental attitude for the moral public servant.

The moral virtues of the Boy Scout oath are widely accepted in the United States. But, as Boy Scouts get older, they are faced time and again with the disturbing fact that contexts exist within which it is impossible to be both kind and truthful at the same time. Boy Scouts are trustworthy. But what if they are faced with competing and incompatible trusts (e.g., to guard the flag at the base and to succor a distant wounded companion)? Men should be loyal, but what if loyalties conflict?

Winds Above the Timber Line

To the morally-sensitive public servant, the strains of establishing a general value framework for conducting the public business is nothing compared to the strains of re-sorting specific values in the light of changing contexts. The dilemmas here are genuine. If value priorities are shifted with every passing wind, the shifter will suffer from his developing reputation as an opportunist. If value priorities are never adjusted, the saints come marching in and viable democratic politics goes marching out. To be consistent enough to deserve ethical respect from revered colleagues and from oneself; to be pliable enough to survive within an organization and to succeed in effectuating moral purposes—this is the dilemma and the glory of the public service.

In general, the higher a person goes on the rungs of power and authority, the more wobbly the ethical ladder. It is not the function of the junior civil servant in a unit of a branch of a bureau to worry about Congressional relations—except on specific mandate from above. But a bureau chief, an assistant secretary, under-secretary, or secretary of a department may find himself contextually conditioned to respond frequently to Congressional forces whose effect it is to undermine the integrity of the hierarchical arrangements in the executive branch. The heroic proportions of the Presidency become clear when one recognizes that the winds are fiercest and most variable above the timber line. The very fact that the President has fewer moments in the day than there are critical problems to be solved, and that crises often emerge unheralded, means an unevenness in the application of his time and attention to adjusting or influencing the moral niceties of any single issue. Dean Appleby understood this when he wrote, "On many matters he [the President] will appear rather neutral; beyond enumerating items in messages and budgets he can expend his time and energies on only a few things. On as many matters as possible he normally yields for the sake of larger concerns."[11] The crucial word is "yields." Put in another way, if the President had more time and staff assistance he would "yield" to far fewer private and petty claims than he presently supports tacitly or openly.

During the Kennedy administration, the President called together a small group of top legislators, cabinet officers, and executive office staff to advise him on whether he should support the extension of price supports for cotton. His staff reminded him of the bonanza which price supports gave to the biggest and wealthiest cotton farmers. Legislative and cabinet leaders reminded him that a Presidential veto on an important agricultural bill could mean forfeiting key and critical legislative support on subsequent domestic and international matters of over-riding importance to the nation's security and welfare. The President agreed not to veto the bill, but the moral torment was there. According to one witness, he stared at the wall and mumbled to himself, "There is something wrong here. We are giving money to those who don't need it. If I am re-elected in 1964, I'm going to turn this government upside down."

President Eisenhower was an honorable chief executive. Yet he publicly lied about the U-2 affair. The context was the crucial determinant.

If the heat in the ethical kitchen grows greater with each level of power, no public servant is immune from some heat—some concern with context. As Dean Appleby has written, ". . . a special favor, in administration even—as by a traffic policeman, to a blind person or a cripple—would be regarded as a political good when it appears an act of equity compensating for underprivilege."[12]

There is not a moral vice which cannot be made into a relative good by context. There is not a moral virtue which cannot in peculiar circumstances have patently evil results.

The mental attitude which appreciates this perversity can be led, of course, into a wasteland of ethical relativity. But this is by no means either inevitable or in the American culture even probable. Where this attitude tends to lead the mature public servant is toward a deep respect for the inconstant forces which swirl around public offices, and toward a deeper understanding of the reasons why moral men sometimes appear to make unethical public decisions. An old American Indian proverb is relevant: "Do not scoff at your friend until you have walked three miles in his moccasins." Because it is not easy for any man to place himself empathetically in the arena of moral dilemmas faced by another man, charity is a difficult moral virtue to maintain with any constancy. But as we shall review more fully below, charity is an essential moral quality in the public service of a democracy.

Paradoxes of Procedure

The third mental attitude which the public servant of a free society must cultivate is a recognition of the paradoxes of procedures. Justice Frankfurter once wrote, "The history of American freedom is, in no small measure, the history of procedure."[13] Rules, standards, procedures exist, by and large, to promote fairness, openness, depth of analysis, and accountability in the conduct of the public's business. Those who frequently bypass or short-cut established means are thereby attacking one aspect of that most precious legacy of the past: the rule of law. Official whim is the enemy of a civilized social order. Not only does it sow the seeds of anarchy in organization, it denies to a new idea the tempering which the heat of procedural gauntlets normally provides. John Mill's "market place" is of little utility if an idea is never allowed to enter the town at all.

But, alas, if procedures are the friend of deliberation and order, they are also at times the enemy of progress and dispatch. Furthermore, there are procedures and procedures. There are apt procedures and inept procedures. The only really bitter comments in *Morality and Administration* are reserved for those members of the legal profession who believe that administration should be circumscribed by precise legal norms, and that a series of administrative courts should be the effective arbiters and sanctioners of administrative discretion.[14] And this, of course, is only one aspect of the problem. Juridic procedures aside, both administration and legislation are frequently encumbered by rules and clearances which limit both responsiveness and the accountability they were presumably designed to enhance. The Rules Committee of the House of Representatives is not only the guardian of orderly procedures, it is the graveyard of important social measures. The contract and personnel policies of many agencies, federal, state, and local, have frequently led to what Wallace Sayre has termed "the triumph of technique over purpose." Anyone who has been closely associated with reorganization studies and proposals knows that every shift in organization—in the structural means for accomplishing governmental ends—is pregnant with implications for the ends themselves. Only a two-dimensional mind can possibly entertain seriously the notion that the structural and procedural aspects of government are unrelated to competing philosophies of substantive purpose.

The public servant who cannot recognize the paradoxes of procedures will be trapped by them. For in the case of procedures, he who deviates frequently is subversive; he who never deviates at all is lost; and he who tinkers with procedures without an understanding of substantive consequence is foolish. Of all governmental roles, the administrative role is procedurally the most flexible. But even here procedural flexibility in the public interest is achieved only by the optimistic, the courageous, and the fair.

Moral Qualities

If mental attitudes related to the moral ambiguities, contextual priorities, and procedural paradoxes of public life are necessary prerequisites to ethical behavior on the part of public servants, they are insufficient to such behavior. Attitudes must be supported by moral qualities—by operating virtues. A list of all relevant virtues would be a long one: patience, honesty, loyalty, cheerfulness, courtesy, humility—where does one begin or stop? One begins beyond the obvious and ends where essentiality ends. In the American context, at least, the need for the virtue of honesty is too obvious to need elaboration. Although Dean Appleby has a chapter on "Venality in Government," he properly dismisses the issue with a single sentence: "Crude wrong doing is not a major general problem of our government." And he continues with the pregnant remark, "Further moral advance turns upon more complicated and elevated concerns."[15]

The three *essential* moral qualities in the public service are optimism, courage, and fairness tempered by charity.

Overcoming Ambiguity and Paradox

Optimism is an inadequate term. It connotes euphoria, and public life deals harshly with the euphoric. But optimism is a better word than realism, for the latter dampens the fires of possibility. Optimism, to paraphrase Emerson, is the capacity to settle with some consistency on the "sunnier side of doubt." It is the quality which enables man to face ambiguity and paradox without becoming immobilized. It is essential to purposive as distinct from reactive behavior. Hannah Arendt once commented that the essence of politics is natality not mortality. Politics involves creative responses to the shifting conflicts and the gross discomfortures [sic] of mankind. Without optimism on the part of the public servants, the political function is incapable of being performed. There is no incentive to create policies to better the condition of mankind if the quality of human life is in fact unviable, and if mankind is in any case unworthy of the trouble.

Optimism has not been the religious, philosophical, or literary mood of the twentieth century. But, in spite of a series of almost cataclysmic absurdities, it has been the prevailing mood of science, education, and politics. It is the mood of the emerging nations; it is the mood of the space technologist; it is the mood of the urban renewer. Government without the leavening of optimistic public servants quickly becomes a cynical game of manipulation, personal aggrandizement, and parasitic security. The ultimate corruption of free government comes not from the hopelessly venal but from the persistently cynical. Institutional decadence has set in when the optimism of leadership becomes a ploy rather than an honest mood and a moral commitment. True optimism is not Mr. Micawber's passive assumption that something will turn up; true optimism is the affirmation of the worth of taking risks. It is not a belief in sure things; it is the capacity to see the possibilities for good in the uncertain, the ambiguous, and the inscrutable.

Organic aging and the disappointments and disaffections of experience often deprive mature individuals of the physical and psychic vitality which in youth is a surrogate for optimism. That is why optimism as a moral virtue—as a life-style—is one of the rare treasures sought by all personnel prospectors whose responsibility it is to mine the common lodes for extraordinary leadership talent. This is true in all organizations; it is especially true in the public service. What else do we mean, when we speak disparagingly of "bureaucratic drones," than that they are those who have entered the gates of Dante's Hell and have "abandoned all hope"?

In the midst of World War II when crises were breaking out at every moment and from every quarter, an ancient White House clerk was caught by a frenetic Presidential aide whistling at his work. The aide asked, "My God, man, don't you know what's going on?" The clerk replied, "Young man, you would be terrified if you knew how little I cared." A sprinkling of such in the public service can be tolerated as droll. If a majority, or even a substantial minority of public servants become jaded, however, especially at leadership levels, an ethical rot settles in which ultimately destroys the capacity of a government to function effectively in the public interest.

A Capacity for Impersonality and Decision

The second essential moral quality needed in the public service is courage. Personal and public life are so shot through with ambiguities and paradoxes that timidity and withdrawal are quite natural and normal responses for those confronted with them. The only three friends of courage in the public service are ambition, a sense of duty, and a recognition that inaction may be quite as painful as action.

Courage in government and politics takes many forms. The late President John F. Kennedy sketched a series of profiles of one type of courage—abiding by principle in an unpopular cause. But most calls upon courage are less insistent and more pervasive. In public administration, for example, courage is needed to insure that degree of impersonality without which friendship oozes into inequities and special favors. Dean Appleby relates a relevant story about George Washington. Washington told a friend seeking an appointment: "You are welcome to my house; you are welcome to my heart . . . my personal feelings have nothing to do with the present case. I am not George Washington, but President of the United States. As George Washington, I would do anything in my power for you. As President, I can do nothing."[16] Normally it takes less courage to deal impersonally with identifiable interest groups than with long standing associates and colleagues upon whom one has depended over the years for affection and for professional and personal support. This is true in relationship to those inside as well as those outside the organization. Part of the loneliness of authority comes from the fact, again in the words of Dean Appleby, that "to a distinctly uncomfortable degree [the administrator], must make work relationships impersonal."[17] Appleby was quick to see that impersonality invites the danger of arrogance, but he also saw that the courage to be impersonal in complicated organizational performance is generally valuable as far as the affected public is concerned. "Its tendency is to systematize fair dealing and to avoid whimsy and discrimination—in other words to provide a kind of administrative due process."[18]

The need for this kind of courage on a day to day basis is probably greater, and more difficult to conjure, in the legislative than in either the executive or the judicial branches of government.

A second area for consistent courage in the public service is to be found in the relationship of general administrators to experts and specialists. It takes quite as much courage to face down minority expert opinion as it does to face down the majority opinion of a clamoring crowd. In some ways it takes more courage, for relationships with experts are usually intimate in the decisional process, whereas relations with the crowd are often distant and indistinct. Both courage and wisdom are reflected in the words of Sir Winston Churchill: "I knew nothing about science, but I knew something about scientists, and had had much practice as a minister in handling things I did not understand."[19]

Perhaps on no issue of public ethics is Dean Appleby more insistent than on the necessity of experts being kept in their proper place—subordinate to politicians and general administrators. "Perhaps," he wrote, "there is no single problem in public administration of moment equal to the reconciliation of the increasing dependence upon experts with an unending democratic reality."[20] The expert, whether professional, procedural, or programmatic, is essential to the proper functioning of a complex and highly technical social system. But the autonomous or disproportionate power of experts, and of the limited worlds they comprehend, is a constant threat to more general consideration of the public good.

During World War II, a twenty-five-year-old civil servant in the soap division of O.P.A. found himself, because of the temporary absence of superiors, dealing directly with the president and legal staff of Lever Brothers. After a few minutes of confrontation the president of Lever Brothers turned scornfully to the government employee and asked, "Young man, what in hell do you know about soap?" A strong voice replied, "Sir, I don't know much about soap, but I know a hell of a lot about price control."

This is the courage needed by a Budget Bureau examiner dealing with the Pentagon; this is the courage needed by an Assistant Secretary of Health, Education, and Welfare in dealing with the Surgeon General; this is the courage needed by a transient mayor in dealing with a career engineer in the public works department; this is the courage needed by a Congressman faced with appraising the "expert" testimony of an important banker in his district.

Perhaps the most essential courage in the public service is the courage to decide. For if it is true that all policies have bitter-sweet consequences, decisions invariably produce hurt. President Eliot of Harvard once felt constrained to say that the prime requisite of an executive was his willingness to give pain. Much buck-passing in public life is the prudent consequence of the need for multiple clearances in large and complex institutions. But buck-passing which stems from lack of moral courage is the enemy of efficient and responsible government. The inner satisfactions which come from the courage to decide are substantial; but so are the slings and arrows which are invariably let loose by those who are aggrieved by each separate decision. The issues become especially acute in personnel decisions. Courage to fire, to demote, to withhold advancement, or to shift assignments against the wishes of the person involved is often the courage most needed and the most difficult to raise.

Man's Sense of Injustice

The third and perhaps most essential moral quality needed in the public service is fairness tempered by charity. The courage to be impersonal and disinterested is of no value unless it results in just and charitable actions and attitudes. Government in a free society is the authoritative allocator of values in terms of partly ineffable standards of justice and the public weal. It requires the approximation of moving targets partly camouflaged by the shadows of an unknowable future. The success or failure of policies bravely conceived to meet particular social evils is more frequently obscured than clarified by the passage of time. As R. G. Collingwood once pointed out, "The only thing that a shrewd and critical Greek like Herodotus would say about the divine power that ordains the course of history is that . . . it rejoices in upsetting and disturbing things."[21]

What remains through the disorder and unpredictability of history is the sense on the part of the public and of working colleagues that power for whatever ends was exercised fairly and compassionately. The deepest strain in our ethical heritage is "man's sense of injustice." The prophetic voices of the Old Testament repaired time and again to this immemorial standard. "Let Justice roll down like waters. . . ." Hesiod, speaking for generations of ancient Greeks, wrote, "Fishes and beasts and fowls of the air devour one another. But to men Zeus has given justice. Beside Zeus on his throne Justice has her seat."[22] Justice was the only positive heritage of the Roman World. The establishment of justice follows directly behind the formation of union itself in the Preamble to the American Constitution.

But the moral imperative to be just—to be fair—is a limited virtue without charity. Absolute justice presupposes omniscience and total disinterestedness. Public servants are always faced with making decisions based upon both imperfect information and the inarticulate insinuations of self-interest into the decisional calculus. Charity is the virtue which compensates for inadequate information and for the subtle importunities of self in the making of judgments designed to be fair. Charity is not a soft virtue. To the contrary, it involves the ultimate moral toughness. For its exercise involves the disciplining of self and the sublimation of persistent inner claims for personal recognition, power, and status. It is the principle above principle. In the idiom of the New Testament, it is the losing of self to find self. Its exercise makes of compromise not a sinister barter but a recognition of the dignity of competing claimants. It fortifies the persuasive rather than the coercive arts. It stimulates the visions of the good society without which government becomes a sullen defense of existing patterns of privilege.

The Essential Humanity

The normative systems of politics and organization which Dean Appleby elaborated in his writings are umbilically related to the mental attitudes and moral qualities of the individual moral actor in the public service. They nourish these attitudes and qualities. They condition and promote public morality. But the reverse is also true. Without proper mental attitudes and moral qualities on the part of the public servant, Dean Appleby's normative systems could neither exist nor be meaningfully approximated.

Bureaucracy and technology are the pervasive realities of modern civilization. Together they have made possible order, prosperity, and mobility in unprecedented magnitudes. But, unfortunately, they have demonstrated a perverse tendency to drain from man the blood of his essential humanity. The nobility of any society is especially encapsulated and made manifest to the world in the personal example of its public leaders and public servants.

Perhaps, therefore, Dean Appleby's writings about morality and government—no matter how wise and how provocative—were of less importance than the lessons of his example as a public servant. For in selecting the mental attitudes and moral qualities of the moral public servant, I have been guided far more by my memories of Paul Appleby than by my perusal of his writings. Dean Appleby in his public career demonstrated an uncommon understanding of the moral ambiguities, the contextual priorities, and the paradoxes of procedures in ethical governance. Of all men of my acquaintance in public life, he was the most completely endowed in the moral qualities of optimism, courage, and fairness tempered by charity. While his wisdom illuminated everything he observed and experienced, his example shone even more brilliantly than his wisdom.

Notes

1. Paul H. Appleby, *Morality, and Administration in Democratic Government* (Baton Rouge: Louisiana State University Press, 1952), p. vii.

2. The intellectual as distinct from the moral implications of hierarchy have been suggested by Kenneth Underwood in his contention that "The policy-making executive is to be distinguished from the middle management-supervisor levels most basically in the excessively cognitive, abstract dimensions of his work." See his paper "The New Ethic of Personal and Corporate Responsibility," presented at the Third Centennial Symposium on *The Responsible Individual*, April 8, 1964, University of Denver.

3. Appleby, *op. cit.*, p. 35.

4. *Ibid.*, p. 214.

5. *Ibid.*, p. 211.

6. *Ibid.*, p. 36.

7. *The Children of Light and the Children of Darkness* (New York: Scribners, 1944), p. xi of Foreword.

8. *The Human Comedy* (London: The Bodley Head, 1937), p. 232.

9. *Op. cit.*, p. 222.

10. Quoted by James Reston, in *The New York Times*, April 11, 1957.

11. *Op. cit.*, p. 127.

12. *Op. cit.*, p. 64.

13. Felix Frankfurter, *Malinski v. New York*, 324, U.S. 401, 414, 1945.

14. See especially, *op. cit.*, Chapter 4.

15. *Op. cit.*, p. 56.

16. *Op. cit.*, p. 130.

17. *Op. cit.*, p. 221.

18. *Op. cit.*, p. 149.

19. *Life*, February 28, 1949, p. 61.

20. *Op. cit.*, p. 145.

21. *The Idea of History* (Oxford: Clarendon Press, 1946), p. 22.

22. Quoted in Edith Hamilton, *The Greek Way* (New York: W. W. Norton and Co., Inc. 1930), p. 292.

5

THE POSSIBILITY OF ADMINISTRATIVE ETHICS

Dennis F. Thompson
Princeton University

Is administrative ethics possible? The most serious objections to administrative ethics arise from two common conceptions of the role of individuals in organizations—what may be called the ethic of neutrality and the ethic of structure. Both of these views must be rejected if administrative ethics is to be possible.

Administrative ethics involves the application of moral principles to the conduct of officials in organizations.[1] In the form with which we are primarily concerned here (ethics in public organizations), administrative ethics is a species of political ethics, which applies moral principles to political life more generally. Broadly speaking, moral principles specify (a) the rights and duties that individuals should respect when they act in ways that seriously affect the well-being of other individuals and society; and (b) the conditions that collective practices and policies should satisfy when they similarly affect the well-being of individuals and society. Moral principles require a disinterested perspective. Instead of asking how an action or policy serves the interest of some particular individual or group, morality asks whether the action or policy serves everyone's interest, or whether it could be accepted by anyone who did not know his or her particular circumstances, such as race, social class, or nationality. Moral judgments presuppose the possibility of a person to make the judgment and a person or group of persons to be judged.

The most general challenge to administrative ethics would be to deny the possibility of ethics at all or the possibility of political ethics. Although a worthy challenge, it should not be the primary concern of defenders of administrative ethics. Theorists (as well as practitioners when they think about ethics at all) have been so preoccupied with general objections to ethics that they have neglected objections that apply specifically to ethics in administration. They have not sufficiently considered that even if we accept the possibility of morality in general and even in polities, we may have doubts about it in organizations.

To isolate more specifically the objections to administrative ethics, we should assume that the moral perspective can be vindicated and that some moral principles and some moral judgments are valid. Despite disagreement about how morality is to be justified and disagreement about its scope and content, we nevertheless share certain attitudes and beliefs to which we can appeal in criticizing or defending public actions and policies from a moral perspective.[2]

The more direct challenge to administrative ethics comes from those who admit that morality is perfectly possible in private life but deny that it is possible in organizational life. The challenge is that by its very nature administration precludes the exercise of moral judgment. It consists of two basic objections—the first calls into question the subject of the judgment (who may judge); the second, the object of judgment (who is judged). The first asserts that administrators ought to act neutrally in the sense that they should follow not their own moral principles but the decisions and policies of the organization. This is the ethic of neutrality. The second asserts that not administrators but the organization (and its formal officers) should be held responsible for its decisions and policies. This is the ethic of structure. Each is called an ethic because it expresses certain norms and prescribes conduct. But neither constitutes an ethic or a morality because each denies one of the presuppositions of moral judgment—either a person to judge or a person to be judged.

I. The Ethic of Neutrality

The conventional theory and practice of administrative ethics holds that administrators should carry out the orders of their superiors and the policies of the agency and the government they serve.[3] On this view, administrators are ethically neutral in the sense that they do not exercise independent moral judgment. They are not expected to act on any moral principles of their own, but are to give effect to whatever principles are reflected in the orders and policies they are charged with implementing. They serve the organization so that the organization may serve society. Officials are morally obliged to serve the organization in this way because their acceptance of office is voluntary; it signifies consent. Officials know in advance what the duties of office will be, and if the duties (or their minds) change, officials can usually leave office.

The ethic of neutrality does not deny that administrators often must use their own judgment in the formulation of policy. But their aim should always be to discover what policy other people (usually elected officials) intend or would intend; or in the case of conflicting directives to interpret legally or constitutionally who has the authority to determine policy. The use of discretion on this view can never be the occasion for applying any moral principles other than those implicit in the orders and policies of the superiors to whom one is responsible in the organization. The ethic of neutrality portrays the ideal administrator as a completely reliable instrument of the goals of the organization, never injecting personal values into the process of furthering these goals. The ethic thus reinforces the great virtue of organization—its capacity to serve any social end irrespective of the ends that individuals within it favor.

A variation of the ethic of neutrality gives some scope for individual moral judgment until the decision or policy is "final." On this view, administrators may put forward their own views, argue with their superiors, and contest proposals in the process of formulating policy. But once the decision or policy is final, all administrators fall into line, and faithfully carry out the policy. Furthermore, the disagreement must take place within the agency and according to the agency's rules of procedure. This variation puts neutrality in abeyance, but "suspended neutrality" is still neutrality, and the choice for the administrator remains to "obey or resign."[4]

Three sets of criticisms may be brought against the ethic of neutrality. First, because the ethic underestimates the discretion that administrators exercise, it impedes the accountability of administrators by citizens. The discretion of administrators goes beyond carrying out the intentions of legislators or the superiors in the organization, not only because often there are no intentions to discover, but also because often administrators can and should take the initiative in proposing policies and mobilizing support for them.[5] The ethic of neutrality provides no guidance for this wide range of substantive moral decision making in which administrators regularly engage. By reinforcing the illusion that administrators do not exercise independent moral judgment, it insulates them from external accountability for the consequences of many of their decisions.

A second set of objections centers on the claim that officeholding implies consent to the duties of office as defined by the organization. While it may be easier to resign from office than from citizenship, it is for many officials so difficult that failure to do so cannot be taken to indicate approval of everything the organization undertakes. For the vast majority of governmental employees, vested rights (such as pensions and seniority) and job skills (often not transferable to the private sector) supply powerful incentives to hold on to their positions. Even if on their own many would be prepared to sacrifice their careers for the sake of principle, they cannot ignore their responsibilities to their families. Higher level officials usually enjoy advantages that make resignation a more feasible option. They can return to (usually more lucrative) positions in business or in a profession. But their ability to do so may depend on their serving loyally while in government, demonstrating that they are the good "team players" on whom any organization, public or private, can rely.

Furthermore, the dynamics of collective decision making discourage even conscientious officials from resigning on principle. Many decisions are incremental, their objectionable character apparent only in their cumulative effect. An official who is involved in the early stages of escalations of this kind (such as aid increases, budget cuts, troop commitments) will find it difficult to object to any subsequent step. The difference between one step and the next is relatively trivial, certainly not a reason to resign on principle. Besides, many decisions and policies represent compromises, and any would-be dissenter can easily be persuaded that because his opponents did not get everything they sought, he should settle for less than what his principles demand. For these and other reasons, an official may stay in office while objecting to the policies of government; a failure to resign therefore does not signify consent.

Proponents of the ethic of neutrality may still insist that officials who cannot fulfill the duties of their office must resign, however difficult it may be to do so. But as citizens we should hesitate before endorsing this as a general principle of administrative ethics. If this view were consistently put into practice, public offices would soon be populated only by those who never had any reason to disagree with anything the government decided to do. Men and women of strong moral conviction would resign rather than continue in office, and we would lose the services of the persons who could contribute most to public life.

Because we do not want to drive persons of principle from office, we should recognize that there may be good moral reasons for staying in office even while disagreeing with the policies of the government. This recognition points to a third set of objections to the ethic of neutrality—that it simplifies the moral circumstances of public office. It tends to portray officials as assessing the fit between their moral principles and the policies of the organization, obeying if the principles and policies match, resigning if they diverge too much. What is important on this view is that in resigning, the individual express [*sic*] "ethical autonomy," which Weisband and Franck, in their otherwise valuable plea for resignations in protest, define as "the willingness to assert one's own principled judgment, even if that entails violating rules, values, or perceptions of the organization, peer group or team."[6] "The social importance of ethical autonomy," they write, "lies not in what is asserted but in the act of asserting." The ethic of neutrality encourages this and similar portrayals of an isolated official affirming his or her own principles against the organization at the moment of resignation. The ethic thereby neglects important considerations that an ethical administrator should take into account in fulfilling the duties while in office.

First of all, as an official you have obligations to colleagues, an agency, and the government as a whole. By accepting office and undertaking collective tasks in an organization, you give others reason to rely on your continued cooperation. Your colleagues begin projects, take risks, make commitments in the expectation that you will continue to play your part in the organization. If you resign, you disappoint these expectations, and in effect break your commitments to your colleagues. A resignation may disrupt many organizational activities, some of which may be morally more important than the policy that occasions the resignation. Presidential Assistant Alexander Haig deployed this kind of argument in October 1973 in an effort to persuade Attorney-General Elliot Richardson to fire Special Prosecutor Archibald Cox. Richardson claimed that he would resign rather than dismiss Cox. Haig argued that resignation or disobedience at this time would jeopardize the president's efforts, which were at a critical stage, to reach a peace settlement in the Middle East.[7] The argument understandably did not convince Richardson (his commitment to Congress and Cox were too clear, and the connection between his resignation and the Middle East settlement too tenuous), but the *form* of the argument Haig invoked was sound. An official must consider his commitments to all of his associates in government and the effect of his intended resignation on the conduct of government as a whole. Officials also have more general obligations to the public. Officials should not decide simply whether they can in good conscience continue to associate themselves with the organization. This could be interpreted as merely wanting to keep one's own hands clean—a form of what some have called "moral self-indulgence."[8]

A third way in which the ethic of neutrality distorts the duties of public administrators is by limiting their courses of action to two—obedience or resignation. Many forms of dissent may be compatible with remaining in office, ranging from quiet protest to illegal obstruction. Some of these, of course, may be morally wrong except under extreme circumstances, but the ethic of neutrality provides no guidance at all here because it rules out, in advance, the possibility of morally acceptable internal opposition to decisions of the organization, at least "final decisions."

The problem, however, is how we can grant officials scope for dissent without undermining the capacity of the organization to accomplish its goals. If the organization is pursuing goals set by a democratic public, individual dissent in the organization may subvert the democratic process. We should insist, first of all, that would-be dissenters consider carefully the basis of their disagreement with the policy in question. Is the disagreement moral or merely political? This is a slippery distinction since almost all important political decisions have moral dimensions. But perhaps we could say that the more directly a policy seems to violate an important moral principle (such as not harming innocent persons), the more justifiable dissent becomes. An official would be warranted in stronger measures of opposition against decisions to bomb civilian targets in a guerilla war than against decisions to lower trade barriers and import duties.[9] In cases of political disagreement of the latter sort, straightforward resignation seems the most appropriate action (once the decision is final). Dissenters must also consider whether the policy they oppose is a one-time incident or part of a continuing pattern and whether the wrongness of the policy is outweighed by the value of the other policies the organization is pursuing. Furthermore, dissenters must examine the extent of their own involvement and own role: how (formally and informally) responsible are they for the policy? What difference would their opposition make to the policy and to the other policies of the organization? To what extent does the policy violate the ethics of groups to which they are obligated (such as the canons of the legal or medical professions)?

These considerations not only determine whether an official is justified in opposing the organization's policy, but they also help to indicate what methods of dissent the official may be justified in using to express opposition. The more justified an official's opposition, the more justified the official is in using more extreme methods. The methods of dissent may be arrayed on a continuum from the most extreme to the most moderate. Four types of dissent will illustrate the range of this continuum and raise some further issues that any would-be dissenter must consider.

First, there are those forms of dissent in which an official protests within the organization but still helps implement the policy or (a slightly stronger measure) asks for a different assignment in the organization. In its weakest form, this kind of dissent does not go much beyond the ethic of neutrality. But unlike that ethic, it would permit officials to abstain from active participation in a policy they oppose and to continue their protest as long as they do so in accordance with the accepted procedures of the organization.[10]

One danger of this form of protest is what has been called the "domestication of dissenters."[11] A case in point is George Ball, who as undersecretary of state in the Johnson administration persistently argued against the government's Vietnam policy in private meetings:

> Once Mr. Ball began to express doubts, he was warmly institutionalized: he was encouraged to become the in-house devil's advocate on Vietnam. . . . The process of escalation allowed for periodic requests to Mr. Ball to speak his piece; Ball felt good . . . (he had fought for righteousness); the others felt good (they had given a full hearing to the dovish option); and there was minimal unpleasantness.[12]

In this way dissenters can be "effectively neutralized," and contrary to their intentions, their dissent can even help support the policy they oppose. It is important therefore to consider whether this effect is inevitable, and, if not, to discover the conditions under which it can be avoided.

In a second form of dissent, officials, with the knowledge of, but against the wishes of their superiors, carry their protest outside the organization while otherwise performing their jobs satisfactorily. This is the course of action taken by most of the 65 Justice Department attorneys who protested the decision to permit delays in implementing desegregation decrees in Mississippi in August of 1969.[13] The attorneys signed and publicized a petition denouncing the attorney-general and the president for adopting a policy the attorneys believed violated the law and would require them to act contrary to the ethical canons of the legal profession. They also believed that resignation would not fulfill their obligation to act affirmatively to oppose illegality. Several of the dissenters argued for stronger actions that would directly block the policy, and some gave information to the NAACP Legal Defense Fund, which was opposing the Justice Department in court. Most of the attorneys declined to engage in these stronger actions, however, on the grounds that obstruction would weaken public support for their dissent.

This kind of dissent usually depends, for its efficacy as well as its legitimacy, on the existence of some widely accepted standards to which the dissenters can appeal outside the organization. Professional ethics or even the law may not be sufficient, since people disagree on how to interpret both, but appealing to such standards may at least reassure the public that the dissenters are not using their office to impose the dictates of their private consciences on public policy. When dissenters oppose democratically elected officials, they must find ways to show that they are defending principles that all citizens would endorse.

The third form of dissent is the open obstruction of policy. Officials may, for example, withhold knowledge or expertise that the organization needs to pursue the policy, refuse to step aside so that others can pursue it, or give information and other kinds of assistance to outsiders who are trying to overturn the policy. A few officials may adopt this strategy for a short time, but organizations can usually isolate the dissenters, find other officials to do the job, and mobilize its own external support to counter any opposition that arises outside the organization. In any such event, the dissenters are not likely to retain much influence within the organization. Effective and sustained opposition has to be more circumspect.

We are therefore led to a fourth kind of dissent: covert obstruction. Unauthorized disclosure—the leak—is the most prominent example. Leaks vary greatly in purpose and effect. Some simply provide information to other agencies that are entitled to receive it; others embarrass particular officials within an agency but do not otherwise subvert the agency's policies; others release information to the press or public ultimately reversing a major government policy; and at the extreme, still others give secrets to enemy agents and count as treason. Short of that extreme, we still may want to say that unauthorized disclosure is sometimes justified even when it breaches government procedures or violates the law, as in the release of classified documents.

An analogy is sometimes drawn between official disobedience and civil disobedience. Many democratic theorists hold that citizens in a democracy are justified in breaking the law with the aim of changing a law or policy, but only in certain ways and under certain conditions. Citizens must (1) act publicly; (2) commit no violence; (3) appeal to principles shared by other citizens; (4) direct their challenge against a substantial injustice; (5) exhaust all normal channels of protest before breaking a law; and (6) plan their disobedience so that it does not, in conjunction with that of other citizens, disrupt the stability of the democratic process.[14]

Even if one thinks that civil disobedience is justifiable, one may not agree that official disobedience is warranted. Officials cannot claim the same rights as citizens can, and, it may be said, the analogy does not in general hold. But the analogy may not hold for the opposite reason. In extreme cases of governmental wrongdoing, so much is at stake that we should give officials greater scope for disobedience than we allow citizens. In these cases we might be prepared to argue that the standard conditions for civil disobedience are too restrictive for officials. If we insist for example that disobedience always be carried out in public, we may in effect suppress much valuable criticism of government. Fearful of the consequences of public action, dissenting officials may decide against providing information that their superiors have declared secret but that citizens ought to know. The point of relaxing the requirement of publicity would be not to protect the rights of dissenters for their own sake but to promote public discussion of questionable actions of government. We may wish to retain some form of the requirement of publicity, perhaps by establishing an authority to whom a dissenter must make his or her identity known. But this requirement, as well as the others, should be formulated with the goal of maximizing the responsibility of governmental officials, not with the aim of matching exactly the traditional criteria of civil disobedience.

The important task, with respect to disobedience as well as the other forms of dissent, is to develop the criteria that could help determine when each is justifiable in various circumstances. The ethic of neutrality makes that task unnecessary by denying that ethics is possible in administration. But, as we have seen, that administrative neutrality itself is neither possible nor desirable.

II. The Ethic of Structure

The second major obstacle to administrative ethics is the view that the object of moral judgment must be the organization or the government as a whole. This ethic of structure asserts that, even if administrators may have some scope for independent moral judgment, they cannot be held morally responsible for most of the decisions and policies of government. Their personal moral responsibility extends only to the specific duties of their own office for which they are legally liable.

Moral judgment presupposes moral agency. To praise or blame someone for an outcome, we must assume that the person is morally responsible for the action. We must assume (1) that the person's actions or omissions were a cause of the outcome; and (2) that the person did not act in excusable ignorance or under compulsion. In everyday life, we sometimes withhold moral criticism because we think a person does not satisfy one or both of these criteria. But since usually so few agents are involved and because the parts they play are obvious enough, we are not normally perplexed about whether anyone can be said to have brought about a particular outcome. The main moral problem is what was the right thing to do, not so much who did it. In public life, especially organizations, the problem of identifying the moral agents, of finding the persons who are morally responsible for a decision or policy, becomes at least as difficult as the problem of assessing the morality of the decision or policy. Even if we have perfect information about all the agents in the organizational process that produced an outcome, we may still be puzzled about how to ascribe responsibility for it. Because many people contribute in many different ways to the decisions and policies of an organization, we may not be able to determine, even in principle, who is morally responsible for those decisions and policies. This has been called "the problem of many hands,"[15] and the assumption that it is not soluable [sic] underlies the ethic of structure.

Proponents of the ethic of structure put forward three arguments to deny the possibility of ascribing individual responsibility in organizations and thereby to undermine the possibility of administrative ethics. First, it is argued that no individual is a necessary or sufficient cause of any organizational outcome.[16] The contributions of each official are like the strands in a rope. Together they pull the load: no single strand could do the job alone, but the job could be done without any single stand. Suppose that for many decades the CIA has had a policy of trying to overthrow third-world governments that refuse to cooperate with their operatives, and suppose further that many of these attempts are morally wrong. No one presently in the agency initiated the practice, let us assume, and no one individual plays a very important role in any of the attempts. If any one agent did not do his or her part, the practice would continue, and even particular attempts would still often succeed. How could we say that any individual is the cause of this practice?

A second argument points to the gap between individual intention and collective outcomes. The motives of individual officials are inevitably diverse (to serve the nation, to help citizens, tò acquire power, to win a promotion, to ruin a rival). Many praiseworthy policies are promoted for morally dubious reasons, and many pernicious policies are furthered with the best of intentions. In many organizations today, for example, we may well be able to say that no official intends to discriminate against minorities in the hiring and promoting of employees; yet the pattern of appointments and advancements still disadvantages certain minorities. Here we should want to condemn the pattern or policy (so the argument goes), but we could not morally blame any individual official for it.

A third argument stresses the requirements of role. The duties of office and the routines of large organizations require individual actions which, in themselves harmless or even in some sense obligatory, combine to produce harmful decisions and policies by the organization. Although the policy of the organization is morally wrong, each individual has done his or her moral duty according to the requirements of office. The collective sum is worse than its parts. In a review of the policies that led to financial collapse of New York City in the mid-1970s and endangered the welfare and livelihoods of millions of citizens, one writer concludes that no individuals can be blamed for the misleading budgetary practices that helped bring about the collapse: "The delicately balanced financial superstructure was a kind of evolutionary extrusion that had emerged from hundreds of piecemeal decisions."[17]

If we were to accept these arguments, we would let many guilty officials off the moral hook. Without some sense of personal responsibility, officials may act with less moral care, and citizens may challenge officials with less moral effect. Democratic accountability is likely to erode. How can these arguments be answered so that individual responsibility can be maintained in organizations?

First, we should not assess an official's moral responsibility solely according to the proportionate share he or she contributes to the outcome. "Responsibility is not a bucket in which less remains when some is apportioned out."[18] If a gang of 10 thugs beats an old man to death, we do not punish each thug for only one-tenth of the murder (even if no single thug hit him hard enough to cause his death). Further, in imputing responsibility we should consider not only the acts that individuals committed but also the acts they omitted. Even though in the CIA example no one initiated the wrongful policy, many officials could be blamed for failing to try to halt the practice. Admittedly, there are dangers in adopting a notion of "negative responsibility."[19] One is that such a notion can make individuals culpable for almost anything (since there seems to be no limit to the acts that an individual did not do). But in the context of organizations we can more often point to specific omissions that made a significant difference in the outcome and that are ascribable to specific persons. Patterns of omissions can be predicted and specified in advance.

The force of the second argument, which points to the gap between individual intention and collective outcome, can be blunted if we simply give less weight to intentions than to consequences in assessing moral culpability of officials, at least in two of the senses that "intention" is commonly understood—as motive and as direct goal. It is often hard enough in private life to interpret the motives of persons one knows well; in public life it may be impossible to discover the intentions of officials, especially when the motives of so many of those questioning the motives of officials are themselves questionable. Insofar as we can discover motives, they are relevant in assessing character and may sometimes help in predicting future behavior, but administrative ethics does better to concentrate on actions and results in public life.[20]

What about officials who directly intend only good results but, because of other people's mistakes or other factors they do not foresee, contribute to an unjust or harmful policy? Here the key question is not whether the officials actually foresaw this result, but whether they should have foreseen it.[21] We can legitimately hold public officials to a higher standard than that to which we hold ordinary citizens. We can expect officials to foresee and take into account a wider range of consequences, partly because of the general obligations of public office. Where the welfare of so many are at stake, officials must make exceptional efforts to anticipate consequences of their actions.

Moreover, the nature of organization itself often forestalls officials from plausibly pleading that they did not foresee what their actions would cause. Organizations tend to produce patterned outcomes; they regularly make the same mistakes in the same ways. While officials may once or twice reasonably claim they should not have been expected to

foresee a harmful outcome to which their well-intentioned actions contributed, there must be some (low) limit to the number of times they may
use this excuse to escape responsibility. In the example of discrimination
in employment, we would say that officials should recognize that their
organizational procedures (combined with social forces) are still producing unjust results in personnel decisions; they become partly responsible
for the injustice if they do not take steps to overcome it as far as they
can.

The requirements of a role insulate an official from blame much less
than the earlier argument implied.[22] The example of the New York City
fiscal crisis actually tells against that argument as much as for it. Mayor
Beame was one of the officials who disclaimed responsibility for the allegedly deceptive accounting practices on the grounds that they were part
of organizational routines established many years earlier and could not be
changed in the midst of a crisis. But Beame had also served as comptroller
and in the budget office during the years when those accounting practices
were initiated.[23] In ascribing responsibility to public officials, we should
keep in mind that it attaches to persons, not offices. It cannot be entirely
determined by any one role a person holds, and it follows a person
through time. These features of personal responsibility are sometimes ignored. Public officials are blamed for an immoral (or incompetent) performance in one role but then appear to start with a clean slate once they
leave the old job and take up a new one. This recycling of discredited public figures is reinforced by the habit of collapsing personal responsibility
into role responsibility. Another way that officials may transcend their
roles should also be emphasized. Even when a role fully and legitimately
constrains what an official may do, personal responsibility need not be
completely extinguished. Officials may escape blame for a particular decision, but they do not thereby escape responsibility for seeking to change
the constraints of role and structure that helped produce that decision,
and they do not escape responsibility for criticizing those constraints.
Criticism of one's own past and current performance, and the structures
in which that performance takes place, may be the last refuge of moral responsibility in public life.

Administrative ethics is possible—at least, the two major theoretical
views that oppose its possibility are not compelling. We are forced to accept neither an ethic of neutrality that would suppress independent
moral judgment, nor an ethic of structure that would ignore individual
moral agency in organizations. To show that administrative ethics is
possible is not of course to show how to make it actual. But understanding why administrative ethics is possible is a necessary step not only toward putting it into practice but also toward giving it meaningful content in practice.

Notes

1. It may be assumed that there is no important philosophical distinction between "ethics" and "morality." Both terms denote the principles of right and wrong in conduct (or the study of such principles). When we refer to the principles of particular professions (e.g., legal ethics or political ethics), "ethics" is the more natural term; and when we refer to personal conduct (e.g., sexual morality), "morality" seems more appropriate. But in their general senses, the terms are fundamentally equivalent. For various definitions of the nature of morality or ethics, see William Frankena, *ethics,* 2nd ed. (Englewood Cliffs, N.J.: Prentice-Hall, 1973), pp. 1–11; Alan Donagan, *The Theory of Morality* (Chicago: University of Chicago Press, 1977), pp. 1–31; G. J. Warnock, *The Object of Morality* (London: Methuen & Co., 1971), pp. 1–26.

2. Cf. the method of "reflective equilibrium" presented by John Rawls, *A Theory of Justice* (Cambridge: Harvard University Press, 1971), pp. 48–51.

3. For citations and analysis of some writers who adopt part or all of the ethic of neutrality, see Joel L. Fleishman and Bruce L. Payne (eds.), *Ethical Dilemmas and the Education of Policymakers* (Hastings-on-Hudson, N.Y.: The Hastings Center, 1980), pp. 36–38. Cf. John A. Rohr, *Ethics for Bureaucrats* (New York: Dekker, 1978), pp. 15–47.

4. Cf. George Graham, "Ethical Guidelines for Public Administrators," *Public Administration Review,* vol. 34 (January/February 1974), pp. 90–92.

5. Donald Warwick, "The Ethics of Administrative Discretion," in Joel Fleishman *et al.* (eds.), *Public Duties* (Cambridge: Harvard University Press, 1981), pp. 93–127.

6. Edward Weisband and Thomas M. Franck, *Resignation in Protest* (New York: Penguin, 1976), p. 3.

7. J. Anthony Lukas, *Nightmare: The Underside of the Nixon Years* (New York: Bantam, 1977), p. 588.

8. On "complicity," see Thomas E. Hill, "Symbolic Protest and Calculated Silence," *Philosophy & Public Affairs* (Fall 1979), pp. 83–102. For a defense against the charge of moral self-indulgence, see Bernard Williams, *Moral Luck* (Cambridge: Cambridge University Press, 1981), pp. 40–53.

9. For an example of the latter, see Weisband and Franck, p. 46.

10. Cf. Graham, p. 92.

11. James C. Thomson, "How Could Vietnam Happen?" *Atlantic* (April 1968), p. 49. Also see Albert Hirschman, *Exit, Voice and Loyalty* (Cambridge: Harvard University Press, 1970), pp. 115–119.

12. Thomson, p. 49.

13. Gary J. Greenberg, "Revolt at Justice," in Charles Peters and T. J. Adams (eds.), *Inside the System* (New York: Praeger, 1970), pp. 195–209.

14. See Rawls, pp. 363–391.

15. Dennis F. Thompson, "Moral Responsibility of Public Officials: The Problem of Many Hands," *American Political Science Review,* vol. 74 (December 1980), pp. 905–916.

16. John Ladd, "Morality and the Ideal of Rationality in Formal Organizations," *Monist,* vol. 54 (October 1970), pp. 488–516.

17. Charles R. Morris, *The Cost of Good Intentions* (New York: W. W. Norton, 1980), pp. 239–240. For some other examples of structuralist analyses, see Herbert Kaufman. *Red Tape* (Washington, D.C.: Brookings, 1977), pp. 27–28; and Richard J. Stillman, *Public Administration: Concepts and Cases,* 2nd ed. (Boston: Houghton-Mifflin, 1980), p. 34.

18. Robert Nozick, *Anarchy, State and Utopia* (New York: Basic Books, 1974), p. 130.

19. Cf. Bernard Williams, "A Critique of Utilitarianism," in J.J.C. Smart and Williams, *Utilitarianism* (Cambridge: Cambridge University Press, 1973), pp. 93–118.

20. But cf. Joel L. Fleishman, "Self-Interest and Political Integrity," in Fleishman *et al.* (eds.), pp. 52–92.

21. But cf. Charles Fried, *Right and Wrong* (Cambridge: Harvard University Press, 1978), esp. pp. 21–22, 26, 28, 202–205. More generally on "intention," see Donagan, *Theory of Morality,* pp. 112–142; and J. L. Mackie, *Ethics* (New York: Penguin, 1977), pp. 203–226.

22. On role responsibility, see H.L.A. Hart, *Punishment and Responsibility* (New York: Oxford University Press, 1968), pp. 212–214; and R. S. Downie, *Roles and Values* (London: Methuen, 1971), pp. 121–145.

23. Dennis F. Thompson, "Moral Responsibility and the New York City Fiscal Crisis," in J. Fleishman *et al.,* pp. 266–285.

Part TWO

Solving Ethical Dilemmas

Clearly, the scholars whose work is reprinted in Part 1, who represent the first three decades of public administration scholarship, were concerned about administrative ethics and trying to sort out just what it means to be ethical in the realm of administration. As thinking evolved, the original debate between controlling behavior and trusting continued, with more people entering the fray. The theme of decision making emerged. Should the ethical administrator make decisions or simply provide information to decision makers? If the administrator does the problem solving, what criteria shall be used?

In Part 2, the first article (Chapter 6) was published in 1974 to stimulate thinking about criteria for solving ethical dilemmas. George A. Graham, representing the National Academy of Public Administration, wrote "Ethical Guidelines for Public Administrators: Observations on Rules of the Game" for the section of *Public Administration Review* called "From the Professional Stream: Currents and Soundings." At the beginning of the article, *PAR*'s editor noted, "It seems clear that in the immediate future there will be an intensified interest in the ethical aspects of public administration." These guidelines were printed to "stimulate thought and discussion about how administrators ought to behave and how they ought to use discretion."

Graham's list of ethical guidelines is a set of standards developed by two standing committees of the National Academy of Public Administration. They provide direction in the areas of the administrator's role in representative government, the limits of compromise, and policy implementation. They also introduce the role of due process in administrative life.

Why had the need for such guidelines become clear in 1974? The Watergate scandal that occurred in 1972 had taken most people by surprise. Previous trust in government was forced into question, and public administrators were operating in the shadow of political mistrust. Questioning of professional responsibilities and professional accountability intensified. Were public administrationists culpable in Watergate? No longer were debates about administrative ethics academic exercises. Being judicious, prudent, and moral had become a practical necessity, as well as theoretically correct behavior. When written, the guidelines were a reaction to the failure of public administration to identify and prevent the events leading to Watergate. Today, they are a checklist for those who want to responsibly address ethical dilemmas in government service.

After Watergate, public administrationists became reflective about solving moral dilemmas and very concerned about identifying, preventing, and controlling corruption in government. The late 1970s and early 1980s were a period of transition in public administration thinking about the role of government. Yet the ethical thinking continued to pivot around the same issues that Friedrich and Finer had debated. Can we rely on public administrators to be moral and conscience driven, or are codes and controls necessary to ensure responsible government? The final three chapters in Part 2 assume and discuss public employee morality.

The second article (Chapter 7 here) was published in 1982. Written by Martin Wachs, it is entitled "Ethical Dilemmas in Forecasting for Public Policy." For Wachs, the central ethical dilemma of forecasting comes from the unreflective use of technology, which implies value-neutral data and predictions. Wachs points out that nothing is value neutral and that policy forecasting requires value judgments. He is worried by the limited number of ethical guidelines available to those who make the decisions that affect people's lives, but he also trusts that public administrators are able to engage in moral decision making. This is a consciousness-raising piece that prompts reflection on the sources of one's assumptions in decision making and the impact of one's decisions.

The final two articles in Part 2 were both published in *PAR* in 1984. York Willbern, in "Types and Levels of Public Morality" (Chapter 8 here), clarifies the difference between individual moral behavior and the moral content of public policy—a difference he believes is important. To this end, he presents a taxonomy of morality for public officials, ranging from "basic honesty and conformity to law" to "compromise and social integration," where compromise can actually become a moral act. This recognition that both micro and macro levels of morality exist and affect both behavior and perceptions of behavior expands the field of administrative ethics. With Willbern's work, we begin to see the complexity of administrative ethics and the futility of looking only at the Friedrich-Finer polarity.

Chapter 9 presents Debra Stewart's "Managing Competing Claims: An Ethical Framework for Human Resource Decision Making," the first article about administrative ethics in an ASPA-sponsored journal written by a woman. It is also the first to examine the line manager as an ethical agent. Thus, it is practical as well as scholarly. Stewart identifies three competing claims for the manager's attention and action, then offers a framework by means of which a manager can "do good."

Whereas the first three authors in Part 2 provide guidelines and a framework for resolving ethical dilemmas, Stewart goes one step further. She goes beyond the normative argument that public administrators should be ethical, presenting a realistic way to act ethically and assurances that ethical action is possible.

So ends Part 2. It has provided guidance for solving ethical dilemmas and the assurance that ordinary people are capable of being moral actors in their organizations. Like the chapters of Part 1, the material presented here is timeless. The serious student of organizations must consider Graham's guidelines and recognize the range and complexity of ethical dilemmas. Although the other ethical themes soon to be addressed present particular challenges, it is in Part 2 that one gains a sense of one's own responsibility for moral behavior and one's obligation to act, whatever the particular ethical dilemma being confronted.

6

ETHICAL GUIDELINES FOR PUBLIC ADMINISTRATORS: OBSERVATIONS ON RULES OF THE GAME

George A. Graham
National Academy of Public Administration

An experienced administrator learns in time that the most serious and difficult ethical problems arise out of conflicts of loyalty and conflicts of involvements, activities, and commitments outside of his job which would bias his judgment on the job, or reduce his motivation to do a good job in the public interest.

Conflicts of loyalty tend to be more difficult to contain. They result from the growing size and complexity of governmental organizations, the wide range and interaction of governmental functions, and the necessary practice of vesting discretion in officials at various points and many levels of the governmental organization. This delegation of discretion is authorized by law on the assumption that it will be exercised wisely and in good faith, and it is done because it is necessary in order to secure high performance. The administrative system that has evolved thus rests equally on a foundation of professional competence and personal integrity.

Where there is discretion, there is uncertainty, and there may be conflicting obligations and loyalties. In dealing with this situation, the administrator is subject to a double hierarchy of authority, one impersonal and one personal, which defines his obligations. The hierarchy of law (constitu-tional, statutory, administrative) is impersonal. The chain of direction or command, into which he fits somewhere, is quite personal. The law in its various forms frequently is stated in general terms, which must be inter-preted, and the courts, which formally and potentially have the last word in interpretation, never get around to definitive interpretations on the vast majority of issues that arise administratively. It thus falls to the administra-tive authorities to interpret and delineate the law through policies, pro-grams, instructions, rules, procedures, and an infinity of decisions. Neither the formal law nor the administrative law is always internally consistent; and public officials, both political executives and professional administra-tors, do not always agree in their interpretation of the law and its imple-mentation through policies and programs. They can and do disagree about what is lawful, about what is proper, and about what is wise or in the pub-lic interest. Disagreements grow out of different values, out of different de-grees, of ignorance or understanding, and out of different purposes. Here is where the most difficult ethical issues arise for administrators. They are not mindless minions of the organization, but are pledged by the system to employ their brains, not just their brawn, in the public service. They are pledged to think and to be honest in their thoughts.

The ethical problem is further complicated by the daily necessity of melding different interpretations of what is lawful, what is proper, and what is in the public interest. An administrator learns, no matter where he is in the hierarchy, that he seldom can get his own way in the sense that the decision made or action taken is exactly what he personally thinks it should be. His "in-put" to the decision is important, but it is only one of many. Accepting decisions that are less than perfect, judged by his lights, is a daily necessity for the administrator, if there is to be orderly government.

Participative management, organizational decision making, and group judgments are not merely a common and/or optimal mode of operation in government, as they may be in the private sector of American life. They are also more or less mandated by one of the most basic ideas of American public law, the principle of "due process of law" enunciated in the Consti-tution of the United States, and elaborated over the years by decisions of the courts. Although most of these decisions deal with regulatory processes of government, the doctrine of due process is broad in its impact and can be said to permeate all public administration.

Due process may be thought of as a basic principle of the unwritten con-stitution of the land which requires all administrators in exercising the power and discretionary authority with which they are entrusted to be in-formed, to be fair, to be rational, and to be reasonable. These guidelines must be accepted by a public administrator for himself. In this respect they are a constraint. But they also indicate what he has a right to expect of other administrators with whom he deals, superiors as well as subordinates, and also his peers in other parts of the organization. The concept of due process in fact comprises a set of "rules of the game" for persons in the public sector which are enduring (and still evolving), although not always respected.

Accepting the melding process as a necessity in organized representative government in a democratic society, and guided by the principles of due process which are embedded in the public law of the land, how then can the public administrator deal with the ethical dilemmas which arise inevitably, and do so within the rules of the game? Most of the hard questions fall into three categories: (1) How shall he make his in-put to decisions? (2) What are the limits of compromise in the melding process? (3) How shall he perform in the action phase of implementing decisions or carrying out programs? The following guidelines for conduct in answering these questions may be suggested.

The In-Put to Decisions

The administrator's role in a democratic society under representative government, i.e., the United States, requires him to:

1. Inform others participating in the decision-making process (supervisors, peers, subordinates) of significant information which is properly relevant to their role in the decision.
2. Interpret the data, explain their meaning, and argue the case for their impact on policy as he sees it, while making sure he has no personal conflict of interest, and at the same time revealing the value base from which he approaches the issue.
3. Be guided in the extent and intensity of his advocacy by the importance of the issue, his position in the hierarchy, and the extent to which the issue falls within his cognizance and his competence. (No requirement to go to Armageddon for petty issues peripheral to his cognizance and competence.)
4. Accept decisions made within the "rules of the game" even though he deems them unwise (i.e., the decision has been made rationally by informed persons, acting within their authority, and attempting to be fair and reasonable).
5. Recognize that he may be required to defend a decision which he personally rejects, if it has been made according to the rules of the game, if it falls properly within his official role and cognizance, without volunteering his contrary views; but that he is not required under any circumstances to testify falsely as to the facts or as to his personal judgment.

The Limits of Compromise

To be true to his professional role, and the rules of the game, the public administrator must

1. Recognize that the rules of the game permit him to contest a decision made by his own organization, but not yet final, by going over his superior's head, or by going to other organizations within the government (including the legislative branch) only when he can honestly assure himself (1) that a mistake is being made on an issue of major public importance, (2) that his judgment is unbiased by personal or partisan, as opposed to public interest, considerations, (3) that the risk he runs of being forced out of the government is justified by the importance of the issue, and (4) that what will be lost by the decision outweighs the value of his probable future usefulness to the government if he continues in the government.
2. Recognize that he is not required to sign documents within his sphere of responsibility which he does not approve, and that he should not do so, although he may be required to prepare them for the signature of others.
3. Uphold, enforce, and comply with the law, insofar as it is within his sphere of responsibility and discretion.
4. Resign if he cannot accept valid interpretations of the law by higher administrative authorities which would control his action (where the interpretation of the law has not been determined judicially).

Correlatively, the understandings of American public administration forbid an administrator to order or instruct a subordinate to

1. Take any illegal action.
2. Suppress significant information which is normally or properly public, misinterpret the true facts, or engage in a deliberate deception.
3. Assume responsibility for a decision which the subordinate opposes and for which the superior could himself assume responsibility.
4. Require a subordinate to sign documents which are within the subordinate's sphere of responsibility, which the subordinate does not approve (although the subordinate may be required to prepare them for another's signature).

Implementing Decisions

Assuming that a decision or plan of action is final and that its legality is not in doubt, an administrator is obligated if it falls within his sphere of responsibility to carry out the action to the best of his ability, in good faith, whether or not he agrees with the merits of the decision.

Assuming that a decision or plan of action is final, but that its legality is in doubt and is being contested, the administrator (insofar as it is within his sphere of responsibility) may "go slow" until the legality is determined.

The alternatives in either case are to ask for transfer to other duties not involved in the action in question, or to resign.

Underlying these guidelines is the principle that all administrators, elected officials, appointed political executives, and professional administrators alike are bound by the law of the land, and where there is discretion in interpreting and applying it, they are obligated to use their power in good faith in the public interest. A second basic principle is that no public official or administrator, high or low, owns the government, his organization, or his office. The government belongs to the public, and the administrator's role is that of a trustee, not a proprietor, in the use of his authority.

Elected officials and their political appointees have a special problem. They must remember that their electoral mandate authorizes them to use their power and exercise their discretion—but only within the "rules of the game." No matter how large the electoral victory which brings them to office, public officials are still obligated to be informed, to be fair, to be rational, and to be reasonable. In view of the normal complexity of election issues which influence voters in casting their ballots, it would be presumptuous for any political executive to assume that he may arbitrarily and alone determine what the election means on an issue within his cognizance, or that he is exempt from "administrative due process."

7

ETHICAL DILEMMAS IN FORECASTING FOR PUBLIC POLICY

Martin Wachs
University of California, Los Angeles

Introduction

Forecasts are part and parcel of policy making. Governments deploy military forces and construct weapons systems on the basis of forecasts of actions by potential future enemies. Transit systems, power plants, hospitals, and airports are constructed only after forecasts have demonstrated that a "need" exists for their services and that their costs are justified by expected benefits. Testimony before Congress advocating increased expenditures for housing or education is considered incomplete unless forecasts of future need are carefully detailed. Economic forecasts are so influential as to be the subject of national media coverage, and of evaluations of national monetary or employment policy by competing candidates for high office.

The requirement to prepare forecasts is written into law and government regulation. For example, highway networks built in American metropolitan areas have been based upon a "comprehensive, continuing, and cooperative" planning process, institutionalized by the Highway Act of 1964. This act was interpreted as requiring that highway plans be evaluated against a 20-year forecast of travel demand, with the 20-year forecast being updated periodically to ensure that the plans remain valid. The Urban

Mass Transportation Administration requires that state and local governments submit "alternatives analyses" as part of requests for funds under its capital grants program. The analysis must show that the course of action for which funding is sought clearly constitutes a superior use of public funds in comparison with all reasonable alternatives. Guidelines for the program require, among other things, that cost and patronage levels be forecast for each alternative. Similarly, airport authorities produce long-range forecasts of air traffic in their regions to arrive at proposals for new facilities, metropolitan planning organizations base housing programs on forecasts, and national energy policy debates have been motivated by competing forecasts of the demand for and availability of fuels.

Forecasts can be made by politicians, clairvoyants, philosophers, or prophets. In policy making, however, forecasts taken seriously for any practical purpose are likely to be produced by technical experts, and it is technical forecasting to which this study is addressed. In a society influenced by technology and technique, prediction is accomplished by applications of standardized methods to carefully collected files of information. Forecasts in most instances are produced by manipulations of computers which are probably understood by relatively few of the people who act on the basis of the results. Forecasters are usually experts, serving as staff or consultants to those in decision-making positions. Public officials who employ forecasts as the basis for action rarely comprehend all of the mathematical procedures involved in the predictions. They are likely to be unfamiliar with the data series employed and unaware of the technical assumptions hidden under the cloak of expert judgment.

The political salience of many forecasts and the technical complexity of the forecasting process combine to create for the forecaster an important ethical dilemma. Forecasts which support the advocacy of particular courses of action are often demanded by interest groups or public officials. Forecasters must rely upon so many assumptions and judgmental procedures that it is usually possible to adjust forecasts to the extent that they meet such demands. On the other hand, forecasters are likely to view themselves as technical experts rather than politicians, loyal to supposedly objective criteria according to which their work is judged in technical terms rather than political ones. Public policy heightens this dilemma by requiring through laws and regulations forecasts which are supposedly technically objective and politically neutral, while distributing political rewards to those whose forecasts prove their positions most emphatically.

Consider a situation described by Peter Marcuse, who changed the name of the community in which it occurred in order to avoid embarrassing those involved:

> In Oldport, the mayor retained a planning firm as consultant to develop a comprehensive twenty-year plan for urban renewal, housing, schools, and so-

cial service facilities. The planners' preliminary report projected moderate population growth but a dramatic and continuing shift in racial composition, with minority groups reaching a majority in twelve years. A black majority was predicted within five years in the public schools.

The mayor reacted strongly to the preliminary report. If these findings were released, they would become a self-fulfilling prophecy. All hope of preserving an integrated school system and maintaining stable mixed neighborhoods or developing an ethnically heterogeneous city with a strong residential base would disappear.

The planners were asked to review their figures. They agreed to use the lower range of their projections—minority dominance in the public schools after eight years and a majority in the city in sixteen. The mayor was not satisfied. He told the planners either to change the figures or to cut them out of the report. They refused, feeling they had bent their interpretation of fact as far as they could. Without a discussion of these facts, the balance of the report could not be professionally justified.

The mayor lashed out at them privately for professional arrogance, asked a professional on his own staff to rewrite the report without the projections, and ordered the consultants not to release or disclose their findings on race under any circumstances. The professional on the mayor's staff initially demurred from rewriting the report but ultimately complied. The consultants remained silent, completed the formal requirements of their contracts, and left. The mayor never used professional planning consultants again.[1]

Here we have in a nutshell the central ethical dilemma of forecasting. Those who use forecasts, prepare them, or critique them, invariably use the language of technical objectivity. A model used for prediction is assumed to be unbiased, a tool in the hands of a forecaster who is a technical expert rather than a decision maker—a scientist more than a politician. Yet, so many technical assumptions are required to make any forecast that the process can ultimately be quite subjective, while the consequences have great significance. By choosing particular data or mathematical forms, many a forecast can easily be changed to transform increases into decreases; growth into contraction, gain into loss. These transformations can produce rewards or remove threats for those who accomplish them, they can often be made to masquerade as technical details rather than value judgments, and the outcome is frequently unverifiable.

Little attention has been given in the field of public administration to the role which forecasting plays in decision making. Even less attention has been given in the education of policy makers and technical experts to the ethical dimensions of forecasting. Without pretending to prescribe appropriate courses of action for those engaged in forecasting, this paper explores the nature of this dilemma. Its roots are sought in both the technical aspects of forecasting and the political uses to which forecasts are put. This explication of this dilemma should help forecasters recognize the volatile situations in which it appears, and to address it more effectively in the education of policy makers.

The Inherent Dilemma of Circularity

The role of forecasts in policy making is fascinating largely because it always involves an inherent dilemma of circularity. The future is made by people, and is not beyond our control. But to choose wisely from among alternative actions we seek information about conditions which will form the context of those actions. We want to know what the future will be like so that we can act, yet actions will determine what the future will be, and may negate the forecast. Because of this circularity, rarely may the accuracy of a forecast made in the public policy arena be literally verified.

A forecast of dire future events is made for the purpose of bringing about actions to avert that future. Having taken action and thus avoided the gloomy prospect, we can never be sure that the forecast events would have happened in the absence of that action. For example, if responsible medical authorities forecast that a particular disease will reach epidemic proportions unless mass inoculations are undertaken, a prudent government would surely conduct an inoculation program before victims begin to expire. If they did so, an incorrect forecast—with no epidemic in the offing—would yield the same measurable result as a correct one. The accuracy of the forecast could only have been proven had no action been taken and had the epidemic come about. Prudent policy makers would surely avoid the possibility of proving such forecasts correct, largely because of the dangerous potential consequences of inaction. Unless a forecast is considered frivolous, the salience of its consequences may be more influential than the probable accuracy. The international attention recently given to the Club of Rome's forecast of world ecological disaster follows more from its tenebrous visions than from its probable accuracy.[2]

A forecast of growing demand for some service, facility, or commodity and its provision in response to the forecast, give rise to a similar dilemma. The demand which is later observed might have been "correctly" forecast, or it might have been instigated by the forecast and the action which it spurred. In past decades, for example, electric utilities foresaw enormous growth in the demand for electricity, and expanded their generating capacity accordingly. Later, having huge capacity, they advertised electric appliances, lowered the price of electricity to users of large quantities, and invented new uses for electricity. Do the earlier forecasters of great demand now have the right to claim that their forecasts were "accurate"? Only in a superficial sense were they correct. It is the intertwining of forecast and action which is more important than any mathematical measure of consistency between forecast and actual consumption of electricity. Such examples serve to illustrate that there can be no absolute criteria of accuracy in forecasting for public policy, and that the supposed accuracy of any forecast can nearly always arouse suspicion among skeptics. From the inherent dilemma of circularity there follow many questions for those who prepare forecasts for government agencies, and those who employ their forecasts.

Forecasts Require Numerous Assumptions

Many authors have drawn a distinction between forecasts on the one hand, and projections or extrapolations on the other. A projection or extrapolation is merely a calculation of the likely consequences of mathematical relationships between variables. A simple population projection, for example, would extend in time the relationships, among birth, death, and migration rates. A forecast is more than a projection, for it involves also committing oneself to the selection of particular values of the variables which are involved. Thus, a forecast of population requires first that certain birth, death, and migration rates be selected as those most likely to prevail, and secondly, projecting the consequences of the specific rates selected. Clearly, the estimation of appropriate future values for these rates is a much more challenging task than calculating their implications. Technical expertise, however, contributes far more to one's ability to do the calculations than it does to one's ability to form the appropriate assumptions about future values of the parameters.

In a complex society, policies set by one organization or institution are inherently dependent upon the actions of many others. The demand for automobiles, for example, depends partly upon decisions made in Detroit, but also upon international politics, current wage rates, residential preferences, investment programs in highways and transit, changes in economic and family roles of men and women, and many other underlying conditions. Health care, housing, energy, and educational programs all present challenges to understanding and forecasting which are equally complex. These intricate interrelationships among the areas of modern society make it difficult to isolate clear cause and effect sequences which would allow forecasting with confidence. This is why Michel Godet has observed: "Forecasting in the classic sense of the word is possible only when man, through his past actions, has overcommitted his future to such a degree that the outcome can only take one or two forms,"[3] Unable and unwilling to exert tyrannical control over events, we instead make forecasts which are conditional upon many assumptions about the likely behavior of some factors, so that we can estimate probable variations in others. Even a simple projection involving relationships among five or six variables would yield an unmanageable range of combinations of future conditions unless some of the variables were constrained by assumptions about the limits of their future values.

Without assumptions, forecasting would be impossible. But assumptions can be self-serving, and in the end can dominate the outcome of the forecast. William Ascher studied the accuracy of forecasts made over a period of 50 years in the fields of population, economic, energy, transportation, and technological forecasting. He concluded that "core assumptions" were more important determinants of the accuracy of any forecast than were any other factors:

> The core assumptions underlying a forecast, which represent the forecaster's basic outlook on the context within which the specific forecasted trend develops, are the major determinants of forecast accuracy. Methodologies are basically the vehicles for determining the consequences or implications of core assumptions that have been chosen more or less independently of the specific methodologies. When the core assumptions are valid, the choice of the methodology is either secondary or obvious. When the core assumptions fail to capture the reality of the future context, other factors such as methodology generally make little difference; they cannot "save" the forecast.[4]

Reliance on assumptions is heightened by the fact that forecasts are often necessarily based on historical trends in variables, yet archives of data on social systems frequently provide historical information for only one or two points in time. It is difficult to project a trend on the basis of few data points, but this is often done by assuming a particular mathematical form for a curve and "calibrating" the trendline on the basis of only one or two observations. On technical grounds it may be quite risky to project a trend forward some 10, 20, or 50 years if the trendline is based upon information extending backward in time only 10 or 15 years, yet this is frequently done for practical reasons.

Extending a trendline based upon inadequate evidence of a relationship between variables is often a manifestation of a problem in forecasting which Ascher refers to as "assumption drag," and which he considers to be "the source of some of the most drastic errors in forecasting."[5] Assumption drag consists of reliance upon old core assumptions, sometimes after they have been positively disproven. He shows, for example, that population forecasters working in the late 1930s and 1940s continued to assume declining birthrates into the fifties and sixties, although the assumption of declining birthrates had already been authoritatively invalidated. Similarly, feminists point out that, while the majority of married women are today in the work force, many predict future household and labor force characteristics on the assumption that the single-worker household will continue to be the norm.

Assumption drag is due, in large part, to the simple fact that it is often more appropriate to incorporate into a forecast an historical trend than it is to anticipate a future deviation from that trend. The forecaster who projects the continuation of past trends may risk criticism for failing to anticipate systemic changes. Conversely, the analyst who forecasts coming systemic changes always risks criticism for going out on a limb, following hunches, or departing from conventional wisdom or established practice. It is usually difficult to decide whether a recent deviation from a long-term trend is a temporary secular variation or a permanent change in the trendline. It may take many years to recognize a systemic change in a policy variable. Furthermore, most forecasters are specialists who use information produced by other specialists as raw materials for their work. A forecaster of transportation or electricity demand may know far less about demography than a population forecaster, but may rely upon population forecasts as a source of change in transportation or electricity usage. While up-to-date on the latest analyses in his or her own area of expertise, the transportation or electricity forecaster may have access only to published population analyses which are out of date, and may not know of newer theories or conclusions in that area of study.

For these several reasons, analysts often conclude that variables which have been stable will continue to be so during the period for which a forecast is being prepared. Forecasting models may even reflect an assumption of stability by omitting from the model a variable deemed to be stable and hence less influential than others which are more volatile. This can have disastrous consequences if the passage of time proves the assumption incorrect. Consider the elaborate set of models widely used to forecast highway traffic throughout the world. These models, involving hundreds of equations, have been institutionalized through the widespread availability of standardized computer packages. The forecast procedures have been in use for more than 20 years, and were developed at a time when gasoline was inexpensive and in ample supply. Thus, while the models are notable for their level of detail, they do not explicitly represent the price or availability of gasoline as determinants of travel. When the forecasting models were formalized, gasoline was so widely available and inexpensive that statistical associations between these variables and the frequency or duration of trips were difficult to identify. The decision to omit these factors seemed rational on technical grounds. With hindsight, having experienced large changes in the price and availability of fuel and consequent fluctuations in travel, we may certainly question the wisdom of omitting them. The omission illustrates Godet's contention that: "certain forecasting errors are explained by our tendency to look at the 'better lit' aspects of our problems. The light dazzles us and hides from us what lies behind it."[6]

We more often assume stability than discontinuity, so assumption drag introduces into forecasting a systematic tendency toward conservatism. The centrality of core assumptions in forecasting makes this a serious problem, although attempting to overcome the conservative bias often means adopting critical assumptions on the basis of little supporting evidence. This dilemma contributes to the ethical quandary which forecasters face, because the absence of evidence supporting assumptions can easily reduce forecasts to statements of advocacy.

Technical Expertise in Forecasting

Despite the fact that assumptions play a larger role in forecasting than do the methods which elaborate upon them, forecasters are usually drawn from the ranks of social scientists, engineers, and planners whose education and professional identity are based primarily upon technical methodological skills. They are likely to believe and promote the belief that forecasting is impossible without the use of computers, mathematical methods, and complex data sets.

Sophistication in the technique of forecasting is more apparent, however, than real. Computers are used because there is often a great deal of data: many variables, many units of analysis for each, several time periods. These conditions lead to the requirement for training and experience in mathematics, statistics, data manipulation, and computer programming. But together, such skills ensure no special perspective on the future, and there is relatively little theory derivable from the social sciences to help one arrive at reasonable core assumptions.

Most forecasts result from extrapolations and assumptions rather than theoretical models incorporating representations of causality. Curve fitting and statistical tests of association may be employed, but extending a quadratic polynomial 25 years beyond the present is disturbingly similar to sketching a simple line on graph paper if the extrapolation is based on goodness of fit rather than an understanding of the underlying phenomena. Mathematical finesse enables one to connect models in series with the outputs of one forming the inputs to others, but if the models are associative rather than causal, errors may multiply so rapidly that they quickly dominate the forecasts. For these reasons, the technical elegance of some forecasting models is an elusion, obfuscating the central importance of assumptions which require or utilize no special expertise.

It would seem obvious that complex social or environmental phenomena can be forecast best using models which capture their complexity by representing the causal chains which underlie them. Thus, a simple model, predicting crime rates or air pollution on the basis of one or two indicators, is likely to be inadequate because we know that crime and air pollution result from many factors working in concert. In technical terms, simplistic models of complex phenomena are likely to have large "specification errors"—they fail to represent the processes by which outcomes are actually determined. By adding complexity—linking larger numbers of variables in longer causal chains—more sophisticated forecasting models can be developed which would appear to promise better predictions.

But complex models raise other problems. As more and more variables are included in the mathematical representation of a social or technical process, more data are required to use such a model in the preparation of a forecast. Of course, every bit of data used in a model is subject to error, and as more variables are used these "measurement errors" tend to increase more rapidly than the number of variables employed. A tradeoff must be made. Simple models, involving few variables, minimize measurement errors at the expense of large errors of specification. Complex models, involving many variables and equations, may reduce errors of specification, but only at the price of rapidly escalating measurement errors. An "optimum" forecasting model would be designed to the level of complexity which would minimize the sum of errors of the two types, but for most real phenomena analysts have no way of actually estimating the magnitude of each kind of error. Many feel that forecasting models of social, economic, and environmental phenomena have been developed to such a level of complexity that measurement errors are multiplied dramatically.[7]

Complex models are attractive for tactical reasons: They appear to be sophisticated and for this reason lend credibility to the advice given by those who understand them. Their very complexity makes it difficult to criticize or question their validity. In reality, they may be no more valid than very simple forecasting models which require less technical expertise.

There is a dangerous impression that forecasting is nothing more than data processing and extrapolation. Often, prescribed steps are followed to get a result even though the connections among the variables may not be known to be causative. No matter how accurate the data used and whether or not the structure of the model is appropriate, the specificity of the results often make them more plausible and authoritative than they ought to be.[8]

The Political Uses of Forecasts

Governments with limited resources to allocate, and citizens who rely upon public services and pay their costs, would seem on the surface to assume that forecasts of future need and cost are executed with objectivity. The complexity of pluralistic and technological societies, however, places many burdens upon those who prepare forecasts, which make objectivity difficult to attain. Public resource allocation is competitive in that the decision to fund a project in one jurisdiction may deprive another of a similar opportunity. Political influence, financial gain, jobs, and prestige all flow from "winning" competitions for public projects. Technical experts are often employed by agencies which advocate particular solutions to certain problems: nuclear vs. fossil fuel plants for power; highways vs. rapid transit for urban transportation, and so on. A forecaster might be in the employ of an engineering firm which received a small contract to estimate the need for a bridge. If the bridge is shown to be justified, additional consulting fees for design and engineering may produce hundreds of times the income derived from the preparation of the forecast itself. If the bridge is shown to be unnecessary, no further contracts may be awarded. In such settings, it is obvious that forecasters are under pressure to adjust their predictions for self-serving purposes.

This pressure is intensified by the issues mentioned earlier: (1) a forecast is inherently unverifiable; (2) the outcome of a forecasting exercise is to a great extent determined by its core assumptions; and (3) the activity of forecasting is technically complex, revealing to most users its results but not its mechanisms or assumptions. It is indeed difficult to withstand pressures to produce self-serving forecasts which are cloaked in the guise of technical objectivity. By politely agreeing to speak of forecasts as objective, planners, engineers, or economists who prepare them can maintain their self-respect and professional identity. Simultaneously, advocates of particular positions gain strength for their arguments by virtue of the supposedly "unbiased" technical analyses which they can cite. And politicians who finally make resource allocations calmly accept forecasts which confirm their particular preconceptions with far less critical review than those which do not. All three sets of actors—technical forecasting experts, advocates for a particular point of view, and politicians—gain by pretending that a forecast is an objective scientific statement, and gain more if it is also an effective statement of advocacy in a struggle for resources.

In keeping with the illusion of technical objectivity, when the passage of time has shown the vast majority of demand and cost forecasts for public services to have been inaccurate, critics generally have contended that "imperfect techniques" and "inadequate data" were the sources of the problems. Rarely has it been argued that forecasts have deliberately been designed to place certain projects in a favorable light and others at a disadvantage. Rarely has it been argued that the structure of governmental decision making makes such ethically troublesome uses of forecasts inevitable.

Consider, as an example, the well-known case of San Francisco's Bay Area Rapid Transit System (BART). Capital cost forecasts for the 71-mile system, which formed the basis for the 1962 bond issue election, amounted to $994 million in construction cost plus $70 million for rolling stock. The final capital cost is now actually estimated to have been in excess of $2.4 billion (deflated to 1962 dollars). Design changes contributed to the deviation from the initial estimate, but there is no doubt that the initial estimate of capital costs was simply too low. The cost estimates may have been deliberately kept unrealistically low for political reasons. The value of general obligation bonds that could be sold was limited to $792 million, 15 percent of the assessed valuation of the real property in the proposed district which for 1960–61 was $5.3 billion. It appears that the estimate of the construction cost was at least influenced by legal restrictions on the borrowing limit of the district.[9]

The example of BART illustrates an age-old problem in forecasting the demand for and the cost of public works. If demand for a water supply system, bridge, or port facility is overestimated and cost is underestimated, the benefits of the project can easily be made to seem to outweigh the costs. Once the decision to build the project has been made, and expenditures of public monies have taken place, the realization that initial cost estimates were too low will rarely kill the project. Somehow, more money will be found to finish a project, which is already underway. This was well understood by Robert Moses, as he planned and built the parkways, bridges, and parks of New York City. His biographer, Robert A. Caro, has written:

> "Once you sink that first stake," he would often say, "they'll never make you pull it up." . . . If ends justified means, and if the important thing in building a project was to get it started, then any means that got it started were justified. Furnishing misleading information about it was justified; so was underestimating its costs.
>
> Misleading and underestimating, in fact, might be the only way to get a project started. Since his projects were unprecedentedly vast, one of the biggest difficulties in getting them started was the fear of public officials . . . that the state couldn't afford the projects (which) . . . beneficial though they might be, would drain off a share of the state's wealth incommensurate with their benefits.
>
> But what if you didn't tell the officials how much the projects would cost? What if you let the legislators know about only a fraction of what you knew would be the project's ultimate expense?
>
> Once they had authorized that small initial expenditure and you had spent it, they would not be able to avoid giving you the rest when you asked for it. How could they? If they refused to give you the rest of the money, what they had given you would be wasted, and that would make them look bad in the eyes of the public. And if they said you had misled them, well, they were not supposed to be misled. If they had been misled, that would mean that they hadn't investigated the projects thoroughly; and had therefore been derelict in

their own duty. The possibilities for a polite but effective form of political blackmail were endless.[10]

The situation described is indeed an ethical dilemma because of the ambiguity and competing allegiances inherent in forecasting. The forecaster, in all likelihood, was educated according to a tradition of scientific-technical rationality, having allegiance to a set of methods and techniques rather than to particular outcomes in a policy debate. It is necessary to make assumptions so that the techniques can produce useful forecasts, and reasonable assumptions are not necessarily a betrayal of a commitment to technical objectivity. The agency for which the forecaster works, however, has a commitment to certain programs or solutions and believes that they can be shown to be superior to others on the basis of reasonable criteria.

In addition to commitment to a body of tools and techniques, the forecaster must also have loyalty or responsibility to the agency which he or she serves, either as employee or consultant. The employee wishes to advance and wants to be considered both competent and cooperative by his or her superiors. The consultant wishes to be considered for future contracts. Rewards flow from effective service as an advocate for the interests clearly identified by the organization. Should the forecast be made on the basis of core assumptions which seem most favorable to the furtherance of the organization's goals? Forecasts often require so many assumptions that there is leeway to allow the forecaster to satisfy both organizational goals and technical criteria. Indeed, if he or she has become a "team player" and has internalized the goals of the agency, there may not even appear to be a conflict between the two loyalties. In cases where the forecaster is aware of the conflict, and where reasonable technical judgment may deliver forecasts which the agency would rather not hear about, the forecaster faces the problem of choosing between advocacy and objectivity. The rewards for advocacy are clear, while even the criteria for judging objectivity are ambiguous.

Dahl and Lindblom observed: "someone must control those who run the calculations and machines. Someone must control the controllers, etc. At every point there would be opportunities for attempting to feed into the calculator one's own preferences. Doubtless, pressure groups would organize for just such a purpose."[11] It is critically important that public administrators recognize the limits of technical forecasts. There are few ethical guideposts included in the education of professionals, the canons of professional societies, or the processes of public policy making to suggest how such choices should be made. The choices are personal and sometimes troublesome. Frequently, the options boil down to serving the agency or leaving its employ. Because the agency itself, and the political process in which it is embedded, continue to describe, respond to, and reward advocacy, as if it were technically objective and neutral expertise, only the most sensitive of analysts would choose not to serve as advocate. The result is that many forecasts are statements of hope and intention, while analysts, agency boards, and politicians cooperatively maintain the fiction that they are value-free projections of trends. Few forecasters engage in blatant falsification in order to receive a commission or promotion. Many, however, are transformed in subtle steps from analyst to advocate by the situation in which they perform their work.

Notes

1. Peter Marcuse, "Professional Ethics and Beyond: Values in Planning." *Journal of the American Institute of Planners,* Vol. 42, No. 3 (July 1976), pp. 264–274.

2. Donella H. Meadows, Dennis L. Meadows, Jorgen Randers, and William W. Behrens, III. *The Limits to Growth: A Report for the Club of Rome's Project on the Predicament of Mankind.* Second Edition (New York: Universe Books, 1973).

3. Michel Godet, *The Crisis in Forecasting and the Emergence of the Prospective Approach* (New York and Oxford: Pergamon Press, 1979).

4. William Ascher, *Forecasting: An Appraisal for Policy-Makers and Planners* (Baltimore and London: Johns Hopkins University Press, 1978), p. 199.

5. *Ibid.,* p. 202.

6. Michel Godet, *The Crisis in Forecasting and the Emergence of the Prospective Approach,* p. 15.

7. William Alonso, "Predicting Best with Imperfect Data." *Journal of the American Institute of Planners,* Vol. 34, No. 3 (July 1968), pp. 248–255.

8. Solomon Encel, Pauline K. Marstrand, and William Page, *The Art of Anticipation: Values and Methods in Forecasting* (London: Martin Robertson and Company, Ltd., 1975), p. 66.

9. Martin Wachs and James Ortner, "Capital Grants and Recurrent Subsidies: A Dilemma in American Transportation Policy." *Transportation,* Vol. 8 (1979), pp. 3–19.

10. Robert A. Caro, *The Power Broker: Robert Moses and the Fall of New York* (New York: Vintage Books, 1975), pp. 218–219.

11. Robert A. Dahl and Charles E. Lindblom, *Politics, Economics, and Welfare* (New York: Harper, 1953).

8

TYPES AND LEVELS OF PUBLIC MORALITY

York Willbern
Indiana University

Students of government and public administration, from Plato to Wilson and from Weber to the proponents of the "new public administration," have nearly always known that what public officials and employees do has a central and inescapable normative component, involving values, morality, and ethics,[1] although they may have differed as to the degree to which this component could be separated, either analytically or in practice, from aspects of administration involving facts, science, or technique. Discussions about moral considerations involving public officials, however, frequently deal with significantly different types of forces and phenomena.

The most obvious distinction is that between consideration of the ethical behavior (honesty, rectitude) of the official and consideration of the moral content of the public policy or action the official promulgates or carries out.[2] Most public criticism of public ethics focuses on the former; the concerns of adherents of the "new public administration" were on the latter.

Serious attention to the ethical and moral components of public officialdom suggests that there are other important distinctions also. This essay is primarily one of taxonomy; it attempts to identify and characterize particular components or facets of official ethics and morality in an effort to lay out a rough map of the terrain.[3] Classification is difficult in this area not only because of the overlapping of the concepts and the activities, but be-

115

cause of the ambiguities of the words used to describe them. Nevertheless, such an effort may be helpful in joining discussion and in making it more likely that people talk about comparable rather than different things.

While for some purposes it would be valuable to distinguish the ethical problems involving elected or politically appointed officials from those involving civil servants, or among those in particular aspects of public service (i.e., public works, social work, university teaching, or others), no concentrated attention will be given here to such differences.

It is suggested that six types, or levels, of morality for public officials can be discerned, with, perhaps, increasing degrees of complexity and subtlety. There are, of course, substantial interrelationships among these levels, but they are different enough to be analytically interesting. They are: (1) basic honesty and conformity to law; (2) conflicts of interest; (3) service orientation and procedural fairness; (4) the ethic of democratic responsibility; (5) the ethic of public policy determination; and (6) the ethic of compromise and social integration.

In general, the first two or lower levels (and in some degree the third) concern aspects of personal morality and, hence, the ethical conduct of the individual public servant; the other, or higher, levels deal more with the morality of the governmental decisions or actions taken by the official or employee. Public scandals and outrage at unethical behavior focus mainly on the lower levels. Most public officials and employees are confronted with choices, as individuals, which involve ethical concerns at these levels. At the higher levels, most actions and decisions and policies in modern complex governments and bureaucracies are more collective, corporate, and institutional in nature, in which the individual moral responsibility is shared with others in complex ways. This is true even for chief executives; even if "the buck stops here," the bulk of the work in preparing "the buck" and its possible alternatives will have been done by others.

Basic Honesty and Conformity to Law

The public servant is morally bound, just as are other persons, to tell the truth, to keep promises, to respect the person and property of others, and to abide by the requirements of the law. The law—the codes enacted or enforced by the legitimate organs of the state—usually embodies these basic obligations and provides sanctions for violating them. The law also includes many other requirements, and there is a moral obligation to conform, with arguable exceptions only in the most extreme circumstances. An orderly society cannot exist if individuals can choose to follow only those laws with which they agree; civil disobedience is an acceptable moral tactic only in very extreme situations. Conformity to law is especially necessary for public officials and employees.

These behaviors are basic requisites of an orderly society, which exists only if people can be reasonably secure in their persons and belongings, can normally rely on the statements and commitments of others, and can expect others to conform to the established norms of conduct. There are, of course, liars and thieves and law breakers in the public sector, as there are in the private, and it is transgressors of this kind which are particularly noticeable and which bring public condemnation.

In general, the difficulties in interpreting and following these broad mandates are about the same for public servants as for others. Definitional problems (What is true, and should all the truth be told? What property belongs to whom? What is the law?) which produce moral dilemmas are probably no more difficult in the public sector than in the private.

Even at this level of basic honesty and conformity, however, there may be some ways in which the public service differs. To some observers, the fact that public officials are vested with the power of the state produces more danger and more opportunity for transgression of the basic moral code. Power and access to public goods may provide more temptation; the necessity to communicate and deal regularly with the public may lead to more occasion to prevaricate or to ignore promises and commitments.

This may be more true in other societies than in America. In this country, two factors seem to limit, in some degree, the relative danger of official misbehavior at this basic level. One is the obvious fact that power is less concentrated in the government. The power that is lodged in private economic institutions and aggregations, especially apparent in the United States, may be no less corrupting than the power of public officials. Ours is a rather pluralistic society, with countervailing powers scattered quite widely. A second and related factor is the existence of stronger and more independent control mechanisms in our system, especially stemming from the judiciary and the press. In the United States, every public official (even the president, as the last decade demonstrated) lives in the shadow of the courthouse. And in America, unlike many other systems, it is the same courts which exercise control over public officials and private citizens. Moreover, the American press is particularly vigorous in trying to exercise surveillance over public officials and employees.

The visibility of public life may well make dishonest behavior less frequent there than in private life. Public officials are expected not only to be honest, but to appear to be honest. Both Caesar and Caesar's wife are to be above reproach, and departures from that norm are noticed. There is almost certainly less tolerance of public employees than of private employees who deviate from accepted standards in such personal matters as marital behavior, sexual deviance, and use of alcohol and drugs, as well as in basic honesty.

Some would argue that the nature of political discourse in a democratic system greatly increases the likelihood of falsehoods and insincere and broken promises. There is no doubt that political campaigns and even the prospect of such campaigns produce statements that are at least selective in their veracity, and that neither the makers nor the recipients of campaign promises seem too surprised if the promised performances do not fully materialize. Without questioning the immorality of campaign falsehoods and forgotten promises, the fact that knowledgeable listeners to puffery of this sort do not really take it too seriously nor depend upon it for their own decisions may mitigate somewhat the seriousness of the sin. The same sort of salt is applied to advertising and salesmanship assertions in the private marketplace; regulations such as those of the Federal Trade Commission and the Securities and Exchange Commission attempt, without complete success, to limit inaccurate allegations and promises. Campaign puffery aside, however, the importance of veracity and adherence to direct interpersonal political commitments is widely recognized.

There are, on the other hand, areas of public official behavior where deceit and lying are not only condoned but approved. The police use undercover agents and "sting" operations to try to catch criminals. Official falsehoods and deception certainly accompany foreign intelligence and some national defense activities. In covert operations in particular countries, public employees may go well beyond falsehood in contravening the normal moral code. These are very difficult ethical areas, where the end is presumed to justify the means, and *raison d'etat* provides shaky moral justification.

Conflict of Interest

The ethical problems associated with conflicts of interest in the public service are even more complex and difficult. The general presumption is that the moral duty of an official or employee of a unit of government is to pursue the "public interest"—i.e., the needs and welfare of the general body of citizens of the unit. His own interests, and the interests of partial publics of which he may be a member, are to be subordinated if they differ from the broader, more general, public interest—as they almost inevitably will, from time to time.

In their cruder manifestations, conflict of interest transgressions fit clearly into the category of ethical problems discussed above, the obligation to respect the property of others and to conform to the law. Embezzlement of public funds, bribery, and contract kickbacks are all actions in which the offenders have pursued their personal interests in obvious contravention of the public interest, as well as in violation of the law. Expense account padding is a more common illustration of both conflict of interest and of theft. There are generally laws against the more obvious conflicts of interest.

But there are also very difficult and subtle conflicts of interest that are not so clearly theft, and which may not involve law violation. At a simple level, to take a trip at public expense which may not have been necessary but which enabled the official to visit family or friends, or just to have a semi-vacation without using leave time, presents a problem of conflict of interest ethics, as does nepotism, or the appointment or advancement of a relative or friend as is the case involving political party patronage systems.

Every public employee belongs to other groups than his governmental agency—church, professional, local community, racial, or ethnic group. Most officials and employees, especially those in public service for only limited periods, worked for and with someone else before the government, and may anticipate such employment after their government service. It is very easy to presume that the interests of those groups coincide with the interests of the entire public, but others may disagree. Moreover, officials have private financial investments which can be affected by public policy decisions.

Among the most difficult and subtle of the public service conflict of interest problems are those relating to the obvious and inevitable interest of a person or group or party to win elections. This is related to the ethic of democratic responsibility, to be discussed later. It is sufficient to note at this point that to award contracts or jobs or shape public policies in such a way as to reward people or groups for their past or expected campaign support rather than on the merits of the public purpose involved raises tough ethical questions.[4] Campaign financing, for example, may be one of the most vulnerable spots in a democratic system. Those who contribute to a successful campaign usually expect, and get, a degree of access to decision makers that raises questions about the even-handedness of decisions and actions.

There are conflicts of interest in private life, as well. In the private as in the public sector, people are imbedded in collective entities—corporations, firms, associations—and they are confronted with many occasions in which their personal or small group interests may conflict with those of the larger entity. The potential, and frequently real, conflicts of interest between the management and the stockholders of a corporation, or between management and rank-and-file employees, are obvious illustrations.

There is a very important difference between conflicts of interest in public life and in private life. A basic cornerstone of the Western economic system is that the vigorous pursuit of self-interest by each participant is the most effective way to secure the general interest—the "invisible hand" of the market will transform selfish pursuits into the general welfare. The presumption that what is good for General Motors is good for the country, and vice versa, seems a truism in the capitalist economic system. In spite of the variety of exceptions that modern economists will make, the power and pervasiveness of this idea make conflicts of interest in the private sector considerably different than in the public.

This vigorous pursuit of self-interest by private economic entities, in their relationships to government, is one of the great causes of moral problems in the public sphere. Modern government has great impact on economic activity, and every economic entity needs and wants to influence public policy in its own interest. Government can give and withhold privileges of great value. The tendency to presume that what is good for the particular group or social segment of which a person is a member is also good for others is almost irresistible.

Lincoln Steffens, in attempting to explain the cause of corruption in government, compared the situation to that in the Garden of Eden. The trouble, he said, was not the serpent—that was his nature. Nor was it the weakness of Eve, nor of Adam—they also did what was natural. The fault, he said, was in the apple.

It can be argued that the political world is also a marketplace, where the pursuit of self-interest by all the varying segments will produce a harmonious general welfare. This was essentially the argument of Madison in Federalist Paper number 10, suggesting that the enlargement of the polity would increase the number of interests participating in the political market, and thus make more likely the achievement of a general rather than a particular interest.

But governmental decision making is far more institutionalized than the decision making of a free economic market, and the public official is always torn between acting as proponent of an interest (his own, or that of his department or agency, or of his profession, or of his faction or party) and acting as an arbiter among competing interests. Should U.S. Senator Richard Lugar support the interests of Indiana coal miners in dealing with acid rain? Can a real estate developer serve impartially on a zoning board? A longtime public servant coined an aphorism that is now widely known in the public administration community as Miles' Law: "Where a man stands depends on where he sits."

Since both potential and real conflicts of interest are so pervasive, major efforts are made to provide a degree of protection by procedural safeguards (a subject to be considered further in connection with the next level of public morality). Public acknowledgement of outside interests is required, and arrangements are made for officials to refrain from participation in matters where their interests may conflict. But these safeguards are far from sufficient to remove the moral responsibility of the individual employee or officer.

Here, as in so many other moral matters, degree may become crucial. Some conflict of interest is inevitable; the question becomes, how much conflict of interest taints a decision or action so much as to make it unethical?

Service Orientation and Procedural Fairness

We now enter areas where the overlap with private morality, while still present, is less noticeable, and where the problems are more peculiarly those of public officials and employees.

The purpose of any governmental activity or program is to provide service to a clientele, a public. This is true even if the activity is in some degree authoritarian, a regulation or control. It is sometimes easy for this moral imperative to be obscured by the fact that government, and government officials, have and exercise power. The auditor at the Internal Revenue Service, the policeman on the beat, the teacher in the classroom, the personnel officer in an agency, are there to serve their clients, but they also exercise authority, and there is real moral danger in the possibility that the authority comes to overshadow the service.

Attitudes and the tone and flavor of official behavior are morally significant. Where power is being exercised, arrogance can easily replace humility, and the convenience of the official becomes more important than the convenience of the client. Delay and secrecy can become the norm. Procedures are designed for official purposes, not those of the public. This may well be the kind of corruption Lord Acton had in mind, rather than thievery or bribery, when he said that "power corrupts."

The effort to provide some degree of protection for the clients against the potential arrogance of officials is one of the reasons why procedural fairness is one of the central components of public morality. The concept that a person threatened with the power of the state has firm procedural rights is a very ancient one. The right to a trial, a public trial, or a hearing, with proper notice of what is alleged or intended, the right to counsel, the right of appeal, are built into administrative as well as judicial procedures. "Procedural due process" is a cornerstone of public morality.

In addition to the need to protect citizens against the corrupting power of the state officialdom, there is another important ground for a procedural component of public morality. As will be noticed further in connection with the sixth (highest?) level of morality to be discussed here, it is inevitable that in a complex society interests will be opposed to each other, that not all can be satisfied, and that often not even a Pareto optimality can be achieved. The public decision-making process may not be a zero-sum game, with inevitable losses accompanying all gains, but the difficulty of satisfying all makes it necessary that the *process* of arriving at decisions about action, or policy, be a fair one.

The Ethic of Democratic Responsibility

In our consideration of various types and levels of public morality, another transition occurs. The first three levels deal with the conduct of public officials as they go about their business, the last three with the content of what they do. It is upon these first three levels (particularly the first two) that attention is usually focused in discussions of official ethics. They are important, and difficult, but they may not be as central as the considerations affecting the moral choices involved in deciding *what* to do, in pursuing the purposes of the state and the society. The first set might be said to deal with collateral morality, the latter set with intrinsic morality.

The dogma of the morality of popular sovereignty is now general throughout the world, and nowhere is it more strongly entrenched than in the United States. To be democratic is good, undemocratic bad. Observers acknowledge the existence of elites, even power elites, but the suggestion is that their presence is unfortunate and, by implication at least, immoral. Citizen participation is encouraged, even required, in governmental programs. Hierarchy is suspect, participatory management the goal, even within an agency or institution.

In spite of almost universal adherence to the dogma, there are some reservations about its practice. Government by referendum does not always arouse enthusiasm. "Maximum feasible participation"—the legal requirement for several national programs—was certainly not an unqualified success; U.S. Senator Patrick Moynihan called it "maximum feasible misunderstanding." Many have reservations about open records, open meetings, public negotiations—all justified on the grounds of the public's "right to know." But these reservations are still only "reservations"; the basic notion of popular sovereignty is seldom challenged.

In its simplest logic, the legitimacy of popular control is transmitted to operating public servants through a chain of delegation. The legislature is supposed to do what the people want, while the public executive and administrator are to conform to legislative intent. The politically chosen official, either elected or appointed by someone who was elected, has the mandate of the people. The civil servant is ethically bound to carry out the instructions of these politicians, who derive their legitimacy from the people. The military is subordinate to politically chosen civilians. The "career" officials or employees are supposed to carry out Republican policies during a Republican administration, Democratic policies during a Democratic administration, because that is what the people want. For public employees to substitute their own judgments as to what the people want for the judgment of those who have the electoral or political mandate is unethical, according to this logic. They may advise to the contrary, but they are to carry out the instructions of their political superiors to the best of their ability. If they cannot conscientiously do so, their only ethical choice is to resign their posts.

In reality, of course, the situation is never as clear as the simple logic suggests. In this country (more, probably, than in other practicing democracies), there are usually multiple rather than single channels for the expression of the public will. Both the legislature and the executive (sometimes many executives), and sometimes the judges, are elected by the people, and they may emit different signals from their popular mandates. A statute, or a constitutional provision, may be considered to embody the popular mandate better than instructions from a political superior. Arrangements for direct citizen participation through hearings or advisory commissions may complicate the process further. A public employee may have considerable range of choice in choosing which popular mandate to respond to. But, in principle, strong support would be given to the concept that a public official in a democracy has a moral responsibility to follow the will of the people in his or her actions.

This ethic of democratic responsibility, the logic of which is quite powerful, produces difficulty for public employees. The employees may have goals and values which differ from those transmitted through the political channels. Or, the political superiors, even the people themselves, may not be fully informed. There may be no better illustration than the resistance which professors in a public university might make to instructions from a board of trustees or a legislature as to what to teach or who should teach it.

The conflict is particularly severe when the logic of democracy conflicts with the logic of science or of professional expertise. What is the ethical position of the public employee when the people, directly or through their properly elected representatives, insist on the teaching of "creationism" which is repugnant to the scientist? Or when the certified experts say that fluoride in the water is good for people but the people say no? To put it in the simplest terms, should the public official give the people what they want or what he thinks they ought to want?

To some, the voice of the people in a democracy may be equivalent to the voice of God. But, for most public officials in most circumstances, that axiom will not provide answers that allow them to escape their personal responsibility to make moral choices based on their own values. The voice of the people will not be clear, it will not be based on full knowledge, it will conflict in small or large degree with other persuasive and powerful normative considerations.

Here, as in other situations, the most popular (perhaps the best) answer may be a relativistic one. The official may be responsive to democratic control and his political superiors, but not too much. Democracy may be interpreted not as government by the people, but as government with the consent of the people, with professionals (either in a functional field or as practicing political leaders) making most decisions on the basis of standards and values derived from sources other than a Gallup poll, and submitting to only an infrequent exercise of electoral judgment as to the gen-

eral direction of policy. Civil servants carry out the instructions of their political superiors with vigor and alacrity if they agree with them, and with
some foot dragging and modification if they disagree. They try to give the
people, and the political officials representing them, what they would want
if they had full information, meaning of course, the information available
to the particular person conducting the activity.

The Ethic of Public Policy Determination

Perhaps the most complex and difficult of all the moral levels is that involved in determining public policy, in making actual decisions about what
to do. The problems of honesty and conformity to law, difficult as they
sometimes are, are simple compared to those in decisions about public policy. And these are inescapably *moral* judgments; some policies, some actions, are good, some bad. Determinations about the nature of the social
security program and how it is to be paid for, for example, turn only in minor degree on technical information; they depend chiefly on basic considerations about human values.

There can be no doubt that normative determinations are made at all
levels of public service. They are not made just by legislatures, or by city
councils, or school boards. They are also made by the street level bureaucrats—the policeman on the beat, the intake interviewer at the welfare office, the teacher in the classroom. These individuals make decisions in their
official capacity that involve equity and justice and order and compassion.
Rules, regulations, and supervision of others in a chain of command
stretching back, in theory, to the sovereign people may provide a framework for decisions, but not a very tight framework. Every teacher knows
that the department chairman and superintendent really have very little to
do with how the job is actually done, and every cop knows the same thing
about the police chief.

Though right and wrong certainly exist in public policy, they are frequently—usually—difficult to discern with confidence. There are degrees
and levels of right and wrong. A medieval English verse about the enclo-
sure of the village commons by the nobles goes:

> The law locks up both man and woman
> Who steals the goose from off the common,
> But lets the greater felon loose
> Who steals the common from the goose.[5]

The perpetrator of a regressive tax, or of a regulation which permits water
or air used by thousands to be polluted, or of a foreign policy position
which produces or enlarges armed conflict, may do far more harm to far

more people than hundreds of common burglars. But is he or she a greater criminal? Or more immoral? The regressive tax may be better than leaving an essential public service unfunded; the pollution may result from a highway that allows people to go about their affairs expeditiously, or a power plant that permits them to air condition their homes; many reasonable people believe that the most effective way to deter armed conflict is to threaten, with serious intent, to initiate or escalate armed conflict.

The judgments that must be made about the rightness or wrongness of a public policy or decision involve at least two types of considerations—one, the benefit-cost calculation, and the other, the distributional problem (who gains and who loses).

Benefit-cost calculations are generally more difficult in the public arena than in the private, for two reasons. One is the matter of measurement—the currency in which the calculations are made. There are, of course, non-monetary considerations in many private decisions, but they are more pervasive in public determinations. The other reason is the greater necessity for concern about externalities, for spillover costs and benefits. This is an important but usually secondary consideration in a private decision, but often central in a public one. The making of good benefit-cost calculations may be more a matter of wisdom (either analytical or intuitive) than of morality, but normative consideration in choosing factors to consider, and assigning weights to them, are inescapable.

Ethical considerations are particularly salient in determinations about *distribution* of benefits and burdens in a public activity or decision. Here we confront squarely the problems of equity and justice and fairness. Any attempt to define these concepts (which have occupied philosophers a long time) is obviously beyond the scope of this short paper. But a few reflections may be offered.

Policies which do not provide equal treatment for all, or which enhance rather than diminish inequality, are usually condemned as unjust and unfair. But equity is not synonymous with equality. Equity may require similar treatment for those who are similarly situated—but not all are similarly situated. Many public policies do, and should, discriminate. The critical question is whether the basis for differentiation and the kind of differentiation are appropriate. It is appropriate and desirable for public policy to reward desirable behavior and punish undesirable behavior. To give an A to one student and an F to another, and to admit one to graduate school and turn the other down, certainly discriminates, but it may be just and fair and equitable. A central purpose of social policy is to elicit desirable behavior, and discourage undesirable.

It is also usually considered appropriate to differentiate on the basis of need—to provide things for the widow and the orphan and the physically and mentally handicapped that are not provided for others. Compassion would certainly seem a morally defensible ground for such discrimination. And there are many other grounds for such discrimination, many of them morally debatable. For example, is it appropriate (ethical) to provide free education for a citizen but not for an alien? Is it ethical to deport a refugee from economic privation but not a refugee from political oppression? Is it inequitable, unjust, and unconstitutional to deviate from one man–one vote apportionment in electing members of state legislatures and city councils, but not in electing U.S. senators?

The Ethic of Compromise and Social Integration

To some, morality means uncompromising adherence to principle. To compromise with evil, or with injustice, is immoral. But "principle" and "evil" and "injustice" are not always certain, especially in complex social situations. One man's social justice may be another man's social injustice. Lincoln's classic formulation, "with firmness in the right as God gives us to see the right," seems to carry with it the implication that God may give someone else to see the right differently, and that he also may be firm.

We must live with each other, adjust to each other, and hence make compromises with each other. This is a central feature of politics and of a bureaucratic world that is also political. We are all involved in politics—the only place without politics was Robinson Crusoe's island before Friday came. As every successful politician knows, it is necessary upon occasion to rise above principle and make a deal. Thus, compromise can be viewed as a highly moral act—without concessions to those who disagree, disagreement becomes stalemate and then conflict.

If sincere people hold to differing values, there must be institutional arrangements which legitimize courses of action which certainly can not satisfy all and may not fully satisfy any, and there is a moral obligation for both citizens and officials, but particularly officials, to participate in and support such arrangements. These institutional arrangements are, in large degree, procedural, permitting and encouraging public policy discourse and mutual persuasion and, finally, resolution of differences. The needed public policy discourse is more than the discourse of a marketplace which involves bargaining between and among economic self-interests. It is somewhat different than the discourse in the "republic of science," in which evidence and proof (or at least disproof) can be marshalled. It may never attain the level of discourse which Habermas calls an "ideal speech situation." But it must be social discourse with a strongly moral component.

Since complete *substantive* due process, measured by the standards of a particular participant in the political process, can rarely be achieved, a large measure of *procedural* due process is a moral necessity, not only to protect an individual against the power of the state, but to make legitimate the process of public decision making. Complete reconciliation, or social integration, will always be elusive, but social cohesion, loyalty to and participation in a group, and in larger communities, is a moral goal of the highest order.

T. V. Smith put it this way: The world is full of saints, each of whom knows the way to salvation, and the role of the politician is that of the sinner who stands at the crossroad to keep saint from cutting the throat of saint. This may possibly be the highest ethical level of the public servant.

Notes

1. To the cynic, of course, the phrase Public Morality is an oxymoron—like Holy War, or United Nations, or Political Science.

2. This distinction has been pointed out by several writers—particularly by Wayne A.R. Leys in "Ethics and Administrative Discretion," *Public Administration Review* 3 (Winter 1943), and in *Ethics for Policy Decisions* (New York: Prentice-Hall, 1952).

3. This outline map differs from others—and they differ from each other. Several which have been particularly suggestive, even though they differ, are the items by Leys cited in note 2, above; a particularly rich two-volume collection of papers edited by Harlan Cleveland and Harold Lasswell, *Ethics and Bigness* and *The Ethic of Power* (New York: Harper, 1962); two substantial essays by Edmond Cahn, *The Sense of Injustice* (Bloomington: Indiana University Press, 1964) and *The Moral Decision* (Bloomington: Indiana University Press, 1966); a volume by George A. Graham, *Morality in American Politics* (New York: Random House, 1952); and a lecture (unfortunately unpublished) given by Dwight Waldo at Indiana University in Bloomington in 1977.

4. A very sensitive description of such problems, based largely on his own experiences as mayor of Middletown, may be found in Stephen K. Bailey, "The Ethical Problems of an Elected Political Executive," in Cleveland and Lasswell (eds.), *Ethics and Bigness, op. cit.,* pp. 24–27.

5. I borrowed this from George Graham, *op. cit.,* p. 33. I'm sure he borrowed it from someone else.

9

MANAGING COMPETING CLAIMS: AN ETHICAL FRAMEWORK FOR HUMAN RESOURCE DECISION MAKING

Debra W. Stewart
North Carolina State University

The core personnel management functions of the line manager are to select, develop, and evaluate people. Historically, public sector managers accepted implicit norms which formed the basis for these personnel management decisions. As Herbert Simon pointed out in his perceptive analysis of administrative decision making, such norms established the "decision premises" for the manager.[1] These premises reflected contemporary prevailing values and evolved with those values, a process well documented in Herbert Kaufman's classic *Public Administration Review* article, "Administrative Decentralization and Political Power." Kaufman describes a cycle, with shifts in values and outlook over time: " . . . [T]he administrative history of our governmental machinery can be construed as a succession of shifts . . . each brought about by a change in emphasis among three values: representativeness, politically neutral competence, and executive leadership."[2] To Kaufman, this process is part of the normal expression of interest in the American political system. Central to Kaufman's analysis is the assumption that while no value is ever totally ignored, one value will always transcend others. The new emphasis comes to displace an earlier emphasis as a pressure experienced by managers.

While Kaufman's model works well to describe administrative history in American public service, observers today note a change. Rather than one interest gaining marked ascendance, interests seem to establish footholds that prevent displacement. Thus, new interests emerge to flourish simultaneously with old interests, each pressing competing claims on government decision-making procedures and practices. It is in this context that we examine the personnel activities of the line manager.

In performing the core personnel management functions of selecting, developing and evaluating people, the line manager today is asked to act on decision premises rooted in three distinct criteria. These premises emerge from different historical contexts, are advocated by different societal groups, place competing claims before the decision maker, and each leads ultimately toward the institutionalization of practices which may impede successful achievement of important goals which other groups promote. The challenge of the 1980s is to balance competing claims, deferring to the just interests of all parties through management strategies which maintain the flexibility necessary to respond to those evolving interests. The scholar's task is to help administrators find the best path toward that objective.

Guided by this task definition, we identify these three decision premises, describe the social interests each represents, and analyze the rationale for institutionalizing each premise. Next we explore the competing claims these diverse interests place on the manager and consider whether managers should play a passive role or whether the public interest calls managers to play a more self-consciously ethical role in balancing competing claims. Concluding that the public interest is best served by administrators with the courage to make "hard choices," we finally propose an ethical framework that helps structure the decision-making process implied by that ethical agent role.

The Collective Negotiations Premise

The public sector unionization movement is the driving force behind the first premise addressed. Generally speaking, the same empirical conditions that led employees to organize in the private sector shaped unionization in the public sector—growth in the size of organizations, increased bureaucratization, deterioration of material and social standing, and changing social and economic conditions. Until the 1960s, in many jurisdictions, employees as diverse as sanitation workers, police, teachers, social workers, and nurses shared important work experiences: low pay, poor working conditions, and often intolerable job pressures. Public unions evolved to provide employees with resources to cope with these conditions.[3]

Public sector trade unions have pressed to participate in management decision-making processes that affect the employee's livelihood. This power sharing has become institutionalized, and ranges from informal to formal roles which correlate with the specific type of collective association behind the action. Mutual benefit organizations, the earliest form of employee organization, typically attempt to advance employee interests through lobbying. A more formal employee management relationship is signaled by dues checkoffs and willingness of top government executives to listen, meet, and confer with employee representatives. A still higher level of institutionalization is reflected in a full blown collective bargaining statute which regulates the bargaining process in the public sector. Beyond basic collective bargaining rights, employee participation becomes increasingly institutionalized as traditional management prerogatives are gradually included as negotiable items at the bargaining table.

Though managers often see the collective negotiations process as an exercise in power politics seldom regulated by moral principles, "rights" issues remain the hidden dimension underlying all labor-management relations. A straightforward rationale gives rise to the notion of a right to negotiate collectively. In capitalism individuals enter into contracts with employers to provide labor in exchange for money. But as individuals, employees are at a disadvantage in the interactions. In order to give the employee the power necessary to ensure fairness in the negotiation with the employer about the nature of the employment contract and the interpretation of this contract, collective bargaining rights are necessary. In fact, to make capitalism work as a fair system, some such provisions are essential.

Students of American politics recognize this as a fundamentally pluralist political argument. It is consistent with pluralist democratic theory for the employee unions (interest groups) to organize politically and to bargain with management (government officials) to advance their own interests. The ideal behind the practice is that sharing in decision making that affects one's livelihood is a basic human right.[4] The operational definition of substantive interests changes over time, often responding to economic exigencies—beginning with the basic "bread and butter" issues, shifting to higher level need issues, and then shifting back to basic survival issues in the face of economic recession. Generally, the less confidence employees have in their management to act fairly regarding matters which affect their livelihood, the more they favor expanding the scope of participation.

The Merit Premise

The second decision premise on which managers are asked to act in personnel decision making is that of merit. The meaning of the term "merit" is disputed in the public personnel literature, with definitions ranging from merit as "the best," to merit as "the most deserving."[5] As defined here, merit means employment actions based upon qualification, with resources being allocated to the best candidates through a selection process consisting of competitive tests. As a norm for regulating public managerial practices, merit was born of a reform ideology based upon three propositions:

1. Government employment was an open arena where the best could prove themselves.
2. Only the best would produce efficient administration.
3. Public interest is served if the best govern.[6]

In the earliest expression of this ideology the civil service reformers of the 1860s and 1870s saw merit as a vehicle for purifying a government riddled by patronage and corruption. The social interests behind the early merit movement were reform interests which saw that if the best qualified were hired in public jobs, these able office holders would be freer to do a better job than their compromised predecessors. But as the reformers of the late 19th century passed their reform work on to the progressives of the 20th century, reform came to represent distinct social class interests. Historians disagree about the precise shape of those interests, but are united on the point that the impulse for civil service reform did not come from the working class.[7]

The point developed in this historical analysis is that the history of "reform" suggests the thrust was not simply to replace bad men with good, but to change the occupational and class orientation of decision makers.[8] Merit in this historical context was the vehicle through which this displacement would occur. The role of merit is well illustrated in reviewing popular literature from the heyday of municipal reform. For instance, the Voter's League of Pittsburgh described in a pamphlet the qualifications for a school board member and pointed out that certain occupations inherently disqualified a man from serving. Ordinary laborers, small shopkeepers, clerks, and workmen in many roles were cited as types whose "lack of educational advantage and business training" rendered them unable to manage effectively.[9] The important point gained from a review of the social history of the reform movement with the merit principle serving as the moral impetus is an awareness of the class bias involved.

But to say that merit historically, and today, better represents some social interests than others does not really denigrate the concept of the merit system. As a decision premise, merit embodies basic Aristotelian notions of procedural justice which call for treating equals equally and treating unequals unequally. The way to ensure that merit is the regulating principle in employment actions is to institutionalize it through establishing civil service examinations and vertical advancement practices. The efficiency and validity of selection methods become the focus of attention; their value is confirmed by their capacity to distinguish employees or applicants with the greatest merit.

The current day spokespersons for the social interest advocated by the reformers are the personnel professionals. Glenn Stahl voices this value orientation clearly: "the merit method has no substitutes in providing the conditions of competence and continuity that are essential to the operation of the complex administrative machine of modern government."[10] Frederick Mosher notes that merit achieves this purpose both negatively by eliminating irrelevant considerations in assessing an employee, and positively, by measuring relative capacity to perform a specific type of work.[11]

Tension between the first two decision premises discussed, collective negotiations and merit, is clear. The very different social interests behind each premise voice quite different definitions of how managers should carry forth their core activities of selecting, developing, and evaluating people. The public administration literature called attention to the diverse implications of these two premises nearly 20 years ago when Muriel Morse wrote of the need to acknowledge the impact of collective bargaining on merit systems. Morse advised that ". . . the decision is not where to draw the line [on collective bargaining]. The decision is about two kinds of personnel systems, and they have different concerns. We can no longer believe we can be half collective bargaining and half merit system."[12] But the manager of the 1980s knows that both premises have remained in place and still a third standard has been added since Morse expressed this concern. That new decision premise is equal employment opportunity.

The Equal Employment Opportunity Premise

The third premise managers are asked to adopt in managing people comes out of the equal employment opportunity movement. Actions in support of equal access are actions which diminish barriers to full participation for historically disadvantaged groups. These interests are advanced by those groups in the population which, by virtue of some racial, ethnic, gender, age, or physical/mental impairment, gain special legal protection against discrimination in the workplace. Their social interests are diverse in terms of the way each group has historically related to the employment situation. However, blacks, women, older citizens, and handicapped persons are all tied together by their experience of discrimination. The interest at stake in each case is to remove that discrimination which inhibits equality of access to positions in work organizations.

The procedures for dismantling discrimination so as to facilitate equality of access have been developed principally on the basis of the experience of racial minorities and women. The process has been guided by a definition of discrimination which has become progressively more subtle over time.

The most common and earliest understanding of discrimination is at the level of the prejudiced individual and the consequent attitudes and behaviors of employers. Typically considered as a motivational or a moral prob-

lem, it was this definition that informed the thrust of various state and local human relations commissions in the 1960s. Discrimination tended to
be viewed as a series of isolated and distinguishable events, due largely to
ill will on the part of identifiable individuals.[13] Personnel officers whose
stereotyped beliefs about women and minorities justified placing them in
low pay or low status jobs, or white male managers who would rely exclusively on the old boy network to recruit male junior executives, are examples of such actions.[14]

The second stage of thinking in the evolving definition of discrimination
saw discrimination as an organizational phenomenon: though practiced by
individuals it was reinforced by policies, practices, and rules of the organization. Height and weight requirements that excluded females from certain
jobs or "last hired, first fired," seniority rules in recently integrated organizations are examples of such policies.

The final stage in reflection on the meaning of discrimination sees a third
self-sustaining discriminatory process best labeled as structural discrimination. Attention here focuses on the classic cycle of discrimination which re-
produces itself. Taking racial minorities as an example, discrimination in
housing channels minorities into inferior schools. This inferior early education impedes minorities from gaining the higher education credentials necessary to get a good job; inability to get a good job confines one to the
same neighborhoods and thus promises the same limited opportunity for
one's children. The cycle is closed. The cumulative effect of the process of
discrimination (individual, organizational, and structural) is to produce a
self-reinforcing cycle magnifying the disadvantage experienced by one generation in one area to future generations in many related areas.

In juxtaposing the EEO decision premise with the merit and collective
negotiation premises, defining the problem of discrimination becomes central. If equal access requires only the observance of nondiscrimination.
EEO poses no direct barrier to achieving goals advanced by the other decision premises. But if it prescribes positive action, EEO rapidly preempts the
place of competing goals. Minorities and women today are advocating the
institutionalization of positive action rather than simply nondiscrimination. Their reasoning is as follows: A nondiscrimination policy premised
on the assumption that the problem is individual prejudice makes sense
only under limiting conditions. Nondiscrimination is a reasonable approach to providing equal access in employment only if those who compete
have an equal opportunity, controlling for natural ability, to acquire the
characteristics that make one a likely choice for a position in the absence of
active intentional discrimination. However, in the absence of equal opportunity to acquire the proper characteristics, positive measures must be
taken, not only to ensure that subtle organizational practices are not limiting opportunity but also to break the cycle described above in the discussion of structural discrimination. Given the fact that intentional discrimi-

nation, though still present in many contemporary organizations, is only part of the problem, current approaches call for affirmative action programs (positive action) designed to change results. The thrust here is literally to place women and minorities into positions in which they have been historically underrepresented, rather than simply depending on the good intentions of nondiscrimination policies in competing for those positions. Theoretically, this would result in a change in organizational practices inhibiting access and contribute toward the breakdown of structural discrimination.

Competing Claims and Managerial Response

From the vantage point of the manager these three decision premises converge in the competing claims of organized interests, each demanding that procedures for serving their goals be institutionalized and each exacting high accountability from the manager in attending to these goals. Even in this era of relative deregulation, each interest is typically backed by an arbitrator ready to correct managerial missteps. Unions have grievance arbitration panels, merit advocates promote merit systems boards, and the EEO uses the judicial system.

In this context the role of the manager *can* be reduced to simply ensuring access to effectively organized groups and ratifying the agreements and adjustments worked out between competing leaders.[15] Neither the interest pursued nor the justification for one selection criterion over another is a matter for the manager to resolve. The process justifies the result.

The question we must raise is whether or not this definition of the manager's role, as a manager of process, is desirable. Some might argue that the role of the manager in managing competing claims among human interests in the organization is to manage the process effectively. Good managers know how to observe rules and regulations strictly, and when to seek further clarification and codification where ambiguity and vagueness exist. But this argument is fundamentally flawed. Three points highlight the need for an understanding of the manager's role in competing claims controversies that leads beyond managing process.

First, to suggest managers are only managers of process treats human resources as something apart from all other resources in the organization. While managers are expected to manage other material and financial resources toward program objectives, people, the most important resource, are managed by rules and regulations to which line managers can only react. While it is certainly true that personnel issues are special in organizations because they deal with human beings, there is no obvious reason to assume that when interests conflict, institutionalized decision rules will result in a more favorable outcome than one produced by the sensitive reflection of a line manager.

In fact, there are cases where the practice of holding administrators accountable for monitoring processes rather than achieving ends can produce significant goal displacement from the vantage point of the organized interest at stake. The collective bargaining process illustrates this point. Because the collective bargaining approach is based on an adversary model of manager/employee relationships, unions advocate various forms of job protection including formalization of job descriptions, clarification of job jurisdictions, and general rigidification of work elements.[16] The effect of this action is to reinforce a regressive expectation system in which neither management nor unions expect workers to take responsibility for the work process apart from their detailed job descriptions. Possibilities for managers to seek participation from employees in shaping managerial decisions are diminished by the very process designed to protect these possibilities at a lower level.

The second basis for rejecting the image of the manager as a "manager of process" relates to the nature of management work. The familiar tendency to restrict discretion of line managers in personnel decision making flows from dubious assumptions about public administration and the role of personnel management in that context. One questionable assumption defines power, in public organizations, as a fixed quantum lodged in the hands of the agency head and dispersed gingerly to those below.[17] When applied to managing people this concept translates into a belief that good personnel practice requires retaining all significant choice in the personnel office while curbing the discretion of the line manager to include only those options personnel sanctions. The "rule of three" practice in many civil service selection systems is an expression of such assumptions.

Neither of these assumptions finds broad support in the literature today despite their operational vitality in some organizations. On the contrary current literature suggests that managerial work involves the exercise of power—a power which is typically created, destroyed, and applied at all levels of a public organization.[18] Administrators not only do, but should exercise power, for often the presumed lack of power can be as corrupting for a public manager as a surfeit of discretion.[19] Think of the manager who justifies the patronage hiring of a legislator's daughter on affirmative action grounds when confronted by a disgruntled white male applicant who was rejected. "The personnel office made me do it" response diminishes the integrity of the hiring official even if there is no deception involved. But a system which removes the onus of responsibility from the hiring official invites invidious manipulation of the kind suggested in this example.

The actual character of the manager's job today demands that managers exercise power. Managing effectively toward organizational objectives means actively managing all the organization's resources, including human resources. Since human resources are often the most important factor in determining organization success, solutions to competing claims controversies which exclude managers from an active role in human resource management must be rejected.

The third difficulty with defining the role of the public executive as "process management" is that it blurs responsibility for actions which can have adverse consequences. As many managers know this deflecting of responsibilities often fails to buy protection anyway. Irate losers in competing claims controversies often hold the individual manager accountable no matter how institutionalized the decision premise guiding his or her acts. Think of the city manager who is called on the carpet by the city council for negotiating a union contract which ignores the council's public commitment to affirmative action. Consider the program manager who is named as a defendant in a reverse discrimination suit after bending merit system regulations to hire a black woman over a white man in accord with an agency affirmative action plan. When disputes over competing claims are resolved it may be an individual manager who is exonerated or blamed.

But in cases where this focus on managing processes does work to diminish personal accountability, is this desirable? In our judgment the public interest is not served by a system which explains actions that produce hurt in terms of a faceless bureaucrat's meticulous implementation of procedures. In any situation where values are being allocated it is important to be clear about the criteria for choice, not merely the purity of process. In fact, public managers may be uniquely positioned for making such choices.

In advancing this case, Douglas Yates argues that major responsibility for examining "hard choices" and justifying public decisions in normative terms should be assigned to the bureaucracy rather than the legislatures. He cites two especially persuasive reasons. First, managers typically enjoy a longer tenure in office than elected officials and thus are better able to put value conflicts in a "long run" perspective—a perspective vital to effective management of human resources. Second, to the extent the value analysis requires substantial informational and analytical resources the bureaucratic setting may be the best host for the activity.[20]

In sum we argue that managers must be acknowledged as more than managers of process in human resource decision making. We conclude this because the process focus often fails to serve the very human interests it presumes to advance, because it reflects a flawed understanding of the role of managers in personnel decisions, and because the public interest is best served by a system in which those with operational responsibility for making hard choices among competing claims are also charged with the value analysis that supports those choices. Institutional strategies which erode the administrator's capacity to judge not only impede attainment of program goals and objectives, but, just as importantly, hamper meeting the basic moral obligation that derives from the definitions of the manager's role advanced here. Where the substantive objectives behind processes conflict, we must fall back on the moral character of the manager charged with implementation. Responsibility in bureaucratic decision making requires careful attention to the treatment and definition of values in these competing claims encounters. Bureaucratic responsibility means that the manager becomes an active ethical agent in this context.

If managers are to become active value assessors in competing claims controversies, we must begin abandoning the two conventional responses to the current situation encountered in the literature. One is descriptive, and sees the manager as immobilized by competing pressures. The second is prescriptive, and admonishes the manager to resist the drive for institutionalization. Both responses fail to provide positive guidance to the manager, because the driving force behind these competing expressions of interest is a legitimate fear of the potential harm individuals may suffer at the hands of the organization. The situation calls for a more sensitive and creative response—one which casts the manager in the role of an active moral agent in the process.

But simply ordaining managers as ethical agents in competing claims controversies is not enough. To make hard choices managers must be given frameworks for value decision making much as we develop analytical tools for policy making more generally. While Stephen Bailey may be right in his observation that ". . . the most essential courage in the public service is the courage to decide,"[21] responsible decisions in the competing claims area hinge on adopting a mode of analysis which highlights the impacts of alternatives on affected groups and provides a framework for allocating costs. In other words, managers need an ethical framework for human resource decision making, a device to empower them as ethical agents in competing claims decision making.

Before offering a framework which prescribes action for the manager, one controversial assumption must be justified. This essay assumes that it is possible to cast the manager as a moral agent in the decision-making process. However, it might be argued that this focus on the individual manager is misplaced because personnel policy in contemporary government organizations is a function of a complex organizational, interorganizational, and intergovernmental decision-making system. In fact, in many governmental organizations the decision premises discussed are so heavily institutionalized that questions of individual ethics are "academic." Some important insights are imbedded in this critique.

Significant ethical questions do emerge at the level of the organization as a whole and a valid distinction can be made between personal ethics and organizational ethics. Organizational norms set the context within which personal ethical decisions about right and wrong are forged. People may turn first to their immediate organization, its climate and procedures, for help when ethical dilemmas arise.[22] In some respects an organization can be viewed as a moral community, often a referent for determining right from wrong in the balancing of competing interests.[23] But, notwithstanding the substantial influence of the organization, it is still the individual manager who singularly or collectively establishes and implements policies which give primacy to some interests over others. While the level at which the interests converge to create a competing claims situation varies by jurisdiction and by issue, the experience of the individual manager at the point of convergence is the same. There are competing interests advocated by distinct stakeholders, each insisting the manager is obligated to act on a particular decision premise. Even if an individual manager concludes in a particular case that the decision authority resides elsewhere in the organization, thus aborting his or her further involvement, that very judgment is part of a moral choice process. While it is true that this choice obviates the need to select between interests, the need to make a choice about where obligation resides is stimulated by competing claims pressure.

If, then, the manager is to be cast as a moral agent in these competing claim controversies, analytical tools are needed to reduce the pervasive ambiguity around issues of obligation, authority, and responsibility for personnel actions. The following ethical framework has been produced from extensive discussions of and reflections on a series of "ethical dilemma" cases written by government managers. (See note for discussion of cases.)[24] The framework aims to empower managers as ethical agents in competing claims decision making.

Ethical Framework for Human Resource Decision Making

Specifically the framework offered here does three things. It provides a way of identifying those interests that should be taken into account by managers, it provides analytical tools for assessing the relative degree of obligation each interest generates, and it invites reflection on issues of authority and responsibility in managerial decision making.

The first step is to identify those interests that must be taken into account in any competing claims situation. For this analysis we turn to what is called "stakeholder theory," a theory developed in an effort to incorporate the claims of broader publics into private sector management decision making.[25] Adapted to this analysis, stakeholders are individuals, groups, or classes whose lives are affected by management decisions. In other words, they are "parties at interest" in a particular decision context. An organization is dependent on and responsible to the stakeholders whose lives it affects. While no one group of stakeholders has total claim to what constitutes appropriate conduct for an organization, when management decisions impinge, stakeholders have a right to say they are injured. An organization must respond in a way that ensures that its activities don't harm those it affects—an obligation which binds despite the current state of regulation or deregulation. While this doesn't require acceding to every stakeholder demand, it does require that managers seek to understand stakeholder concerns and proposals arising out of a serious expectation of potential harm.

In seeking to understand stakeholder demands and management's obligations vis-à-vis those demands, a simple conceptual framework makes the distinction initially between negative and affirmative obligation and suggests that negative responsibilities are more stringent than affirmative responsibilities. The responsibility to avoid injury to others is a more stringent obligation than the responsibility to help others. In his writing on corporate ethics, Michael Rion uses a simple example to illustrate this point:

> Suppose you encounter a beggar soliciting donations as you walk down the street of a large city. Should you make a contribution? Should you aid her to find shelter or even take a continuing interest in her welfare upon returning to your home town? The answers are not obvious, for they depend upon your understanding of why persons must beg, your charitable commitments and priorities, and your financial means. Judging affirmative responsibilities to do good to others can easily lead to disagreements about values and appropriate roles but if asked whether you should intentionally push the begger off her chair into the rain puddle, surely all moral agents would say that you should not. Morally, we agree that we should not harm others.[26]

Customarily, ethics in public administration means the obligation to avoid injury. Avoiding injury is the principle behind the public's insistence that managers avoid waste and public deception. Our scheme for guiding managers in competing claims decision making focuses on such negative responsibilities. Obviously this does not restrict managers merely to avoiding and correcting injury. Some even argue that, in the last decades, the role definition of the public manager has expanded to include the pursuance of social justice. But this essay's analysis of competing claims is concerned with the avoidance of injury rather than a more expansive notion of "doing good."

No one disputes that the administrator bears a negative obligation to avoid injuring others in the execution of public service. But the nature of injury requires careful analysis. Take the case of a manager charged with drafting a Reduction in Force (RIF) policy for an agency. Assume the agency acknowledges the American Federation of State, County, and Municipal Employees (AFSCME) as the representative of the nonprofessional employees. The professional staff has, for the most part, been selected and promoted through a civil service system relying heavily on test scores and formal credentials. But in the last three years the total staff has gone from 2 percent to 20 percent representation of minorities in all positions, and women, always well represented in non-professional slots, have increased their presence in professional jobs from 2 percent four years ago to 18 percent today. These gains are due largely to an aggressive affirmative action program implemented by the agency.

In this situation the manager is challenged to understand the nature of harm involved in any particular RIF action and then balance that action against another potential harm inflicted by an alternative action. Clearly this case presents potential for injury on a number of fronts. In order to analyze the nature and extent of injury, the manager first asks who the potential "stakeholders" are in this dilemma. Again, stakeholders are the parties affected by a decision. Next managers ask what rights or interests each party has. Finally, the manager considers the nature of all the conflicting values among the stakeholders and rates the relative importance of each value. Doing harm to the interest of some stakeholders might derive from avoiding injury to other stakeholders. In this ethical dilemma the stakeholders would include at least the following:

- union AFSCME and union membership (nonprofessional)
- professional staff selected and promoted through the merit system
- new women professional staff
- new minority employees, professional and nonprofessional
- agency beneficiaries/clients
- agency head
- administrator reporting the dilemma

Each of these parties could be injured by the administrator's response. Avoiding injury to every party is not possible in this case. Typically, this kind of ambiguity dominates decision making in the public sector. But the task of the administrator is to sort out these potential injuries, and within his or her authority, to select the least injurious decision from the value rankings derived from thoughtful analysis. Viewed from this perspective, though the most stringent obligation of the administrator is to avoid doing harm, defining this obligation in a particular context admittedly is difficult.

In this sorting and shifting process, managers are guided by their own ethical systems. Ethicists describe such systems as ". . . an ordered set of moral standards and rules of conduct by reference to which, with the addition of factual knowledge one can determine in any situation of choice what a person ought or ought not to do. . . ."[27] Two distinctively different ethical systems give rise to two ethical standards which guide action. The first system, deontological ethics, asserts that certain features of acts render them good or bad irrespective of consequence. Classic examples of good acts are keeping promises and telling the truth. We ought to always tell the truth, and to keep agreements, because of the value inherent in the acts—in other words, because it is right. The second ethical system, utilitarian ethics, sees an act as right if it produces a greater balance of good over evil. In this second system, the moral quality of actions is dependent on what they bring about or try to bring about.[28] If the consequences are "good," then the act is right.

Most managers are neither pure deontologists, nor pure utilitarians, but rather operate according to a kind of ethical pluralism. Guided by this synthesis of moral systems, managers typically might conclude that the moral reason for or against some action resides in its consequences, while the rationale for or against other actions stems from their being of a kind required or prohibited by duty. When acting out of ethical pluralism, managers need to develop a capacity for sensitive moral judgment, for often one must apply both sorts of moral reasoning to the same actions. It might be that the consequences of some action would be so bad that it should not be undertaken even though one has a *prima facie* obligation to do it.

Taking the RIF example above, clearly one has an obligation to keep the long-standing commitment made to the union to lay off employees according to seniority and in the absence of moral reasons against it, seniority would be the prime determinant of RIF decision making. But, in this particular context, the consequence of such a decision-making rule would be to lay off 90 percent of the minority nonprofessional employees in the organization and only 2 percent of their white coworkers. The consequences of following the seniority decision rule are so bad in terms of adverse impact on minority employees, that a manager may reject the seniority criterion notwithstanding the long-standing commitment to the union to follow it.

The assumption of this essay up to this point has been that the manager or the organization has been sufficiently involved in the injurious act to trigger an obligation to cease the injury or to compensate. But often in organizations, particularly in instances of competing claims, the whole issue of responsibility to act is problematic. In many real life situations, before managers even get to the "what is right?" issues, they want to know when it is even appropriate to exercise their own moral judgment. Clearly if they are personally involved in causing the injury, moral judgment is called for, as illustrated in the RIF policy-making discussion above. But sometimes managers are also obliged to correct injury caused by others.

The conditions triggering obligatory action are enumerated in an ethical decision rule called the "Kew Gardens Principle," a label borrowed from the widely publicized murder in the Kew Gardens section of New York City, witnessed by 30 to 40 silent bystanders. The principle suggests action is obligatory to the extent that the following conditions prevail:

1. *Need*—There is a clear need for aid. . . .
2. *Proximity*—The agent is "close" to the situation, not necessarily in space but, certainly in terms of notice; . . .
3. *Capability*—The agent has some means by which to aid the one in need without undue risk to the agent . . . .
4. *Last Resort*—No one else is likely to help. . . . [29]

In reflecting back on the RIF example, assume that the individual manager is not responsible for drafting the RIF policy, but simply for implementing it. Hence, there is no specific injury implicated by implementation action. However, if a manager is in a position to make a more accurate assessment of the injury suffered by certain stakeholders as the result of a RIF and to feed that information into the construction of an organization-wide policy, the character of obligation may change. Take this example:

> Assume you are a division head directing an engineering division in an agency about to undergo a 30 percent RIF. The RIF policy developed by the staff of the agency head has determined to cut positions in the professional ranks beginning with the lowest civil service positions first. The historically all white engineering division has diversified in recent years, through the efforts of a highly committed personnel unit. The division has been able to recruit and maintain minority engineers so that the division's engineering workforce is 10 percent minority. Because the minority engineers joined the unit in entry level positions, they are currently concentrated in the 1/3 lowest civil service grades. The chief of the personnel unit in the department has just been replaced and the new chief clearly does not share the commitment to minority recruitment and retention. Because of the more relaxed EEO regulatory environment, generally you believe there is a little sentiment in the organization as a whole for continuing to press EEO issues. You are sure that implementing the policy of achieving the reduction by eliminating the lower grade positions is tantamount to RIFing all of the minority engineers.

The question is: does this manager have an obligation to try to reshape the policy or at least secure an exemption in his unit? The Kew Gardens Principle suggests that an obligation might exist. The minority group employees have been injured by a discriminatory policy in the past and through a nonconsciously discriminatory policy are now about to lose their jobs (need). The manager in this case is close enough to the situation to have the vital information about the impact of a position-based RIF (proximity). Whether or not he or she could act without jeopardizing his or her job or future effectiveness in the organization is uncertain (capability). It does appear that the manager in this case may be the only one who can come to the aid of the minority engineers (last resort).

To sum up this presentation of an ethical framework for human resource decision making, the basic moral principle counsels managers to avoid hurting others. Sensitive ethical analysis is required to actually define an injury in terms of all stakeholders involved and to weight injuries caused by a particular action. But even managers who avoid doing injury to others may be further obligated to correct or prevent injury caused by others, according to the Kew Gardens Principle. This principle offers a blueprint for those areas where there is a less stringent obligation than in the requirement to avoid injury, but a more stringent obligation than the affirmative obligation to do good.

Conclusion

In the late 1970s Warren Bennis described the expression of competing interests in organizations as "the politics of multiple advocacies—vocal, demanding, often 'out of sync' with each other."[30] Bennis spoke for many public sector executives when he described his organization as analogous to an anvil on which a fragmented society hammers. Today the society remains fragmented and groups still hammer, though the force of their blows may be lightened by deregulation. This article argues for moving beyond the anvil imagery of the analogy.

The image and fact of paralyzed managers, able only to reflect imprints of competing interests, must change. Change will come from a more self-conscious definition of the human resource manager as a morally responsible actor. The challenge for the public sector manager is to move beyond lamenting the expression of strong group interests and toward responding sensitively and fairly to expressions of hurt. We do not claim to tell managers how to weigh different expressions of hurt. Moral reasoning may lead individual managers to give primacy to different decision premises in similar cases. Still, whatever social interest is served by a particular decision, this article presents ethical reflection as a mode of response which rejects the imagery of the human resource manager as a passive actor, buffeted to and fro on a sea of competing claims and imprisoned in a role devoid of conscience. The manager as a self-consciously ethical decision maker is an active listener who sensitively and thoroughly considers the competing interests at stake, exercises informed moral judgment regarding the balance of these interests, and purposefully adopts the decision premises guiding action.

Notes

1. The term "decision premise" is taken from Herbert Simon's classic work, *Administrative Behavior*, 2nd ed. (New York: Free Press, 1965). It suggests a starting point for decision making which accepts as "given" both goals or values

to be achieved and a specified set of alternative strategies for achieving those goals.

2. Herbert Kaufman, "Administrative Decentralization and Political Power," *Public Administration Review* 29 (January/February 1969), 3.

3. For a detailed discussion of these conditions see Margaret Levi, *Bureaucratic Insurgency* (Lexington, Mass.: D.C. Heath Company, 1977), 19.

4. M. Chandler, *Management Rights and Union Interests* (New York: McGraw Hill, 1964), 64; *The Public Interest in Government Labor Relations* (Cambridge, Mass.: Ballinger Publishing Co., 1977), 19.

5. Enid F. Beaumont, "A Pivotal Point for the Merit Concept," *Public Administration Review* 34 (September/October 1974), 426.

6. Wilber C. Rich, *The Politics of Urban Personnel Policy: Reformers, Politicians, and Bureaucrats* (Port Washington, N.Y.: Kennikat Press, 1982), 25.

7. One stream of scholarship sees the drive to put "merit" in government through structural reform as an effort to gain ground for the emerging middle class values of administrative efficiency and professionalism—values which embody the attributes of middle class life style and experience (see George W. Mowry, *The California Progressives* (Berkeley and Los Angeles, 1951), 86–104; Richard Hofstadter, *The Age of Reform* (New York, 1955), 131–269; Alfred D. Chandler, Jr., "The Origins of Progressive Leadership," in Elting Morrison, *et al.* (eds.), *Letters of Theodore Roosevelt* (Cambridge, Mass., 1951–54), VIII, Appendix III (1462–64). But Samuel Hays presents evidence that it was the upper class, leading business groups and professional men closely identified with them, who forced reform at least in municipal systems (Samuel P. Hays, *American Political History as Social Analysis* [Knoxville: University of Tennessee Press, 1980]), 209.

8. Hays, 218.

9. Hays, 281.

10. O. Glenn Stahl, *Public Personnel Administration,* 6th ed. (New York: Harper and Row, 1971), 41.

11. Frederick C. Mosher, *Democracy and the Public Service,* 2nd ed. (New York: Oxford University Press, 1968), 203–204.

12. Muriel M. Morse, "Shall We Bargain Away the Merit System?" *Public Personnel Review* 24 (October 1963), 239–243.

13. See Congressional Oversight Hearings, H.R. Rep. No. 92–238, 92nd Cong., 1st Sess., reprinted in (1972) U.S. Code Cong. and Ad. News 2143–44.

14. This discussion is based upon the analysis of discrimination provided in U.S. Commission on Civil Rights, *Affirmative Action in the 1980s: Dismantling the Process of Discrimination,* Clearinghouse Publication 65 (January 1981), 10 ff.

15. See Theodore J. Lowi, *The End of Liberalism,* 2nd ed. (New York: W. W. Norton and Company, 1969), 51.

16. See G. David Garson, "The Future of American Public Administration" (MPA and CUACS Joint Paper Series, JPS-01, North Carolina State University, 1980), 9.

17. Donald P. Warwich argues this is the basic notion that we must lay to rest in order to develop a meaningful managerial ethics. See Donald P. Warwich, "The Ethics of Administrative Discretion" in Joel Fleishman, Lance Liebman, Mark H. Moore, *Public Duties: The Moral Obligations of Government Officials* (Cambridge, Mass.: Harvard University Press, 1981), 125.

18. Warwich, 125.

19. Warwich, 125.

20. Douglas T. Yates, Jr., "Hard Choices: Justifying Bureaucratic Decisions" in Joel Fleishman, Lance Liebman, Mark H. Moore, *Public Duties: The Moral Obligation of Government Officials* (Cambridge, Mass.: Harvard University Press, 1981), 48–49.

21. Stephen K. Bailey, "Ethics and the Public Service" in R. C. Martin (ed.), *Public Administration and Democracy* (Syracuse: Syracuse University Press, 1965), 296.

22. James S. Bowman, "The Management of Ethics: Codes of Conduct in Organizations," *Public Personnel Management* 20 1(1981): 61.

23. Ann-Marie Rizzo and Thomas Patka, "The Organizational Imperative in Supervisory Control," *Public Personnel Management* 10, 1(1981): 103.

24. Valid scholarship in management ethics must be closely linked to moral quandaries as they are experienced by managers. This analysis has grown from discussions with government executives participating in the North Carolina Government Executive Institute (GEI). The GEI is an executive development program available to state, local and some federal executives. (For GEI purposes executives are defined as managers of managers.) In preparation for our management ethics session I ask participants to complete a management ethics case writing assignment. The core of the case assignment reads:

Reflect back to a situation where you experienced an ethical dilemma arising from a conflict between action dictated by your own personal code of ethics and that expected by the formal or informal norms of your agency or the public you serve. Describe the dilemma in one paragraph, changing names (if used) and/or department so as to protect your anonymity and that of others involved.

Of the 150 executives participating in the GEI over the past two years, 45 have chosen to submit ethics cases for class discussion. About half of these cases dealt with human resource management issues and centered on competing claims pressed on the manager. The ethical framework presented is a product of (1) my understanding of the decision premise advocated by competing interests in our society, (2) discussion and reflection on the experiences of managers at the point where divergent interests converge and jointly press for primacy, (3) application of ethical theory to these cases.

25. For a discussion of stakeholder theory application see Henry B. Schacht and Charles W. Powers, "Business Responsibility and the Public Policy Process" in Thornton Bradshaw and David Vogel (eds.), *Corporations and Their Critics* (New York: McGraw Hill, 1981), 25–32.

26. Michael Rion, "Ethical Principles" (Columbus, Indiana, 1980) (mimeographed).

27. Paul Taylor, *Principles of Ethics* (Dickenson Publishing Company, 1975), 12.

28. William K. Frankena, *Ethics,* 2nd ed. (Englewood Cliffs, N.J.: Prentice-Hall, 1973), 23.

29. John G. Simon, Charles W. Powers, Jon P. Gunneman, *The Ethical Investor* (New Haven: Yale University Press, 1972), 22–25.

30. Warren Bennis, "Where Have All the Leaders Gone?" Technology Review (March/April 1977), 39.

Part THREE

Corruption

Despite the optimism and wisdom of the ethics scholars, everyone in public service does not engage in moral reasoning, or even obey the laws and policies governing their behavior. Corruption raises its ugly head too often in government service, and that is the concern of the scholars represented here.

Chapter 10, "A Scandal in Utopia," written by Herbert Emmerich in 1952 for *PAR*, is an impassioned response to irregularities in the collection of national revenues and the effect of interstate gambling syndicates on local and state law enforcement, covering as well the general movement away from the powerful wartime government to one more responsive to the people of the United States.

The early 1950s was a period of transition. People were still frightened and viewing those near them as potential threats to the newly established peace. In 1947, President Truman had issued an executive order to establish a program to find and deal with subversives in the federal bureaucracy, and by the 1950s, Senator Joseph McCarthy was on a crusade to find and eliminate Communists employed in government.

This was an uneasy time, and Emmerich describes it well. He is concerned that widely publicized instances of malfeasance will either "allow government work as a vocation to be libeled" or "fail to admit the serious nature of these occurrences" of corruption. Thus, he offers suggestions for dealing with the "current scandals in the government" and calls for other readers of *PAR* to "revise and to extend and to debate" the points he has raised.

A close check of *PAR* from 1952 to 1960 reveals that no one was sufficiently concerned with corruption to respond to Emmerich or to elaborate on his thinking. Indeed ASPA journals are strangely silent on ethical issues until the crisis of Watergate demanded attention be paid to the subject.

Chapter 11, "Reflections on Watergate: Lessons for Public Administration," appeared in *PAR* in 1974. In it, James L. Sundquist calls for public administration professionals to examine themselves by asking the question "Where did we go wrong?" For Sundquist, Watergate and Vietnam are twin demons produced by an excessively strong presidency that created both a corrupt presidency and a crisis of confidence in our entire system of government. The blame, he believes, rests partly on the shoulders of the profession of public administration, which has collectively denied the reality of Lord Acton's statement: "Power tends to corrupt and absolute power corrupts absolutely." Sundquist thus offers several suggestions for curtailing the power of the president as a means of eliminating corruption in that office.

In 1977, Gerald and Naomi Caiden began their *PAR* article, "Administrative Corruption" (Chapter 12 here), by declaring, "The increased visibility of administrative corruption has become a persistent and disturbing feature of our times." Acknowledging that research into corruption had not heretofore been deemed respectable, they define the term, discuss the ramifications of different definitions over time, and offer a research agenda for the study of corruption. Unlike Sundquist, who focuses on the leader who uses political power to advance the self, the Caidens address systemic corruption that is the institutionalized subversion of the public interest.

In 1983, Simcha Werner offered "New Directions in the Study of Administrative Corruption" in *PAR* (Chapter 13 here). He identifies four theoretical tenets of corruption that he believes have stifled its study: (1) corruption is an inseparable by-product of modernization and development, (2) corruption is a functional influence of political and economic development, (3) corruption is a self-destructive process, and (4) corruption is an individual action committed by the occasional immoral official for personal benefit. These tenets are followed by a comprehensive literature review on the subject that is especially important for this volume as none of the viable research on corruption had been published before in an ASPA-sponsored journal. Werner concludes his article by calling for more systematic development of research and description of administrative corruption.

These articles about corruption were beginning efforts to address and solve the problems corruption creates. Corruption in American public administration has not been a popular area for study, perhaps because Americans are in collective denial about the possibility and prevalence of corrupt acts. Corruption in countries other than this one, however, is both studied and discussed. Scholars and moral administrators alike acknowledge the potential for corruption and work to learn how to prevent or curtail it, whereas Americans seem to believe that the corrupt public servant is an anomaly. It is telling that much of the work now being done by the Caidens and Werner is international in nature.

10

A SCANDAL IN UTOPIA

Herbert Emmerich
Director, Public Administration Clearing House

I

The recent disclosures of serious irregularities in the management of our national revenue collection system should not pass unnoticed in the pages of this journal. The American Society for Public Administration, which publishes this *Review,* is dedicated to the advancement of the standards of honest and efficient public administration. We who constitute its membership cannot fail to be aroused by the apparent deterioration of a service which for many years has enjoyed a high reputation. When we add to these disclosures those made by the Senate committee headed by Senator Kefauver inquiring into the effect on local and state law enforcement agencies of commercialized interstate gambling syndicates, we must feel that a pretty thorough stocktaking is in order. It is appropriate for us to ask ourselves some searching questions about the state of American public administration in these critical times. It is important not only to put these occurrences in their proper perspective but to bend our energies to building upon the current interest in these matters to obtain lasting improvements in the public service in directions which many of us have been advocating for a long time. The purpose of this article is to start a discussion which I hope will be continued in the pages of *Public Administration Review.*

In approaching this unpleasant topic it seems to me that those engaged in government service must, in the interest of their profession, avoid two pitfalls. One pitfall is to allow government work as a vocation to be libeled by failing to supply facts when exaggerated and sensational generalizations are drawn from specific instances of wrongdoing. The other pitfall is to fail to admit the serious nature of these occurrences, the need for their correction, and the threat they constitute to the reputation and prestige of public administration.

Unfortunately these revelations come at an embarrassing time from both the domestic and the foreign points of view. At home we are engaged in a large mobilization effort to defend ourselves and the rest of the free world against a dangerous threat. The volume of public administration is expanding enormously. We are drafting young men for military service, spending great sums on defense and foreign aid, and taxing and regulating our citizens and private institutions to an extent never before attempted except in a period of all-out war. In the extraordinarily difficult task of administering these programs we need the best people we can get. It is a time which calls for confidence of citizens in their government so that they will be ready to accept the necessary sacrifices and prepared to render public service in the national effort. Not the least serious result of these disclosures, particularly when they are blown up into blanket defamations of the government service, is that they make harder the already difficult job of attracting and retaining the able people that the present great effort requires.

The fact that these revelations come at the beginning of a presidential election year increases the possibility that they will be damaging both at home and abroad. The free election of our chief executive is one of the glories of our republic, yet in a partisan political campaign more heat than light is apt to be shed on matters of this kind. The hard thinking and difficult decisions needed to cope with this and other complex problems are apt to be postponed at a time when we habitually tend to divide into two camps and reduce issues to two simple choices which, expressed in lowest terms, are to "*throw* the rascals out" or to "*keep* the rascals out." The effect abroad is likely to be particularly bad. The election campaign of 1952 threatens to be one of the most unashamed exhibitions of dirty linen to the entire world in which any country has ever indulged. Today we have not only the problem of face saving but of preserving the international leadership that only this country with its skills, vitality, and resources can supply to the free international community. It will be very important for political campaigners and for the press, while not suppressing these disclosures, to refrain from sensationalism and hyperbole.

The most serious danger of a wholesale castigation of the integrity of American democratic government at this stage of world history is the effect it will have on other countries. We cannot sell the extension of democratic government if we recklessly assert that its entire machinery is corrupt. Having pledged our resources to assist other nations in a common enterprise to resist aggression and to spread the areas of freedom and well-being by means of money, materials, and the exchange of skills and know-how through technical assistance, we find ourselves in a new role of telling other peoples how to manage their affairs and, indeed, how to govern themselves. The assumption has grown in the underprivileged nations that the United States, having demonstrated such great technical prowess and productivity, such a high standard of living, such generosity and dynamic leadership in world affairs, must have things pretty well managed at home. The fact is that we have an abundant supply of good things to export in addition to our industrial, scientific, and military skills and products. In the last fifty years we have made great improvements in the techniques of our public administration, and in this field we have many sound methods that other lands need and can profitably adapt to their own institutions. I refer not only to the techniques in general administrative management, but also to those in special fields such as education, health, and agriculture, in all of which we have very special, though not exclusive, contributions to make. Neither we nor the other free nations can afford to turn off this rich source of help because of what may seem to be "A Scandal in Utopia" to peoples who look with envy on our abundance and efficiency.

It is important to put the current revelations in proper perspective not only to insure a fair interpretation of their meaning abroad but also to gain the maximum benefit for the improvement of the public service. Robert Ramspeck, chairman of the United States Civil Service Commission, is rendering a valuable service by his "campaign of facts." He is insisting that while the necessary steps are taken to correct the situation, the revelations not be allowed to become a wholesale castigation of the federal service, which is preponderantly honest, able, and industrious.

It occurs to me that three approaches may be helpful in getting a proper perspective in our thinking about the current scandals in the government. One is the historical approach, another is through analysis of the environment in which government operates, and a third is through an assessment of postwar trends in American public administration.

II

I believe the point can be made that we have come a long way in increasing the respect of citizens for the public service and in raising the standards which they expect it to uphold. The very things that are now causing surprise and indignation as deviations from the standard were at many times in our history unfortunately taken for granted and considered normal operating procedure. We have only to remember the low standards prevailing in the latter part of the nineteenth century to perceive the great change that has come about. In the period of westward expansion, with its ruthless exploitation of immigrant labor and natural resources, predatory interests bought state legislatures, which in turn elected United States senators, who in turn "appointed" unqualified political hacks to government posts. The federal service, with some notable exceptions, was generally held in low esteem—a place for hangers-on and incompetents who were supposed to run the errands and do the favors for special interests through a system of political brokerage. As the big cities grew and as frontier towns sprang up there was a similar decline in the moral tone of focal government. It took the assassination of President Garfield to dramatize to the nation the evils of the patronage system and to give the pioneer reformers a chance to get their plans adopted.

The British as usual were ahead of us in governmental reform, but lest we get an inferiority complex we may recall that the British patronage and rotten borough systems lasted into the nineteenth century and were not eliminated until after the Civil Service and the Reform Acts were passed. Even in more recent times there have been occasional lapses on the part of British public men, but when these occur we do not jump to the conclusion that because of individual transgressions everyone in His Majesty's magnificent service is venal and corrupt.

To compare the present state of public indignation to the relative callousness of bygone days we need not go back to the scandals of the Grant administration, or the "embalmed beef" disclosures after the Spanish American War, or the Teapot Dome revelations involving two Cabinet officers in the Harding administration. Most of us can still recall the nightmare of the prohibition era of the 1920's when corruption in large segments of all levels of government was accompanied by a general spirit of lawlessness in our communities and a general cynicism among citizens toward government. All levels of government and of society were besmirched in this disgraceful era in our history. Not the least of the good results of the Twenty-first Amendment were the tremendous improvements it brought about in the local, state, and federal services and in the reversal of attitude of citizens toward law-enforcement and other government officials. The fact that we have reacted so indignantly to the present crop of disclosures is evidence of the high standard of expectation we have reached in regard to the integrity of public servants. We are shocked not because we have a low regard for public officials, but because we expect them to have so high a standard of integrity.

On the positive side, it may be noted that in the period of greatly enlarged governmental activities and expenditures of the New Deal and World War II there was evidence of a greatly improved standard of public administration. In spite of the large delegations of authority to the executive during the Roosevelt administration, both in peace and in war, dozens of investigating committees disclosed practically no scandals and none of major national proportion. The crusading honesty of such Cabinet members as Harold Ickes and Henry Morgenthau became a watchword that helped create an atmosphere of integrity and ethical handling of the public business.

A brief examination of the environment in which public administration operates in our democracy will also help to put the current examples of official misconduct in proper perspective. In a country that is committed to the largest possible measure of individual freedom and initiative and variety in its private enterprises, public administration cannot operate in a vacuum. It must touch, and be touched by, private interests. Indeed, with the growth of big government, which regulates, taxes, finances, and contracts with private enterprise and litigates with private interests, these contacts are more pervasive and important than ever before. In some instances the government service is a training ground for, and stepping-stone to, remunerative private careers. Government in the United States operates in a "business civilization," as James Truslow Adams has described our culture. Men going into government from business must understand that certain practices that are accepted in large parts of the business world, such as liberal entertainment and exchange of gifts, are not accepted in the official world. It is essential that persons working for the government at all times be above suspicion of favoritism to their friends, to their political backers, or to persons who might advance their future careers.

In a democracy the public service must operate in a political atmosphere. It is right and proper that members of Congress and congressional committees should be interested in facts regarding government policies and procedures. They have the right and the duty to scrutinize and review both policy and practices. In the determination of policy, the special needs of industrial and occupational interest groups and of widely varying localities and regions cannot be ignored; but in the application of policy to particular cases, these special claims frequently cannot be granted. Here there is need for continuing vigilance and for perhaps a degree or kind of administrative awareness we have not yet demonstrated.

In considering the environment in which government operates, we must look at the problems created by the organized professions and guilds, their pressures for representation and for special exemptions from the merit system. The lawyers have enjoyed some special exemptions from civil service rules, but they are by no means the only group that needs to reconsider its relationship to government service.

It has also become a part of the environment of our democracy for many persons to serve their government part-time or for short tours of duty. There is need in a free society for this kind of mobility between public and private employment. It is particularly important in times of crisis. Today we are again begging persons whose skills are particularly needed in the defense effort to come into the government service. In recruiting such persons for short periods of service or for part-time consulting work, we must insure that merit and fitness are the sole criteria in selection. Such appointments, however, do not involve tenure rights, and they do not need to be made through formal competitive tests. Once a person of this type has entered on duty, however, he should no more represent an interest group than he should represent a local political club. He is in the service of the government of the United States and while in that service he owes his undivided loyalty to it and to the standards which have come to characterize it. There is a much more subtle form of disloyalty and corruption than the obvious forms that we generally hear about, and it is to a degree an unconscious one. It is a lack of loyalty to the general interest resulting from conflicting specialized loyalties.

A third way of getting a better perspective on the significance of current scandals in the government service is to try to measure or assess the postwar trends in American public administration. There are two distinct postwar trends that can be identified; the first gets on the front page, the second rarely gets any notice of importance.

Although there has been less "letdown" after World War II in the standards of public service and in citizen morale than after other wars in our history, there has been a trend in this direction. In addition to the government scandals, there have been athletic scandals and an unusual number of bank defalcations. We are still reaping some of the fruits of the prohibition days, and the scions of the bootleggers have turned to commercialized gambling and other shady businesses which have sought and sometimes found special protection through bribing hitherto honest but underpaid police departments and undermanned law-enforcement agencies. There has been an abundance of private employment at higher rates of pay and with less danger to health and reputation than the hazardous government service offers. This situation has naturally drawn off talented men from Washington. There have been cases where the President, who has made earnest and persistent efforts to find good men to fill important jobs, has mistakenly shown the same loyalty to persons deficient in a proper sense of public deportment that he has shown to outstanding men of high character that he thought were being unfairly attacked. Some of the young New Dealers may have been fanatically hostile toward business in the excitement of the early relief and recovery days. As a reaction to this feeling, in the postwar period the pendulum in some cases may have swung too far to the other extreme.

But when one considers the enormous expansion of governmental services in every field, the amount of delegated discretion, the vast sums of money for loans, guarantees, contracts, and subsidies, and the extent to which governmental action touches private interest at every point, it is remarkable how free federal officials have been of wrongdoing and favoritism in comparison with previous times. The sensational emphasis given to the back-sliding trend is partly because it has news value, partly because of partisan considerations; but I believe the indignant reaction is also an evidence of the higher standard of public morality and expectation of governmental integrity to which we have become accustomed.

The positive and less glamorized and publicized trend in postwar public administration in the United States is as clearly identifiable as the negative one. This is the trend of a really astonishing amount of improvement at all levels of government that has taken place since 1945.

In our cities there has been a veritable upsurge of administrative and governmental improvement. Citizen organizations and professional associations of public officials have both contributed to this progressive trend by the interchange of information on improved methods and by the stimulation of continuing programs of improvement. In city after city citizen campaigns have led to new charters and improved forms of government. The number of cities with the council-manager form of government has doubled since 1945; today 1060 cities are operating under this plan. Other cities have adopted new charters with interesting innovations; Philadelphia and Boston are the most recent examples of large cities that have made thoroughgoing changes in both structure and personnel. Every big city but Chicago has eliminated the ward system. Important steps have been taken in city-county consolidation and in improved metropolitan and regional governmental arrangements. Between the last two censuses over 10,000 small local taxing units were abolished. Great forward strides in the quality of municipal service have resulted from the adoption of better techniques in many specialized fields.

The states have not lagged in undertaking administrative improvement. In recent years a number have completely renovated outmoded constitutions or have adopted amendments to open the way to improvements in administration. Some thirty-five states have had their Little Hoover Commissions; their recommendations are resulting in many reforms.

In recent years there has been a further great decline in the patronage system at the state and local levels and a great improvement in the way in which the merit system is administered. In spite of the headline rackets that the Kefauver Committee has uncovered, today, in 1952, we need no longer apologize with Lincoln Steffens for "the shame of the cities," or deplore with James Bryce the failure of local government in the American commonwealth.

A resolution adopted by the American Municipal Association in December, 1951, is evidence of the spirit of self-improvement and of pride in the prestige of the public service that now animates municipal officials.

RESOLVED that the American Municipal Association reaffirm its vigorous desire to eliminate the forces of corruption in local government, since it was official action by the American Municipal Association which first called public attention to organized crime syndicates operating in some of our cities.

RESOLVED FURTHER that the American Municipal Association recognize that the great majority of public servants and officials are honest, efficient and loyal, and that the Association express its desire to see the loyal servants duly recognized and honored by the respective citizens of respective local governments in order that good persons may be induced to render service in the future.

RESOLVED that we communicate these sentiments to the Congress of the United States, and that we request that any further investigations be specific on designation of wrongdoing, in order to avoid blanket condemnation of local government, and to prevent the destruction of citizen confidence in public officials.

Even at the much flagellated federal level the postwar period has been, on balance, one of progress. The work of the President's Committee on Administrative Management (the Brownlow Committee) and of the Commission on Organization of the Executive Branch (the Hoover Commission) has provided the impetus for continuing executive and legislative action for improvement. It is not generally appreciated what earnest cooperation President Truman gave to ex-President Hoover's work and the extent to which he has continued to follow up on the recommendations of the Hoover Commission. A large percentage of these recommendations has been adopted and installed according to the testimony of the Citizens' Committee on the Hoover Report—testimony that cannot be said to be biased in favor of the present administration. In addition to reforms in the fields of administrative management, fiscal operations, procurement, and personnel, there has been real progress in the centralization of policy and decentralization of day-to-day work. Department after department and bureau after bureau have made managerial studies and have followed them up with reorganizations and the installation of improved methods and procedures. The modernization of procedures in such agencies as the Patent Office, the Bureau of Land Management, the Customs Bureau, Bureau of Reclamation, and the Coast Guard may be cited as just a few examples of this trend. The archaic federal accounting system is in the process of being thoroughly renovated through the joint accounting project, in which the General Accounting Office is working with the cooperation of the Treasury Department and the Bureau of the Budget to accomplish one of the biggest managerial reforms in federal executive history. In all of these reforms, the responsible officials have taken the initiative and have enlisted the help of advisory committees, task forces, special consultants, management engineers, and professional associations.

There is still, of course, vast room for improvement at all levels, and day-by-day efforts of citizen associations and professional organizations of officials, working with the aid of an enlightened press, will be needed to achieve it. The fields of county administration and of judicial administration deserve and are receiving increased attention. The Commission on Organized Crime of the American Bar Association, of which the late Secretary of War, Robert P. Patterson, was chairman and Judge Morris Ploscowe is executive director, advocates that district attorneys and their staffs be taken entirely out of politics.

The improvement of our legislative bodies must also receive attention. With increased delegation of authority to executive bodies and the gradual elimination of patronage, the elected official will, I believe, be judged more and more by the quality of his performance. Many authorities are of the opinion that television will do even more than radio has done to improve the caliber of the people that the electorate chooses.

A great deal of attention has been given to mechanical devices for the improvement of Congress, such as better staffing, but none of the recent official or unofficial studies has given enough attention to the problems arising out of the fact that the job of being a congressman has become full-time. Short terms and poor compensation, the necessity for conducting increasingly expensive political campaigns every two years, the need to be in Washington almost all year round, and the difficulty of attending to one's private business—all of these factors have completely changed the original concept of the occasional tour of duty in Washington and the continued maintenance of a business or profession to which the congressman could go back. In the face of the demands which are on them, it is to their credit that congressmen and senators, by and large, have conducted themselves well. It is important, however, in the current investigations of scandals in the executive branch that we recognize the enormous pressures exerted on congressmen by constituents, which, in turn, sometimes become powerful pressures on appointed officials for special treatment in favored cases.

III

In the light of these perspectives, what can we do about the current scandals in government? How can we emphasize the positive trend in public administration and arrest the negative trend? I think the answer lies in two directions. One is to accelerate the rate of putting into practice the things we already know about the art and science of administration and the other is to accelerate the rate of practical research and invention on the points about which we are ignorant. This article does not pretend to exhaust the avenues of approach, but the story would not have an ending if I did not give one or two examples of what I mean.

The tone of the front office sets the tone of any administration, and I cannot refrain from criticizing from an administrative point of view some of the things that have happened in the front office in the Truman administration that have generally been attacked from a political point of view. I have served the government during the Truman administration as a consultant and as a member of the President's Advisory Committee on Management and have come to respect the many good things that have been done. But the tone in some sections of the front office has not been good.

After 150 years without help, the President of the United States in 1939 was given a White House Staff and an Executive Office to assist him, and they, like Caesar's wife, must be above suspicion. Even more important than the obvious improprieties which have been publicized is the danger that the top office will intervene in departmental operations. It is not enough that the Executive Office should set a tone and create an atmosphere for the departments and agencies to emulate in respect to honesty; the members of the Executive Office must lean over backward to be sure of "operating at the proper level," as Dean Paul Appleby puts it. The Executive Office and the White House staff cannot escape having political duties and responsibilities. But in the main these responsibilities must be confined to the policy field and the President must insist that his staff refrain from becoming centers of influence or back doors for special pressures in individual cases. Nor should the President have a gestapo at his disposal for gumshoe work or surveillance in the departments and agencies of the government. The fine work that this administration has done to foster management improvement and to decentralize responsibility must not be impaired by intrusions from above into day-to-day operations for which department and agency heads are responsible.

The Secretaries of the departments, in turn, have a duty to create an atmosphere which the bureaus and agencies should emulate and to avoid interfering in detailed operations. As the managerial heads of large operating staffs, they also need a system of managerial audits of the performance of the agencies under their supervision. Here again I do not advocate a kind of detective service to uncover irregularities that a good current accounting audit should uncover, but constructive managerial surveys, audits, and inspections carried on by a qualified staff at the department or large bureau level. Such surveys should come to the attention of the bureau chiefs and department heads and should serve to encourage good practices and to discourage poor practices.

I think it has been amply demonstrated that at the operating level the patronage system is obsolete and dangerous. A regional or field office is particularly susceptible to political pressures, and the revelations in the Bureau of Internal Revenue have once more indicated that even career people with civil service status are not immune to temptation when the collector or the deputy collector, who are their bosses, have political loyalties other than to their chief in Washington. Whatever the shortcomings of our present civil service system, recent events lead me to conclude that we need to extend civil service at the regional and field level.

Perhaps the time has come also for another special review of the status of lawyers in the government, both in Washington and in the field. It may be that we are ready for the forward steps of selecting United States attorneys and their staffs through a merit system and of giving them permanent status.

Better methods are needed in recruiting and training temporary and part-time executive and technical personnel, both for home assignments and for overseas missions. Hit-and-miss recruiting and inadequate briefing methods are now used for such personnel. Increasingly, attention is being given to the suggestion that a United States civilian reserve corps be established to secure and develop this kind of talent.

On the side of research and invention, I believe we need a thorough reconsideration of the training and indoctrination that government employees receive upon entrance into the public service and at critical periods in their careers. I know of no governmental in-service training programs that discusses the environment in which government operates or the points of ethics involved in standards of good government practice. The code of ethics that has been recommended by the Subcommittee on the Establishment of a Commission on Ethics in Government would be useful as a starting point, but each agency has special problems the answers to which are not so obvious as one might think, and even within an agency ethical problems vary among the various fields of work. I have seen many pure scientists and rigid executives enter the government service determined to "have nothing to do with politics or politicians," and I have seen many inexperienced persons enter the government service assuming that it was smart and accepted governmental practice to do favors for elected officials and their friends. New government officials are presumed to know the rules, and there is surprising lack of indoctrination on proper conduct. There are surprisingly few departmental conferences to develop or to teach desirable standards of conduct. Here there is room both for research and for invention. We need new methods to overcome these unrealistic assumptions, for the good government servant must have an unusual combination of flexibility and firmness. He must understand the principle of compromise that underlies the policy-making processes of a democratic state and appreciate that it does not involve a compromise of principle in the application of policy to individual cases.

Two quotations from recent pronouncements of men in high public office strike me as timely and appropriate in the consideration of the problems that I have discussed in this article.

The following paragraphs appeared in an article by Senator Paul H. Douglas of Illinois in the *New York Times Magazine* January 6, 1952. Senator Douglas is the chairman of the special Subcommittee on the Establishment of a Commission on Ethics in Government which issued the stimulating report *Ethical Standards in Government* in the autumn of 1951. This report is a landmark in the field—a fine basis for public discussion and for further study by legislators and administrators.

As we of the Eighty-second Congress meet to resume our work, we need to strengthen ourselves in the best of the qualities developed by those who have preceded us. We need the rugged honesty of old Bob La Follette; we need the courage to battle for the general welfare exemplified by the late George W. Norris, and perhaps we need most of all the ability shown by the late Arthur Vandenberg to put the national interest above partisan advantage.

We shall be meeting, moreover, in a Presidential year when partisan spirit runs high, and when men and parties contest for the high stakes of fame power and position. But we shall also be meeting in a period of grave national danger when the whole free world is exposed to the threat of attack by Soviet Russia and its allies.

It will be proper to discuss and to criticize policies parties and individuals. But it will be equally important for us not to carry this criticism to the point where it will destroy national unity or where it will split the country into bitter parties whose dislike for each other exceeds their common interest. For we must constantly remember that the interests and ideals which we all share together are more important than the issues upon which we differ. We are Americans before we are Republicans or Democrats, before we are Northerners, Westerners or Southerners, native-born or of foreign stock, liberals or conservatives, employers or employees. In all our debates, we have a solemn obligation to hold these truths in mind and to govern our tongues and our acts accordingly.

If we in Congress can fuse unity and determination with some degree of charity and mutual understanding, we can then make wise decisions on the main problems which face the nation. And in so doing, we can help to knit together in a greater degree of fellowship what is likely otherwise to be a bitterly divided nation.

*   *   *

Unquestionably we need a moral revival on all levels of our society so that our basic standards of integrity may not be undermined by the temptations of cheap materialism and meretricious success. But certain institutional changes such as those suggested by the Subcommittee on Ethical Standards in Government, of which I had the honor to be chairman, would reduce the temptations of the weak and furnish a guide for those who are somewhat perplexed and uncertain. Among these are: (1) the enactment of a code of ethical proprieties, violation of which on the part of a public official would be grounds for dismissal from office and on the part of interested private individuals the revocation of certain rights and privileges such as contracts, etc.; (2) the development of a more adequate system for limiting and reporting the total contributions to political campaigns and of having these costs more democratically shared; (3) the full disclosure of the incomes by amount and source of all important elected Federal officials and of administrative officials with a salary of $10,000 a year or more. We should be vigorous in exposing official wrongdoing wherever it manifests itself and in replacing guilty or unduly negligent public officials. But we shall not have adequately protected the public interest unless we also consider and adopt some such constructive steps permanently to improve our political and social behavior.

The following is an excerpt from President Truman's Annual Message to Congress on the State of the Union delivered before the two Houses on January 9, 1952.

The United States and the whole free world are passing through a period of grave danger. Every action you take here in Congress, and every action I take as President, must be measured against the test of whether it helps to meet that danger.

This will be a Presidential election year—the kind of year in which politics plays a larger part in our lives than usual. That is perfectly proper. But we have a great responsibility to conduct our political fights in a manner that does not harm the national interest.

... our shortcomings, as well as our progress, are watched from abroad. And there is one short-coming I want to speak plainly about.

Our kind of government above all others cannot tolerate dishonesty among its public servants.

Some dishonest people worm themselves into almost every human organization. It is all the more shocking, however, when they make their way into a government such as ours, which is based on the principle of justice for all. Such unworthy public servants must be weeded out. I intend to see to it that Federal employees who have been guilty of misconduct are punished for it. I also intend to see to it that the honest and hard-working majority of our Federal employees are protected against partisan slander and malicious attack.

I have already made some recommendations to the Congress to help accomplish these purposes. I intend to submit further recommendations to this end. I will welcome the co-operation of the Congress in this effort.

I also think that the Congress can do a great deal to strengthen confidence in our institutions by applying rigorous standards of moral integrity in its own operations—and by finding an effective way to control campaign expenditures— and by protecting the rights of individuals in Congressional investigations.

In closing this article, may I express the hope that other readers of this *Review* will feel encouraged to revise and to extend and to debate the points that I have discussed, and to increase their efforts in their communities and in their vocations to press on with the work of improving both the practice and the prestige of public administration in our country.

11

REFLECTIONS ON WATERGATE: LESSONS FOR PUBLIC ADMINISTRATION

James L. Sundquist
The Brookings Institution

If a great epidemic swept the land, the public health profession would look in upon itself, I suppose, and ask, "Where did we go wrong?" And if they didn't, someone else would look to them and ask, "Where did *you* go wrong?" It is now just as incumbent upon those in public administration to look upon themselves and ask that question, "Where did *we* go wrong?" For Watergate—whatever else one may call it—*was* public administration. It was the breakdown of public administration, to be sure, as an epidemic is a breakdown of public health. But it is the business of both professions to prevent pathology. The question, "Where did we go wrong?" needs to be asked very seriously—and answered.

It might not be so significant if Watergate, and all that that term conveys, were an isolated episode. But it followed right on the heels of another breakdown, which is called Vietnam. What follows is the product of reflection on not just one of those but both. Together, they have created a crisis of confidence in the entire system. Never—at least never during the period that polls have been taken on the subject—has the public respect for government, and the people in it, been so low.

So, what *did* go wrong? We start from the fact that what has brought the country to this low state is the way in which presidential power has been used—or abused, or misused, whichever one prefers. In the one case a President got the nation deeply mired in a war that the people did not know they were getting into, that the Congress did not consciously authorize, that turned out to be a ghastly mistake in almost everybody's view—and then kept the country there long after it wanted only to get out. And in the other case, those who exercised presidential authority did all manner of things—that need not be recited here—to misuse the agencies of government for partisan ends and bring disgrace upon a President, and a party, and a whole governmental system.

Public Administration Has Glorified the Presidency

And what did the profession of public administration have to do with that? Quite a bit, I think. The profession has devoted 40 years to aggrandizing presidential power. It has consistently sought—and contributed in no small measure to the consequence—to strengthen the President at the expense of all the other elements that make up the governmental system. Or, to put it in a more invidious way, to undermine the checks and balances that have existed in the American system—put there partly by accident and partly by design for the specific purpose of keeping the President from gaining too much power.

Sometimes we in public administration repeated Lord Acton's phrase, "Power tends to corrupt, and absolute power corrupts absolutely," but we didn't really believe it. Instead, we believed Louis Brownlow when he said, "during the whole history of the thirty-two Presidents, not one has been recreant to his high trust—none has used his power to aggrandize himself at the expense of our settled institutions."[1] And that may have been true enough when it was said—in 1947.

The literature of public administration is shot through with the doctrine of the strong executive (influenced, no doubt, by the literature from business administration, from which so many of its early theses were taken). Indeed, until very recently, there was not even any rival doctrine. One can reread the works written before the late 1960s by the men who have represented the mainstream of thinking in the profession—the men who, for example, like Brownlow, have been presidents of the American Society for Public Administration—and find not so much as one dissenting word. Every writer was for a strong presidency. Absolutely nobody was for a weak one.

In his pioneering article of the 1930s. "Notes on the Theory of Organization," for instance, Luther Gulick put forward the doctrine of the strong executive categorically and confidently. "Coordination," said Gulick, is "mandatory," and one of the two ways coordination is achieved is "by orders of superiors to subordinates, reaching from the top to the bottom of the entire enterprise." "Organization requires . . . a system of authority," he goes on, and that "requires . . . a single directing executive authority."[2]

The Brownlow Committee on Administrative Management, of which Gulick was a member, applied that doctrine to the Executive Branch of the United States government. Its object was to make the President the "single directing executive authority" by giving him in an Executive Office of the President the staff assistance he needed for that purpose. The plan was adopted, the office created, and then those who sought to aggrandize the President could pursue their mission from the inside. William Carey, a member of the Executive Office staff almost from its beginning, wrote of that mission a generation later in words Gulick would have approved: the object of a presidential staff was to help the President attain "command and control."[3]

It did this in many ways, through protection and development of the functions assigned the office, particularly those of budgeting, legislative clearance, and the preparation of government reorganization plans. The presidential staff constantly asserted the President's prerogatives in his struggles with the Congress, on matters that the Nixon Administration has now carried to the ultimate, like impoundment of funds and the doctrine of executive privilege. Not least important were the reorganization plans. Power was systematically taken from bureau chiefs and placed in department heads, for the latter were the President's men, and whatever strengthened the President's men enhanced the President's own control. One of the two criteria by which any reorganization plan should be judged, wrote Herbert Emmerich, was whether "the ability of the President to see that the laws are faithfully executed" was "strengthened."[4]

I do not suggest that this was any kind of sinister conspiracy. Of course, in aggrandizing the President, public administration did aggrandize itself. But there is nothing reprehensible about that. To be a good member of the public administration profession, one must love and respect administration just as a good lawyer reveres the law or a good doctor venerates the practice of medicine. One has to believe in one's own calling: otherwise, who in the world would believe in it? But administration is what the executive does. So our reverence, our veneration, went to the Executive Branch: and particularly to the President as the chief of that branch, and it was our purpose in life, bred into us from our earliest days in graduate school, to advance our professional ideals by aggrandizing him.

And all the while we forgot Lord Acton. We forgot that the power to do great good is also the power to do great harm. If we strengthen the presidency for *our* purposes—all of them noble, of course, we will strengthen it also for the purposes of *others* whose ends may turn out, in our eyes if not in theirs, to be less than noble.

And So Has Political Science

If the public administration fraternity was bound by its very nature to exalt presidential power, could one look to the political scientists to take a broader view? The answer is no; they, too, were part of the cult of the executive. Most leading political scientists since the 1930s, after all, have been liberals, believers in strong government; if they weren't, they probably wouldn't have been drawn into political science in the first place. But, more, they were Franklin Roosevelt, New Deal liberals. They had lived through the 1930s, and so they could have no doubt whatever it was a strong and activist President, and no one else, who had rescued the country from despair and set it right again. The other branches of government, at best, fell in behind the presidential leadership or, at worst, obstructed. Roosevelt took an honored place in the galaxy of national heroes, so many of whom, as it happens, were also strong Presidents—from Washington and Jackson and Lincoln in the last century to Theodore Roosevelt and Woodrow Wilson in this one. After the war, Harry Truman saved Europe from communism. The liberals chafed during the Eisenhower hiatus; but then came Kennedy and Johnson, and the country was back in the pattern of activist Presidents carrying the banner for liberal causes—that is, until things went sour in Vietnam.

Thomas Cronin has drawn a composite picture of the presidency as it is presented in standard political science textbooks. Here are some phrases that Cronin lifted from those works: The presidency is "the great engine of democracy," the "American people's one authentic trumpet," "The central instrument of democracy," a "glittering mountain peak," "the chief architect of the nation's public policy," "he symbolizes the people [and] also runs their government," "Presidential government is a superb planning institution," "He is . . . a kind of magnificent lion who can roam widely and do great deeds."[5]

The cult of the executive reached its zenith, perhaps, with publication of Richard Neustadt's influential book, *Presidential Power.* Neustadt wrote that book with the explicit purpose, he explains in the preface, of teaching activist Presidents about "personal power . . . how to get it, how to keep it, how to use it." A President seeking to "maximize his power" energized the government, said Neustadt. What is good for the President, he concluded, is therefore good for the country.[6]

Overlooked: The Potential for Abuse

In all of this, there is surprisingly little concern about the potential for abuse of all that power. The public administration literature all but ignores the possibility. Paul Appleby, after praising the President as "the symbol of all the government's executive power," simply assures us that "through

Congress, and through elections, it is a power popularly controlled."[7] Emmerich strikes a similar note: "The centrifugal forces in our society are so strong and the checks and balances in our governmental system so powerful that we are in danger not of giving too much power to the President but of having many conflicting, mutually-cancelling centers of power that will defeat the general interest."[8] The political scientists had sounded no warnings either. Neustadt worries only about the non-use, not about the use, of presidential power. Cronin summarizes the theme of all the textbooks as one of simple faith: "whoever is in the White House [will turn out to be] the right man."

But the two Presidents last elected to that office were subsequently adjudged by overwhelming popular majorities to have been the wrong men, the public opinion polls make clear. Now, as one looks back on history, one can reach the same verdict on other Presidents as well. The New Deal years bring to mind not just Franklin Roosevelt but also Herbert Hoover— honorable, well-motivated, unlucky, but surely the wrong man to have in the White House for those long years between October 1929 and March 1933.

"Checks and Balances" Turn Out Not to Be There After All

What of Paul Appleby's assurance that through the Congress and elections presidential power is controlled? And Emmerich's similar reliance upon the checks and balances of our governmental system?

We can dispose of elections simply: Yes, they are a control, but only when they happen. Unlike many other democratic countries, the United States votes only by the calendar. The Johnson adventure in Vietnam ran for more than three years before the people could call him to account. Now, assuming that impeachment fails, the country will be constrained to limp along with a government discredited by scandal for almost four full years. Hoover was useless as a national leader for longer than three years. Elections as an ultimate check, yes. As a timely check when desperately needed to restore presidential leadership, no.

And the Congress? We learn now that the checks and balances are really not there, after all. Their existence has been mostly a myth. All it took was a couple of Presidents back to back, with the temperament of monarchs, determined to press their powers to the full, with a penchant for secrecy, to demonstrate that.

We get the idea that the checks are checking and the balances balancing because almost every day's newspaper tells us how the President and the Congress are in one conflict or another, each branch of government blocking and stalemating the other. But the effective stalemating is primarily in one field of governmental action—legislation. There Emmerich is quite right in talking about "mutually-cancelling centers of power."

The legislative power *is* divided, with each branch given a veto over the other.

But not so the executive power. The Constitution gives the Congress no role in the execution of laws once they are enacted—save for the power in the Senate to ratify treaties (and Presidents have learned that if agreements with other nations are embodied in documents other than treaties this senatorial check can be evaded). Beyond that, executive power is assigned wholly to a single branch of government—the Executive Branch. The Congress has no right to share in the executive power, or even any right to be consulted.

That does not mean that the Congress does not find ways of "horning in," but it does so with very blunt and indirect instruments. Sometimes, if the Congress does not like the way the President is executing the laws, it can deal directly with the matter, by passing new legislation to make its intent clear. But the President can veto that kind of legislation and, if upheld by one-third plus one of either house—and normally he can expect to have at least that much support from members of his own party alone—he can go on doing as he pleases. Moreover, this recourse is of no avail at all if the intent of the Congress was clear all along—which seems to be the case most of the time—and the President is just choosing to ignore it. Take, for instance, the President's recent attempt to liquidate the Office of Economic Opportunity in open defiance of the law and of the clear intent of Congress. There would not have been much point for the Congress to pass still another law reiterating that intent.

The vaunted power of the purse is similarly limited. It can be used directly only to prevent, but not to compel, executive action. It might have been used to force an earlier end to the war in Vietnam, for instance; but if the problem is, say, the use of the FBI or the Internal Revenue Service by a President against his political enemies, the Congress cannot get at that matter by cutting the budgets for those agencies. That would only mean that more criminals would run loose and more tax evaders would go undiscovered.

The power of the Senate to confirm presidential appointees is even more ineffectual. At the time an appointee comes up for confirmation, the Senate rarely knows what kind of an administrator he is going to be and what commitment it needs to extract from him. One need only point to the number of Watergate figures who had been confirmed easily by senators who could not know how the appointees were going to behave in circumstances that had not arisen and could not be foreseen.

Finally, there is the general right of the Congress to inquire and to expose—the congressional investigation. Here the Congress can be frustrated, initially, by the exercise of executive privilege to withhold information, even if that turns out to be a not unlimited right. But when the Congress does obtain the information it wants about what the executive is doing, it cannot order him to change his ways. It can heckle, entreat, bulldoze, and threaten, but it cannot tell him what to do. A congressional investigation is essentially an appeal to public opinion, which a determined or obsessive President can ignore. In the end, the President's responsibility under the Constitution for the execution of the laws remains exclusive.

So if the Congress wants to restrain the President, what it is compelled to do most of the time is resort to a kind of blackmail: The members who are aggrieved threaten to use against the President the powers they *do* share with him—the legislative powers, including the power of the purse. Sometimes this works, but more often it does not, because the President's position is much the stronger one. In the first place, threats run both ways. The President can bring senators and congressmen into line by using *his* powers against *them*—by granting or withholding all kinds of favors, in appointments, projects, legislative bargaining, and all the rest. In the second place, the Congress is not organized to bargain effectively with the President. The 535 members are divided into two houses, two parties, and a multiplicity of committees and subcommittees; they have no way of arriving at a common strategy to combat a monolithic Executive Branch, and they have not delegated to their leaders the responsibility to strike deals on their behalf.

That leaves the courts. True, the judiciary provides a check of sorts, if a case can be brought (Vietnam, for instance, was not litigable), if executive secrecy can be breached—which, as has been demonstrated, is not easy—and if retribution is the only object. But if the basic need is institutional mechanisms that will *prevent* the damage from occurring in the first place—that will forestall the abuses of power that cause the loss of confidence of the people in their government—then putting people in jail long after the damage has been done is not quite good enough. Moreover, the legal processes only cover outright violations of the law. There is a wide range of circumstances where presidential power can be used legally enough but unwisely, from simple mistakes to egregious folly. The courts are useless here. And the same limitations apply also to that ultimate remedy—impeachment—which is a judicial-type process based upon a concept of the illegal use of power.

The checks and balances, such as they are, operate either long *before* the fact, in the case of the confirmation power, or else *after* the fact—after the damage has been done. None of them operate *during* the fact, while the executive power is being used—and abused—which is the crucial time if the damage is to be prevented. They can be marginally improved here and there within our present constitutional system—the War Powers Act was one such improvement—but basically they are barriers to presidential power made of very thin stuff.

The Internal Checks: Cabinet and Bureaucracy

What of checks and balances provided internally within the Executive Branch? Time was that the cabinet meant something. During the first century of the Republic, the United States had cabinets patterned on the British model. Presidents chose as department heads men who represented a broad spectrum of the party's top leadership—prominent members of the Congress, party leaders from the largest states, major rivals for the presidential nomination, all with independent political strength and power bases. So men of the stature of Hamilton and Webster, Clay and Calhoun, Seward and Sherman and Bryan, sat in presidential cabinets. And they were used as a consultative body. Presidents made decisions in cabinet, rather like kings-in-council.

But Presidents have now discovered, in these days of direct communication between them and the people, that their political strength is highly personal. It is not compounded from the strength of other party leaders assembled in a cabinet. That being the case, they can avoid the pain of surrounding themselves with department heads who have independent sources of political strength. Such men or women can be defiant, and cause trouble; they have to be conciliated, because if they resign they can do so with a splash. Far better, Presidents have learned to appoint nameless and faceless men, who are wholly dependent upon the President who gave them what stature they can claim. They can be counted on not to defy the President—or, if by any chance they do and he is forced to fire them, their departure will go unnoticed and unregretted. John Ehrlichman described the modern version of the ideal cabinet member shortly after the Miami convention in 1972; "The Cabinet officers must be tied closely to the chief executive, or to put it in extreme terms; when he says jump, they only ask how high."[9] A cabinet so composed would hardly be worth much as a collective consultative body to check the presidential judgment—which may be one reason that no President since Eisenhower has even tried to use his cabinet that way.

Finally, these days, public administrators are taking some considerable pride that the bureaucracy has acted as a check upon the President. Career civil servants have been tarnished very little by Watergate, and in the FBI and the Criminal Division, the IRS, and the CIA, they did act as a restraint upon the President—which is why the "plumbers" were forced to operate directly out of the White House. But those who talk about encouraging bureaucratic restraints upon Presidents as a kind of general principle are surely grasping at the wrong straw. Bureaucratic foot-dragging may save the Republic from unwise or illegal conduct, now and then, but in the normal course the bureaucracy simply has to be effectively subordinated. A few questions should settle any doubts: Should the military establish its own war policies and conduct its own operations, outside of civilian control? Should the FBI make its own policies about wiretapping and privacy? Should the foreign service have its own foreign policy, whether or not that is in accord with the policy of the President and the Secretary of State? The answers are obvious. If a career civil servant objects to presidential policies, he may argue his case as forcefully as he wishes, but if the decision goes against him he has the choice to either accept it or resign. If he resigns, he can take his case to the public to get the decision changed, but if he stays he has no right to obstruct, or countermand by indirection, his superiors' policy. The object must not be to encourage the defiance of political decisions by those whose job it is to execute them, but rather to take steps to get better political decisions made in the first place.

The Safeguard of Plural Decision Making

Here is where public administration as a profession, as a branch of the social sciences, should take a careful look at other institutions. That examination would at once reveal a basic principle of institutional design that has been applied all but universally in the English-speaking world: the principle that major decisions shall be made not by one man acting alone but by a collective body of some kind. I say "all but" because of that great and glaring exception, the Executive Branch of the United States government (as well as the executive branches of the state governments and some city governments that are patterned after it). Legislatures are all plural bodies. So are the higher courts, and juries. So are regulatory commissions. In corporations and labor unions and voluntary service organizations the ultimate authority is in plural boards of directors, who select and supervise the managers. Likewise the universities and the public schools, as well as most local governments—particularly those whose form of government is the one that reformers and public administrators designed and most admire, the council-manager form. In political parties the authority is in conventions and committees. That is true of most churches that took form in the English-speaking world, Indeed, in the entire institutional structure, public and private, it is difficult to find an organization of any size or consequence that is not subject to the direct control of a plural body—except, to repeat, the executive branches of the national and state governments and some cities.

In other English-speaking countries, even those exceptions do not exist. Executive authority there rests not in lone individuals but in plural cabinets. That is largely true in non-English-speaking democracies as well.

The principle is often violated, of course. In many organizations where authority is formally vested in a plural body—notable in private organizations, such as corporations and labor unions—the executive is able to dominate the organization, even to the point of controlling the selection of members of the governing body. But this is a corruption, commonly recognized as such when it occurs. The *form* of organization is designed to protect against such executive bossism, and the basic right of the governing body to impose its will on the executive remains unimpaired—and is even enforceable in the courts. It is the model, not necessarily its application in every instance, that embodies the folk wisdom evolved over centuries of experience with human organization.

To put power in one man, societies have learned over and over again, is inherently dangerous. A single man may be erratic or impulsive or obsessive in his judgments. He may be arbitrary and unfair. He may be incompetent, a bungler. He may be lazy, or negligent, or corrupt. He may pervert the ends of the organization for his own benefit, whether that be to gain money or punish enemies or reward friends or simply to perpetuate himself and his followers in office.

And so, in almost every organization, a restraint of collective decision making has been forced upon the leader. He is made subordinate to, or required to act as a member of, a plural body of some kind. It may be called by many names—commission, council, board, committee, Senate, House, cabinet—but the important thing is that its members have a degree of independence from the leader. Then if the leader is impulsive, cooler heads can prevail. If he is unfair or arbitrary, his colleagues can refuse to go along. If his policies are unwise, they can be corrected. If he is negligent, he can be goaded. If his tendency is to corrupt the system, he can be watched and checked. If he tries to pervert its purposes for his own ends, he can be overruled.

Plural decision making has its own drawbacks, obviously. It can mean delay and caution and conservatism. But the folk wisdom, over the centuries, has weighed the disadvantages against the merits and given its verdict: the plural body, not the single leader, is better to be trusted.

Yet in the case of this one great office—the presidency—the office with the greatest consequences for good or ill in all our lives—the folk wisdom has been violated. Enormous power is in a single man, unrestrained by any requirement of collective decision making. The Founding Fathers, interestingly enough, were not unanimous on that. A significant minority in the Constitutional Convention desired a plural executive, a three-man presidency, but they were outvoted, seven states to three, by those who argued that, in Luther Gulick's later words, a hierarchical organization requires "a single directing executive authority." So now the people are left to worry about what Arthur Schlesinger, Jr., calls "the imperial presidency" or "the runaway presidency" or "the revolutionary presidency," like so many Frankensteins wondering what this monster they have created—with all the same innocent enthusiasm of Baron Frankenstein—will do next. So what can be done?

One school of thought says, nothing much has to be done. The nation will have learned great lessons from Vietnam and Watergate. No President for a long time will dare to embark on any such headstrong foreign adventures as Lyndon Johnson did. No President will be so careless in choosing subordinates as Richard Nixon was, or so lax in supervising them. The elements of the bureaucracy that stood up well against the presidency will stand up even better next time. Besides, any remedy might make things a good deal worse, because—to put the shoe on the other foot—any measure that restrains the President's power to do bad things will also restrain his power to do good things. In other words, those who sought to aggrandize the power of the President were right all along. The nation does need a strong President, for all of the reasons given by public administrators and political scientists for 40 years. Those who believe in liberal causes should not let themselves be led by the clamor of the moment to impair the instrument that they correctly and wisely saw was necessary for their purposes. Clean the system up a bit around the edges, but don't attempt any fundamental constitutional change.

This seems to me to leave entirely too much to luck. There is so much risk—given our selection system—of putting the wrong man in the White House that I would like to find some means of forcing upon our chief executive some of the restraints of collective decision making that in this country we routinely insist upon in lesser organizations. There is something about the White House, as George Reedy has suggested, that can bring out latent traits of megalomania in any human being who finds himself there. And let's face it: it is not inconceivable that a President could become mentally or emotionally unstable while in office—as has happened to the heads of other governments—yet not be removable for disability nor guilty of impeachable crime.

Dismantle Presidential Power?

Another school of thought looks at all that concentrated power and sees the answer in taking some of it away. All kinds of proposals are heard: Give power back to the Congress, elect the key members of the cabinet, take certain sensitive agencies such as the Department of Justice out of the Executive Branch, limit by law the size of the White House staff, and so on. A few of these proposals—a permanent independent prosecutor, for instance—may have merit but, generally speaking, most of these proposals seem to move in the wrong direction. For, no matter how doubtful it may seem at the moment, the public administration fraternity *has* been right all along in its arguments for a powerful presidency. Governmental functions do need to be directed and coordinated from a single point of leadership. There does need to be "command and control," in Carey's words, so that within limits set by law there can be worked out a coordinated economic policy, a military policy and a foreign policy and a food policy consistent with one another, a coordinated system of intergovernmental relations, and all the rest. If the functions of the Executive Branch were to be scattered among persons of independent authority, any chance of the government's making sense with what it tried to do would be lost, and the cry would immediately arise: Give the President the authority to make order out of this shambles. Indeed, a strong case can be made for giving some additional powers to the President—for instance, clear control over the personnel management functions of the Civil Service Commission (as distinct from its inspection and policing functions) and over the activities of the Federal Reserve Board, which now has the authority to pursue a monetary policy that can cancel the President's fiscal policy and thus prevent the government from having any effective economic policy at all, and the power to raise and lower tax rates, within limits, for fiscal policy purposes. In short, there is no substitute for a powerful presidency in the complex modern world, for all the reasons public administrators have given from Gulick and Brownlow to the present time.

Or Try to Pluralize the Exercise of Power?

But—and this is all-important—a powerful presidency under equally powerful control. That suggests looking for the answer in a third direction. Instead of trying to reduce the presidential power, can a way be found to heed the folk wisdom of the ages by pluralizing that power in its exercise? In other words, by establishing institutions that would force the President into some kind of collective process in making major national decisions.

Where are the people of independent stature with whom the President could be forced to consult? Not the cabinet, obviously, or any other group of Executive Branch subordinates; a President cannot be required to appoint strong men to the Executive Branch, or permit them to restrain him. The only people around, apart from the President and Vice President, who are elected, and hence who have any independent power base at all, are the members of Congress. But to force the President into a closer relationship with the Congress—which, as a practical matter, would have to mean the leaders of the Congress—would clearly require some additional sanctions in the hands of the Legislative Branch, so that he could not just ignore its leaders or defy them, as he does now.

I think that sanction has to take the form of a simpler way of removing Presidents. That object would serve a double purpose.

First, it is a necessary end in itself, in view of the limitations of the courts and of the impeachment process. It does not take high crimes or misdemeanors to destroy the capacity of a President to lead and inspire and unify the country, as he must. If one starts from the proposition that the United States needs at all times an effective government, that it cannot afford to wait for as long as three years or more if its President loses his ability to lead and govern, then one has to conclude that the present removal process is too limited.

Second, it would tend to impose upon the President, to some degree, the restraint of collective decision making. If the Congress had a greater discretion in removing Presidents, he would have to keep its confidence. And to keep its confidence, he would have to take its leaders into his. He could not hide from them essential information. He could not abuse his powers and then defy them to do anything about it. He would have to make sure, through consultation in advance, that major decisions met with their concurrence.

The problem is to strike exactly the right balance in making presidential removal easier. The presidency obviously should not be destabilized too much. If the opposition party has a majority in the Congress, which is so often the case, it should not be able to turn out a President for trivial or partisan reasons. Perhaps the British system comes closest to the model: there, prime ministers normally serve their full five-year term (assuming that the governing party has a clear parliamentary majority, which it usually has), but when a prime minister botches his job and so loses the confidence of the country—and hence of the House of Commons and its governing majority—the majority does have means to force him out and get the country off to a fresh start under a leader who can lead and a government that can govern. So when prime ministers can no longer govern, they step—or are pushed—aside, as Neville Chamberlain gave way to Winston Churchill after Narvik, and Anthony Eden to Harold Macmillan after Suez. In the American system, a Neville Chamberlain would hold onto his office as a kind of property right even if, in the judgment of the country, he had no capacity to lead the people in time of peril.

Alternative Constitutional Amendments

Several types of constitutional amendments to ease the removal process have been suggested. One idea is just to broaden the impeachment clause—by adding after the phrase "high crimes and misdemeanors" five little words, "Or for any other reason." Removal would then become a political rather than a juridical type of action, taken through a "no confidence" vote, as in the parliamentary countries. But under this amendment two-thirds of the Senate would still be required to remove the chief executive, and that seems to embody the wrong principle. To govern effectively, a President needs to sustain the confidence of the majority of the country and of the legislature, not just a one-third-plus-one minority.

A proposal by Congressman Bingham runs into the same objection. He would empower the Congress by law to call a new presidential election at any time. This is somewhat like the recall provisions of some state constitutions, except there the recall is initiated by petition of a specified number of voters. But the Bingham proposal to act by statute would require a two-thirds vote of both houses, in order to override the inevitable presidential veto.

Congressman Reuss has tried to meet the objection to the two-thirds requirement by providing for a "no confidence" removal by 60 per cent of both houses. But that still violates the majority principle while at the same time probably making removal too easy. Sometimes the opposition party in the Congress by itself has a 60 per cent majority.

My favorite approach, therefore, is this: Empower Congress to act by a simple majority to remove the President and call a new election. But, to deter the Congress from acting from trivial or fractious causes, require that the Congress upon removing the President itself be dissolved and all its members forced to face a new election. They would have to take their decision, in effect, to a referendum. That would surely be a very great restraint upon the exercise of the congressional prerogative. Those who know the Senate have difficulty visualizing any circumstance in which its members would voluntarily subject themselves to an election when they did not have to. But perhaps that strikes the right balance. A procedure for removing incompetent or unstable or discredited Presidents would be available to a national majority as expressed through its representatives—which is not now the case, at grave risk to the nation—but the process would be sufficiently unattractive to assure that it would be used only when absolutely, and incontrovertibly, necessary, and when public support was overwhelming.

Perhaps better ideas will be heard as this whole problem is considered. The important thing is that the country begin talking seriously about what should be done about the presidency—about how that awesome concentration of power can somehow be hedged in with the kind of restraints that our society tries to make sure exist in every other lesser organization.

Notes

1. *The President and the Presidency* (Chicago: Public Administration Service, 1949), a compilation of lectures given in 1947.

2. Luther Gulick and L. Urwick (eds.), *Papers on the Science of Administration* (New York: Institute of Public Administration, 1937), pp. 6–7.

3. William D. Carey, "Presidential Staffing in the Sixties and Seventies," *Public Administration Review*, Vol. 29, No. 5 (September/October 1969).

4. *Essays on Federal Reorganization* (University, Ala.: University of Alabama Press, 1950), p. 8.

5. "The Textbook Presidency and Political Science," paper prepared for delivery at the annual meeting of the American Political Science Association, 1970.

6. *Presidential Power* (New York: John Wiley and Sons, 1960), pp. vii, 181–185.

7. *Big Democracy* (New York: Knopf, 1945), p. 124.

8. *Essays on Federal Reorganization, op cit.*, p. 147.

9. Quoted by Harold Seidman in National Academy of Public Administration, Preliminary Papers, Conference on the Institutional Presidency, March 1974, p. 40.

12

ADMINISTRATIVE CORRUPTION

Gerald E. Caiden and Naomi J. Caiden
University of Southern California

The increased visibility of administrative corruption has become a persistent and disturbing feature of our times. Almost every issue of the daily press brings, it seems, fresh examples of allegedly corrupt behavior on the part of responsible public and private figures. This growing prominence of corruption has coincided with increased academic interest in a subject long deemed inappropriate for serious research, and still not regarded as a respectable topic for study in certain circles. Fortunately, obvious objections to research into corruption—problems of measurement, difficulties of access, bias, and evaluation—have been largely attenuated, if not overcome. It is accepted now that it is the responsibility of social scientists to choose for their research subjects which touch on or embrace problems central to human society, and not merely those convenient to the tools they have to hand.

For those interested in corruption as a social phenomenon, the traditional approach, which treated it in a moralistic manner, was inappropriate. Studies of corruption were vague as to definition, condemned it *a priori,* and looked for explanations in individual behavior. Social scientists demanded precise definitions, objectivity, and some relationship between the workings of society and the existence of corruption. Thus was born a "revisionist" approach (6), which defined corruption in terms of divergence from a specific norm of accepted behavior, explained its existence by reference to social mores and deficiencies in economic and political systems, and enumerated conditions in which it might elicit approval rather than condemnation. Although this approach contains much that is appealing, and has paved the way to more serious study of the problem of administrative corruption by non-revisionists (3) (26) (27) (33), careful examination of its assumptions and conclusions reveals several misconceptions. These arise mainly because, although the revisionists deal with social variables, they still think of corrupt behavior in individual terms without recognizing the existence of systemic corruption.

The Revisionist Approach

Until recently corruption was treated in a moralistic manner. Its cause was seen as the gaining of positions of power and trust by evil and dishonest men. The solution was to "turn the rascals out." Corruption was therefore incidental to the working of society which might be safeguarded by appropriate laws and exhortations. But even as the muckrakers did their work of uncovering graft and corruption in the turn-of-the-century United States, suspicion was growing that these phenomena did not exist in isolation. The arch-muckraker, Lincoln Steffens himself, late in his career drew attention to the role of incentives fostering corruption in the private enterprise society, by providing "ordinary men" with "extraordinary temptations" (30).

A similar disquiet, and concern for corruption as rooted in the mores and institutions of society, stimulated a rejection of moralistic and individualistic explanations by students of comparative administration. As interest grew in non-Western systems of government and in the workings of development programs, those concerned with international aid and development encountered apparent and blatant corrupt administrative practices in poor countries. It was natural to ask "Why do certain societies at particular times appear especially prone to corruption?" Rejecting the answer of comparative moral virtue as somewhat out of keeping with the premises of the comparative administration movement, the revisionists were led to the view that corruption stemmed from norms of polities and administration which differed from those of the West, and might even fulfil political, administrative, and economic needs better than the public ethic fostered by aid officials. Corruption was not incidental but structural: it could therefore be removed from the realm of the moral (and unspeakable) to the neutral (and researchable).

The first problem was "what is corruption?" Definitions have been classified into three types (20): public interest, public duty, and market centered. The first, which has largely been rejected by the revisionists, regards corruption as arising:

whenever a powerholder . . . i.e., a responsible functionary or office holder, is by monetary or other rewards not legally provided for, induced to take an action which favors whoever provides the rewards, and thereby does damage to the public and its interests (17).

Such definition pre-judges the result of corruption, is imprecise (as the meaning of public interest is open to different interpretations), and may preclude recognition of corruption until after the event only when the public interest can be clarified and judged.

The second type of definition, public duty, appears more promising. Though a number of variations exist (3) (5) (21) (24) (26), the basic idea is conveyed by the most often used definition:

> . . . behavior which deviates from the formal duties of a public role because of private-regarding (personal, close family, private clique) pecuniary or status gains; or violates rules against the exercise of certain types of private-regarding influence (28).

As long as no confusion exists regarding the standard from which corrupt practices diverge, i.e., the nature of public duty, corruption may clearly be defined and recognized. Once, however, the public standard is challenged, or regarded as relative to circumstances, then considerable ambiguity enters. Who sets the standard to say what behavior is acceptable and what corrupt? What is *undue* influence? What is *misuse* of authority? What is public *irresponsibility?* If there is no accepted public standard, or if the standards of public office and public duty are regarded as foreign importations inapplicable in given conditions, is there then innocence of corruption (20)? In short, "Are ideas and theories offered by Western scholars about the state of corruption in the developing nations valid in the light of the divergent social norms that govern the conduct of public office in the West and those in the transitional societies of Asia" (19)?

The issue is one of conflict of values. Against the Western, impersonal, and universalistic norms of bureaucracy are set the values of kinship and reciprocity. Are these to be denied validity, and the public servant who fulfils their expectations to be considered as corrupt? After all,

> . . . in a given society, various kinds of norms operate, some congruent, others inconsistent with one another. Legal norms may conflict with moral, religious and cultural norms, so that a sample of behavior defined as illegal may be acceptable using cultural standards (19).

In retaining a residual definition of corruption, but rejecting the specific substantive standard to which it pertains, the revisionists have dissolved corruption. In their conception, corruption is by definition exceptional, the departure from the normal ways of doing business: corruption cannot itself be the norm. Once corruption, in other words, becomes sufficiently widespread as to constitute a normal rather than an exceptional mode of behavior, it ceases to exist.

Analysis is taken beyond public ethics by market-oriented types of definition, such as "Corruption involves a shift from a mandatory pricing model to a free-market model" (31), or "Corruption is an extra-legal institution used by individuals or groups to gain influence over the actions of the bureaucracy" (23). Unlike the public duty-type definitions, there is no doubt as to what "public" ways of doing things represent. It is in the former case a "centralized allocative mechanism" and in the latter a stipulated institutionalized decision-making process. But again, the standard is purely relative, since these institutions are regarded as so inadequate to fulfill the demands placed upon them that corruption provides an alternative means of allocation or of access to decision making. Once again corruption is legitimized in terms of its prevalence and of faulty working of Western-style norms and institutions.

These definitions provide the under-pinning for explanations of why corruption is allegedly more prevalent in certain places, notably poor countries. The "cultural" explanation starts from the assumption that in "developing" countries there exists a gap between law (as imposed Western and alien standards) and accepted informal social norms (sanctioned by prevailing social ethics), i.e., there is a divergence between the attitudes, aims, and methods of the government of a country and those of the society in which they operate (24). The individual who assumes a public role is:

> ... torn between two social forces operating in his world. Because of the rational, impersonal and universalistic norms of the bureaucracy, he must accept that a public office is a public trust, not a personal domain. He must therefore commit himself to serve the national and community's need ahead of his personal and family interests. But there, too, are strong kinship bonds which compel him to look after the needs not only of the immediate members of his family but even those of his extended family system, otherwise he violates a stronger norm which is deeply rooted in the personalistic and familistic outlooks which characterize traditional cultural values. As he imbibes Weberian ideas in school, including possible post-graduate studies abroad, he faces a conflict in regard to his duties to his family and his kin, some of whom may have helped him bear the cost of an expensive education (19).

In the resulting role conflict, the Weberian, bureaucratic role is only one open to the official, and not necessarily the most compelling (13). So-called corruption appears to be consistent with customs and traditions, whereas the laws and ethics that make it illegal and immoral are alien, imported, or super-imposed (1). It is also suggested that traditional values pre-dispose toward corruption, which in turn eases the gap between citizen and government (29). A variation on this theme is the view that corruption is "dislocated" behavior resulting from a lag in the value system of the community in relation to institutional change (32).

The "cultural" explanation blurs into considerations of governmental capacity, which have two major emphases. The first of these might be called "economic," since it relates to the government's inability to provide the services demanded of it. The centralized allocative mechanism breaks down because of disequilibrium between supply and demand, and the market reasserts itself (31). In poor countries the situation is aggravated by cultural factors, rising expectations and demands, the predominance of government as a supplier of resources, and lack of alternatives. Similarly, one can refer to the inability of morally approved structures to fulfill essential social functions (25).

The "political" aspect of the explanation relates corruption to access to power and political institutionalization. Corruption is seen as primarily related to inadequate political channels, and as such simply a special case of political influence (29). Again, poor countries are good candidates for corruption because of the disproportionate impact of government on society, bureaucratic dominance, a weak sense of nation with a high value placed on kinship, and a marked gap between citizen and government. There is a heavy burden for political institutions to carry in terms of capacity and legitimacy, and corruption fills the gap. Corruption is the equivalent of pressure group influence in more politically developed countries, but taking place after the passage of legislation rather than prior to its passage because of factors such as erratic administration or public discrimination against minorities (29). Similarly corruption is regarded as the result of modernization in the absence of political institutionalization (21). Reference is made to the disruptive effects of changes in values (e.g., ascription to achievement; acceptance of public role), the creation of new sources of wealth and power, the expansion of governmental functions and regulation, and the lack of strong political parties. Corruption has much the same function as violence (and acts as an alternative). Its emergence is inversely related to the degree of social stratification in the society. The lack of opportunities outside government leads to the use of public office to build private fortunes, and foreign business activities tend to encourage local corruption (29).

As these explanations have strong functional overtones, they stress the positive effects of corruption. Since attention is on "developing" countries, the main issue raised is the probable effect of corruption on economic, political, and, to a lesser extent, administrative, development. On the whole, considerations relating to administrative development are the most pessimistic, for obvious reasons, since corruption undermines bureaucratic norms. Cited are non-achievement of goals, rise in the price of administration, diversion of resources from public purposes, erosion of morale, lowered respect for authority, a poor example enhancing lack of political courage, diversion of energies into lobbying, fiddling, etc., resulting in argument and bitterness, delays, and the use of inappropriate criteria in decisions (5). On the other hand, corruption is also regarded as a means of surmounting either traditional laws and/or bureaucratic regulation (21) and considered as a means of cutting down uncertainty in decision making (29). Nepotism may even result in the appointment of more competent bureaucrats (2).

As far as economic development is concerned, however, corruption is seen as positive in effect, on the assumption that governmental administration acts as a stifling force against private initiative. Thus corruption may impel better choices, increase the allocation of resources to investment, improve the quality of public servants, increase the responsiveness of bureaucracy and through nepotism substitute for a public works system (5). While admitting that corruption may lead to capital outflow, investment distortions and aid forgone, it may be functional as a source of capital formation, cutting red tape and offering private incentives to entrepreneurs given certain conditions, *viz.,* a tolerant culture and dominant groups, perceived security by elites, and certain societal or institutional restraints. Corruption funnels capital to struggling entrepreneurs, minimizing wastage of resources, wresting control of trade and industry from aliens, and promoting investment through politicians (2).

Finally, corruption is seen as making a positive contribution to political development, usually viewed in terms of national integration and the strengthening of political parties. Corruption is cited as an acceptable alternative to violence (21) (28) and as aiding national unification and stability, helping integration by bringing in groups otherwise alienated, and increasing participation in public affairs (21) (2). It is also argued that corruption reduces pressure for policy change and weakens the governmental bureaucracy, both of which are regarded as functional for political institutionalization (21). Others stress elite integration: the bourgeoisie can buy its way into the elite, and corruption can cement together a conservative coalition, while holding back or cancelling out the effects of growing collective demands and humanizing government for non-elites. Finally, corruption contributes to the strengthening of political parties and will itself be defeated in the long run, since vigilant and strong political parties will tend to reduce opportunities for corruption (21).

In sum, poor countries for cultural and historical reasons have a propensity toward corruption, seen as a violation of Western norms. To this propensity may be added a breakdown in the allocative mechanisms of society, or economic, political, and administrative reasons, so that corruption steps in to fulfill the missing functions. Corruption is thus legitimized in terms of its prevalence, and of its functionality: indeed, given the inappropriateness of Western norms and inadequacy of Western institutions, corruption does not really exist at all—it is simply a different way of doing business. Before such conceptualization can be accepted, however, we have to ask two questions. First, does corruption really disappear once it becomes normal behavior, or is it a substantive phenomenon, which may exist as normal behavior itself? Second, whereas corruption may arise because a system is failing to achieve its purpose, might not that purpose be better served by reforming the system than acquiescing in corruption?

Administrative Corruption as a Norm

Up to this point, corruption has been treated simply as divergence from an acknowledged standard, whose applicability is now felt in some quarters to be in doubt. It is assumed, therefore, that until this standard came into being in Western Europe at the end of the 18th century, corruption did not exist: corruption was, in effect, the creation of bureaucracy.

Before the clear distinction between public and private standards of behavior which emerged with the ideas of the French Revolution, the argument runs, many practices now regarded as corruption, such as venality and nepotism, were not against the law and were even exploited to their own benefit by rulers. Corruption, in accordance with a public duty definition, did not and could not exist since no concept of public duty existed. Behavior now thought of as corrupt might at most be seen as a special category of "proto-corruption," regarded as normal and legitimate by contemporaries (29).

It is true that current concepts of corruption date from the ideas of the French Revolution, which swept away private monarchical government and replaced it with representative government (9). Office became a public trust, and officials servants of the community. Public and private were separated. Privilege and hereditary tenure were replaced by qualification for office. Venality and nepotism were abolished and office holders ceased to have private rights in their office. Officials became full-time, and were paid by salary, not from private profits gained from conducting the government's business. A clear distinction was made between the personal lives of officials and the conduct expected from them in their work by the enforcement of rules. Public accountability entailed continued hierarchical bureaucratic control, as opposed to sporadic, dilatory judicial intervention (11).

It is also true that before this transformation practices now thought of as corrupt provided the basis of government. Nepotism, venality, exploitation of public function for private profit, were not only usual but also served needs of the crown which could not be fulfilled through more legitimate channels. But even while such practices were commonplace, they were by no means accepted. As long ago as the ancient empires, before even money was in common use, corruption was recognized and vigorous attempts made to combat it, as for example in the bureaucracy of Mauryan India (18) (22). In the Athenian city-state, a public audit was instituted in order to check corruption and enforce a public role upon officials (7). In republican Rome, even while provincial officials and others were making their fortunes at the expense of the state and its subjects (the current joke was that a governor needed three years to make his fortune—one to pay off his debts, one to provide a nest-egg for himself, and one to bribe his judges when he returned to Rome [4]), awareness of corruption existed and orators such as Cicero spoke out against it. Machiavelli attempted to analyze corruption in the Italy of his day (8). The monarchies of Europe all instituted some machinery to combat corruption, even though to serve their own needs, they sometimes acquiesced in its subversion (10) (14) (15) (16).

Lack of bureaucratic standards, entrenchment and pervasiveness, functionality for the short-run purposes of the regime or participants, did not mean that corruption did not exist. Though widespread and prevalent, the phenomenon of corruption was well recognized and its consequences realized. As a frequent, and sometimes normal, accompaniment of government, it was not an exception from the norm: it was the norm itself, although regarded as wrong.

Administrative Corruption as Functional

That corruption should at times serve certain interests, even those of the state itself, is not surprising: its very *raison d'être* indicates that someone is profiting. The revisionists, however, have made a link between corruption and development, by indicating that where political and administrative systems are deficient, corruption may compensate and prove of general benefit to development.

The problem is to what exactly the revisionists are referring. They link "corruption" defined in residual rather than substantive terms, and "development," a concept which has come to mean all things to all men (12). Further, the relationship may be far from positive, i.e., rather than "corruption" (whatever it might be) aiding "development" (in mythic terms of whatever one would like it to be), a particular kind of development may tend to be accompanied by corruption. Often there is an uneasy ambivalence regarding which is to be the dependent variable, development (or modernization) or corruption.

Beyond the semantic problem, however, lies the issue of functionality. It is generally accepted that system survival is bound up with a system's ability to adapt and survive, in turn dependent on its ability to absorb and benefit from change. The revisionists handle the problem of change along classic functional lines, i.e., corruption is a dysfunction of the system, which arises because the system cannot accommodate change—it is thus a *functional* dysfunction, whereby the new (and therefore functional) norms it represents replace outmoded norms. Exactly where this fits into the argument regarding cultural norms or propensity to corruption is unclear: for here the new norms are, in fact, the old (pre-development, non-Western) norms. There is a further ambiguity in the "cultural" argument, which does not make it altogether clear whether we are discussing actual traditional norms held by "traditional man" (if he exists) or the breakdown in these norms impacted upon by Western-type development. There is also a missing link in the analysis, which should explain the actual dynamic whereby new norms are evolved, and what kind of norms these will be.

Leaving aside the ambiguities, we have to ask whether the norms of corruption have been able to accommodate the needs of societal change. In the case of the transition to bureaucratic norms and public responsibility in Western countries, they failed to do so. In the end the old ways of conducting state business simply could not cope with the state's needs for increased mobilization of resources, effective and honest disbursement of funds, public trust in government, and control over its activities (9).

The entrenchment of corruption prevented these changes taking place on an orderly basis. In the most extreme example, that of 18th-century France, corruption helped suppress and funnel opposition to the regime until it reached disastrous proportions, on the analogy of landscape along a fault line which remains unaffected by repeated shocks for a long period and then is completely transformed by a catastrophic earthquake. In other words, the more that corrupt practices approached the dimensions of a norm, or accepted standard of behavior, the more they impeded both administrative and societal changes. The impulse for change had to come not from within, from the continuing development and modification of accepted and corrupt means of administration, but from reformers promoting innovation and new norms. Though corruption might prove functional to the interests of certain individuals and groups, and to the system insofar as it shares those interests, its very functionality is a symptom or indication of the need for reform. Corruption does not disappear when it becomes entrenched and accepted: rather it assumes a different form, that of *systemic* as opposed to *individual* corruption.

Individual and Systemic Corruption

Although revisionists have recognized corruption as a social fact, with structural causes and consequences, it is our contention that they have continued to think of it in individual terms. The definitions they suggest are well suited to individual corruption—the individual who strays from a prevailing norm of official public behavior. Several of the hypotheses they put forward may even be plausible as long as they are thought of in individual terms—informal organizational short-cuts; the occasional accommodation of personal favor; mutual "understandings." These may, according to circumstances, be condonable or reprehensible, but they still bear the vital characteristics of individual corruption—they can be coped with and minimized (though rarely if ever eliminated) within a reasonably effective control system, and they do not subvert or sabotage organizational purpose.

The conceptions of the revisionists, however, do not appear to stretch to encompass the significance of what they often appear to describe, which is systemic corruption—a situation where wrong-doing has become the norm, and the standard accepted behavior necessary to accomplish organizational goals according to notions of public responsibility and trust has become the exception not the rule. In this situation, corruption has become so regularized and institutionalized that organizational supports back wrong-doing and actually penalize those who live up to the old norms. Such systemic corruption is found today in many countries and jurisdictions, particularly where society prizes organizational loyalty over the public interest, where past standards of public rectitude and personal integrity have been eroded, and where notions of public responsibility and trust have been thrust aside with exploitation of public office for private gain. The key is not so much the techniques of organizational method, e.g., bureaucracy, as organizational goals and the qualities necessary to support and maintain them, *viz.,* honest administration and public accountability. The issue only becomes tangled where goals are displaced, so that specific, substantive, and public goals are transposed into, on one level, generalized and hazy development goals, and on another particularized benefits for privileged individuals or groups.

Systemic corruption has not been subject to much specific research. Examples readily come to mind in many large-scale organizations and at different levels of government. The Watergate affair showed that the White House was not immune. The Fitzgerald revelations indicated that defense contracting was riddled with systemic corruption, and other brave whistle-blowers have questioned law enforcement agencies, regulatory commissions, and public inspection bodies. Systemic corruption occurs whenever the administrative system itself transposes the expected purposes of the organization, forces participants to follow what otherwise would be termed unacceptable ways, and actually punishes those who resist. Deviant conduct is so institutionalized that no individual can be personally faulted organizationally (not morally) for participating, and dysfunction is actually protected. In systemic corruption:

A. the organization professes an external code of ethics which is contradicted by internal practices;

B. internal practices encourage, abet, and hide violations of the external code;

C. non-violators are penalized by forgoing the rewards of violation and offending violators;

D. violators are protected, and when exposed, treated leniently; their accusers are victimized for exposing organizational hypocrisy, and are treated harshly;

E. non-violators suffocate in the venal atmosphere; they find no internal relief and much external disbelief;

F. prospective whistle-blowers are intimidated and terrorized into silence;

G. courageous whistle-blowers have to be protected from organizational retaliation;

H. violators become so accustomed to their practices and the protection given them that, on exposure, they evidence surprise and claim innocence and unfair discrimination against them;

I. collective guilt finds expression in rationalizations of the internal practices and without strong external supports there is no serious intention of ending them;

J. those formally charged with revealing corruption rarely act and, when forced by external pressure to do so, excuse any incidents as isolated, rare occurrences.

The point to be stressed above all is that few corrupt practices can be conducted without collusion. Few can be kept secret for any length of time. Violations of public norms are known to all.

As we have previously illustrated, some revisionists argue that, moral judgment apart, if public business is conducted according to systemic corruption, that is how things are, that is how public power is exercised, that is the operational norm of public administration, and can no longer be considered corruption. It is merely an extra-legal device to gain influence over public policy, to fill vacuums left by inadequate public laws, to get around unrealistic administrative norms, to bridge lags in the value system of the community in relation to institutional change, to reallocate resources and services when disequilibrium arises between supply and demand, to stabilize the political system and replace violence, to cut down uncertainty in decision making, to cut through bureaucratic red tape, and to increase the responsiveness and sensitivity of public organizations. Systemic corruption may do all these things and more, but when one reduces the term to specific actions, then the dangers are self-evident and its institutionalization is obviously dysfunctional to society. In most cases, the practices constitute theft, bribery, or extortion and probably involve deceit, hypocrisy, and false testimony, and so are indictable offenses, even if they fall into the category of victimless crime.

Individual cases of corruption can be rooted out by the application of organizational sanctions. The wrong-doer is taxed with the evidence, penalized for minor offenses, and dismissed, and possibly prosecuted under the criminal code, for major offenses. The scandal is localized and steps are taken to prevent repetition. Systemic corruption cannot be handled so easily. There is no guarantee that if the most serious offenders are dismissed, or if everyone who is guilty is replaced, corruption will not persist. The old patterns will continue with new players. Further, the scandal will have a reinforcing effect. Successors will make sure they will not be caught so easily by examining where their predecessors went wrong and so reorganizing to make any repetition of exposure much harder. The people may change, but the system persists. Moreover, in the wider society, systemic corruption impedes rather than aids change.

A. Systemic corruption perpetuates closed politics and restricts access, preventing the reflection of social change in political institutions.

B. Systemic corruption suppresses opposition contributing to increasing resentment. Thus corruption far from being an alternative to violence is often accompanied by more violence.

C. Systemic corruption perpetuates and widens class, economic, and social divisions, contributing to societal strain and preventing cohesion.

D. Systemic corruption prevents policy change, particularly where this works against immediate market considerations. Individual or sectional interests are not the best guide to the public interest.

E. Systemic corruption blocks administrative reform, and makes deleterious administrative practices profitable, e.g., induced delays.

F. Systemic corruption diverts public resources and contributes to a situation of private affluence, public squalor, especially serious where affluence is confined to the few.

G. Systemic corruption contributes to societal anomie in shoring up or transmuting traditional values into inappropriate areas.

H. The effects of systemic corruption are not limited to a specific case: there is an accumulator effect upon public perceptions and expectations which subverts trust and cooperation far beyond the impact upon the individuals immediately concerned.

I. Systemic corruption is not confined to poor, developing, or modernizing countries, but found in all organizational societies.

These hypotheses might better form the starting point for serious research into administrative corruption than the historically inaccurate assumptions and often unfounded assertions of the revisionists, who have confused individual and systemic corruption. In contemporary public administration, the issue is not so much individual misconduct in public office, serious as that is, as the institutionalized subversion of the public interest through systemic corruption.

References

1. Abueva, J., "What Are We in Power For? The Sociology of Graft and Corruption," *Philippine Sociological Review,* Vol. 18 (July-October 1970), pp. 203–210.
2. _____. "The Contribution of Nepotism, Spoils and Graft to Political Development," *East-West Center Review,* Vol. 3 (June 1966), pp. 45–54, reproduced in A.J. Heidenheimer, *Political Corruption: Readings in Comparative Analysis* (New York: Holt, Rinehart and Winston, 1970).
3. Alatas, S.H., *The Sociology of Corruption. The Nature, Function, Cause and Prevention of Corruption* (Singapore: Donald Moore, 1968).
4. Arnott, P.D., *The Romans and Their World* (London: St. Martin's Press, 1970).
5. Bayley, D.H., "The Effects of Corruption in a Developing Nation," *Western Political Quarterly,* Vol. 19 (December 1966), reproduced in A.J. Heidenheimer, *Political Corruption: Readings in Comparative Analysis* (New York: Holt, Rinehart and Winston, 1970).
6. Ben Dor, G., "Corruption, Institutionalization and Political Development: The Revisionist Theses Revisited," *Comparative Political Studies,* Vol. 7 (April 1974), pp. 63–83.
7. Boeckh, A., *The Public Economy of the Athenians* (London: John Murray, 1828).
8. Bonadeo, A., *Corruption, Conflict and Power in the Works and Times of Niccolo Machiavelli* (Berkeley: University of California Press, 1973).
9. Bosher, J., *French Financial Administration 1770–1795: From Business to Bureaucracy* (Cambridge: Cambridge University Press, 1970).
10. _____. "Chambres de Justice in the French Monarchy," in J. Bosher (ed.), *French Government and Society 1500–1850* (London: Athlone, 1973).
11. Caiden, G.E., *The Dynamics of Public Administration* (New York: Holt, Rinehart and Winston, 1971).
12. Caiden, N., and A. Wildavsky, *Planning and Budgeting in Poor Countries* (New York: Wiley, 1974).
13. Carino, L.V., "Bureaucratic Behavior and Development: Types of Graft and Corruption in a Developing Country," paper presented at the Conference on the Political Economy of Development, Manila, 17–18 December 1974.
14. Dent, J., "An Aspect of the Crisis of the Seventeenth Century: The Collapse of the Financial Administration of the French Monarchy 1653–61," *Economic History Review* (August 1967).

15. _____. *Crisis in France: Crown, Financiers and Society in Seventeenth Century France* (Newton Abbot: David and Charles, 1973).
16. Durand, Y., *Les Fermiers Generaux au XVIII Siecle* (Paris: Presses Universitaires de France, 1971).
17. Friedrich, C.J., "Political Pathology," *Political Quarterly,* Vol. 37 (1966), reproduced in A.J. Heidenheimer, *Political Corruption: Readings in Comparative Analysis* (New York: Holt, Rinehart and Winston, 1970).
18. Gopal, M.H., *Mauryan Public Finance* (London: Allen and Unwin, 1935).
19. Guzman, R.P., et al., "Graft and Corruption: Issues in and Prospects for a Comparative Study of a Specific Type of Bureaucratic Behavior," paper prepared for the IDRC Project Development Meeting on Bureaucratic Behavior and Development, Baguio City, January 26–30, 1975.
20. Heidenheimer, A.J., *Political Corruption: Readings in Comparative Analysis* (New York: Holt, Rinehart and Winston, 1970).
21. Huntington, S., *Political Order in Changing Societies* (New Haven: Yale University Press), reproduced as "Modernization and Corruption" in A.J. Heidenheimer, *Political Corruption: Readings in Comparative Analysis* (New York: Holt, Rinehart and Winston, 1970).
22. Kautilya, *Arthasastra* (Shamasastry translation) (Mysore: Mysore Printing and Publishing House, 1961).
23. Leff, N., "Economic Development through Bureaucratic Corruption," *American Behavioral Scientist,* Vol. 8 (November 1964), pp. 8–14.
24. McMullan, M., "A Theory of Corruption," *The Sociological Review* (Keele), Vol. 9 (July 1961), pp. 181–200.
25. Merton, R., *Social Theory and Social Structure* (New York: Free Press, 1957).
26. Monteiro, J.B., *Corruption: Control of Maladministration* (Bombay: Manaktalas, 1966).
27. Myrdal, G., *Asian Drama: An Inquiry into the Poverty of Nations II* (New York: Twentieth Century, 1968), reproduced in A.J. Heidenheimer, *Political Corruption: Readings in Comparative Analysis* (New York: Holt, Rinehart and Winston, 1970).
28. Nye, J.S., "Corruption and Political Development: A Cost-Benefit Analysis," *American Political Science Review,* Vol. 61 (June 1967).
29. Scott, J.C., *Comparative Political Corruption* (Englewood Cliffs, N.J.: Prentice Hall, 1972).
30. Steffens, L., "Los Angeles and the Apple," in J.A. Gardiner and D.J. Olson (eds.), *Theft of the City: Readings on Corruption in Urban America* (Bloomington: Indiana University Press, 1974).
31. Tilman, R.D., "Emergence of Black-Market Bureaucracy: Administration, Development and Corruption in the New States," *Public Administration Review,* Vol. 28, No. 5 (September/October 1968), pp. 432–444.
32. Van Roy, E., "On the Theory of Corruption," *Economic Development and Cultural Change* (October 1970), pp. 86–100.
33. Wraith, R., and E. Simpkins, *Corruption in Developing Countries* (New York: Norton, 1964).

13

NEW DIRECTIONS IN THE STUDY OF ADMINISTRATIVE CORRUPTION

Simcha B. Werner
University of Manitoba

Administrative corruption was long a neglected area of research in American public administration. This neglect was due primarily to the axiomatic belief of earlier scholars that American public administration was inherently moral. Given the scientific origin of the discipline of public administration, and given Woodrow Wilson's division of politics and administration, this is not surprising. But developments after the Second World War not only made Wilson's dichotomy obsolete, but also led to new ethical dilemmas. Nevertheless, while dealing with these dilemmas,[1] the discipline of public administration continued with its *a priori* premise that public administrators remained "philosopher-kings."[2]

During the 1960s, the ethos of public administration was affected by the advent of policy analysis and by the developmental and structural-functional approaches in political science. These approaches were responsible, as will be demonstrated, for the existing gap between corruption in American social institutions and scientific knowledge about the various causes of, and remedies for, corruption. Mark Lilla commented in his essay on the ethics of policy analysis:

The year 1960 proved to be a turning point for the field of public administration and the democratic ethos it embodied. The ... "whiz-kid" in the

191

Kennedy Administration . . . was prepared to apply the latest "scientific" management and analytic tools to the problems of public policy. . . . Professors, with their bulging analytic tool-kits in hand over-ran Washington attempting to "rationalize" everything from defence procurement to government budgeting. . . . However inadequate the old public administration was in analytic sophistication, it did embody an ethos which prepared the student, through an informal moral education, to take his place within a democratic government. Public policy has no such ethos. . . . Students flocked to public policy programs . . . [and] found out that they would simply be taught analytic techniques. And the techniques themselves, it was claimed, were "biased" in favor of those in power and had led to inhumane policies at home and abroad. In short, policy analysis was immoral.[3]

In building up "applied ethics," policy analysis, according to Lilla, became a new form of medieval casuistry,[4] a "political ethic" developed during the 17th century and adopted by the Jesuits as a science, art, or reasoning to resolve cases of conscience by applying the general rules of religion and morality to particular instances in which there appears to be a conflict of duties.

While domestically, American policy analysts rationalized the need for applied ethics, students of the structural-functional approach shifted attention to the developing countries, pointing to the functional contributions of political and bureaucratic corruption to political and economic development. The functionalists came to regard corruption as an inherent aspect of the normal growth-decay life cycle, and challenged the moralist school which deemed corruption to be ultimately pathological and, therefore, destructive. Corruption received a "sympathetic understanding"[5] and, instead, was classified as a "functional dysfunction." According to Nye,[6] the functionalists echoed Bernard Mandevill's aphorism: "Private vices, by the dextrous Management of a skillful politician, may be turned into Publick Benefits." This is to say that corruption is merely the price to be paid for certain advantages. However, as Nye argued, whether ". . . the benefits of corruption . . . outweigh the costs depends on its [corruption's] being limited. . . ."[7] This, in turn, suggested the following theoretical tenets: (1) Corruption as an inseparable byproduct of modernization and development; (2) corruption as a functional influence in political and economic development; (3) corruption as a self-destructive process; and (4) corruption as an individual action committed by the occasional immoral official for personal benefit.

These tenets stifled investigation of the apparently ubiquitous phenomenon of corruption by unconsciously introducing a fatal ennui. If, for example, corruption was associated with political development and apparently withered away with political maturation, then, since western nations are mature, corruption is by now restricted to non-western nations. Moreover, as it assists them in developing it concomitantly destroys itself. Its "transitory" nature obviated the need for study.

During the 1970s, as a result of American scandals, public administration and political science research was characterized by a rather prolific growth in the literature of corruption in developed countries, particularly in the United States. This new literature is coalescing into a distinctive "post-functional" approach to the study of administrative and political corruption. At present, this emerging approach can be best identified by a growing body of descriptive studies that: (a) point to the reckless generalizations and intellectual inconsistencies of the functionalists; (b) contradict the theoretical tenets and premises of the functionalists; (c) warn that academia, state, and society must rouse themselves from the auto-narcotic effects of the "functional corruption" myth, and develop multi-dimensional strategies to defeat corruption; and (d) fail to offer a new deductive theory of corruption.

The Definition of Corruption

Kirkegaard, the stern moralist of the 19th century, has argued that "aesthetics" is the true ethics. Similarly, Peter Drucker calls our attention to the replacement of ethics by "ethical chic," because the latter describes a media event rather than a moral or philosophical absolute.[8] Both "aesthetics" and "ethical chic" are, as terms relative, for beauty (or corruption, in this case) lies in the eyes of the beholder. Also, corruption is determined in large part by prevalent cultural norms.

Despite the obscurity of relevant concepts, definitions of corruption have been categorized[9] into three groups: (1) public office-centered definitions which involve the deviation from legal and public duty norms for the sake of private benefits, be it for pecuniary or status gains, or influence; (2) market-centered definitions which view corruption as a "maximizing unit," a special type of stock-in-trade, by which public officials maximize pecuniary gains according to the supply and demand that exist in the marketplace of their official domains; (3) public interest-centered definitions which emphasize the betrayal of public interests by preference of particular to common interests.

Peters and Welch[10] classified corruption according to its legal, public interest, and public opinion bases. While the first two bases are not unique, the third deserves scrutiny because it does not so much define corruption as ask who determines what is corrupt. This was based upon Heidenheimer's "litmus test," which deemed corruption to be black, gray, or white, depending upon the commonality of perception by the public and its officials. If the public and its officials agreed that a specific "bad" action was to be either condemned or condoned, then that act would be an example of, respectively, either black or white corruption. A lack of accord produced a gray area.

Peters and Welch, then, took the next logical step in categorizing a corrupt act in accord with its four components: the donor, the recipient, the favor, and the payoff. They wrote that corruption would be perceived as "limited" when: the recipient public official acts as a private citizen; a constituent pays a public official as opposed to the official "putting his hand in the till"; the favor is a routine part of the public official's job or benefits the public interest; and the payoff is small, long-range, general (e.g., an unspecified, future electoral consideration), or in the form of support rather than money. In the final analysis, then, a "bad" political act is deemed less corrupt if it is performed for the "good" of the constituency.

Also, in 1978, Dobel published his essay on "The Corruption of a State," in which he discusses the relative nature of corruption. Dobel defines corruption as, essentially, a factor of specific cultural attitudes regarding loyalty, morality and the usurpation of the public good.[11] This definition assumes that there are levels of loyalty and interest, such as can be found by differentiating between the welfare of the state and the welfare of the individual. It also assumes that corruption is, therefore, more venal as it is more avaricious, and less corrupt as it is less individual.

Thus, for example, the news of Lockheed bribing overseas buyers need not have been regarded as evidence of corruption, because Lockheed, in developing and increasing its markets, was working for the benefit of a large constituency, the company, its employees, and their families, and, more implicitly, for the benefit of the United States' economy, business, and political community.

This concept of "noble" or "patriotic" corruption contradicts traditional definitions of corruption as betrayal of the public trust for private gain. Lilla[12] and Drucker[13] noted the revitalization of such "casuistry" in government and business, and deemed it to be ultimately dysfunctional. As Schwartz observed in his study of Soviet public enterprises:

> Not infrequently an evasion of the law begins with expediency and is allegedly dictated by "business interests," and gradually, almost imperceptibly, is transformed into common thefts where the "noble objectives" serve as cover for private gain.... If one must falsify for the good of the cause, then why not add a little more for one's self.[14]

Vulnerability to Corruption

Influenced by the developmental approach of the 1960s, corruption was associated with the process of modernization. Every modernizing system was regarded as being susceptible to corruption, as was the case in Western societies which evidenced peak levels of corruption as they experienced socio-political development. Developing countries, therefore, were assumed to allow corruption to become a usual and expected part of the national maturation process.

It, thus, became simplistic to attribute corruption in developing countries to cultural heritages which produced "supportive values." In these countries, where citizens have negative attitudes toward public authority, "gift-giving" practices have been transformed into corruption only by the imposition of western values.[15] In these countries, "there exists a gap between law (as imposed by western and alien standards) and accepted informal social norms (sanctioned by prevailing social ethics). . . . "[16] In sum, these countries demonstrate a "folklore,"[17] a "climate,"[18] and a "way of life"[19] with regard to corruption.

However, in rebuttal to the "self-destructive nature" theory of corruption, common wisdom in the United States indicates that corruption has now become part of the national lifestyle. A growing body of literature suggests that corruption may well be endemic to United States politics,[20] businesses, and social institutions.[21] Similarly, corruption as a *modus operandi* has been observed throughout most of the world.[22] This implies a lack of boundaries to corruption imposed by political ideology or development. Corruption, for example, is a feature of communist countries[23] and nations now in the final stages of political development.[24]

Therefore, the theoretical tenet that corruption is a dependent variable of development is false. Corruption is universal. It can thrive and propagate itself in any level of political and bureaucratic development. More contemporary research suggests that:

1. Patron-client networks which border on corruption can thrive at any level of political development or institutionalization;[25]
2. Socio-economic or political inequalities stimulate corruption;[26]
3. A consumer-oriented society and the gap between desire and the means of fulfillment is now becoming universal;[27]
4. Too little or too much government control tends to enhance corruption;[28]
5. Too little or too much institutionalization tends to enhance corruption;[29]
6. Expanded governmental functions in less-developed countries, and extensive welfare programs in more-developed countries (e.g., food stamps) provide open invitation to major corruption;[30]
7. Economic scarcity and inflation can turn ordinary citizens to relatively minor crimes, such as the view of England as "a nation of petty thieves";[31]

8. American politicians are susceptible to foreign bribery (as demonstrated in Abscam), and to organized crime;[32] and
9. Weak administrative detection and control mechanisms combine with leadership apathy and limited knowledge of corruption to produce cross-cultural, cross-developmental corruption.

Given the prevalence of corruption, perhaps even its inevitability, it is necessary to determine whether it has beneficial aspects.

Dysfunctional Versus Functional Corruption

The functionalists identified the following functional propositions:

Economic Market Propositions: Corruption brings with it a wider range of economic choices by encouraging foreign investment and strengthening the private vis-à-vis the public sector. It is, therefore, a means of bypassing cumbersome, genuinely hampering, governmental economic regulations.[33] Bayley argued that corruption is an "accommodating device" a "'must' for successful development."[34]

The Integrative Function: Corruption allows citizens access to public officials and thereby fosters the integration of immigrant or parochial groups.[35]

Institutionalization Initiative: Either corruption encourages institutionalization and party-building,[36] or an honest, merit-oriented and incorruptible bureaucracy hampers the rise of political leadership.[37]

Administrative Advocacy: Corruption brings elasticity and humanity to rigid bureaucracies.[38] It may also serve to increase the caliber of public servants because corruption brings with it opportunities for supplemental income which may compete with co-optive forces arriving from the non-governmental job market.[39]

Pacifistic Corruption: In the absence of structural reform, violence as the other alternative to corruption threatens the stability of already unstable systems: "He who corrupts a system's police officer is more likely to identify with the system than he who storms the system's police station."[40]

By the end of the 1960s, functionalism came under attack. A scathing condemnation of the supposed morality of the functionalists was sounded by Singapore's Minister of Foreign Affairs and Labor, S. Rajaratnam:

I think it is monstrous for these well-intentioned and largely misguided scholars to suggest corruption as a practical and efficient instrument for rapid development in Asia and Africa. Once upon a time, Westerners tried to subjugate Asia ... by selling opium. The current defense of Kleptocracy is a new kind of opium by some Western intellectuals, devised to perpetuate Asian backwardness and degradation. I think the only people ... pleased with the contributions of these scholars are the Asian Kleptocrats.[41]

Academics, too, began to criticize openly the "opportunistic rationalization of corruption,"[42] and the tendency of the functionalists toward ". . . shallow research, reckless generalizations and loosely formulated plans of action."[43] This sloppy reasoning of the functionalist school became the focus of post-functionalist research.

Even assuming that corruption is functional, the question arose: ". . . at what point does the 'least developed' country develop to the point where such corruption is no longer functional."[44] If corruption indeed enhances the opportunities for modernization, then there should be some element in the functionalist theory ". . . which should explain the actual dynamics whereby the new norms evolve, and what kind of norms these will be."[45]

Studies were performed, and the claims of the functionalists for the benefits of corruption to developing systems were shattered. Tilman[46] pointed out that in the Philippines under the Marcos regime, martial law had to be enforced as a means to recover a decaying economy long tainted by institutionalized corruption. McHenry[47] demonstrated that food donated to Bangladesh is politically controlled. Only 10 percent of U.S. aid reached those in the rural areas who needed it most. The rest was used to keep the Bengali government in power by rationing it out to the political constituency in urban areas. The dysfunctional results are smuggling, a black market economy, and disincentive effect on domestic agriculture, not to mention mass starvation. Goodman[48] proved that political corruption in Yucatan, Mexico, inhibited evolution toward universalistic norms by protecting incompetence rather than by rewarding the efficient producer.

Studies on bureaucratic and political corruption in India[49] indicated that corruption is so rampant that government reform policies based upon law were inadequate for their task. Instead of assisting in the development of a functional party system, corruption generally aided in strengthening the dominance of one party, weakened the economy and fostered national disintegration. Eventually, concerned Indians came to regard corruption as a "multi-faced monster" against which "war" must be declared, a war which could be won only if India underwent a "moral revolution."[50] Developed countries and those nearing the final stages of development also failed to provide proof of the assertions of the functionalists.

Mamoru and Auerbach[51] have shown that venality is still intrinsic in the contemporary Japanese political system. The culturally rooted concepts of *takari* (to be a hanger-on) and *nareai* (illicit collusion) explain why corrupt officials are condoned. In the Japanese system, then, while "patronism" can lead to the trivialization of corruption, the intrinsic system of bribery can lead to the actual purchase of votes. Ben-Dor's study[52] of the Israeli case demonstrates that corruption serves only itself. After Israel was established as an independent state, it absorbed immigrants from diverse cultures and countries. Corruption did not foster the integration of those immigrants into the political system. Instead, "opportunities" for corruption were selective. The mass of immigrants could not find the channels to the centers of influence.

In the fully-developed countries of the West, corruption manifests dysfunctional aspects almost entirely. The growth of pilfering and related "minor" examples of corruption in England constitute an entire "hidden economy."[53] Pilfering is known as, "larceny by servants" and is, according to Henry, an everyday phenomenon in factories, shops, and offices. It became a method of survival, a response to rapid inflation, high prices, scarce money, restrained income, crippling taxation, and a government policy which offered "equality of sacrifice."[54]

Comprehensive studies[55] of political and administrative corruption in the United States also carry the seeds of a post-functionalist thesis. As corruption becomes institutionalized and systemic, it "involves the loss of moral authority, weakens efficiency of government operations, increases opportunities for organized crime, encourages police brutality, adds to [the] taxpayers' burden . . . undermines political decisions, leads to inefficient use of resources, and benefits the unscrupulous at the cost of the law abiding."[56]

These observations led to a rather contradictory confluence of views between the functionalists and the post-functionalists. The premise of the functionalists that corruption is a "self-extinguishing catalyzer," brought with it the corollary that political development and corruption are interlocked in a "moving equilibrium."[57] The more corruption fosters development, the more it undermines the conditions of its own existence.

However, in arguing that corruption is dysfunctional, the post-functionalists made an argument for its self-perpetuating nature. Corruption feeds upon itself, blocking organizational change and societal reform. As reform is blocked, it becomes increasingly onerous to achieve, and more corruption is fostered as a remedy to existing corruption. Demonstration of a dynamic corruptive mechanism will lay the foundations for further empirical research and subsequent change. Such a corruptive mechanism is the "spillover effect."

The Spillover Effect

If left to itself, corruption will grow. "spilling over" and affecting increasing portions of a given organization or society. This effect is abetted by complacency, naiveté and lethargy on the part of the functionalists and the new casuists. However, three specific spillover mechanisms can be demonstrated, and the knowledge derived can be used as a beginning of a formulation of a strategy to reverse the multiplicative tendency of corruption. These three spillover mechanisms are:

I. Leader-Follower Spillover

The spillover effect is evidenced to the greatest extent by the leaders of a given entity. Leaders, by definition, play a large role in shaping public opinion and societal behavior. Therefore, the corruption of leaders tends to affect the trust, loyalty, and personal integrity of their followers.

Machiavelli observed that "what the prince does the many will also soon do—for in their eyes the prince is ever in view." Corruption of leaders is dangerous because leaders are the paradigms of the body politic. Equally important, the leaders are usually those individuals charged with rooting out corruption.

Halayya[58] has pointed out a gap between verbal condemnation of corruption and action to thwart it. For example, Pandit J. Nehru, Prime Minister of India, announced that the corrupt "should be hanged from the nearest lamp post," but did nothing to combat corruption and even shielded some of his corrupt ministers. In the United States, the Commission on Law Enforcement and Administration observed: "Derelictions of corporations and their managers, who usually occupy leadership positions in their communities, establish an example which tends to erode the moral base of law and provide an opportunity for other kinds of offenders to rationalize their conduct."[59] Also, white-collar crime has a definite spillover effect on blue-collar workers.[60]

The failure to condemn corruption will result in the administrative equivalent of a permeable membrane through which corruption is diffused in an osmotic manner. Consider, for example, the effects of Stalin's slogan for the first Soviet Five Year Plan: "Victors of production are not judged."[61] Levi Eshkol, the late Prime Minister of Israel, when questioned about a corrupt official, replied with a quote from Deuteronomy 25:4: "Thou shalt not muzzle the ox when he treadeth out the corn."

Rationalization of corruption enhances the negative effects of the leader-follower spillover effect. This occurs in three distinct ways:

1. By the leaders designating themselves as the only ones capable of differentiating between "honest" and "dishonest" graft. Also, by support of the proposition that leaders who act for the good of the organization are "entitled" to compensation beyond their salaries.
2. By arguing, as the casuists did, that certain circumstances require "alteration of the rules," and that it is the responsibility, even the loyal duty, of leaders to commit corruption for the "good" of their organization. As Peter Drucker observed, rulers think they "have to strike a balance between ordinary demands of ethics which apply to them as individuals and their social responsibility to their subjects, their kingdom or their company";[62]

3. By the legitimization technique which occurs after corruption
    becomes prevalent. Those who are caught will blame the system
    rather than find guilt in themselves.

In sum, the corrupt behavior of leaders—whether by excessive use of
perquisites or by massive abuse of the system—is certain to be emulated by
members of the leaders' organization. This is the essential truth of the
Latin proverb: "*corruptio optimi pessima*—the corruption of the best is the
worst."

II. The Dimensions of Corruption Spillover Effect

The previously-mentioned classifications of corruption are useful, but they
are also too static, failing to elucidate the mechanism(s) by which corrupt
acts change in intensity. Heidenheimer[63] argued that gray corruption is the
most destructive, because it is the most difficult to define, detect, and punish. This paper proposes that white corruption best evidences the spillover
effect and, therefore, is the most destructive.

The salient characteristic of white corruption is its being a petty and borderline type, which neither the public nor public officials regard as being
punishable. Often, white corruption does not clearly violate the law. While
every code of law does define corruption, it also "carries the seeds of its
own neutralization,"[64] because it does not account for extenuating circumstances. White corruption is psychologically condoned or rationalized because it is so prevalent. By attributing little or no importance to a corrupt
act, trivialization and rationalization function as a self-perpetuating mechanism.

Schwartz observed that, in the Soviet Union, minor types of corruption
are regarded by the government as truisms in social life. The press, on the
other hand, complains that official tolerance of petty violations leads to "a
general sense of impunity, and that this encourages more serious types of
corruption."[65] In the United States, McGee and Anzelmi[66] have shown in a
case study that "there is no such thing as a free ride," in that "friendship"
between a police service professional and a businessman can turn subtly
into a pitfall.

The rationalization of white corruption, as well as the failure of the system to determine when corruption becomes destructive, cause the formulation and subsequent enforcement of control strategies to be severely constrained. Unchecked, white corruption is a growth industry. When a
corrupt act is regarded as being innocuous, that act is removed from previous definitions of corruption. The acceptance of white corruption as being
"legitimate" tends to contribute to the legitimization of other types of corruption. The gray and black shades become progressively lighter, and a further momentum of spilling over is established.

III. Institutional Spillover

The influence of specific behavior patterns of different organizations, or groups within the same organization, has not been well documented. However, it is reasonable to deduce that effective institutional corruption will reproduce itself. If, for example, aircraft manufacturer A consistently loses contracts to aircraft manufacturer B, who has an unwritten policy of providing "sales commissions" to influential governmental officials, then aircraft manufacturer A will be induced or compelled to follow suit. Furthermore, there is evidence of a coalition of corrupt politicians, law enforcement officers, businessmen, and labor officials in the United States[67] and, in the underdeveloped countries, coalitions of businessmen, politicians, and administrators.[68]

Whatever the arrangement, corrupt leaders allow their corruption to spread from one institution to another. This spread is either desirable, for corruption has been seen to produce benefits without substantive cost, or is imperative, a means of successfully competing. Dobel has observed that corruption spreads beyond the political realm and cripples the structures "which generate reasonably disinterested loyalty and civic virtues."[69] Also, corruption spreads from family to school, and from organized religion to other voluntary social organizations. Finally, even the army can become loyal to those who pay it.

The Diffusion of Corruption: Systemic Versus Individual

A basic area of contention between the functionalists and their successors is that of the diffusion of corruption. Gerald and Naomi Caiden correctly point out that, although advocates of functional corruption of the 1960s "deal with social variables, they still think of corrupt behavior in individual terms without recognizing the existence of systemic corruption."[70] The corollary of this functionalist premise comes from their definition of corruption as a legal deviation, optical illusion, and intellectual inconsistency. "If corruption is illegal, it tends to appear as occasional acts of dishonesty on the part of civil servants. . . . The root of corruption lies exclusively in the *appetitus divitarum infinitus,* the insatiable avarice that is one of the human weaknesses. . . ."[71]

The Caidens suggest that within an organization, systemic corruption implies the existence of an external code of ethics which is contradicted by internal practices.[72] These internal practices encourage and conceal violations of the external code.

Violators of the external code are protected, although non-violators are penalized, particularly in the case of "whistle-blowers." Systemic corruption thus prevents policy change and blocks administrative reform. From the perspective of the spillover effect, it is perhaps the most significant type of corruption because of its thorough permeation of an organization.

According to the post-functionalist view, systemic corruption occurs primarily because a series of isolated incidents—accidental or intentional—have proven their value. The organization, therefore, follows the path of least resistance, and will continue to do so until an insurmountable barrier or an unacceptable cost is placed in its path. Furthermore, when corruption becomes systemic within an organization, spilling over and affecting an increasing portion of that organization, a corrupt code of conduct will replace the legal code, and institutionalization of corruption will become a *modus operandi* for subsequent organizational goals. Two possible examples of this later case include the corruption of entire United States police departments,[73] and the built-in corruption in land-use and building regulation statutes throughout the United States.[74]

More cynical observers of the American scene have come to accept that, even if corrupt officials are removed from office, they will be replaced by equally corrupt officials who have benefitted from the mistake of their predecessors. This is perhaps the ultimate dysfunction of corruption.

In assuming that any given political system is vulnerable to corruption, one is forced to assume that the system does not reflect the will of the people in the intended manner. In other words, corruption becomes the unofficial but actual political or administrative order. Such a situation demands violent reform as a corollary of citizen frustration. In lieu of reform, the morality and loyalty of the citizens may become further factionalized.

Control Policies:
Toward Multi-Dimensional Control Strategy

In assuming that corruption is individual, functional, and self-destructive, the functionalists deny the need for remedy. If there is no diagnosis of sickness, then there can be no attempt to provide a cure. The post-functionalists have, on the other hand, demonstrated anxiety about the problem and subsequently proposed a number of remedies.

If, as political economists have argued, corruption is a variant of economic choice, then the remedy is to reduce the benefits while increasing the costs of corruption.[75] One means of accomplishing this is to increase organizational accountability. Another remedy might mandate payment of exorbitant sums, multiples of the original payoff, for individuals caught in a corrupt act. However, these sanctions will be to no avail without increased efforts to detect corruption.[76] However, when corruption of state and society reflects the privatization of morality and a loss of loyalty to communal institutions, reducing opportunities and incentives will not change the motive for corruption. It will instead force the corrupted person to adapt and to make his technique for bypassing administrative and legal barriers more sophisticated. Those who corrupt will raise the bid to make the sale of public officials' "stewardship power" once again worthwhile.

When corruption is institutionalized, systemic, or an intrinsic part of everyday life, the traditional wisdom that corruption can be effectively contained or eliminated only by legal and police measures is disproved. Not only is every law limited by its definition, but also, the punishments prescribed neither reform nor deter "unless the punished respects both the punishers and the norms underlying the penalty."[77] Dobel observed ". . . that only when the vast majority of citizens spontaneously accept the laws even when they disagree with them can law be a tool for community direction and reform."[78] Others point to the dysfunctional utility of prohibitory regulations because—as in the case of trade, customs, gambling, liquor, drug, and prostitution laws—the prohibitory regulations themselves can become an incentive for corruption.[79] Therefore, "the objective should be to create an atmosphere of reform which the law will serve to consolidate."[80]

During the past decade, the "whistle-blowing movement"[81] grew out of this concern for the deterioration of morality. Although the strategy is, at present, to incorporate whistle-blowing into policies designed to improve overall accountability of public agencies, it involves a conflict of "loyalty to conscience" and "loyalty to team."[82] Drucker[83] pointed out the destructive import of whistle-blowing. Similarly, students of criminology and white collar crime have argued that people, not laws, make things work.[84] It is not the police and the law which prevent crime, it is the community. Studying the anemic "hidden economy" in England, Henry has argued that only by community justice, can we ever hope to "liberate" society from the hypocrisy of its attitudes toward crime and only then will be capable of controlling it.[85]

Community justice, according to Henry, enables us to understand the perspectives of all parties to a corrupt or criminal offense, as well as the context of the crime and allows for the involvement of all parties it affects. Decentralized, popular community tribunals are used successfully in socialist countries, primarily in the Soviet Union and China. In Great Britain, where borderline crime and corruption is rampant, the Schweppes Company is experimenting with factory tribunals where management and labor representatives act as judges. Although, community justice seems a return to the old pre-development commonplace of justice, it may be a potential productive means to supplement the inadequacy of formal legal systems in dealing with contemporary systemic corruption. As the corrupted tend to rationalize their offenses by blaming an impersonal system rather than themselves and so neutralizing or mitigating the effects of their offenses upon otherwise unidentified individuals, community, informal justice may be more effective, because of its internalization of peer pressure.

The post-functionalists have not yet articulated a "community justice strategy." They have, however, set forth the necessity of developing a "communal and societal strategy" to combat corruption by consciously endeavoring to achieve and sustain public concern and scrutiny. In a recent provocative essay on corruption in the contemporary American presidency and administration, Theodore Lowi has observed: "In the age of large and growing government, we had better cultivate the art of political criticism, or we will have to learn the science of revolution."[86]

Conclusions

In the study of corruption, research of the 1970s has pointed to the reckless generalizations and logical inconsistencies which the functionalist school of the 1960s displayed. This new research, however, can best be described as a growing but nevertheless inconsistent body of descriptive studies which loosely attempts to theorize on the general phenomenon. It is premature to even attempt to articulate a new deductive theory of corruption. The articulation of such a theory requires that, in the next period of research, greater attention must be given to the following areas of corruption that are under-represented in extant empirical work:

A. The scope, nature, and dynamics of systemic corruption.
B. The causes and values of corruption. If, for example, case studies on mature systems yield insufficient data about how corruption changes in intensity, then the focus should be shifted to those countries now making the final stages toward development. These countries provide sufficient institutionalization so that the battle, between dysfunctional corruption and functional growth can be more clearly observed.
C. The scope, nature, and dynamics of patriotic corruption, or what Peter Drucker and Mark Lilla referred to as the new casuistry.

If the field of administrative corruption is to become more theoretical and less descriptive, it must develop a framework and methodology that will permit comparative analysis. Also, it cannot ignore asking questions on the rather amorphous problems of corruption, such as whether corruption is a learned behavior, where values are diffused through a process, and by agents, of socialization. In this sense, the concept of the spillover effect, while lacking sufficient theoretical depth, does serve as a transitional phase between the inadequacies of past research and the need for more theoretical research. While post-functionalists point to the need for articulating a multi-dimensional strategy to control corruption, the newly introduced concept of "community control," has not yet sparked noticeable academic enthusiasm. It seems, however, that it deserves more theoretical elaboration and experimentation to learn about its potential importation into social institutions in western democracies. The need for these studies is both imperative and immediate, for corruption threatens the very pillars of the democratic experience.

Notes

1. See, for example, H. P. Appleby, *Morality and Administration in Democratic Government* (Baton Rouge: Louisiana State University Press, 1952); K. S. Bailey, "Ethics and the Public Service," *Public Administration Review*, Vol. 24 (November-December 1974), pp. 234–243; H. Cleveland and H. D. Lasswell (eds.), *Ethics and Bigness: Scientific, Academic, Religion, Political and Military* (New York: Harper and Brothers, 1962); T. R. Golembiewski, *Men, Management and Morality: Toward a New Organizational Ethics* (New York, McGraw-Hill, 1965); D. Waldo, "Development of Theory of Democracy Administration," *American Political Science Review*, Vol. 64 (March 1982), pp. 81–103.

2. M. E. Gunn, "Ethics and the Public Service: An Annotated Bibliography and Overview Essay," *Public Personnel Management*, Vol. 10, No. 1 (1981), pp. 172–178.

3. T. M. Lilla, "Ethics, and Public Service," *The Public Interest*, Vol. 63 (Spring 1981), pp. 7–9.

4. *Ibid.*, pp. 11–13.

5. M. McMullan, "A Theory of Corruption," *Sociological Review*, Vol. 9, No. 2 (July 1961), pp. 181–201.

6. J. S. Nye, "Corruption and Political Development: A Cost-Benefit Analysis," *American Political Science Review*, Vol. 61 (June 1967), p. 417.

7. *Ibid.*, p. 424.

8. F. P. Drucker, "What Is Business Ethics?" *The Public Interest*, Vol. 63 (Spring 1981), pp. 18–36.

9. A. J. Heidenheimer (ed.), *Political Corruption: Readings in Comparative Analysis* (New York: Holt, 1970).

10. J. G. Peters and S. Welch, "Political Corruption in America. A Search for Definition and Theory; Or, If Political Corruption Is in the Mainstream of American Politics. Why Is It Not the Mainstream of American Politics Research?" *American Political Science Review*, Vol. 72, No. 3 (September 1978), pp. 974–984.

11. J. P. Dobel, "The Corruption of a State," *American Political Science Review*, Vol. 72, No. 3 (September 1978), p. 960.

12. Lilla, *op. cit.*

13. Drucker, *op. cit.*

14. A. C. Schwartz, "Corruption and Political Development in the USSR," *Comparative Politics*, Vol. 11, No. 9 (July 1979), pp. 431–432.

15. J. C. Scott, *Comparative Political Corruption* (Englewood Cliffs, N.J.: Prentice-Hall, Inc., 1972), p. 11.

16. E. G. Caiden and N. Caiden, "Administrative Corruption," *Public Administration Review*, Vol. 37, No. 3 (May-June 1977), p. 303.

17. G. Myrdal, *Asian Drama* (New York: Twentieth Century Fund, 1968).

18. McMullen, *op. cit.*

19. V. T. LeVine, *Political Corruption: The Ghana Case* (Stanford: Hoover Institution Press, 1975).

20. See, for example, G. Benson, *Political Corruption in America* (Lexington: Lexington Books, 1978); L. L. Berg, H. Hann and J. R. Schmidauser, *Corruption in the American Political System* (Morristown, N.J.: General Learning Press, 1976); S. Rose-Ackerman, *Corruption: A Study in Political Economy* (New York: Academic Press, 1978).

21. L. Sherman, *Scandal and Reform: Controlling Police Corruption* (Berkeley: University of California Press, 1978); G. Amic, *The American Way of Graft* (Princeton, N.J.: The Center for the Analysis of Public Issues, 1976).

22. LeVine, *op. cit.*

23. Schwartz, *op. cit.;* J. M. Kramer, "Political Corruption in the U.S.S.R.," *Western Political Quarterly,* Vol. 30, No. 2 (June 1977), pp. 213–224.

24. See, On Israel, G. Ben-Dor, "Schitut, Misud Ve'itpatchut Politit," *Rivon Le'Mechkar Chevrati* (August 1973), pp. 5–21 (Hebrew); On Japan, S. Mamoru and H. Auerbach, "Political Corruption and Social Structure in Japan," *Asian Survey,* Vol. 17 (June 1977), pp. 556–564; On Mexico, M. Goodman, "Does Political Corruption Really Help Economic Development: Yucatan, Mexico," *Polity,* Vol. 7, No. 2 (Winter 1974), pp. 143–162.

25. Ben Dor, 1973, *op. cit.*

26. Dobell, *op. cit.;* S. Dasgupta, "Corruption," Seminar 185 (January 1975), pp. 35–38.

27. Dasgupta, *idem;* Schwartz, *op. cit.*

28. S. P. Varma, "Corruption and Political Development in India," *Political Science Review,* Vol. 13, Nos. 1–4 (January-December 1974), pp. 157–179.

29. G. Ben Dor, "Corruption, Institutionalization, and Political Development: The Revisionist Thesis Revisited," *Comparative Political Studies,* Vol. 7 (1974), pp. 63–83.

30. A. Wildavsky, *Speaking Truth to Power: The Art and Craft of Policy Analysis* (Boston: Little, Brown and Company, 1979), p. 118.

31. *The Baltimore Sun,* "We All Pay," August 9, 1976, p. 2.

32. J. W. Chamblis, *On the Take: From Petty Crooks to Presidents* (Bloomington: Indiana University Press, 1978).

33. H. D. Bayley, "The Effects of Corruption in a Developing Nation," *Western Political Quarterly,* Vol. 19, No. 4 (December 1966), pp. 719–732; N. H. Leff, "Economic Development Through Bureaucratic Corruption," *American Behavioral Scientist,* Vol. 8 (November 1964), pp. 10–12; Nye, *op. cit.*

34. Bayley, *ibid.,* p. 719.

35. Bayley, *idem;* Scott, *op. cit.*

36. J. V. Abueva, "The Contribution of Nepotism, Spoils, and Graft to Political Development," *East-West Center Review,* Vol. 3 (June 1966), pp. 45–54; S. I. Huntington, *Political Order in Changing Societies* (New Haven, Conn.: Yale University Press, 1968); R. K. Merton, "Some Functions of the Political Machine," pp. 72–82, in R. K. Merton, *Social Theory and Social Structure* (New York: Free Press, 1957).

37. R. Braibanti, "Public Bureaucracy and Judiciary in Pakistan," in J. LaPalombara (ed.), *Bureaucracy and Political Development* (Princeton: Princeton University

Press, 1963); W. F. Riggs (1963), "Bureaucrats and Political Development: A Paradoxical View" in J. LaPalombara (ed.), *idem.*

38. Nye, *op. cit.;* Bayley, *op. cit.*

39. Bayley, *op. cit.*

40. Huntington, *op. cit.*

41. Manuscript of speech given at the Second Public Service International Asian Regional Conference in Singapore, Nov. 14, 1968. Reproduced in Heidenheimer (ed.), *op. cit.,* p. 54.

42. Myrdal, *op. cit.*

43. R. O. Tilman, "Emergency of Black Market Bureaucracy: Administration, Development and Corruption in the New States," *Public Administration Review,* Vol. 28, No. 5 (September/October 1968), pp. 437–444.

44. Ben-Dor, 1974, *op. cit.,* p. 68.

45. Caiden and Caiden, *op. cit.,* p. 305.

46. R. O. Tilman, "The Philippines Under Martial Law," *Current History,* Vol. 71, No. 422 (December 1976), pp. 201–204.

47. F. McHenry, "Food Bungle in Bangladesh," *Foreign Policy,* Vol. 27 (Summer 1977), p. 72–88.

48. Goodman, *op. cit.*

49. L. M. Hager, "Bureaucratic Corruption in India: Legal Control of Maladministration," *Comparative Political Studies,* Vol. 6, No. 2 (July 1973), pp. 179–219; M. Halaya, *Emergency: A War on Corruption* (New Delhi: Chand and Co. Ltd., 1975); Varma, *op. cit.*

50. Halayya, *ibid.,* pp. 134–135.

51. Mamoru and Auerbach, *op. cit.*

52. Ben-Dor, 1974, *op. cit.*

53. Henry, *op. cit.*

54. *Ibid.,* p. 11.

55. Benson, *op. cit.;* J. Gardiner and T. Lyman, *Decisions for Sale: Corruption and Reform in Land-Use and Building Regulation* (New York: Praeger, 1978); Rose-Ackerman, *op. cit.;* Sherman, *op. cit.*

56. N. Caiden, "Shortchanging the Public," *Public Administration Review,* Vol. 39, No. 3 (May-June 1979), p. 295.

57. Nye, *op. cit.,* p. 419.

58. Halayya, *op. cit.,* p. 128.

59. Quoted in R. D. Cressey, "White Collar Subversives," *The Center Magazine,* Vol. 11, No. 6 (November/December 1978), p. 48.

60. *Idem.*

61. Quoted in Schwartz, *op. cit.,* p. 430.

62. Drucker, *op. cit.,* p. 22.

63. Heidenheimer, *op. cit.*

64. D. Matza, *Delinquency and Drift* (New York: John Wiley and Sons, 1964), p. 60.

65. Schwartz, *op. cit.,* p. 440.

66. P. F. McGee and F. J. Anzelmi, "There Is No Such Thing as a Free Ride," *Public Personnel Management,* Vol. 10, No. 1 (1981), pp. 161–164.

67. Chamblis, *op. cit.*

68. A. H. Somjee, "Social Perspectives on Corruption in India," *Political Science Review,* Vol. 13, Nos. 1–4 (January–December 1974), pp. 180–186.

69. Dobel, *op. cit.,* p. 970.

70. Caiden and Caiden, *op. cit.,* p. 301.

71. Van Klaveren, "Corruption as a Historical Phenomenon," in Heidenheimer (ed.), *op. cit.,* pp. 67–75.

72. Caiden and Caiden, *op. cit.,* pp. 306–307.

73. Sherman, *op. cit.*

74. J. Darton, "Construction Industry: The Graft Is Built In," *New York Times,* July 13, 1975; *Corruption in Land Use and Building Regulation: An Integrated Report and Conclusions* (Washington, D.C.: U.S. Department of Justice, 1979).

75. Sherman, *op. cit.*

76. Amick, *op. cit.;* Corruption in Land Use, *op. cit.*

77. Cressey, *op. cit.,* p. 45.

78. Dobel, *op. cit.,* p. 971.

79. Varma, *op. cit.,* p. 164.

80. Hager, *op. cit.,* p. 217.

81. J. Bowman, "Dissent in Government: A Bibliography and Resource Guide on Whistle-Blowing." Paper presented at the annual convention of the American Society for Public Administration, San Francisco, April 1980.

82. E. Weisband and T. M. Frank, *Resignation in Protest: Political and Ethical Choices Between Loyalty to Team and Loyalty to Conscience in American Public Life* (New York: Grossman, 1975).

83. Drucker, *op. cit.*

84. M. Frome, "Blowing the Whistle," *The Center Magazine,* Vol. 11, No. 6 (November-December 1978), pp. 50–58.

85. Henry, *op. cit.,* p. 173.

86. T. J. Lowi, "The Intelligent Person's Guide to Political Corruption," *Public Affairs,* Vol. 82 (September 1981), p. 6.

Part FOUR

Codes of Ethics

Codes of ethics are often proposed as the solution to administrative misconduct, and they have been under discussion in public administration since the early 1950s. Prior to that, the focus was on establishing legislated standards of conduct. Such standards carried with them sanctions for violation, and they focused on observable and measurable behavior. These standards were the kinds of rules that Finer had argued were needed to ensure honest government.

In response to what has been called the "mid-century mess in Washington,"[1] described by Emmerich in Chapter 10, the Douglas subcommittee of the Senate was created. From that committee's deliberations came a 577-page report called *Ethical Standards in Government*[2] and a book. During the hearings by the subcommittee, a number of witnesses commented favorably on the suggestion that a code of ethics be developed.

The first chapter in Part 4 was published in 1953 in *PAR*. In "A Code of Ethics as a Means of Controlling Administrative Conduct" (Chapter 14 here), Phillip Monypenny suggests that "a measure of skepticism seems in order." His concern is one that later scholars will also raise, and that is the tension between an ethical code as a control device and as a "pious declaration" of what we ought to be doing. He suggests that ethical standards are essentially personal and that "conformance to a code is a matter of conversion that takes place from the inside." Sanctions are imposed by the conscience of the individual and are not controllable by external rules. From this perspective, he questions the value of a written code of ethics that is incorporated into administrative rules and examines the pros and cons of ethics codes, as he sees them. Monypenny concludes that an ethical code would seem a useful device.

TABLE IV.I   Code of Ethics for Government Service

Any Person in Government Service Should:

1. Put loyalty to the highest moral principles and to country above loyalty to persons, party, or Government department.

2. Uphold the Constitution, laws, and legal regulations of the United States and of all governments therein and never be a party to their evasion.

3. Give a full day's labor for a full day's pay; giving to the performance of his duties his earnest effort and best thought.

4. Seek to find and employ more efficient and economical ways of getting tasks accomplished.

5. Never discriminate unfairly by the dispensing of special favors or privileges to anyone, whether for remuneration or not; and never accept, for himself or his family, favors or benefits under circumstances which might be construed by reasonable persons as influencing the performance of his governmental duties.

6. Make no private promises of any kind binding upon the duties of office, since a Government employee has no private word which can be binding on public duty.

7. Engage in no business with the Government, either directly or indirectly, which is inconsistent with the conscientious performance of his governmental duties.

8. Never use any information coming to him confidentially in the performance of government duties as a means of making private profit.

9. Expose corruption wherever discovered.

10. Uphold these principles, ever conscious that public office is a public trust.

SOURCE: U.S. Code of Federal Regulations: 21CFR 19.6.

This "useful device" did not come into being at the federal level until 1958, when the Code of Ethics for Government Service[3] was adopted by Congress. It was passed with no fanfare and no recognition in ASPA-sponsored journals, yet it is still the operable ethics code for federal employees. It is reproduced in Table IV.I and stands as an aspirational statement for moral public administrators. It represents the type of professional standards that Friedrich idealized in the original Friedrich-Finer debate. It would later prove to be insufficient as a guide to ethical actions in government.

Twenty-nine years were to pass before the next ASPA article devoted to Codes of Ethics appeared! By the early 1980s, a debate about codes of ethics in public administration was going on behind the scenes at ASPA.

Since ASPA was one of the few professional associations without a code of ethics, there was impetus to create a code specifically for ASPA members. After thorough consideration by its Professional Standards and Ethics Committee, the National Council voted in 1981 against establishing a code of ethics for ASPA members. Citing the great diversity in the field and reiterating all the difficulties with legislating morals, the council voted to establish a statement of principles instead of a code of ethics.

In 1982, *State and Local Government Review* published "Ethics in the Public Service" (Chapter 15 here), written by Joseph Zimmerman. It detailed the history of the development of ethics codes for public service. First to appear were the conflict of interest laws. Then came codes of ethics, financial disclosure acts, public meeting laws, freedom of information laws, and privacy acts. After weaving the history of city, state, and federal development of ethics codes, Zimmerman argues that the most intractable ethical problems are violations of time rules, sick leave abuse, whistle-blowing, and abuse of citizen participation. His solution to the problems of immoral behavior is to institute more rigorous screening of job applicants and to provide an adequate salary. Although he does not negate the value of a code of ethics, he sees such codes as of minimal utility.

The January/February 1983 issue of *Public Administration Review* contained a reaction to the ASPA National Council action of 1981. Ralph Clark Chandler, a member of the Professional Standards and Ethics Committee, wrote to clarify "why codes of ethics are in disrepute among many, but why others believe a code is highly appropriate at this juncture of American administrative history." His article, "The Problem of Moral Reasoning in American Public Administration: The Case for a Code of Ethics" (Chapter 16 here), argues for an affirmation of the basic goodness of humankind. He offers the "Athenian Oath" to demonstrate the role of the community as the arbiter of what is ethical behavior and suggests that those who pledged their "their lives, their fortunes, and their sacred honor to secure the blessings of liberty" to the founding of this United States demonstrate the possibility for moral decision making that is rooted in heroic behavior—behavior not controlled by sanctions but by internal standards.

One would not learn from any ASPA-sponsored journal the outcome of the code of ethics debate in the society. The debate did continue. Ralph Chandler and other members of the Professional Standards and Ethics Committee moved to involve the ASPA membership around the country in discussions, even as they developed the first ASPA Code of Ethics, which was approved in 1985. Today, the slightly revised ASPA Code of Ethics is a vital part of what it means to be a professional public administrator, and it is printed on the cover of every issue of *Public Administration Review*.

Notes

1. H. C. Nixon, "Ethics and Politics," *Public Administration Review* 12, no. 4 (Autumn 1952):284–286.

2. U.S. Senate Subcommittee of the Committee on Labor and Public Welfare (1951), *Ethical Standards in Government.* Washington, D.C.: U.S. Government Printing Office.

3. U.S. Code of Federal Regulations, 21CFR19.6, pp. 187–188.

14

A CODE OF ETHICS AS A MEANS OF CONTROLLING ADMINISTRATIVE CONDUCT

Phillip Monypenny
University of Illinois

The recent surge of popular interest in the standards of administrative conduct has its parallels in the work of students and practitioners of administration. During an earlier period the academic students of government were often skeptical of the usefulness of any deliberate effort to set out standards of administrative ethics. Among nonacademic observers there has always been a great deal of skepticism that any other standard than the crudest conception of self-interest was active in the world of polities and government. A distinguished Jefferson City correspondent of the St. Louis *Post-Dispatch* once assured the writer, then working on a thesis on personnel standards in state government, that no one ever got a job in state government unless somebody got something out of it. But of late there has been a growing interest among the academic specialists in the values that determine administrative actions—an interest obviously related to a study of the ethical purposes that administrative activity serves.[1] The British writers on the civil service have always paid explicit attention to the high ethical standards of their own civil servants and Fritz Morstein Marx in a study of the German civil service before Hitler stressed the ethical standards of the service and the means of enforcing them.[2] A similar interest in ethical standards among writers in administration is fairly recent in the United States. The high point in popular interest has undoubtedly been the publication of the report and hearings of the Douglas subcommittee on governmental ethics.[3] The work of that subcommittee has already produced two volumes on the same general subject, one by its chairman, one by the head of its research staff.[4]

This paper has another purpose than to go over ground so ably covered before. Both in the subcommittee report and in the hearings there is a suggestion that a code of ethics might be a useful thing for governmental officers generally and for administrative employees in particular. The subcommittee even proposed a commission to draw up such a code and to apply disciplinary standards on the basis of it. During the hearings, a number of witnesses were asked to comment on the possibility of such an undertaking and did so; most of them distinctly favored it.

A measure of skepticism seems in order with respect to the changes in administrative conduct that would result from such a code. There are statutes already on the books which prohibit some of the transactions most subject to public censure. Would not a code of ethics be just another official pronouncement without any force of itself to secure the standards which it develops? There are reasons for believing, however, that under appropriate circumstances a deliberately formulated ethical code might be of use in controlling administrative conduct, that it might result in another standard of conduct than would be achieved by the spontaneous development of individual or group standards among administrative personnel.

This paper is addressed to the possible differences between a situation in which any standards that develop arise out of the unguided adjustment of individuals to each other, and to the environment in which the agency works, and the situation in which there has been a deliberate attempt to formulate standards. If there are differences, then an ethical code may function as a control device and not simply as a pious declaration.

If we take a situation in which a number of persons are participating in various decisions of some consequence for persons inside and outside an agency, we may assume a number of factors that enter into the decisions that are made. Some of these factors will be deliberately controlled by those who take the responsibility for controlling the work of the agency. There will be a division of labor, a system of authority, standard procedures, and the orderly presentation of grounds of decision, both factual and nonfactual—and implicit in the nonfactual, which we may call agency policy, the values to be maximized in the decisions taken. But there is obviously an area not subject to deliberate control, except as the selection of the staff may have determined some of the characteristics of staff members which affect their work. The decisions reached by individuals on the basis of even the most careful control of the factors supposed to affect decision-making will not ordinarily be identical. There will be standards present peculiar to individuals and there will be a group standard evolving—and these are only partially within the control of the superior officers of the agency. Actions taken may vary considerably from formal prescriptions.

The departure of decisions from the formal standards set out in agency regulations is not easily controlled through supplementary means of exercising authority. Only a relatively small number of decisions may be reexamined to see whether the specified grounds account for the result or whether others seem to have entered. Those in authority cannot oversee directly the work that finally embodies the agency purposes, except in the very smallest agencies. They must act through others, and these through still others. Great reliance must ordinarily be placed on the immediately-undirected compliance of many individuals with the agency standards of action. To reduce the area of uncertainty there has been a considerable elaboration of measurement of all kinds—unit cost taking, statistical reporting, and other means of discovering indirectly whether the authorized standards are being followed. But in the end the informal standards are known only to those who are applying them.[5]

Suppose however, that an attempt is made to set up a code of ethical conduct, thus attempting to deal by definition with some of the intangibles that are not easily included in official regulation. Such a code will be a body of statements containing grounds for decision of somewhat general applicability. It will specifically exclude certain grounds of decision. It will codify the implicit assumptions of disinterestedness and devotion to official policy not expressed in official regulations. It will have no legal effect, since we assume that it serves another purpose than rules and regulations. To be sufficiently specific to be a reliable guide, it will probably have to be based on the operations of particular administrative units. Thus, it may have a meaningful content with respect to the ordinary run of decisions. But even if it is assumed that it embodies the virtues of specificity and practicality, will it not be a set of statements like official rules and regulations endorsed by higher authority as an appropriate guide to conduct, but not necessarily accompanied by appropriate activity? Is there anything which will translate such formulas into action? Is there any system of sanctions more effective than the cumbersome sanctions that may attend formal violation of regulations?

In ordinary discussions, ethical standards are often treated as peculiarly personal, like habits of bathing or table manners. You either have them, or you don't. A person measures up, or he does not. A standard may be stated, but only the individual himself can bring about the transition within himself suggested by acceptance. Conformance to a code is a matter of conversion that takes place from the inside. If this is so, then the only value in an ethical code, whether general or particular, is to present a more explicit statement of good conduct than might otherwise be obtainable. In the degree that it is explicit it may be a better vehicle for achieving conversion than the example of others and the implicit expectations of the other actors on the scene. If conversion takes place, action will follow. But obviously conversion cannot be controlled except, of course, by unusually skillful evangelists.

But if one looks more closely it is obvious that there are more powerful administrative tools than evangelism to convert ethical standards into ethical conduct. It is true that the words of any code are only words, that it is people who act. But it is not necessary for all of the personnel of an agency, or even a majority of them, to be converted in order for a code to be an effective standard of conduct. What is required is action to effectuate it on the part of a number of persons in positions of authority, whether their authority be formal or informal. The code becomes for this authoritative group, if they are willing and able to use it, a more or less exact standard by which the conduct of agency members can be judged. It becomes a standard not for the review of specific acts, but for the judgment of the whole official performance of agency members. During the probationary period, persons who do not show a ready sense of the standards contained in the code may be dropped. When jobs which are the key to future opportunities become available, those who by the standards rank high may get them. When junior members are selected to share in discussions of pending policies, the ones who conform will be the ones invited to participate. When more intimate associations develop within the range of junior-senior relationships, it will be those who meet the standards who get the friendly nod, the invitation to coffee, the invitation to walk home. Those who do not meet them will be excluded from the sphere of informal discussion and cut off from the opportunities to show their capacity for more demanding duty.

As this process develops the junior employees who find their own standards appropriately mirrored in the official code will evaluate their associates by these standards and those who fail to measure up will be excluded in many ways from the more intimate association of their colleagues. Men on the same level in an organization affect one another's future in many ways and those who are not generally accepted will fall behind those who form part of a congenial company of men with common standards. These are sanctions of no small effect, more continuously operative than the major sanctions which are attached to legal regulation.

Now it is true that such a process goes on in every working group. There is always some standard that develops out of shared activity. But there is a great deal of difference between the piecemeal elaboration of a working code in immediate response to the various demands of the working situation and a considered review of the implicit purposes which are being served. Presumably one kind of code will be some sort of reasonable variation from the other. Men's purposes are not only cherished in their minds; they are evident in their acts. But since they are at least partially knowing animals and since knowing is not an automatic process, the setting within which the view is taken will determine what is seen. And purposes in the heat of the event, partially apprehended, may not be the purposes which will be willingly affirmed when a span of events is covered. There is reason to think, therefore, that a deliberately-developed code will be somewhat different from one that is implicit in day-to-day activity.[6]

Once a code is enunciated it becomes common property in a way in which implicit codes are not. Everyone can know its provisions. It has the blessing of legitimacy. There is no need for individuals to doubt their own understanding of the situation. Here it is stated for all to see. It is easier to follow as it is accepted by the individual and easier to implement through sanctions of one kind or another. It is in this quality of sanctions that a code of ethics shows its primary difference from ethical standards individually held. The sanctions imposed by conscience, or if you will, the superego, are not subject to administrative control. But the sanctions that may be attached to a code of ethics, a standard initially, at least, external to the individual, are. Since the sanctions are for offenses too difficult of definition to be punishable as infractions of regulations, they must be both restricted and flexible—a matter for subtle judgment rather than formal rule. But sanctions they may be for all that.

The individual faced with an ethical code to which various sanctions are attached is therefore in a very different position from the individual faced with the pain of departure from his own personal standards. He may find the internal pain reduced through many departures from his original standards, or he may avoid it entirely by a redefinition of his standards. But the sanctions of a code are less escapable. A code may have definite consequences attached to it as a private standard may not. It presents more clearly differentiated alternatives by which a choice may be made. And it will not be surprising if, after a period of acting according to externally imposed consequences, the standard of action becomes an internal one as well—a habit of action which it takes considerable effort to displace.

It is obvious that there is nothing self-enforcing about an ethical code. It can be enforced only when a sufficient number of persons in appropriate positions accept it as a guide to their own action with respect to their fellows. But unlike personal conversion, it does not require that all of the members of a working group accept it. It does not even require a majority. Rather, it must be accepted only by those who by their action are able to affect in significant ways the careers of their associates and subordinates. This fact also indicates a limitation—a code cannot set a higher standard than is apt to be followed by such a strategic group. In all probability it must be worked out with their cooperation. Furthermore, in the nature of things, the strategic group is likely to differ only in a limited degree from the others whose conduct it is desired to affect. They live largely in the same world, they reached their positions in comparable ways, they are responsive to about the same forces. However they are likely to differ somewhat, and if they do, an ethical code has some possible usefulness.

The other limitations of a code are obvious. A code of any kind is useful only to the degree that its principles can be applied to the normal range of business of the agency so as to give answers which will be approximately the same for all those who are attempting to find them. This suggests that for greatest usefulness a code should be formulated in relation to the business to which it applies. Its seeming generalities must have rather specific meaning to those who apply them. It must cover the kind of decisions they are making, the situations which for them contain conflicts between immediate expediency and long-run standards. A code promulgated by the legislature or by a specially appointed commission, for example, will be limited in effect. A code is more likely to be effective in agencies with established functions than in those which are exploring new kinds of activity. It will be most effective among people who expect to be working together for a long time and who see their future as depending on the judgment of their fellows.[7]

Yet, despite all of these limitations an ethical code would seem to be an important device for administrative control—useful in reducing to systematic statement the highest standards of perception and devotion which are active within an agency and securing their general adoption.

Notes

1. Wayne A.R. Leys, *Ethics for Policy Decisions: The Art of Asking Deliberative Questions* (Prentice Hall, 1952), 428 pp.; Paul Appleby, *Morality and Administration in Democratic Government* (Louisiana State University Press, 1952), 261 pp.; Herbert A. Simon, Donald W. Smithburg, and Victor A. Thompson, *Public Administration* (Alfred A. Knopf, 1950), 582 pp., ch. 3.

2. H. E. Dale. *The Higher Civil Service of Great Britain* (Oxford University Press, 1941), 232 pp.; Fritz Morstein Marx, "Civil Service in Germany," in Leonard D. White and others, *Civil Service Abroad: Great Britain, Canada, France, Germany* (McGraw-Hill Book Company, 1935), pp. 161–275.

3. *Ethical Standards in Government.* Report of a Subcommittee of the Committee on Labor and Public Welfare, United States Senate, 82d Cong. 1st sess., Committee Print (United States Government Printing Office, 1951), 89 pp.; *Establishment of a Commission on Ethics in Government,* Hearings before a Subcommittee to Study Senate Concurrent Resolution 21 of the Committee on Labor and Public Welfare, United States Senate, 82d Cong., 1st sess. (United States Government Printing Office, 1951), 577 pp.

4. Paul H. Douglas, *Ethics in Government* (Harvard University Press, 1952), 114 pp.: George A. Graham, *Morality in American Politics* (Random House, 1952), 337 pp.

5. Once the author was an unimportant unit in a chain of communications relaying reports on ammunition stocks to higher headquarters. It was at the end of the war and the figures were always the same. Then during a period of unusual alertness, battalions were ordered to inventory their ammunition and make good the deficiencies needed to come up to combat readiness. There was a tremendous requisitioning, though there had been no previous indication of shortage.

6. For a technical analysis of this matter see Muzafer Sherif, *The Psychology of Social Norms* (Harper & Bros., 1936), ch. 1. For the dynamic quality of group decision as opposed to exhortation in effecting a change in conduct see Kurt Lewin, "Forces behind Food Habits and Methods of Change," in National Research Council, Committee on Food Habits, *Problem of Changing Food Habits* (The Council, 1943).

7. These limits on scope and effect are treated more fully in an article by the author, "A Code of Ethics for Public Administration," 21 *George Washington Law Review* 423–44 (March, 1953).

15

ETHICS IN THE PUBLIC SERVICE

Joseph F. Zimmerman
State University of New York at Albany

Ethics was of great concern to Old Testament authors and Greek philosophers, including Socrates, who was accorded the title "Father of Ethics." Derived from a Greek word meaning "custom," ethics is the science of morals. It was enshrined in the form of the decalogue in the Old Testament.

Since the beginning of recorded history, organized societies have established rules of conduct or ethical standards, such as the prohibition of peculation, for the guidance of citizens and public officials. English Common Law, followed in amended form by the U.S. Government and forty-nine states,[1] establishes ethical standards for public officials. To cite one example, common law provides that a contract between a municipality and one or more of its officers is invalid.

Governments in the United States have been plagued by unethical behavior of certain public officials and employees since the colonial period [15, pp. 1–2]. Common in the nineteenth century, bribery, embezzlement of public funds, macing, sinecures, and nepotism have not been eliminated totally today.[2]

The National Institute of Law Enforcement and Criminal Justice in 1978 published the following:

Corruption has three main components that are controllable and one that is not. The three controllable ones are opportunity, incentive, and risk: the uncontrollable one is personal honesty. Many public servants over a long period of time have had the freely available opportunity to be corrupt, a large incentive to do so, and little risk of being found out if they did, but have refused because "it wouldn't be honest" [12, p. 5].

Government actions to raise and maintain ethical standards in the public service can be seen in the creation of conflict of interest laws, codes of ethics, financial disclosure acts, public meeting laws, freedom of information laws, and privacy acts. Our discussion will be limited to ethical problems faced by appointive officials in the executive branch of government. We will first consider conflict of interest laws.

Conflict of Interest Laws

The first laws enacted by legislative bodies in the United States to ensure that public officials and employees act in accordance with the highest moral standards were conflict of interest laws. These dealt with "black and white" situations in which the overwhelming majority of citizens would recognize overt unethical conduct—such as bribery or embezzlement.

To promote public integrity and ensure that private interests and self-serving government employees do not benefit unfairly from governmental operations, statutes have been enacted over the years forbidding public officials and employees to use confidential government information for their private benefit, requiring competitive public bidding on most government contracts, prohibiting public officials and employees from acting as agents or attorneys in the sale of land to the government, forbidding the offering of bribes to public officials and the accepting of bribes, and making it illegal for suppliers to offer and public officials to request or accept commissions or bonuses from suppliers. These statutory provisions undoubtedly have reduced the amount of outright corruption and graft in the conduct of the public's business [4, pp. 176–79, and 11].

In an increasingly complex society, outright dishonesty is only one facet of the problem of unethical conduct in government service. Recognizing that anticipating every conceivable ethical question is impossible, legislative bodies in recent years have enacted codes of ethics containing standards and guidelines for situations falling in the "gray area" between what is clearly ethical behavior and outright unethical behavior. These codes also provide sanctions for violations of the standards.

Codes of Ethics

The Municipal Reform Movement, which originated at the turn of the century, had as one of its major goals the elimination of corruption and the raising of ethical standards in government service. Venal officials, open to bribery, were relatively common in many cities at that time [16, pp. 19–20]. Municipal reformers incorporated Richard S. Childs's 1909 council-manager plan of administration as a plank in their programs of corrective action on the grounds that professional management would raise ethical standards in municipalities as well as improve economy and efficiency. Ten years after its formation, the International City Managers' Association in 1924 adopted the City Manager's Code of Ethics for the guidance of association members.[3] The code includes the provisions that a manager should "seek no favor; believe that personal aggrandizement or profit secured by confidential information or misuse of public time is dishonest" [3, p. 9]. Many other professional associations, such as dentistry, law, and medicine, have adopted codes of ethics.

Government codes of ethics have three major objectives:

1. Maintaining high ethical standards in government service.
2. Increasing public confidence in the integrity of public officials and employees.
3. Assisting officials and employees in determining the proper course of action when they are uncertain about the propriety of a contemplated action, thereby preventing them from unwittingly entangling public and private interests.

According to the International City Management Association, "it is desirable . . . to include legal provisions in a code of ethics, without imputation of lack of integrity, in order to maintain common minimal standards. Practically all else in a code should be voluntary and directed at an ever-increasing refinement of ideals and conduct" [21, p. 6].

Public officials and employees in effect live in glass houses and consequently must avoid giving the appearance of a conflict of interest or other form of unethical behavior. Hence, the propriety of the social contacts of officials and employees merits inclusion in a code of ethics. The code might urge officials and employees to choose with care their social associates because of the danger of giving the impression of being engaged in unethical practices.

How detailed should a code of ethics be? A code should deal more specifically with certain matters than do conflict-of-interest laws. Nevertheless, a brief code is preferable to a highly detailed and rigid code. A specific standard cannot be written to cover every conceivable situation that might arise—especially a subtle one involving unethical conduct.

Codes of ethics stress that holding office is a public trust and that standards of political morality are higher than those of the marketplace. Section 1A of the code of the Village of Glen Ellyn, Illinois, emphatically states that "what is acceptable in private business may not be proper conduct by elected and appointed officials." The Rockville, Maryland, code of ethics—ordinance 6-74, § 15-1.01—opens with a declaration of policy: "That no man can fairly serve two masters whose interests are, or may be, in conflict is a principle of ancient and respected lineage. A particularly serious application of this principle occurs where one who is employed as a servant of the public has a financial or personal interest that in a particular situation conflicts, or may conflict with the public interest."

Should all provisions of a code of ethics apply to all officials and employees or should specific provisions in the code apply only to certain officers? An examination reveals that most codes do not include provisions applicable to specific officials other than members of the legislative body. It is apparent, however, that administrative officials and employees with inspection or regulatory responsibilities have a greater opportunity than others to engage in unethical activities. As a consequence, the Smithtown, New York, Code—§4—contains specific provisions relating to the town attorney, building inspector, justices of the peace, assessor, town engineer, and director of planning. The building inspector, for example, is forbidden by section 4 (b) to "engage in the real estate, insurance, building contracting business, or building materials business, directly or indirectly, . . . during the course of his employment."

Failure of full-time government officials and employees to devote the required time to their official duties clearly is unethical. The Geneva, New York, Code of Ethics—art. XV, § 15.2—contains a section stipulating that "appointive officials and employees shall adhere to the rules of work and performance established as the standard for their positions by the appropriate authority." The New Orleans Code of Ethics—§5A (1)—contains a similar provision: "Full-time employees shall perform a full day's work each and every working day."

Problems of ethics most often involve acceptance of a favor or a gift, favored treatment for a business firm, use of public equipment and personnel for private purposes, disclosure of or use of confidential information to further the official's or employee's personal interests, incompatible employment, and personal interest in a proposed law or contract. The personal interest in a proposed law or contract frequently involves a relative.

Advisory Opinions

A code of ethics should require public officials or employees to notify their superiors in writing whenever they suspect that present or anticipated actions may violate the code. Whether the potential violation is real or only apparent is of concern. Many potential conflicts are minor and inconsequential, unavoidable in a complex society. All requests for advice should be considered confidential information.

The superior should be responsible for making a written determination and notifying the person seeking the advice whether the action poses a threat to the public interest, and this should be done within a specified period of time. The superior should be free to request the advice of the board of ethics if there is such a board, and any determination made by the superior should be appealable to the board. This procedure provides a relatively simple mechanism whereby a public official or employee can be protected against a possible code violation.

If the supervisor fails to make a written determination within the specified period, the matter should be automatically referred to the board of ethics. If the board fails to make a written determination within a specified period, the code should provide that failure of the board to act shall be deemed an advisory opinion and that the facts and circumstances of the particular case do not constitute a code violation. The rendered or deemed-rendered opinion, unless amended or revoked, should be binding on the board of ethics in any subsequent case involving the official or employee who sought the opinion and acted on it in good faith, unless the official or employee omitted or misstated material facts in the request for the advisory opinion.

The Board of Ethics

Experience has revealed that a complex society needs a governmental mechanism to deal with subtle conflicts-of-interest of public officials and employees that are not amenable to statutory definition. The best mechanism is an official or a board charged with responsibility for (1) rendering advisory opinions on the propriety of proposed actions in uncharted areas, (2) investigating charges of unethical behavior, and (3) reporting findings to the appropriate officials. The official or board could perform an additional service by suggesting to the legislative body needed code amendments revealed by experience.

The federal Ethics in Government Act of 1978–92 STAT. 1864, 5 U.S.C. 5316 (1978 Supp.)—established in the Office of Personnel Management an Office of Government Ethics, headed by a director charged with 14 specific responsibilities.

At the state level, commissions such as the Alabama Ethics Commission and the Ohio Ethics Commission perform duties similar to those of the Federal Office of Government Ethics. In borderline ethical cases, rendering advisory opinions may be assigned to the attorney general.

Most local boards of ethics consist of five members appointed for a three- or five-year term by the local legislative body or the local chief executive, with approval of the legislative body. Some local boards also have *ex officio* members such as the corporation counsel.

The major function of the board of ethics is to issue advisory opinions to officials and employees. Published advisory opinions, with deletions preserving the anonymity of the official or employee involved, will guide officials and employees who may encounter similar future situations involving ethical questions. In small municipalities, however, it may be impossible to publish advisory opinions without invading the privacy of an official or employee.

The New York General Municipal Law—§805-a (1) (McKinney 1974)—forbids a municipal official to disclose "confidential" information acquired "in the course of his official duties." Similar provisions are found in other state statutes and in many local codes of ethics. A board of ethics can provide guidance about what constitutes confidential information. The board, for example, might inform inquiring officials that they could disclose information that their superiors had classified as confidential purely for partisan political reasons.

The International City Management Association's *Guidelines for Professional Conduct* stipulates that an association member should not accept a gift "under any circumstances in which it could reasonably be inferred that the gift was intended as a reward for any official action on his part" [3, p. 16]. However, the *Guidelines* stresses that "it is important that the prohibition of unsolicited gifts be limited to circumstances related to improper influence. In such de minimum situations as cigars, meal checks, etc., some modest maximum dollar value should be determined by the member for his guidance" [3, p. 16].

One can argue that a code of ethics should stipulate that a public official or employee should accept no gift of "economic value." On the other hand, it is possible to argue that there is nothing unethical about a police officer accepting a small gift given in the same spirit as gifts given to postmen and newspaper boys. No one will argue with a code provision stipulating that a government official or employee should not accept, directly or indirectly, a gift of "economic value" if doing so might give the impression of compromising the impartiality of that person's position or impairing the independence of judgment in the exercise of official duties. Especially in a period of inflation, there obviously is a need for developing standards of value. A board of ethics can develop a body of precedents dealing with the gift problem, i.e., a common law developed on a case-by-case basis.

The New York City Board of Ethics has had the most experience in rendering advisory opinions. Opinion number 53 is typical. An assessor from the city tax commission inquired whether the city's Code of Ethics prohibited him from investing in private real estate transactions in an area of the city "which he does not currently assess." The board ruled that such investment would constitute a code violation.

Although the writer may not be assigned to the area assessing the property in question, his interest in such property is in our opinion sufficient to create a conflict of interest because the property in question is part of the assessable area under the jurisdiction of the department in which he is employed and for the further reason that assessors are subject to reassignment and in addition all property assessments are the responsibility of the same department and the same class of employees with whom the City employee works side by side.

An ethics code should direct the board to investigate possible code violations upon the written request of the local government's chief executive, a majority of the local legislative body, and the governor. In all other cases, the board should not be allowed to conduct an investigation of possible code violations unless the person making a charge(s) against an official or employee has signed the charge under oath or affirmation or the board has adopted a formal resolution defining the nature and scope of the inquiry. Section 6 of the New Orleans Code of Ethics authorizes "any qualified elector to file written complaints in the form of an affidavit with the Civil Service Commission concerning violations. . . ."

An official may call upon a board of ethics to investigate charges by the media questioning the official's conduct. Manhattan Borough President Percy E. Sutton in 1967 requested the New York City Board of Ethics "to evaluate the propriety of my conduct as a public official with regard to the stories that have appeared in the *New York Post* alluding to improper conduct by me as a public official." The *Post* articles could have led readers to infer that Mr. Sutton had an interest in two multiple dwellings charged with many violations by the city's department of buildings. After an extensive investigation, the board of ethics concluded that "Mr. Percy E. Sutton did not have any interest, direct or indirect, in the ownership of 505 West 142nd Street or 502 West 141st Street properties," and that "there has been no violation of the Code of Ethics and Related Laws and that there has been no impropriety in his conduct during the period of his public service with respect to the properties in question."

Whenever the conduct of officials or employees is under investigation for alleged code violations, the board of ethics should notify the alleged violators at least 30 days prior to a hearing. The alleged violators should have the right to be present and represented by counsel at the hearing, to examine and cross-examine witnesses, and to call witnesses on his or her behalf. It is advisable for the board to arrange for the preparation of a stenographic record or tape recording of each hearing.

The Seattle Code of Ethics—ordinance no. 100435, §4—specifies that "all officers, employees, departments, and agencies of the city shall make available to the board of ethics all books, papers, documents, information, and assistance requested by said board and pertinent or material to any inquiry or investigation being conducted by said board in the performance of its duties under this code."

The board of ethics should conduct its investigation on a confidential basis and report findings of code violations to the concerned officials or employees and their supervisors. Section 6 of the Seattle ordinance stipulates that the appropriate city supervisor must file with the board, within 14 calendar days of receiving the board's decision, a written report of the disciplinary action taken.

The board of ethics should be granted the power to issue subpoenas and have them served and enforced. Persons testifying before the board should be required to testify under oath or affirmation. An individual whose name is mentioned adversely during testimony before the board should be notified and allowed to appear before the board or to file a sworn statement.

Financial Disclosure Acts

Closely related to codes of ethics and often included in such codes are financial disclosure requirements. The federal Ethics in Government Act of 1978–92 STAT. 1938, 5 U.S.C. 5332 (1978 Supp.)—requires the specified officers and employees to file annually by May 15 a detailed financial report.

Except as noted below, reports are filed by covered officials and employees with a designated agency official. The president, vice president, postmaster general, deputy postmaster general, governors of the board of governors of the United States Postal Service, designated agency officials, candidates for president and vice president, and officers whose positions require Senate confirmation file their reports with the director of the Office of Government Ethics. Members of the uniformed services file their reports with the concerned secretary.

Each agency is required within 15 days of receiving a financial disclosure report to permit inspection of the report or to furnish a copy of it to any individual requesting an inspection or copy of the report. The act—92 STAT. 1846—specifically makes it illegal for any individual to obtain or use a report:

A. for any unlawful purpose;
B. for any commercial purpose, other than by news and communications media for dissemination to the general public;
C. for determining or establishing the credit rating of any individual;
D. for use, directly or indirectly, in the solicitation of money for any political, charitable, or other purpose.

Should a code of ethics require all local officials and employees to disclose aspects of their personal finances? The answer must be "no" for at least some local officials and employees. A disclosure requirement not only would be an unnecessary invasion of privacy in certain cases, but also could result in a significant number of officials resigning and many individuals refusing to accept an appointive office because they consider disclosure to be an inordinate burden. To a large extent, local government in smaller municipalities is "part-time" citizen government, relying on citizens serving without compensation or receiving only minor stipends. Who would be willing to serve on a village planning board if all members were required to make a complete personal financial disclosure? Service on a non-paid board or commission represents a sacrifice of time and money. A disclosure requirement might make the sacrifice too great for many competent men and women. If a disclosure requirement is incorporated into a local code of ethics, a distinction clearly must be made between the "full-time" officials and employees and the "citizen" officials serving on a part-time basis.

If a financial disclosure requirement is adopted, should officials and employees be required to disclose all their assets? One answer to this question is provided by Rockville, Maryland, which holds that "a savings account in a bank or other savings institution, or an insurance policy, are not considered to be a financial interest in the bank, institution, or insurance company and should not be reported" [9, p. 2]. Furthermore, "ownership of tangible personal property should not be reported unless it is used for income producing purposes."

A mandated disclosure requirement preferably should be restricted to a listing of sources of income and should not include the amounts received from each source. On June 17, 1976, the New York State Board of Public Disclosure exempted members of the Board of the Municipal Assistance Corporation, who are part-time officials, from the state requirement that officials disclose the value of their assets [18, p. D-12]. The officials, however, are required to identify their assets—such as bank deposits and real estate holdings—without disclosing their value.

The disclosure also might be limited to specified sources of income exceeding a stipulated amount. Individuals should file annual required disclosure reports of the preceding year with the board of ethics on a form prepared by the board. The board should be empowered to investigate charges of violations. The required disclosure statement should contain the name and address of each creditor to whom a specified amount is owed, due date of the debt, interest rate, date and original amount of the debt, existing special conditions, and a statement indicating whether the debt is secured or unsecured. Retail installment debt and mortgage debt on a personally occupied home might be exempted from the disclosure requirement.

Recognizing that a blanket prohibition of stock in a corporation doing business with the town would be unfair, the Bel Air, Maryland, Code—§22-4 (b) (4)—stipulates that the board of ethics "with the unanimous approval of the Commissioners of Bel Air, may specifically authorize any Town official or employee to own stock in any corporation or to maintain a business in connection with an entity participating in any transaction of the Town if, upon full disclosure of all pertinent facts by such officials or employee to the Board and the Commissioners, both the Board and the Commissioners determine unanimously that such stock ownership does not violate the public interest."

In response to a request for his opinion, the New York Attorney General in 1974 advised that "the Town of East Hampton is not authorized to require that, once a year, certain of its officers and employees fully disclose and itemize their status to include all of their assets and all of their liabilities when there is no apparent or potential conflict of interest in the standard of conduct of such officer or employee as it relates to his employment with the municipality" [14, p. 291].

The Recruitment Problem

Recruitment problems associated with financial disclosure requirements for local officials are paralleled on the state level. The only recent New York governor to experience serious problems in recruiting department heads is Hugh L. Carey. His recruitment problems stem in part from issuance of a 1975 executive order. This order requires all employees in exempt, noncompetitive, or unclassified positions in the executive branch earning in excess of $30,000 and heads of state departments and agencies appointed by the governor to make annual public disclosures of their finances by filing with a newly created board of public disclosure in the Department of State a list of assets and liabilities plus a statement of sources of income exceeding $1,000. In addition, the 2,000 affected officers and employees were forbidden to hold a second position with a government or private firm.

The governor expanded coverage of the financial disclosure requirement in 1976 by issuing an amended executive order covering more than 10,000 employees in "managerial or confidential positions" earning more than $30,000. A 1979 amended executive order lowered the salary to $25,000. Many highly qualified business employees and professionals earning more than $30,000 in private employment felt that the governor was asking too big a sacrifice by requiring them to make a public disclosure of their personal finances should they accept a lower-paying state position. Because of recruitment problems. Governor Carey convinced several legislators to resign to become eligible for positions in the executive branch.

Sunshine Laws

So-called "sunshine" laws are designed not only to open official meetings and records to the public, but also to ensure that high ethical standards are

maintained by public officials and employees by making most of their actions visible. These laws generally exempt meetings involving acquisition
of land and buildings, collective bargaining, and personnel management
(appointments and disciplinary actions). Sunshine provisions can be included in a code of ethics since their inclusion may reduce the opportunity
for unethical action of officials and employees and build public confidence
in their integrity. Openness in conducting governmental affairs, of course,
may slow the decision-making process.

The federal Freedom of Information Act of 1966, as amended in
1974–88 STAT. 1561, 5 U.S.C. 552a—is designed to provide for open government. However, it has encountered strong opposition from some bureaucrats who prefer operating in camera. Bureaucratic obstructions raise
serious ethical questions. Professor Samuel J. Archibald, Staff Director of
the House Special Subcommittee on Government Information from 1955
to 1966 reported in 1979 that bureaucrats

> . . . developed secrecy by delay, taking many weeks to answer an initial re-
> quest for access to a public record. They developed secrecy by dollars, charg-
> ing far in excess of costs for copying public records. They used the investiga-
> tory files exemption as a major shield for secrecy. The original FOI Act
> included nine categories of public records which might be exempt from public
> disclosure. One category was investigatory files compiled for law enforcement
> purposes. Federal agencies often claimed their public records were investiga-
> tory files even though the investigation had been completed long ago. When
> all else failed, federal agencies forced insistent applicants for public records to
> go to court [1, p. 316].

To overcome delays in providing requested information, the 1974
amendments established strict time limits that agencies have met readily.
Archibald concludes his article with the statement that "somewhere,
deep within the memory bank of each federal agency, is some sort of
mechanism that tells the bureaucrats how to keep ahead of the lawmakers" [1, p. 317].

A conflict may occur whenever sunshine acts invade the area of personal
privacy. The federal Privacy Act of 1974–88 STAT. 1896, 5 U.S.C. 552(a)
(1974 Supp.)—requires executive agencies to keep confidential personal information, yet the Freedom of Information Act requires agencies to make
executive branch records available for inspection or copying except "to the
extent required to prevent a clearly unwarranted invasion of personal privacy. . . ." (§552(a) (2)).

Professor David M. O'Brien wrote that "the Freedom of Information
Act encourages agencies to err on the side of disclosure by not forbidding
disclosures and by neglecting to provide incentives to safeguard personal
privacy; while the Privacy Act does not supersede the Freedom of Informa-

tion Act, it permits disclosures only when required" [13, p. 325]. He also noted that "disclosure under the Freedom of Information Act might violate the Privacy Act" [13, p. 325].

The federal government in the Sunshine Act of 1976–90 STAT. 1244, 5 U.S.C. 554 (1976 Supp.)—requires the tape recording or transcription of every open and closed meeting of members of each collegial agency. Theodore J. Jacobs, director of the Project for Open Government, reported in 1980 that a tape recording of a meeting of the board of directors of the Export-Import Bank assisted a recent congressional investigation of the circumstances involved in the bank's loan to Rupert Murdoch's company and the endorsement of President Jimmy Carter by Murdoch's *New York Post* [10, p. 22]. Jacobs also reports that "without the requirements of the Sunshine Act, this meeting would never have been taped. The tape proved to be an immense aid in the banking committee's investigation. In the absence of a tape or transcript, it would be one person's recollection against another's" [10, p. 22].

Senator Daniel K. Inouye of Hawaii, in an attempt to shed additional sunshine on federal government operations, field the Federal Reports Authorship Act of 1980—S. 2788—on June 4, 1980. This bill would have required every federal agency issuing a report to reveal whether the report was prepared by agency personnel or by consultants. If prepared by the latter, the bill provided for the disclosure of the amount of the contract and the names of the consultants who prepared the report. In introducing the bill, Senator Inouye stated:

> These government officials are often too busy to devote time to research and writing. Instead, outside consultants and experts are hired to prepare studies which are subsequently released for public consumption. I believe that all government reports, like medicine and foods, should be labeled so that we, in Congress and the American public, can have an opportunity to know what we are going to digest before we swallow it. . . .
>
> The bill will force disclosure of the type of bidding used to let the contracts. Too often sweetheart deals are permitted, because of the supposed sole-source competence of one firm. Too often cost-plus contracts allow a supposedly lowest-cost bidder to escalate the final price far beyond their competitor's original bids. Publishing the type of contracting used in each report will permit the public and the competition to be aware of what contracting procedures were used and allow them to challenge any inequities they perceive [5, p. S6266].

The Florida Sunshine Act of 1967—chap. 67-356, *West's Florida Statutes Annotated*, §286.011 (1)—stipulates that all meetings of all state boards or commissions and local governments "at which official acts are to be taken are declared to be public meetings open to the public at all times, and no resolution, rule, regulation, or formal action shall be considered binding except as taken or made at such meeting." The act does not provide for exempt meetings, "but the role of the courts in exempting aspects of collective bargaining and the decision of the Attorney General concerning the exemption of the Judicial Qualifications Commission demonstrate that there is a balancing of values within the operation of the Florida law as well" [7, p. 5].

The 1974 New York State "Freedom of Information Law"—chap. 578–79, New York Public Officers Law, §§85–89 (McKinney 1980 Supp.)—applies to all local governments as well as to state agencies. Every local government must publish rules making all public records available for public inspection and copying, including the times and places the records are available, fees for copies, and required procedures. Each local government also is required to maintain and make available to the public a detailed list by subject matter of all public records and a record of final votes by each member of every agency.

To prevent undue encroachment on personal privacy, the New York State Committee on Public Access to Records may promulgate guidelines for the deletion of identifying details for specified records that are to be made available. When no such guidelines exist, the law—§89 (2) (a)—allows an agency or municipality to delete identifying details when making records available. Examples of the invasion of personal privacy include disclosure of medical or credit histories and also personal references of applicants for employment without their written permission. In addition, exempt records include those containing information confidentially disclosed to an agency or municipality and parts of investigatory files compiled for purposes of law enforcement.

Intractable Ethical Problems

A review of ethical problems in government service during the past 25 years reveals that the age-old problems of bribery, embezzlement, and use of confidential information for personal gain have not disappeared, but other more subtle ethical problems have become more common. We will briefly discuss six of them.

A "Fair" Day's Work

The concept of a "fair" day's work for a "fair" day's pay is widely accepted. Yet a supervisor is apt to be labelled a Simon Legree for attempting to deal with employees who consistently report late, leave early, and/or take extended coffee breaks. He or she may find other employees defending the violators of time rules. A related ethical problem involving time is the use of work restrictive practices to slow down the pace of the operation.

Sick Leave

Abuse of sick leave is a serious ethical problem disrupting the work of an organization. Sick leave is a fringe benefit preserving the salary of employees unable to work because of health problems. Some employees, however, view sick leave as a right that can be used to augment regular vacation leave. To combat sick leave abuses, supervisors can require documentation for lengthy absences, conduct spot checks—by telephone or in person—of personnel suspected of abuses, and note patterns of absences for possible future disciplinary action. Some governments offer incentives, such as an additional day off or monetary rewards, for employees not using sick leave. Other governments grant "all purpose" days—vacation leave, sick leave, and holidays—that employees use as they please with the understanding that no additional time off will be granted when the "all purpose" days are exhausted.

The Ultra Vires Problem

A particularly difficult ethical problem is the ultra vires problem—employees exceeding their legal authority. In some instances, employees exceed their authority through ignorance. In other instances, government employees knowingly exceed their authority, convinced that they will not be challenged and that the average citizen will assume any reasonable action taken by a government employee is lawful. The Geneva, New York, Code of Ethics—art. 15. §15.2—stipulates that "officials and employees should not exceed their authority or breach the law. . . ."

The Revolving Door Problem

Some have perceived the so-called "revolving door" between government service and private industry as an evil affecting the federal government most seriously. The problem involves an official leaving government service and accepting employment with a private firm affected by the government agency formerly employing him, and vice versa. The Ethics in Government Act of 1978–92 STAT. 1864, 18 U.S.C. 207 (1978 Supp.)—attempts to deal with this problem by prohibiting high level officials leaving a agency to appear, formally or informally, or to make any oral or written communication for a minimum of one year. This post-employment conflict-of-interest provision may increase the difficulty of recruiting highly qualified personnel for the federal service.

"Whistle-Blowers"

Ethical standards in government service can be raised if officials and employees are encouraged to be "whistle-blowers" by reporting other employees' unethical actions to the proper officials. A particularly difficult problem to control without the aid of "whistle-blowers" is use of public equipment and facilities for private purposes.

Naturally, people are reluctant to be labelled as "squealers." Most officials and employees are reluctant to be "whistle-blowers" because of fear of administrative recriminations. So-called informers have been demoted, reassigned to less important positions, excluded from decision-making meetings, and even fired. The problem of administrative recrimination faced by "whistle-blowers" is highlighted by a suit pending in the Supreme Court of Albany County, New York, filed by Paul Thomas against the Temporary State Commission on Regulation of Lobbying. Thomas, an attorney, was fired by the commission's executive director who, according to legal papers, informed Thomas he was being discharged for "personal disloyalty to the Commission." Thomas contends he was fired "for speaking honestly and factually" about the work of the commission, was not given written reasons for his discharge, and was denied a hearing as provided by the State Civil Service Law [8, p. 1]. The firing apparently stems from interviews conducted with Thomas and other commission staff members by the New York Public Interest Research Group (NYPIRG) and Common Cause, two organizations criticizing the work of the commission.

Citizen Participation

The final ethical problem to be discussed involves citizen participation. Commencing with the Housing Act of 1954, federal grant-in-aid programs have mandated citizen participation as a condition for the receipt of funds by state and local governments. More recently, federal agencies have adopted public participation programs [6, pp. 28911–8919]. Cynics speak of "citizen manipulation" rather than citizen participation in agency programs. There can be no denying that government agencies have subverted the intent of citizen participation requirements by various means, including the appointment of unrepresentative "blue ribbon" advisory committees [22, pp. 13–14].

A most serious problem involves deliberate attempts by government bureaucrats to "co-opt" citizens. There is a natural tendency for bureaucrats to want citizen support for government programs. The deliberate manipulation of citizens to win support for a government program clearly is unethical [17]. If a legal requirement for citizen participation in a government program exists, then it is incumbent upon bureaucrats to ensure that citizens receive full information as well as the opportunity to participate in the decision-making process from start to finish.

Supplemental Actions

By containing relatively clear behavior standards and providing a mechanism to generate advice on unusual situations, a code of ethics can help eliminate malversation in public office. It can raise behavioral norms and serve as a basis for disciplinary action. In addition, a carefully drafted code of ethics and a board of ethics can help maintain, or restore if need be, public confidence that public affairs are being conducted in accordance with high ethical standards.

Enactment of a code of ethics should help promote right conduct on the part of government officials and employees. However, the code may prove inefficacious. One would be naive to assume that adopting a code will solve all ethical problems by promoting rectitude in all actions by officials and employees. A good code can help to achieve this goal, but it needs to be supplemented by actions removing or reducing the opportunity or temptation for unethical conduct. Actions by management are emphasized in the following conclusion of the National Institute of Law Enforcement and Criminal Justice:

> Management practices affect both the opportunities for corruption and the risks that attend any act of corruption. Frequently, corruption results from poor management—management that does not use all of the tools at hand to limit the opportunities and maximize the risks. Officials and employees alike feel that they can get away with corruption if they perceive that no one is looking. If nothing bad happens as the results of one or more acts of corruption, it is likely to appear to the actors that nobody cares or even that such acts are condoned. A folklore may arise that corruption is permitted "because salaries are so low," or because the extra compensation is a prerequisite that goes with the job ("supervisors get to take their cars home, and they get all the free gas they want," for example) [12, p. 11].

Adopting adequate control devices can help maintain high moral standards in government. Making rigorous applicant screening part of the recruitment process, for example, will reduce the number of new employees with a proclivity to unethical conduct. Furthermore, good central purchasing, reporting, record keeping, and accounting systems will remove or reduce the opportunity or temptation for unethical behavior. These systems also can reveal improprieties, thereby permitting initiation of corrective action.

In conclusion, each chief executive and governing body should examine the relationship between the salary schedule of the governmental unit and ethical standards. Logic suggests that low pay scales may make some officials and employees susceptible to bribery and other forms of corruption. Employees supporting large families on low salaries or wishing to maintain reasonably high standards of living will have difficulty making ends meet. They may seek to supplement their incomes on the basis of the ability to do favors.

A high salary schedule, however, will not raise automatically moral standards in a government. But an adequate salary schedule has the advantage of attracting a larger number of applicants, thus permitting the government to be more selective in hiring new employees and selecting only men and women of the highest integrity.

Notes

1. Louisiana follows the Napoleonic Code.

2. Macing is the practice of requiring a prospective government employee to agree to contribute part of his salary to the political party controlling the government as a condition for securing and retaining a government position. A sinecure is a paid government position with few or no duties.

3. The name of the Association was changed in 1968 to the International City Management Association.

References

1. Archibald, Samuel J. "The Freedom of Information Act Revisited." *Public Administration Review* 39 (July-August 1979): 311–18.

2. Bollens, John C., and Schmandt, Henry J. *Political Corruption: Power, Money, & Sex*. Pacific Palisades, Calif.: Palisades Publishers, 1979.

3. *City Management Code of Ethics*. Washington, D.C.: International City Management Association, 1972.

4. "Common Cause Model Conflict of Interest Act." *The Municipal Year Book: 1975*. Washington, D.C.: International City Management Association, 1975.

5. *Congressional Record*. 96th Cong., 2nd sess., vol. 126 (June 4, 1980): S 6266.

6. "Environmental Protection Agency: Proposed Policy on Public Participation." *Federal Register* 45 (April 30, 1980): 28911–8919.

7. *Florida's "Government in the Sunshine Law": A Summary Report*. Gainesville: Holland Law Center. The University of Florida, n.d.

8. Freedman, Eric. "Fired for Aid to Probers, He Sues State." *Knickerbocker News*, June 9, 1980, p. 1.

9. *Information/Instruction Sheet, City of Rockville Statement of Employment and Financial Interests*. Rockville, Md.: n.d.

10. Jacobs, Theodore J. "The Federal Sunshine Act Is Paying Off." *New York Times*, June 7, 1980, p. 22.

11. *Model State Conflict of Interest and Financial Disclosure Law*. New York: National Municipal League, 1979.

12. National Institute of Law Enforcement and Criminal Justice. *Prevention, Detection, and Correction of Corruption in Local Government*. Washington, D.C.: United States Department of Justice, 1978.

13. O'Brien, David M. "Freedom of Information, Privacy, and Information Control: A Contemporary Administrative Dilemma." *Public Administration Review* 39 (July/August 1979): 323–28.

14. *Opinions of the Attorney General of the State of New York*. Albany, N.Y.: 1974.

15. Prescott, Frank W., and Zimmerman, Joseph F. *The Politics of the Veto of Legislation in New York State*. Washington, D.C.: University Press of America, 1980.

16. Schiesl, Martin J. *The Politics of Efficiency: Municipal Administration and Reform in America, 1880–1920.* Berkeley: University of California Press, 1977.
17. Selznick, Philip. *TVA and the Grass Roots.* Berkeley: University of California Press, 1949.
18. Smothers, Ronald. "M.A.C. Employee Exempt on Assets." *New York Times,* June 18, 1976, p. D-12.
19. Steffens, Lincoln. *Autobiography of Lincoln Steffens.* New York: Harcourt, 1931.
20. _____. *The Shame of the Cities.* New York: McClure-Phillips, 1904.
21. *A Suggested Code of Ethics for Municipal Officials and Employees.* Chicago: International City Managers' Association, 1962.
22. Zimmerman, Joseph F. "Citizen Participation in Urban Renewal." *Planning and Civic Comment* 29 (December 1963): 13–14.

16

THE PROBLEM OF MORAL REASONING IN AMERICAN PUBLIC ADMINISTRATION: THE CASE FOR A CODE OF ETHICS

Ralph Clark Chandler
Western Michigan University

The ethics debate in American public administration has centered in recent months on a proposed code of ethics for the American Society for Public Administration (ASPA).[1] Is a code desirable? Can the language of a code possibly comprehend the diversity of the field and the complexity of the problems of moral reasoning? The National Council of ASPA has said no and adopted a statement of principles in lieu of a code of ethics in late 1981, doing so on recommendation of its Professional Standards and Ethics Committee.[2] Thus, ASPA remains one of the few professional associations without a code of ethics. It continues to operate on the margins of a professional development continuum which includes systematic theory, clientele-recognized authority, community sanction, professional culture, and a code regulating the relations of professionals with clients and colleagues.[3] Without joining the debate within ASPA's infrastructure about why a particular code was rejected, we might offer some analysis of why codes of ethics are in disrepute among many, but why others be-

lieve a code is highly appropriate at this juncture of American administrative history.

Arguments Against a Code of Ethics

The first argument against a code of ethics is that we should resist moralizing as a practical matter. We live in the residue of the implicit but clearly
understood American tradition that liberty is the first principle of the republic, with prosperity close behind. If the framers had allowed the Presby-
terians to take us too far into a discussion of the public good, the result
would probably have been the kind of regimentation, ordering, and indoctrination that might have worked in Geneva and the Massachusetts Bay
Colony, but was not preferred in New York and Virginia. Theocracy was
out, not because the framers were immoral, but because a self-consciously
moral society would have to put duties first and relegate rights and everything else that is private to a subordinate place in the life of the republic. It
was clear to Publius in *The Federalist* as well as in the debates of the Constitutional Convention, that political liberty and economic energy unavoidably engender some immorality, but that government can control it without the institutional consequences of preaching and being preached to. The
tradition of American public administration came to be that we ought to
live with a moderate degree of immorality and condemn the occasional
self-righteous moralist who forgets that men and women are not angels.
The tradition has served us well.[4]

Another reason some of us are less than enthusiastic about a code of ethics
is that our pathfinders periodically celebrate the unique virtues of consensus
building and proceduralism in American society. By this line of reasoning,
the lack of stated public purpose is one of the nation's fundamental
strengths, because throughout our national history continuing redefinitions
of purpose and compromise of principle have allowed us to make the incremental changes necessary for political stability. They have also permitted us
to flourish at once as a republic and as an empire, as a constitutionally limited federal state governed by law and as an unlimited unitary state with expanded economic and territorial ambitions. Proceduralism is necessary because in a pluralist pressure system an article of faith must be that from the
clash of opposites, contraries, extremes, and poles will come not the victory
of any one, but the mediation and accommodation of all. Truth, unity, and
especially morality can never be forged from one ideal form. They must be
hammered out on the anvil of debate. Thus necessity has become a virtue in
public administration, and consensus is built around the agreement to agree
on nothing substantive. Assent is given not to value, but to value default.
The irony of the proceduralist position, of course, is that as the need for
shared values in an increasingly factionalized and anomic society grows, ad-

versaries who no longer find in their disagreements a basis for common norms are transformed from adversaries into enemies.[5]

A third reason which helps to explain our discomfort with a code of ethics is the lingering influence of both Woodrow Wilson and Max Weber. Wilson maintained that administration stands apart "even from the debatable ground of constitutional study. It is part of political life only as the methods of the countinghouse are a part of the life of society; only as machinery is part of the manufactured product."[6] It follows that where there is no discretion there is no moral responsibility. Weber also spoke of "the bureaucratic machine" in which the honor of the civil servant is vested in his or her ability to execute conscientiously the order of superior authorities, "exactly as if the order agreed with his own conviction. This holds even if the order appears wrong to him, and if, despite the civil servant's remonstrances, the authority insists on the order. Without *this moral discipline* [emphasis added] and self-denial, in the highest sense, the whole apparatus would fall to pieces."[7] Thus Weber's administrator considers it moral to avoid morality, with the result that the organization in which he or she serves becomes incapable of determining how its power should be used. The organization schools itself in moral illiteracy and the administrator becomes the victim of his or her own success. This is the condition Erich Fromm describes as the state of moral confusion where man is left without the guidance of either revelation or reason. The result is the acceptance of a relativistic position which proposes that value judgments and ethical norms are exclusively matters of taste or arbitrary preference and that no objectively valid moral statement can be made.[8]

There are many other arguments against a code of ethics. Although some of us would be uncomfortable with the comparison, a large number of American public administrators agree with the prophet Jeremiah that the laws of right behavior are written on one's heart, not on paper. Others think that professional organizations such as ASPA are too diverse for a code to apply to all parts of it, and that, since an ethics code is largely unenforceable anyway, we should not have one. Still others resist what they call the overly moralistic and preachy language of ethics codes in general, which raises for these critics the specter of the profession caving in to the moral majority.

Arguments for a Code of Ethics

The first argument *for* a code might be called the argument from objectivism. To take objectivism seriously, however, or indeed to take seriously any of the affirmative arguments, one probably must agree with Wallace S. Sayre that administrative discourse at any level of sophistication frequently resolves itself into problems of political theory. This is a difficult saying for pluralists and proceduralists, because they tend to take as an article of faith that the *process* of arriving at consensus is ultimately more important than both theory and the substance of any words agreed upon. Nevertheless, as long as the letterhead of the American Society for Public Administration says it exists to advance the science and art, as well as the processes, of public administration, the analysis of thought and language becomes more than a frivolous exercise.

Objectivism refers to the ancient debate in philosophy about transcendent values. It posits a center of value external to human collectivities and is represented in such concepts as God, the Good, and in Paul Tillich's phrase, "the ultimate ground of being." In a code of ethics it typically is reflected in such phrases as "public morality," "the sovereignty of the people," and in references to *the* law. Objectivism is best understood in comparison to its opposite, subjectivism, which holds that the center of value is somewhere in the human condition. Subjectivism is represented in such concepts as humanism, happiness, and "the dignity of man." In public administration it is thoroughgoing in Simmons and Dvorin's concept of radical humanism. Subjectivists tend to reject "public morality," for example, as a self-contradictory term. They translate "the sovereignty of the people" into "the best interests of the public," and they change *the* law, which has no objective existence, into *laws,* which are culturally determined. Thus morally transcendent ideas become ethically relative ones.

Objectivists maintain that ontological ethics invite the administrator to be ethical, because they encourage him or her to make choices and judgments and to pursue actions. Actions are the predicates of being. Unless one assumes the risks attendant on them, he or she vacates the ethical arena. Objectivist codes therefore frequently employ active transitive verbs rather than intransitive verbs of being. Note the verbs "fight," "revere," "obey," "incite," "strive," "quicken," and "transmit" in one of the best-known of the objectivist codes.

The Athenian Oath

We will never bring disgrace to this our city
by any act of dishonesty or cowardice,
nor ever desert our suffering comrades in the ranks;

We will fight for the ideals and the sacred things of the city,
both alone and with many;

We will revere and obey the city's laws and
do our best to incite to a like respect and reverence
those who are prone to annul or set them at naught;

> We will strive unceasingly to quicken
> the public sense of public duty;
>
> That thus, in all these ways, we will transmit this city
> not only not less, but greater, better and more beautiful
> than it was transmitted to us.

The Athenian Oath also illustrates the second argument for a code of ethics. It is the argument from community. In this view, moral behavior in public administration is not just a matter of private preferences and personal integrity. The determination of what is a gift and what is a bribe rests with the giver as well as the receiver. Judgments about right and wrong are community decisions as well as private ones. The community is the arbiter of what is ethical. The communal "we," with its varied implications of personalized ownership, is strikingly apparent in the Athenian Oath and in other codes. Aristotle warned repeatedly that it is possible to obey laws and regulations and still be unethical. The community looks at the nature of an act in order to decide whether it is moral or not. Stephen K. Bailey wrote: "There is not a moral vice which cannot be made into relative good by context. There is not a moral virtue which cannot in peculiar circumstances have patently evil results."[9] Laws govern all actions of the public service, but it is equally true that actors govern. Laws regulate people, not action, and people are part of a community. They are not islands unto themselves.

Vincent Ostrom has written that any normal science needs general agreement about a basic theoretical paradigm or framework in which "a community of scholars shares common theoretical assumptions, and a common language defining essential terms and relationships."[10] Proponents of a code argue that the self-interestedness of relativism represents a loss of paradigm, and with it a loss of a sense of community. There cannot be a paradigm without a community.

A third argument advanced for a code of ethics is the argument from courage. G. K. Chesterton once remarked that where there is no courage, there is no room for any other virtue. Courage holds up idealism in a field where the practice of *realpolitik* reflects our true learnings that human life is characterized by a little more or a little less justice, and a little more or a little less equity. Theologian Rheinhold Neibuhr has told us why impossible ideals are nevertheless relevant: they function prophetically. They demand the best, while they expose "the impotence and corruption of human nature." Sin-talk is admittedly old-fashioned, restrictive, and somewhat embarrassing, but if this is the only reason that the parlance of idealism is rejected, we also put ourselves out of touch with a rich classical tradition which sought for moral unity and a higher law in conversation that has little to do with sin.

The argument from courage maintains that the criticism of public administration as being amoral is validated in anti-code sentiment. The politics-administration dichotomy appears to be alive and well, despite Nicholas Henry's hope that the public administrator is now forced to make decisions "not on the comfortable basis of efficiency, economy, and administrative principles, but on the more agonizing criteria of morality as well."[11] The collection of anti-code opinions we have variously described as relativistic, proceduralist, and pluralist certainly does not agonize very much. Rather than agonize, it resorts to neutralized language, as when the condemnation of waste and abuse of government funds is transformed into the affirmation of efficient and effective management (see footnotes 1 and 2).

Henry notes that the counter-culture's charge of administrative amorality is essentially a linguistic one. "It holds that the symbols and values of technological society prevent individual men and women from choosing."[12] When the American Institute of Planners surveyed 1,178 planners in 1979, for example, to determine "what planners think is ethical and why," it discovered that professionals who considered themselves "technicians" indicated they were value-neutral 81 percent of the time.[13]

The avoidance of choice affirms the administrator as technician. In its educational dimension, it refuses responsibility for socializing new professionals in a broader view of the science and art of public administration. It pretends once again that public administrators do in fact strictly adhere to value-free decision making. Idealists say further that opposition to the language of ethical choice in a code extends the widespread misunderstanding of what "moral" means. It has become a pejorative term in many circles, probably aggravated by the moral majority movement. It connotes judgment, condemnation, narrow-mindedness, obsessive or compulsive religion, and legalism. "Moral" does indeed involve standards of conduct, but these standards are as much voluntarily assumed as they are enjoined from without. Once assumed, however, the standards do impose obligations of choice, and they withdraw certain areas of conduct from the free option of the individual to do as he or she pleases. That must be the problem.

Further Analysis of the Positions

There is something persuasive in each of these contending positions: the arguments against a code of ethics from practicality, procedure, and administrative theory, and the arguments for a code of ethics from objectivism, community, and courage. Further analysis of the positions suggests nuances of meaning that have important ramifications for the society as a whole. Let us begin where the *anti* statements begin, and that is with history.

The Negative Argument from Practicality. It is true that the founders counseled moderation on moral matters. They said that unbounded moralism is as self-indulgent as any other form of excess. If there was a need for government to control the abuses following from selfishness, given the observed fact that the basic motivation of people is self-interest, there was an equal need to insist that acts of government control ought also to be bounded. The founders were widely acclaimed for such insights into human nature, and for the countervailing instrumentalities of government they devised.

Consider, however, the following conundrum in logic and in historical practice. When James Madison pointed out in *The Federalist* that men, and presumably women, are not angels, he also noted that if they were, no government would be necessary. That meant at the time that government was necessary, and that the Constitution should be ratified. Since government is administered, however, by the same men and women who are not angels, where is Madison's argument if the instrumentalities of government are themselves corrupt? He and other moderates rested their case, after all, on the fact that government can keep public immorality within reasonable bounds.

The problem is that the historical record sustains the view that corruption is endemic in the American political and administrative system and that it constantly assaults reasonable bounds. From the Yazoo land fraud in the 1790s, to the bribery of members of Congress by officials of the Second United States Bank in the 1830s, to the scandals surrounding Union Pacific Railroad land acquisitions in the 1870s, to Teapot Dome and Elk Hills in the 1920s, to the revelations of kickbacks in tax settlements by collectors of internal revenue in the 1950s, to the Vietnam order of battle misrepresentations in the 1960s, to the Watergate phenomenon in the 1970s, to ABSCAM in the early 1980s, and many other instances in-between, our history can be read as a litany of lies, avarice, and greed. In *Capitalism the Creator,* historian Carl Snyder calls the characteristics of the sharpdealer the great force in the building of America.

In addition, consider the opinion of Henry Steele Commager. In "A Historian Looks at Our Political Morality," he discusses the presuppositions of certain national policy decisions. These had to do with our collective responsibility for what he describes as "the conquest and decimation of the Indian," slavery defended as a moral good, the child labor of the industrial revolution explained as the necessary price of progress, and the Vietnam War pursued as the logical result of "better dead than Red." Commager concluded that despite the hopes of Madison, the instrumentalities of government cannot in fact control immorality.

Carl Sandburg in his role of poet as well as historian had a kinder indictment of those burdened with the exigencies of ethical choice. He said we are all liars, just different kinds.

People lie because they don't remember
clear what they say.

People lie because they can't help
making a story better than it was
the way it happened.

People tell white lies so as to be decent
to others.

People lie in a pinch, hating to do it,
but lying on because it might be worse.

And people lie just to be liars
for crooked gain.

What sort of liar are you?

Which of these liars are you?

Perhaps we are the kind of liar Alexander Hamilton was. In trying to help Madison deal with the problem of corrupt human nature, he wrote:

The aim of every political constitution is, or ought to be, first to obtain for rulers men who possess most wisdom to discern, and most virtue to pursue, the common good of society; and in the next place *to take the most effectual precautions for keeping them virtuous.* [emphasis added]

The ink was hardly dry on this issue of *The Federalist* when the Yazoo land fraud case came to light. The state of Georgia, its legislature bribed by New England financiers, sold to private speculators most of what is today the states of Alabama and Mississippi at one and one-half cents an acre. Involved in the graft were two United States Senators, including Robert Morris of Pennsylvania, two Congressmen, three leading jurists, including Associate Supreme Court Justice James Wilson, and assorted civil servants who could have stopped the scheme at almost any point in its development, but remained neutral.

The story is celebrated and involved and eventually resulted in a major Supreme Court decision, *Fletcher v. Peck* (1810). The speculators won out finally because the Marshall Court held invalid an act of a subsequent Georgia legislature repealing the sale. The bribers kept their profits largely through the efforts of their sagacious lawyer, the same Alexander Hamilton who had called for effectual precautions for keeping public officials virtuous.[14]

The Negative Argument from Procedure.   As long as the United States was a land of plenty and had a manifest destiny, the nation was like a good centerfielder. It could outrun many of its mistakes as long as there was expansion room and abundance. Never mind Nicholas Biddle's bribe of Daniel Webster, Henry Clay, John C. Calhoun, and 52 other members of Congress in exchange for the renewal of the charter of the Second United States Bank in 1833.[15] Such shenanigans were an aspect of the ethos of privatism, material ambition, and self-sufficiency, shielded as they were by the rhetoric of personal and national independence.

That rhetoric sounds hollow in the 1980s, however. The opposites of independence: interdependence and cooperation, were once considered weaknesses of the American national character, but now they are necessities. They spring from a sense of common limits. In the old rhetoric, words, like everything else, could be wasted as long as open spaces, empty jobs, and unmade fortunes were the conditions of American life. Now the nation is faced with the prospect of limited growth, scarce resources, and the bankruptcy of privatism. Just as abundance was the natural soil of competitive individualism, scarcity is the soil of mutualism. In scarcity and mutuality words are important. They may not change behavior, but they do other essential things in a circumscribed environment where the vision of administrators is crucial to survival: they inspire, they set a tone, and they create expectations. They provide points of reference for living in the settled land. If proceduralists throw away the words of idealism, perhaps in ignorance of what they mean, they will deprive themselves of a singular source of power in understanding and manipulating the new conditions of American life.

The dilemma of faith in proceduralism and countervailing power versus the requirements of careful talk in mutualism invites more authoritative solutions than those immediately discoverable in the more patient processes of moral reasoning. The classical culture Publius and other founders admired provides the following example of the problem. By the year A.D. 284 the Roman administrative class felt itself so undermined by Christian talk about unselfishness and moral responsibility that it undertook to support Diocletian as a candidate for Emperor of the Roman Empire. He was the person most likely to restore the old glory. The well-springs of that were understood as the proper administration of Rome's vast and still largely undiminished resources. It is true that Diocletian was only half civilized, but he was a professional soldier who believed in consensus, citizen responsibility, restraint, and especially practicality. As emperor he enforced fixed prices to fight inflation. He allowed the patrician class to make money, explaining that some of it would trickle down to the plebeians. He spent millions on national defense. In addition, he cut welfare programs. He also persecuted the Christians. But 20 years later Diocletian abdicated in despair. He retired to a palace built like a fortress in what is today Yugoslavia, and spent the rest of his life raising vegetables. Neither he nor the administrative class who desperately pursued rectitude by honoring the old ways ever really understood how Rome had changed, and how the consensus-building procedures of the old ways were irrelevant for the new.

Constantine did understand, however. Within 20 years of Diocletian's abdication, he had established the Constantinian Settlement, which was not much more than official recognition of Christian idealism as symbolically useful for the new conditions of Roman life. Its language of heroism, transcendence, and mutualism gave rise to a new kind of civilization that would last a thousand years. Constantine admitted that the *Pax Romana* could no longer be imposed. He said that unlimited national power was a myth. He forced the administrative class to acknowledge that it had both discretionary power and the moral responsibility which went with it. This simple reorientation released remarkable new energies in Roman life.

The Negative Argument from Administrative Theory. The anti-code argument from practicality is unconvincing because government cannot control immorality. The anti-code argument from procedure is something of an anachronism because it is out of sync with the changing and changed conditions of American life. The anti-code argument from administrative theory is flawed because the administrative man or woman it posits never really existed and cannot exist psychologically except in the models built by Woodrow Wilson and Max Weber.

Weber's morally neutral administrator who claimed he was not responsible for the crimes of German National Socialism in the 1930s and 1940s, for example, was told at the Nuremberg trials that he was responsible. Wilson's administrative technician who says he cannot seek personal goals within the organization has found himself increasingly a victim of bureaupathology as he therefore attaches himself ritualistically to routines and procedures. He attempts to deny human characteristics which will not be denied.

Administrative theorists such as Michel Crozier and Victor A. Thompson have pointed out that there is no necessary correlation between bureaucracy as a rational system and the irrational behavior of the body of civil servants who are the instrumentalities of government. Civil servants are frequently observed as being aloof, bored, negative, inefficient, impolite, unhelpful, and abusers of the power that official doctrine says they do not have. Thompson says such bureaupathetic behavior is exhibited by people who interpret any challenge to existing rules as a threat to their own security. Robert K. Merton adds that the tendency of bureaucracies to adhere to rules as ends in themselves, which he calls goal displacement, results in a process of sanctification in which bureaucratic procedures are invested with attitudes of moral legitimacy. Procedures are established as values in their own right, and are no longer viewed as merely technical means for expediting administration. Sentiments of devotion to the methodical performance of routine activities are more intense than is technically necessary. Thus instrumental values become terminal values.[16]

The reader will note such words as "ritualistically," "doctrine," "sanctification," "moral legitimacy," and "sentiments of devotion" in the foregoing description. These and similar words appear more and more frequently in modern administrative analysis. They are value-laden and even religious in their affect. One must ask, therefore, if "value neutral" civil servants can pass through a "process of sanctification" to make their enterprises "morally legitimate" (even if bureaupathetic), why can they not also embrace processes of moral reasoning which would produce professional standards from outside the limitations of their organizations and their psyches. White magic may be as good as black magic.

More directly in answer to Wilson and Weber and their modern disciples is the apparent fact that most public policy has as its declared aim some public good. Normative forces in the political order shaped the policy. The moral dimensions of policy warrant, and perhaps demand, examination by those who will execute it. Fleishman and Payne have listed the reasons: (1) the duty of the public official may be unclear because of conflicting obligations or because of conflict between an obligation and legitimate self-interest; (2) the values embodied in policy options may be disputed or insufficiently understood; and, (3) the normative principles guiding policy are themselves frequently unclear or contradictory.[17]

Whatever the doctrine of value neutrality may state, the real decisions of public officials frequently involve ethical choices and the resolution of ethical dilemmas. Administrators choose daily between and among conflicting values in the interpretation of the ultimate goals of policy. Neither legislatures nor courts offer definitive interpretations of the vast majority of issues which arise administratively. Administrators must delineate the law. Their policies, programs, instructions, rules, procedures, and day-to-day decisions may not always agree with the intent of the elected officials who broadly structured the law in the first place, or with the courts who are too busy to define it. Many administrators live in a no-man's land of what is lawful, what is wise, and what is in the public interest. The real question is not whether they inhabit the land of moral ambiguity, but how well equipped they are to survive in it without seeking refuge in bureaupathology. An enhanced and self-consciously developed capacity to engage in moral reasoning, and even an occasional glance at a modern version of the Athenian Oath, might help.

The Affirmative Argument from Objectivism.   The affirmation of transcendent values moves to correct the conditions of Hannah Arendt's remark that authority has vanished in modern society. Statements of objective truth help reduce the moral confusion which the lack of authority brings. Aristotle said we do not do good acts because we are already good, the precise position of the founders of the American republic; we do good acts because they have been prescribed by the requirements of virtue, good manners, the revealed word of God, tradition, the elders, the common law, the Constitution, or some other source of transcendent authority; and in the process of doing good acts, we become good. Aristotle may have been the first behaviorist.

Authority has had a difficult time in ethical theory since the Reformation. Before the Reformation the Christian West was a monolith of values, authority, and the affirmation of objective truth. There were definitive provisions for the resolution of any ethical dispute. The Reformation shattered that sense of certainty with Martin Luther's doctrine of the priesthood of all believers. Competing orthodoxies emerged, and individuals came to believe they were their own mediators of religious and moral truth. John Calvin added to Luther's doctrine that God alone was the Lord of the conscience, and the idea of moral autonomy was born.

It has been a heavy burden to bear. One wonders if Luther and Calvin would have been quite so definite about individualism if they had understood the implications of the work of Copernicus. His calculations dislodged man from his central place in creation and cast him adrift in a universe where there was no absolute point of reference. Later, Charles Darwin's *The Origins of the Species* [sic] did for anthropology what Copernicus had done for physics. Together they made man's place in nature an enigma. Mankind had to ask if the world were a number which came up in a cosmic Monte Carlo game. If man is not the product of divine intention, and if the earth evolved from blind chance, there cannot be moral certainty about anything.

The subsequent atomization of moral philosophy means it has significant disabilities to overcome if it is to respond to its current summons to deal with the ethical crisis of American culture. Among these disabilities are: (1) the language of moral discourse tends to be a collection of fragments of culturally dead large-scale philosophical systems, as when remnants of the medieval doctrine of the just war contend against truncated and secondhand versions of utilitarianism, and both of these are confronted in turn by amateur Machiavellianism; (2) the loss of the vision of the whole means ethics is constantly being rediscovered in American society, rather than being a permanent cultural enterprise, with the result being occasional statements of temporary and fragile moral premises about which there is little agreement and over which there are endless battles of assertion and counterassertion; (3) the inevitable appeal to intuition which moral philosophy must make faces the probability that the prephilosophical intuitions which evaluate the appeal are so dominated by what Alasdair

MacIntyre calls "an unsystematic conceptual archaeology" that rational discourse on moral subjects is impossible in popular forums.

Meanwhile the ongoing celebration of moral autonomy helps to explain why the American Society for Public Administration cannot agree on a code of ethics. Gerald Dworkin says a person is morally autonomous if he or she: (1) defines his or her own moral principles; (2) engages his or her will or volition as the ultimate source of authority; (3) is involved in the decision regarding which moral principles are binding on him or her personally; (4) bears the responsibility for the moral theory he or she accepts and applies; and (5) refuses to accept external moral authority, except as independently filtered.

A moral theory which stresses autonomy will have difficulty with the central moral category of obligation. To be obliged is to be bound, and to be bound is to be restricted. If the individual is the primary moral agent, there cannot be a priori assumptions about the principles which oblige. It does not matter that they are aspects of a moral tradition passed on to one as part of his or her training and/or professional standards, or that they are the principles of Gandhi, Thoreau, Socrates, Confucius, Tolstoy, or Jesus. The tyranny of the self is such that it must mediate all authority claiming to represent objective truth. Theologians used to call that original sin.

The Affirmative Argument from Community.   A good deal has been written about public administration's inability to define itself as a profession and as an academic discipline. Dwight Waldo's idea of the disparate elements of public administration forming a holding company remains the best analogy for what public administration really is. Yet a holding company by definition is able to control other companies by virtue of stock ownership in them. The companies together form a community held together by income derived from the exchange of stock and securities among themselves and with others.

The American Society for Public Administration cannot control even one of its members who may be convicted of fraud, embezzlement, or mismanagement of any kind. There is no legal tender, no commonly agreed-upon currency, the counterfeit of which is the legal basis for expulsion from the Society. The current by-laws provide no standards of professional behavior against which a member can be judged as unprofessional. Theoretically one could sit in prison in violation of fundamental professional norms and simultaneously maintain membership in ASPA, because the organization has never stated its norms in an enforceable code of ethics. Surely this condition militates against the coming of age of public administration in the United States. A community of any kind must have legal tender, not only to establish its own identity, but to gain the sanction of the larger community with which it does business.

The Affirmative Argument from Courage.   In his closing argument in the *Glavis-Ballinger* case of 1910, Justice Louis Brandeis provided the following vision of the public servant:

> They cannot be worthy of the respect and admiration of the people unless they add to the virtue of obedience some other virtues—virtues of manliness, of truth, of courage, of willingness to risk position, of the willingness to risk criticism, of the willingness to risk the misunderstanding that so often comes when people do the heroic thing.[18]

The "heroic thing" puts us back in Athens among those who "revere," "strive," and "transmit," and it recalls those men and women who once pledged their lives, their fortunes, and their sacred honor to secure the blessings of liberty to the young American republic and its posterity. Psychologists tell us that accepting risks and assuming vulnerability are signs of health in a person or an organization. If we are life-affirming people, we do not merely tolerate our tasks from economic necessity, but we find beauty, meaning, and value in the tasks themselves, even if they are mundane administrative chores. Insofar as we find beauty in them, we find the elusive relationship between aesthetics and ethics that Plato said is the essence of the good life. Insofar we find meaning and value in them, we also encounter moral choice and moral talk. Jean-Paul Sartre said that to avoid such talk and such choice is bad *faith*—an interesting choice of words for an atheist. Faith therefore is not merely a religious phenomenon. Faith is saying yes to life in the midst of its tragedies, ambiguities, and hard moral choices. Faith makes felicitous that which in any case is necessary.

Notes

1. The proposed code was developed by a subcommittee of the Professional Standards and Ethics Committee over a two-year period. It included 14 articles, of which the following, Article 8, is an example: "We will neither commit nor condone the commitment of fraud, waste, abuse of government funds or property, or mismanagement of government programs. When it has been established that wrongdoing has occurred, and an innocent colleague is in difficulty because he or she exposed it, we will take appropriate steps to defend that colleague's interests. We will call attention to those agencies which demonstrate a pattern of harassment of persons who attempt to maintain high ethical standards or which ignore wrongdoing when it has been responsibly exposed."

2. The adopted statement of principles included nine articles which constituted a revision of the code. Article 8 of the code became Article 4 of the principles, for example, and reads as follows: "Efficient and effective management is basic to public administration. Subversion through misuse of influence, fraud, waste, or abuse is intolerable. Employees who responsibly call attention to wrongdoing will be encouraged."

3. One of the earliest discussions of the process of professionalization remains one of the most helpful. See Houard M. Vollmer and Donald L. Miller (eds), *Professionalization* (Englewood Cliffs, N.J.: Prentice-Hall, 1966), especially pp. 2–9.

4. See Robert A. Goldwin, "Of Men and Angels: A Search for Morality in the Constitution," in Robert H. Horwitz, ed., *The Moral Foundations of the American Republic,* second edition (Charlottesville: The University of Virginia Press), pp. 1–18.

5. See Benjamin R. Barber, "The Compromised Republic: Public Purposeless in America," in Horwitz, *op. cit.,* pp. 19–38.

6. Woodrow Wilson, "The Study of Administration," *Political Science Quarterly,* Vol. 11, No. 1 (June 1887), in Jay M. Shafritz and Albert C. Hyde (eds.), *Classics of Public Administration* (Oak Park, Ill.: Moore Publishing Company, 1978), p. 10.

7. Max Weber in H. H. Gerth and C. Wright Mills (eds.), *From Max Weber: Essays in Sociology* (New York: Oxford University Press, 1946), p. 95.

8. See Erich Fromm, *Man for Himself: An Inquiry into the Psychology of Ethics* (New York: Fawcett Book Group, 1978).

9. Stephen K. Bailey, quoted in Dwight Waldo, *The Enterprise of Public Administration* (Novato, Calif.: Chandler and Sharp Publishers, Inc., 1980), p. 99.

10. Vincent Ostrom, *The Intellectual Crisis in American Public Administration,* revised edition (University, Ala.: The University of Alabama Press, 1974), p. 13.

11. Nicholas Henry, *Public Administration and Public Affairs,* second edition (Englewood Cliffs, N.J.: Prentice-Hall, Inc., 1980), p. 132.

12. *Ibid.,* p. 134.

13. Elizabeth Howe and Jerome Kautman, "The Ethics of Contemporary American Planners," *The APA Journal,* July 1979, pp. 243–254.

14. See Ralph Clark Chandler, "Ethics and Public Policy," *Commonweal,* Vol. CV, No. 10 (May 12, 1978), pp. 302–309.

15. *Ibid.,* p. 304.

16. See Ralph Clark Chandler and Jack C. Plano, *The Public Administration Dictionary* (New York: John Wiley and Sons, 1982). For a discussion of bureaupathology, goal displacement, Neo-Weherism, and related ideas, especially pages 158–159, 173–174, and 195–196.

17. Joel L. Fleishman and Bruce L. Payne, *Ethical Dilemmas and the Education of Policymakers* (Hastings-on-Hudson, N.Y.: The Hastings Institute, 1980), p. 15.

18. Quoted in J. D. Williams, *Public Administration: The People's Business* (Boston: Little, Brown and Company, 1980), p. 541.

Part FIVE

Enforcing Ethical Behavior

As clarified in Part 4, codes of ethics are aspirational and inspirational. They are necessary, but they are insufficient to control corruption and prevent misconduct. Thus, a continuing theme in administrative ethics is the concern that those working in government cannot be trusted to be honest, trustworthy people of integrity. Finer's early argument remains constant, and the chapters in Part 5 will assert that strict laws establishing correction and punishment for ethical violations are necessary to ensure adherence to standards. Those whose work is included in Part 5 assume that humankind is inherently self-interested and that only various types of sanctions and punishments will ensure ethical behavior by government employees.

Part 5 begins with Robert C. Wood's 1955 *PAR* article, "Ethics in Government as a Problem in Executive Management" (Chapter 17 here). Like the authors of the other two articles included in this book that were written in the early 1950s, Wood is writing in response to gross misconduct by federal officials. He describes the reactions to the Senate Subcommittee on Ethics in Government. He, too, has studied the testimony before that committee and has read the scholarly analysis and recommendations that he denigrates with the words, "Repetitiously, the revelations produce a bundle of literature ranging from Sunday supplements to learned journals. . . ."

Wood rejects the four types of solutions typically proposed: reform society; reform bureaucracy; increase competition between Republicans and Democrats; or professionalize the public service. He suggests that, instead, we must return to the Constitution, in which Article 2, Section 3 provides that the president "take care that the laws be faithfully executed." Citing the laws that are "control devices," he argues that they must be enforced and that "investigatory facilities" must be implemented. The bulk of his article describes how and why these facilities will reduce corrupt behavior. This is the antithesis of the Monypenny argument that conformance to a code comes from the inside and that sanctions are imposed by the conscience of the individual and are not controllable by legislation.

In ASPA-sponsored journals, the burst of debate over how to ensure an ethical public service seems to have stopped with Wood's article. It was not resurrected until over twenty years later in the aftermath of Watergate. Whereas the popular press and several scholarly journals covered the scandals discovered in the post-Watergate era, arguments over how to prevent and eliminate them were slow to appear in ASPA-sponsored journals.

Part 3 of this book includes Sundquist's lament over the culpability of the profession of public administration in Watergate, the Caidens' call for research into systemic corruption, and Werner's offer of four theoretical tenets of corruption. This work opened the way to research into the causes of and solutions for misconduct in government service. These works, however, offer no practical solutions.

Chapter 18 was published in 1980 by James Bowman in the *Review of Public Personnel Administration*. It offers and evaluates one way to enforce ethical behavior: through whistle-blowing. In "Whistle-Blowing in the Public Service: An Overview of the Issues," Bowman introduces the practice that emerged in the late 1960s and early 1970s as a response to the scandals that had erupted at all levels in government. Whistle-blowing was institutionalized in the Civil Service Reform Act of 1978. Bowman describes those most likely to engage in it, then discusses the process for encouragement and protection of whistle-blowing as a means of controlling corruption. He acknowledges that the whistle-blower is not popular and sees the task as both essential and dangerous.

Another form of employee control is embodied in the Inspector General Act of 1978, which also emerged in the post-Watergate fervor. In his 1985 *Public Budgeting and Finance* article, "The Inspector General Concept: Where It's Been, Where It's Going" (Chapter 19 here), Charles Dempsey explains, "Passage of the act resulted in an increased emphasis on the prevention and detection of fraud, waste, and mismanagement in the federal government." Written seven years after the passage of the act, this article evaluates its effect and suggests future directions.

Both whistle-blowing and investigations by Inspector Generals' offices are still a part of government activities to prevent and identify misconduct. They are still areas for research, practice, and debate. They stand alongside codes of ethics as twin pillars to promote ethical behavior. The Friedrich-Finer debate was never won. Morality and control both appear essential to the encouragement and assurance of ethical conduct in public service.

17

ETHICS IN GOVERNMENT AS A PROBLEM IN EXECUTIVE MANAGEMENT

Robert C. Wood
Harvard University

I

Whenever a public official goes astray, a large audience runs at his heels. Disclosures of misconduct and corruption fascinate both the general public and the professional student of government. No matter how frequently instances of misbehavior occur, each generates its own outburst of popular indignation and spate of expert commentary designed to prevent future wrongdoing.

The public outcry is likely to have immediate and decisive political effect. The Internal Revenue Service and Reconstruction Finance Corporation scandals, the mink coats, deep freezes, and five percenters, for example, set off a chain reaction which according to George H. Gallup conclusively determined the 1952 elections.[1] Changes of corruption reportedly figured decisively in the 1953 New Jersey gubernatorial campaign.[2] The recent housing scandals resulted in a shakeup extending to the far corners of the Federal Housing Administration; they appear to have contributed directly to a congressional reorganization of the parent Housing and Home Finance Agency as well.[3]

The effect of scholarly analyses and prescriptions is less certain. Repetitiously, the revelations produce a bundle of literature, ranging from Sunday supplements to learned journals, devoted to suggesting reforms to eliminate misbehavior in government. Yet few of these recommendations have been officially adopted or, to judge from the record, even seriously considered.

Possibly one reason for the unenthusiastic reception given these proposals is their truly radical nature. Most of the suggestions for reform would involve major changes in our established customs or our governmental processes. The extreme ones rest on the proposition that public and private ethics are inseparably intertwined. Accordingly, some witnesses appearing before the Senate Subcommittee on Ethics in 1951 foresaw little improvement in government behavior until all our morals are uplifted. They proposed solving the old problem of the double standard applied to political ethics and community ethics by somehow raising all behavior to the ideal theoretically demanded of the public service.[4] In their opinion society, not bureaucracy, was to blame for official wrongdoing.

Others advance a more restricted version of the "up by the bootstraps" solution. They are content to purify bureaucracy and leave the test of the community to fend for itself: Thus the Douglas Subcommittee itself gave only passing reference to legislative, judicial, and popular ethics, and emphasized the development of special standards for the public service.[5] The committee proposed to backstop its ethical pronouncements by classifying government agencies according to their proclivity to misbehave and by tightening administrative regulations and statutory prohibitions accordingly. But it placed major reliance on the creation of a commission of ethics to promulgate and monitor rules of behavior applicable almost exclusively to administrative officials.

Two other schools of reform take a more pragmatic approach. The politically oriented argue, with the late Senator Tobey, that corruption is the inevitable result of one-party rule for too long a time. Essentially, they accept Lord Acton's analysis of the corrupting effects of power and believe that only if Democrats and Republicans succeed each other at fairly regular intervals can we expect honest administration of our public affairs.

The second so-called practical approach derives from public administration circles and would substitute a corrective secular trend for a purifying cycle of party competition. The burden of this analysis, as set forth by authorities like Keith Callard, is that corruption of public personnel in the United States is a by-product of existing procedures for their selection and employment. In their view, the elimination of irregularities depends upon professionalization of the bureaucracy.[6] Their ideal is usually the British civil service; their means are the development of a responsible administrative class, loyal to its fellows and its craft. This "professionalization" can be accelerated by all sorts of incentives and special dispensations—honors, medals, bonuses, and awards—to make the career man feel secure and proud, but until "some degree of professional autonomy" is allowed, little advance in ethics can be expected.[7]

Without commenting on the relative merits or feasibilities of these programs, or disparaging them in any way, one common characteristic should be noted: they are all long-run solutions. We are not going to improve either community or bureaucratic ethics overnight; nor are we, by current indications, progressing very rapidly in the development of the career civil service. Even the political solution must rely on sporadic house cleanings, for neither party has demonstrated a monopoly on virtue. If these are the only weapons in our armory, we shall have to resign ourselves to a number of years of repeated scandals until we progress painfully into our administrative Utopia or, what is more likely, and impracticable, accept the philosophy of the moral cynic. Even if we grant the soundness of any or all of these suggested reforms, we need to take some steps to deal with the immediate situation and the immediate public agitation.

II

One thing which might be done, to use an old-saw phrase, is "to return to the Constitution," in the sense that it sets guidelines for administrative procedures. Article II, Section 3, provides that the President "take care that the laws be faithfully executed," and most state Constitutions vest similar responsibility in the office of the Governor. Early constitutional interpretations, at least so far as the federal government is concerned, defined this responsibility principally in terms of the establishment and maintenance of proper standards of personnel conduct.[8] Over the years, the federal provision and its counterparts in other levels of government and for other public executives have lost a good part of their original meaning. Today faithful execution seems to imply primarily notions of scientific managerial control, special staff facilities, and professional recruitment and training techniques. For most public administrators the emphasis has become "expert management" or "competent management." Efficiency and economy have tended to supplant the early definition of faithful execution, and to bury it under the managerial paraphernalia of the twentieth century.

An initial attack on the problem of corruption might well begin with the resurrection of the old principle that public officials have the duty to make sure their employees are honest as well as efficient and competent. It seems time to recall that public irregularities are by and large administrative phenomena, and that corruption is a proper subject for organizational and managerial analysis in the limited sense of those words. Administrators, under the law and in the view of the public, must assure the integrity of their subordinates. In common reason, they should have the means to discharge this responsibility.

What kind of procedures and arrangements do administrators need if the faithful execution of the laws is to retain its normative flavor? Obviously, all or most of the control devices installed during the last fifty years are helpful. Published rules and regulations for personal conduct, augmented by sensible in-service training programs, educate and inform public officials and often enable them to dispose courteously of otherwise embarrassing situations. They help to take the pressure off employees in agencies where awards, decisions, and procurement and loan activities increase opportunities for misconduct. Similarly, careful recruitment procedures screen out undesirables and improve the caliber of personnel. Internal audits verify financial transactions and fix individual accountability. The budget process, program inspections, management surveys, reporting, and review systems frequently result in detecting patterns of systematic deficiencies and are useful in evaluating individual performance. A tight hierarchy within a public agency, in which the top official appoints his subordinates directly and delegates functions explicitly and precisely, increases the surety against wrongdoing.

Just as obviously; however, neither in practice nor in logic are these staff arrangements and internal procedures sufficient. Rules of behavior are not self-enforcing; the most comprehensive audit system cannot detect irregularities not evident in financial records. Budget reviews and inspection and reporting systems tend to become routine and cursory. And in any event they will not uncover instances of outside collusion, and should not be expected to, since they have been designed primarily for other objectives. Their effectiveness in reducing misconduct and promoting honesty is strictly a by-product of their major purposes.

What the government executive really needs to assure the integrity of his personnel are devices especially established for that purpose. He needs arrangements which are expertly designed to enable him to discharge this portion of his executive responsibility. He needs them; so do his employees, if their reputations are to be protected against malicious informers and idle gossips; and so does the public if it is to have confidence in the public service. Such arrangements exist, but they are neither generally recognized nor apparently very respectable in the literature of public administration. They are, quite simply, the systematic employment of administrative investigatory facilities.

III

Investigatory facilities are bad words in this country. It is important, however, to know exactly what they are and what they are not, and what they do and do not do, when properly constituted, before judging their utility.

Essentially, administrative investigatory facilities are staff devices that provide an executive with information about the personal conduct of his employees. They are control units that take their place alongside other staff units, with the specific function of reporting to the executive, protecting him against the derelictions of his subordinates, and assuring the compliance of personnel with applicable law, administrative regulations, and generally accepted ethical standards. They have the further function of safeguarding the reputation of employees by enabling administrators to determine quickly and conclusively the validity of allegations and exposing unfounded derogations. By their very existence, they help sustain the good name of the agency.

The point of departure for an effective investigatory program is the establishment of sensible and reasonably specific rules of conduct for the agency.[9] Although in most instances agency heads can depend on their subordinates to exercise common sense and normal discretion, comprehensive and intelligible rules of conduct highlight the sensitive areas in public programs and offer an effective way for the front office to "set the tone," in Herbert Emmerich's words, "of any administration." They provide a clear, written standard to instruct the unthinking or careless employee and to provide an equitable basis for taking disciplinary action where necessary. While the development of these rules is sometimes scorned as the embodiment of administrative puritanism, they enable the executive to say explicitly what conduct he expects from his staff in the grey area where temptations are likely to be strong. As a minimum, rules of conduct should offer guides to the types of outside employment that are acceptable and to the point at which the proper play of social amenities leaves off and the improper acceptance of gratuities begins. Each public agency needs to prepare its own rules, for each has its particular problems of ethics.

Given these ground rules, by far the most important task of an investigatory facility, and the one consuming the bulk of its staff time, is following up on complaints that the administrator receives from the public or his own employees. Almost every administrator has a flow of accusations, rumors, and bits of gossip across his desk in the course of his day-to-day work. When he lacks a competent investigatory staff, he must ignore these complaints, try to evaluate them without first-hand knowledge, place them in the hands of assistants who are at most intelligent amateurs, or turn them over to a law-enforcement agency. Under any of these procedures, he fails to carry out his executive responsibility.

A secondary service is the review of particularly sensitive activities within the agency on the investigatory unit's own initiative. From such periodic checks, the unit can assist in the development of preventive procedures and work systems which speed the detection of misconduct. In company with management and budgetary personnel, the investigatory staff effect better executive control. A properly established facility will usually initiate all personnel investigations within an organization, except such special-purpose investigations as security checks in the federal government, and will complete those within the range of administrative sanction. Where criminal violations are detected, law-enforcement agencies are usually called in to complete the case. The administrative unit participates, however, to the degree necessary to protect its chief, and by reporting directly only to him it makes sure that he controls the investigation to the limit of his discretion.

A few examples drawn from federal experience may indicate more clearly the general usefulness of these facilities at all levels of United States government. In perhaps the most celebrated of the recent scandals, those involving the Bureau of Internal Revenue, the bribery and collusion disclosed by congressional investigations were precisely of a nature with which a properly functioning investigatory unit is equipped to deal. As the King Subcommittee observed:

> One pattern of evidence runs through all the corruption cases. . . . A revenue officer who derives profit from abuse of his office always comes up with an embarrassing surplus of money for which he cannot account. Either he spends it on a scale of living inexplicable for one in his income bracket, or he accumulates property resulting in an unaccountable growth in net worth. To conceal his misconduct he usually omits the illicit income from his personal income tax return, thus becoming a tax evader.[10]

The subcommittee conducted its inquiry by the simple expedients of following tips, making net worth investigations, and auditing employers' tax returns, with highly effective results. Yet, during the period in which the corruption was most widespread the bureau's own self-policing program had failed to show any substantial record of accomplishment. Its failure, according to the Subcommittee Report, stemmed from the improper organization and functioning of the investigatory program.

> Until 1951, ninety-five inspectors, known as Supervisors of Accounts and Collections, were charged with the responsibility of checking the efficiency and honesty of some thirty-one thousand Bureau employees located in offices of Collectors. These Supervisors were instructed to accomplish their purposes by persuasion. They were not authorized to change operating procedures. Indeed, on many occasions Supervisors were threatened with reprisals where they offended the politically appointed Collectors of Internal Revenue whose conduct in office they were supposed to supervise. Reports and recommendations from Supervisors regarding the conditions in certain Collectors' offices had for years been buried in Bureau files unheeded.[11]

Not until October, 1951, when the bureau established an independent Inspection Service, was the basis laid for developing an effective self-policing system. The President's Reorganization Plan No. 1 of 1952 completed the job by creating an Office of Assistant Commissioner for Inspection with direct access to the commissioner. The assistant commissioner now has full responsibility for assuring that employees adhere to proper standards of conduct, that irregularities are detected, and that personnel investigations are speedily conducted independent of the organizational unit involved.[12]

If the remedy provided for the Bureau of Internal Revenue had been adopted throughout the executive branch, the federal government might have been spared some serious headaches. The disclosures in early 1954 in the Federal Housing Authority revealed once again the sort of irregularities which an investigatory unit is tailor-made to uncover. One of the most striking illustrations, developed in Senate hearings, was the testimony that an official whose record was alleged to include embezzlement, larcenies, and bogus checks, twice reported by the Federal Bureau of Investigation, had served for years and that neither report could even be found in the agency's files.[13] In this case, the absence of systematic procedures within the agency to receive and evaluate outside information and to alert the agency head to irregularities—essential functions of an administrative investigatory unit—appears to have negated the early work of the FBI.

The Hoey Subcommittee's investigations of influence in government procurement, popularly known as influence peddling and five percenters, involved as much, if not more, the victimizing of businessmen by persons outside the government as improper conduct on the part of public officials. Where improper activities were carried on by federal employees, in many instances the persons involved appeared to be at the top of the agencies. But as in the case of the American Lithofold Corporation and the RFC, the names of Internal Revenue agents and employees of the RFC; the Air Force, and the Department of Labor cropped up repeatedly in congressional reports in connection with outside employment and activities which seemed questionable.[14] Even in this difficult twilight zone where criminality may not be an issue but impropriety is, the existence of effective arrangements to detect and report the conduct of the employees involved to the agency head would have served to correct a deteriorating situation before agency and personal reputations were blackened.

IV

If the cases just cited demonstrate the services which investigatory staffs can properly perform, some comments are in order on the activities from which these staffs should be barred and the limits to their effectiveness.

Investigatory facilities need not and should not be conceived as an underground administrative octopus with informers in every unit of a public agency, holding every employee under close surveillance and reviewing every action within the establishment. Members of investigatory staffs should never be responsible for evaluating the results of their investigations or determining sanctions. In the context used here, such staffs are not substitutes for law-enforcement agencies responsible for the prevention and detection of criminal acts outside or within their governments or for security programs. Their concern is with the strictly defined administrative irregularities which if unchecked breed criminal activities; their techniques are those of recognized detective work—interrogation, the examination of accounts, and occasional surveillance. Their approach is not all encompassing but rather selective and specialized, designed to avoid the blunderbuss efforts of amateurs working under pressure.

Investigatory facilities are not effective in all situations and against all types of wrongdoing. For example, they are not useful in monitoring important regulatory activities involving discretionary judgment, and they are likely to be excessively expensive when employed in the highly repetitive routine cases of benefit programs. But they do work well in the area where most irregularities have occurred recently: in cases involving impropriety between agency employees and agency clientele, in enforcement activities, and in procurement, lending, and property administration.

Finally, no centralized system of investigatory facilities, authorized to operate throughout the entire executive branch of a government, should be established. These facilities belong properly to the operating agency heads, the responsible administrators, not to a single police chief. To be acceptable, investigatory facilities should be agency staff units with limited responsibility. No uniform pattern for these units should be applied throughout a government, since staff qualifications and working methods vary according to the size and type of activities of an agency. Some agencies need a small unit reporting directly to the top executive; others need units at the lower echelons as well. But properly established and supervised investigatory facilities provide a sensible, reasonable arrangement for protecting the public service and the public from the wrongdoing of a few.

V

The failure of administrative doctrine to consider the value of investigatory staffs probably stems from the instinctive distaste most Americans have for such institutions. We like to believe our associates are honest; and we generally dislike and distrust the policeman and the informer. The history of our investigatory and law-enforcement agencies, especially on the state and local levels, is not always reassuring and abuses of authority are not unknown. The liberal dose of violence and of vigilance committees in our tradition operates to discourage reliance on investigatory organizations.

However wholesale the motives for scholarly neglect may be, the results seem unfortunate. While a few organizations, such as New York City's Department of Investigation and the inspection service of the United States Post Office Department, have records of substantial accomplishment, many public agencies in which improprieties frequently come to light have no investigatory staffs at all—to the detriment of their reputations and programs.[15] Others maintain poorly functioning, incompetent organizations, manned by amateurs and frequently doing more harm than good. Generally speaking, very few attempts have been made in our governments to determine the specific agencies in which these units are needed, where they should be located in the administrative hierarchy, and how they should be supervised.[16]

The consequences of this situation unhappily go beyond persistent and overt recurrences of wrongdoing and failure to prevent and detect irregularities before they become widespread. If we fail to establish small, effective, and responsible investigatory units, less palatable solutions, fundamentally foreign to American institutions and customs, are likely to be pressed upon us. If chief executives are not equipped with the means effectively to discharge their responsibilities, there are others willing and eager to assume them. There are proposals at all levels of government to vest complete authority for the detection of all types of misconduct in central law-enforcement agencies. Such arrangements have strong similarities to the "police state" which critics of administrative investigatory facilities seek to avoid.

Alternatively, legislative bodies, aware of the political capital to be gained in catching the crooks, sometimes show more enthusiasm than competence in "helping" administrators go about their executive duties. Where no arrangements exist within the executive branches of our governments, legislative committees are encouraged to go beyond the scope of their established investigatory responsibilities and engage in gossip mongering, with the objective of headlines rather than fact-finding for the purpose of lawmaking. Exaggeration, misrepresentation, individual injustices, and political backbiting are not the only results of this practice. More fundamentally, the independence of the chief executive is undermined under circumstances in which it is almost impossible for him to defend himself, for the crooks, often as not, are found to exist.

Nor should we be dissuaded from working to increase the number of properly functioning investigatory facilities because they are sometimes described as "gumshoe." Such disdain is even less justifiable than distrust and fear. Behind the title and the emotion is the general argument that investigators are likely to be inefficient or incompetent. It is alleged that they are frequently the sources of as much corruption as they detect or, and this is worse, that they actually lower the morale and ethical standards of other personnel.

This reasoning is contrary to fact. Investigators, like other personnel, can be trained for useful and rewarding careers. More appropriate qualifications have to be established, it is true, and civil service boards need to make provisions for proper standards and training. Recent experience with special police forces shows conclusively that these objectives can be attained. This experience also shows that corruption within investigatory units can be effectively handled—the techniques for "investigating the investigators" are well established. Public administrators, by study and application, have provided regularized means for moving from patronage systems to professional personnel administration and for making budgetary and purchasing operations positive benefits rather than dictatorial techniques. They can also develop satisfactory investigatory units.

VI

No one familiar with the operations of investigatory facilities supposes that they are the complete answer to the problem of public corruption. When compared with the more revolutionary proposals to reform our society, our politics, and our administrative profession, the proposal for the wider use of such facilities is modest and unheroic. Yet there seems to be more danger of underestimating the utility of competent staff organizations of this nature than of developing them to excess. Even after all their potential misuses are explored, it is difficult to justify their almost studied neglect in the literature of public administration. Once the layers of misinformation and unfounded apprehension are peeled off, they appear as invaluable staff adjuncts to the practicing administrator. A public official who does not provide himself with a "personal eye" when he can runs the risk of damage to his own career; he is also derelict in his duty, for the proposition that public office is a public trust—old as it is—remains the first charge of a responsible government servant.

The great advantage of a proposal to accelerate the use of these facilities is that it can be immediately adopted and with immediate effect. While we wait for better men and better communities, we should try to catch the dishonest among us. While we work for the professionalization of the entire bureaucracy, we should perfect at once critical staff units within our public agencies. Certainly, persistent revelations of corruption damage the development of American public administration too severely to allow us to be dilatory or complacent. When so much dynamite is involved for the political leader loyal to his party and the bureaucrat proud of his trade, even a holding action is worth while.

Notes

1. The post-election poll of the American Institute of Public Opinion, dated January 20, 1953, as reported in *The Washington Post*, Jan. 21, 1953.

2. *The New York Times,* Nov. 3, 1953.

3. *The Washington Post and Times Herald,* July 20, 1951.

4. *Establishment of a Commission on Ethics in Government,* Hearings before a Subcommittee to Study Senate Concurrent Resolution 21 of the Committee on Labor and Public Welfare, United States Senate, 82d Cong., 1st sess., June 19–July 11, 1951 (U. S. Government Printing Office, 1951), p. 577.

5. *Ethical Standards in Government,* Report on a Subcommittee of the Committee on Labor and Public Welfare, United States Senate (U. S. Government Printing Office, 1951), p. 89.

6. Keith Callard, "On the Ethics of Civil Servants in Great Britain and North America," in C. J. Friedrich and J. K. Galbraith, eds., *Public Policy, A Yearbook of the Graduate School of Public Administration, Harvard University, 1953* (Graduate School of Public Administration, 1953), pp. 134–56. Callard is among the most forthright of those who advocate this sort of solution. In my judgment, the following accept substantial portions of the philosophy: Paul H. Appleby, *Morality and Administration in Democratic Government* (Louisiana State University Press, 1952), p. 261; George A. Graham, *Morality in American Politics* (Random House, 1952), p. 337; a number of the authors of articles in the March 1952, issue of *The Annals of the American Academy of Political and Social Science,* titled "Ethical Standards in American Public Life"; and, to a lesser extent, Herbert Emmerich, "A Scandal in Utopia," in *Public Administration Review* 1952 (Winter, 1952).

7. Callard, *op. cit.,* p. 156.

8. Edward S. Corwin, *The President: Office and Powers, 1787–1948* (New York University Press, 1948), ch. III. Specific reference is made on pp. 98 and 101 to the opinion of Attorney General Wirt, in 1823, and the judgment of the lower courts in *Kendall v. U. S.*

9. For an analysis of the utility of rules of conduct, see Phillip Monypenny, "A Code of Ethics as a Means of Controlling Administrative Conduct," 13 *Public Administration Rreview* 184–7 (Summer, 1953).

10. *Internal Reader Investigation,* Report to the Committee on Ways and Means, House of Representatives, by the Subcommittee on Administration of the Internal Revenue Laws (U. S. Government Printing Office, 1952), p. 5.

11. *Ibid.,* p. 6.

12. *Reorganization Plan No. 1 of 1952* (H. Doc. 327. 82d Cong., 2d sess.).

13. *The Washington Post and Times Herald,* July 20, 1954.

14. *American Lithofold Corp., William M. Boyle, Jr., Guy George Gabrielson,* Interim Report of Committee on Expenditures in Executive Departments Made by Its Senate Permanent Subcommittee on Investigations, Pursuant to S. Res. 156 (U. S. Government Printing Office, 1952), pp. 11–18.

15. Although the suggestions for investigatory facilities considered in this article are as applicable to state and local governments as to the federal government, few competent studies of their operations and potentialities at these levels seem to exist. An outstanding exception is Harold Seidman, *Investigating Municipal Administration* (Institute of Public Administration, Columbia University, 1941), p. 213, which tracks the history of New York City's Department of Investigation in detail and provocatively explores the general utility of administrative investigatory facilities.

16. According to reports appearing in *The Washington Star* on Sept. 30 and Oct. 1, 1954, and subsequent dates, *The New York Times,* Sept. 30, 1954, and elsewhere, the federal government has undertaken a review of existing procedures and arrangements within executive departments and agencies designed to detect and prevent acts of impropriety, unethical conduct, and other activities short of criminal violations. On the basis of these newspaper reports, it would appear that the new program incorporates many of the principles discussed in this article. It also seems evident from the editorial comment accompanying the press reports that many of the criticisms there advanced against the program are similar to those considered here.

18

WHISTLE-BLOWING IN THE PUBLIC SERVICE: AN OVERVIEW OF THE ISSUES

James S. Bowman
University of Wyoming

Introduction

In recent years ethical issues in politics and government have received unprecedented attention. A series of scandals involving manipulation of gasoline supplies, illegal political contributions and surveillance, excessive executive perquisites, and pay-offs, bribes and kickbacks have been reported in the national media. "Koreagate," Congressional sex scandals, the Bert Lance fraud trial, corruption in the General Services Administration, drug abuse in the White House, "Billygate," the "Abscam" sting of Congressmen, and the first expulsion of a member of the House of Representatives in over one hundred years are only the most prominent ethical questions in the post-Watergate era. In addition to major exposes and questionable actions on the part of high officials, studies have found widespread unethical practices in daily management, the General Accounting Office has received thousands of complaints of wrongdoing over its "hotline," and the Deputy Attorney General recently testified that "wherever we look . . . significant fraud and abuse" is detected.[1]

It should not be surprising, then, that opinion polls have shown a dramatic drop in confidence in governmental institutions; the events of the 1970's had a traumatic effect on the relationship between the public and its government. Yet, if official misconduct has crippled the credibility of authority and weakened the national political consensus, it has also revealed the strength of the foundations of the country. Survey evidence demonstrates that the people have lost faith in the way the system is operated, but have not lost confidence in the system itself.[2] Perhaps one reason why this is so is that whistle-blowers have kept alive the bond of trust between the American government and its citizens. As government becomes more pervasive in these United States, it becomes more essential to control its power. The effort to regain public confidence and restore credibility in government during the 1980's cannot overlook the role of the whistle-blower in responsible public administration.

The objective of this essay, then, is to explore the importance of dissent in bureaucracies in a democratic society. As part of a larger project, and in order to obtain systematic data on this subject, previously unassembled studies were compiled and analyzed. The following pages will explore the development and institutionalization of whistle-blowing in recent years, examine the relationship between the individual and the organization, and consider long-range and short-run reforms to promote integrity in government and reduce the need to blow the whistle (Bowman, forthcoming).

The Emergence of Whistle-Blowing

The late 1960's and 1970's witnessed the initiation of the Age of the Whistle-blower.[3] It was the C-5A military transport, the New York City police department, the Vietnam War, Watergate, and the Kerr-McGee Oklahoma nuclear plant that dramatized whistle-blowing: Ernest A. Fitzgerald exposed defense contract overruns; Frank Serpico spoke out against corruption in city government; Daniel Ellsberg made the famous Pentagon Papers public; the mysterious Deep Throat was instrumental in uncovering the misdeeds of the Nixon administration; Karen Silkwood's death represented the danger in trying to reveal information to the public. While not all conscientious employees become national *cause celebre* [*sic*], they also have been responsible for disclosing problems such as regulatory corruption, merit system abuses, dangers to public health, and conflict of interest irregularities.

Given pervasive group norms in organization, whistle-blowing is, nonetheless, not a frequent occurrence. It is, in fact, a rather extreme manifestation of underlying problems, and provides little evidence where abuse may be widespread, but the whistle is "swallowed" rather than blown. Yet, neither is whistle-blowing merely the product of a series of isolated incidents. Instead, it may be indicative and symbolic of the problems in contemporary politics—Jimmy Carter even campaigned on a promise to protect non-conforming federal workers in 1976. Indeed, while whistle-blowers have brought important issues to light, many trends in bureaucratic ethics began before these events and, in many places, continue. Responsible commentators now believe that corruption is ubiquitous and systemic in American life and cannot simply be dismissed as a part of "post-Watergate morality."[4]

Although dissent at the workplace is as old as humankind, it has only recently crystallized into a movement comparable in content, if not scope, to earlier civil rights and liberation movements. By the late Seventies, whistle-blowing began to be institutionalized as public interest groups formed, professional associations sponsored symposia, universities encouraged research, unions protected members, national conferences convened, and Congress held hearings and passed laws. All of these activities suggest how far society has come in its quest for truth and justice in organizations.

The more sensational examples of official impropriety, in short, have brought into focus latent concerns about the freedom of expression in government. People today are more receptive to these concerns than ever before perhaps because the liberties of the public employee are the liberties of a substantial percentage of the citizenry. Blowing the whistle will continue as government grows larger, as expectations of work rise, as more females, with fresh perspectives on work enter the labor force, as America increasingly becomes a nation of employees, and as corruption persists in bureaucracy. Alan F. Westin writes that "many observers ... believe ... [that] ... demands for new individual rights ... will reach their mature status in the 1980's."[5]

Although it may be true that the public is becoming more sympathetic to whistle-blowers, many bureaucracies remain hostile to them. Congressman William Clay (D.–Missouri) has noted that whistle-blowers are the "new niggers" in organizational society following student anti-war protesters, civil rights activists, and Communists (U.S. Congress, House, 1980: 148). Once attention is focused on the employee, the bureaucracy knows how to deal with the problem. Dissenters are regularly given meaningless assignments, transferred to remote locations, forced to undergo psychiatric examinations, ordered to do work for which they are not qualified, assigned to "turkey farms," fired from their jobs, and otherwise neutralized and retaliated against by having their careers destroyed. By abusing personnel procedures, bureaucracy can rid itself of abnormality. Certainly it is easier to deal with the dissenter than the object of dissent. Public officials rarely welcome challenges to their authority as exemplified by the Nixon White House designation of John Dean as a "bottom-dwelling slug."

Yet the vast majority of these employees are not malcontents, misfits, neurotics, crusaders, nor radicals. Typically, a whistle-blower is a middle manager, a knowledgeable individual who can see policy problems, but who may not have a vested interest in ensuring they are never made public. Most are ordinary Americans with no record of political activism or animosity toward government. Indeed, the act of whistle-blowing is likely to be conservative because it seeks to restore, not change, a pre-existing condition (Weinstein, 1979b: 76). Since the whistle-blower frequently seems to have believed the good government lessons taught in schools, he or she expects problems to be solved when they are brought to the attention of those in positions of authority. When they are not and corruption goes unchallenged, the conscientious employee exposes the problem.

Presidents, senators, professional associations, public interest groups, ethicists, and journalists all have attempted to define whistle-blowing. A useful definition was offered by Alan Campbell, Director of the Office of Personnel Management, during the 1980 Congressional oversight hearings on the subject.

> Quite simply, I view whistle-blowing as a popular shorthand label for any disclosure of legal violations, mismanagement, a gross waste of funds, an abuse of authority, or a danger to public health or safety, whether the disclosure is made within or outside the chain of command.[6]

Thus, a whistle-blower is an employee who reveals information about illegal, inefficient, or wasteful government action that endangers the health, safety, or freedom of the American public.

The difficulties in judging whistle-blowers and the issues exposed are vividly suggested by comparing Judas Iscariot and Martin Luther. Weighing all the dilemmas in blowing the whistle, as Sissela Bok suggests, is not an easy task. The ideal case—where the cause is just, where all administrative appeals have been exhausted, where responsibility is openly accepted, and where the dissenting employee is above reproach—is unusual.

> Given the indispensable services performed by so many whistle-blowers, strong public support is often merited. But the new climate of acceptance makes it easy to overlook the dangers of whistle-blowing: of uses in error or in malice; of work and reputations unjustly lost for those falsely accused; of privacy invaded and trust undermined (*New York Education Quarterly*, 1979: 2–11).

Bok suggests that different instances of whistle-blowing can be distinguished by using the rare clear cut cases as benchmarks to analyze more complex actions. Attorney Peter Raven Hansen advises that such cases may be characterized by a whistle-blower who focuses on the abuse itself, not personalities, uses appropriate administrative channels before "going public," anticipates and documents retaliation, and knows when to give up and move on (*Technology Review,* 1980: 34). Ultimately, the courts have maintained that a balance must be struck between the exercise of free speech and the authority of government to discharge employees for the good of the service. The difficulty in defining this balance is no excuse for permitting the kind of abuse discussed earlier. Dissent in organizations suggests that society questions the idea that management possesses superior ethical wisdom and desires a new balance between employee rights and management prerogatives.

There are at least two significant societal issues related to whistle-blowing. The first is responsibility and accountability in a system of representative democracy. In light of pervasive citizen distrust in government, this is hardly an academic or philosophical problem. Ways need to be found to introduce democratic rights into bureaucracies. The second issue is that in order to assure responsibility and accountability, due process procedures are necessary to protect employees who care about the general interest. Effective methods need to be discovered to balance an individual's duty to his or her employer with his or her duty to the public. In fact, "many of the rights and privileges . . . so important to a free society that they are constitutionally protected . . . are vulnerable to abuse through an employer's power" (Blades, 1967: 1407). Society has a right, in a word, to learn about significant problems in American politics without having those who expose them destroy their careers in the process.

It is critical, in short, that the "I win, you lose," zero-sum approach to dissent in organizations change. Responsible protest should be treated fairly to the benefit of both the employee and the employer. Directing corrective efforts to the dissenter instead of the policy issue in question will not alter the conditions that make whistle-blowing necessary. Disclosure of waste, illegal activity, and abuse of power should be seen as a commitment to make government more worthy of public trust. Open discussion strengthens, not weakens, democracy. Despite the attention that dissent in organizations has received in recent years, whistle-blowing alone will never establish standards of public accountability and credibility that the citizenry deserves and expects. Yet, if the measures reviewed below were instituted, blowing the whistle would be less necessary than it is today. Before these measures are analyzed, however, the environment within which whistle-blowing occurs requires examination.

The Context of Whistle-Blowing: The Individual and the Organization

It is essential to recognize that individual actions occur in an organizational context.[7] Moral judgments reflect group norms; the organization itself is a moral community, the formal expression and endorsement of those norms. One of the principal problems in bureaucracy today is that growth and diversification have diminished the sense of individual responsibility. This diffusion of accountability has meant that many people work in an environment in which nobody can be effectively in charge to set standards.[8]

Since corruption is a part of the human condition, structures are needed to limit, discourage, and channel it (Dobel, 1978: 958–973). That is, institutions must assume at least partial responsibility for the ethical conduct of their employees. Individuals may make decisions based upon personal standards, but employers can control and define the situations in which decisions are made. It is not sufficient, in other words, for the individual to be convinced of his or her own rectitude and integrity. Managers, as moral custodians of collective goals, are strategically placed to recognize the factors that promote and inhibit ethical behavior. Accordingly, they should be responsible for providing an institutional basis for professional conduct and responsible dissent. Without it, individual conscience can be paralyzed when rules of the organization are inadequate to support personal dignity. The pathetic plight of the whistle-blower, however, demonstrates how tenuous the relationship is between the individual and the organization.

The difficulty stems from the fact that bureaucracies resemble authoritarian states which do not permit legitimate opposition. Employees in hierarchical organizations cannot act politically except in disloyal opposition; whistle-blowing is a political phenomenon that occurs in organizations which are not supposed to be political systems.[9] The reason for this is that the prevailing, if long discredited, administrative myth is that bureaucracy is a rational, non-partisan, technical process, divorced from politics.[10] Whistle-blowing punctures the myth of neutrality and consensus in administration. It suggests that bureaucracy is a political system consisting of human beings as purposive actors with a sense of individual responsibility.

However, whistle-blowing occurs in the context of the administrative myth and the fear of hierarchical power and habits of obedience that originate in working etiquette and bureaucratic politeness.

There is a pervasive ethic of loyalty to the team . . . which manifests itself in the sanctity of the organization qua organization. The self-perpetuating propensities of organizations resulting from the teamwork ethic have been variously described . . . as organizational opportunism, bureaucratic self-maintenance, and the institutional imperative (i.e., every action or decision of an institution must be intended to keep the institutional machinery going). By whatever name, this organizational characteristic ensures that whistle-blowing will tend to be perceived as a threatening affront to an organization. . . . Because an organization's behavior can be no more proper . . . than the people within the organization, the job of the internal dissenter can be expected to be an enduring one (Bogen, 1978: 24, 17).

Whistle-blowing is heroic because it requires bureaucrats "to transcend the every day world by naming abuses where none are supposed to exist, by challenging authority when obedience is required, by overcoming narrow self interests, and by inventing and creating novel ways of achieving their goals" (Weinstein, 1979a: 76).

Protecting Dissenters

If whistle-blowing has come of age, it does not automatically follow that effective plans of action are developed and implemented. Since the lack of internal procedures is frequently responsible for whistle-blowing, what changes might serve to protect the rights of dissenters while assuring effective management (Leahy, 1978)? Robert F. Allen (1980: 37) identifies four elements of any successful, long range change program. First, in an effort to deal with the causes of behavior instead of its symptoms, administrators should ask themselves "What did we contribute to this behavior"? Second, instead of relying on simple explanations for organizational problems, thorough understanding involves: (a) analysis of the organization's cultural setting, (b) introduction of new strategies, and (c) evaluation of change and development of a continuing renewal process. Third, by creating answers to such questions as "What behavior is rewarded and penalized by the institution?" a sound data base can be established. Finally, an audit of the organization's ethical and moral results can point the way to constructive change. While this approach does not deemphasize individual responsibility nor ignore scandals, it does address the underlying weaknesses that produce them. Blaming the bearer of bad tidings, after all, is a way of freeing conforming employees and their organizations from complicity in what is happening around them.

Whistle-blowing would not be so necessary if managerial indifference was not so pervasive and if elective procedures were used to incorporate dissent into decision-making. Thus, in the context of long range change, the need to resort to whistle-blowing in the short run can be reduced by providing mechanisms to ensure that managers take criticism seriously.

While it may be that some executives welcome criticism, communication techniques such as suggestion boxes and "open door" policies lack power to compel top management to examine criticisms they are reluctant to deal with, and could turn out to be a trap for the employee. Since she or he is objecting to management policy, it is not reasonable to expect an unbiased review of the dissent or the dissenter. More systematic procedures may not entirely deal with these problems, but they may have a significant deterrent effect if employers know that their actions will be subject to review. Both internal and external checks may be useful depending upon the circumstances.[11] The absence of such safeguards virtually guarantees that dissent will develop into confrontation between management and the employee.

One internal device is an "ethical audit." Used for years in business, the social audit is a methodical review of a corporation's activities in the area of social responsibility (e.g., environmental pollution, affirmative action, community relations). An expanded or refocused effort could include ethical concerns in all areas of decision-making beyond those normally included in a social audit. Since audits are usually done after the fact, an ongoing technique used in some organizations is the appointment of an ethical advisor comparable to a legal or financial advisor. Such a person acts as a "devil's advocate" in policy decisions. The same staff personnel could formulate ethical impact statements, design employee bills of rights, serve as an ombudsman or inspector general, provide space on standard forms for dissenting opinions, and/or serve on review boards.

A second possibility would be to formalize the decision-making process. Policy objectives could be clearly specified and criteria established for all decision-makers so that the procedure and content of decisions would be made more visible and accountable. The organization's standards and how they are being implemented could be part of its major reports. Bureaucratic competition in the form of overlapping jurisdictions and rival organizations may also prevent concentrations of power and guard against corruption.

Since the personnel process is frequently used to harass and remove whistle-blowers, a third internal check would be to emphasize the importance of ethics and employee rights throughout the personnel system. For instance, knowledge of the existence of the organization's code of conduct could be required as a condition of employment. It would then be explained during new employee orientation sessions. The role of dissent could also be made part of management training. The subordinate and the supervisor could discuss ethical conduct in the organization and at the time of performance evaluation. Automatic payroll deductions could be made to provide for legal services for conscientious employees. Leaves of absence or personnel exchanges between organizations could provide administrators opportunities to stand back from their work and refine their perspectives in organizational behavior. One product of such an experience could be a newsletter story or article for a trade magazine. In fact, measures could be taken to ensure that the personnel manager or staff librarian is aware of current books on management ethics, can obtain reprints of relevant articles, and is on the mailing list of organizations that sponsor meetings on topical issues. Finally, outplacement services for separated employees could be sponsored by the agencies.

However helpful such internal mechanisms may be in improving management and protecting individual rights, their limitations must be recognized. Kenneth T. Bogen (1978: 129) points out that "the true protection offered by . . . [any] . . . intra-organizational procedures depends upon the good will of management, the very lack of which often produces whistle-blowing."

External checks on administrative responsibility are, therefore, desirable. Employee unions, for example, can assist whistle-blowers. Historically unions have been more interested in the material conditions of work life than in civil liberties. In point of fact, union membership does not seem to affect the inclination to engage in whistle-blowing (Weinstein, 1979: 41). Nonetheless as members become more sophisticated and educated, activities in this area should grow, as long as employees cannot protect themselves without the union. Many of the same comments also apply to professional societies, most of which have been reluctant to defend the independence of their members. Useful programs that might be undertaken would be to recognize leadership in professional ethics by awarding citations to deserving individuals and organizations, provide ethical consulting services, operate preferential reemployment networks for whistle-blowers, and publicize those organizations which violate professional standards.

The most popular current remedy for organizational abuse is statutory relief for whistle-blowers. Since action is ordinarily not taken against agency management, however, there is little reason not to retaliate against dissenters. Thus, a recent study of eight public laws that include employee protection sections found that such provisions have had limited success (Chalk and von Hipple, 1979: 55). Perhaps the most innovative type of statutory relief would be to extend unlawful discrimination on the basis of race, color, religion, sex, national origin, age, and union membership to political, social, or economic views. Lawrence Blades argues that it is anomalous that the courts provide relief to an employee discharged because of race or religion, but they do not provide protection for an employee discharged because of the exercise of free speech. Indeed, it has been pointed out that as long as federal law denies employees the right to engage in partisan political activities and the right to strike, their constitutional right to petition the government should be broadly construed.[12] Failing that, statutory hiring preferences for abused employees could be enacted.

The most discussed form of statutory protection in recent years has been the Civil Service Reform Act of 1978. Part of the Act established the Merit Systems Protection Board and the Office of Special Counsel with the power to investigate prohibited personnel practices, including reprisals against whistle-blowers. While it may be too early for definitive judgments, initial indications are not reassuring (U.S. Congress, House, 1980).

Although the Special Counsel is required to maintain the anonymity of the whistle-blower, agencies, when requested by the Special Counsel, are permitted to investigate themselves. To date, such investigations have been less than satisfactory. If the Counsel determines that a prohibited personnel practice is involved, the case is referred to the Merit Systems Protection Board. In carrying out its function, the Board has adopted more formal judicial procedures than had existed under the Civil Service Commission which had been called a "whistle-blower's graveyard." The initial, precedent-setting cases before the Board suggest a tendency for the rights of dissenters to be subordinated to the needs of efficiency. Equally significant is that in 1980 the Office of Special Counsel was subject to massive budget cuts which reduced its staff by two-thirds.

As Rosemary Chalk and Frank von Hipple (1979: 55) point out, whatever due process protections "are provided [they] will have little value unless they are embedded in a process which deals effectively with the substance of dissent." The situation of the whistle-blower, in other words, will only be marginally improved unless the issues she or he raises are dealt with. If internal checks are little more than window dressing and external checks are ignored or turned into management tools, little change can be expected and confidence in government can only be further undermined.

Indeed, Congressional hearings on the implementation of the Civil Service Reform Act consisted largely of, in the words of the subcommittee chairwoman, "blowing the whistle on whistle-blowing protections."[13] Most of the testimony claimed that the safeguards were a failure, and that reforms had been transformed to where there is no more protection now (perhaps less) than under the pre-existing system. In a prescient observation, Deena Weinstein (1979b: 124) remarked that:

> All of the proposed reforms of bureaucratic abuses which work within the present system confront a basic dilemma. The ground of hierarchical administrative authority is that a specific group of officials should be held responsible for the conduct . . . of the organization. The presence of abuses . . . shows that officials cannot or will not behave responsibly . . . "Reform of abuses concentrates in making officials accountable to other agencies. Such accountability, however, weakens their autonomy or, in the case of co-option, allows them to be even more abusive . . ." Reform, then, diffuses responsibility and gives officials excuses for their failures.

Stated differently, intentionally developed devices for guaranteeing accountability are as likely as not to formalize techniques of evasion. Weinstein goes on to argue that the reason for this is that there are deep social conflicts over the purposes organizations should serve. "Without the consensual loyalty and trust of the citizenry," J. Patrick Dobel (1978: 969) writes in a treatise on corruption, "reforms will simply be shams to rationalize the continuation of corrupt practices." Reassurances and denials seem to merely confirm official hypocrisy and untrustworthiness.

In short, whistle-blowing is a manifestation of serious problems concerning the legitimacy of American government. Both the long and short run methods discussed above to help protect dissenters may be quite useful in specific organizations and for individuals. Until more basic issues about the conduct of politics are addressed, however, such devices can never be truly effective in reducing the underlying need to blow the whistle.

Summary and Conclusions

This analysis has examined the significance of corruption in American government today, traced the emergence and institutionalization of whistle-blowing as an important social phenomenon, explored the relationship between the dissenting individual and the bureaucratic organization, and discussed both reforms designed to encourage ethical behavior and make whistle-blowing less necessary.

Only once in American history did administrative reform become part of the mainstream of the nation's politics and that was during the Progressive Era. The increasing interest in the public employee as a productive source of information about government suggests that there is an important movement to reaffirm the basic principle that the free exchange of ideas is an integral part of democratic decision-making. Nonetheless, although civil servants have rights and protections, in reality managers successfully retaliate against whistle-blowers. The quest for more ethical government must permit public employees to fulfill their role as autonomous and responsible citizens in American democracy.

Some of the trends discussed in this article suggest that the tension between individual democratic rights and organizational authoritarianism in American life may be resolved in future years. But, until it is dealt with, the daily interactions among employees and institutions that do not provide opportunities for the exercise of integrity will continue the corruption of democracy, and whistle-blowing will remain a dangerous, if essential, task.

Notes

1. See Bowman, 1977: 3–20; U. S. News and World Report, 1979: 38; and Weinstein, 1979: 19. Another indication of the depth of the problem is that the convenor of the 1980 National Conference on Fraud, Waste, and Abuse informed the author many prominent appointed public officials expected illegal honoraria as a condition for speaking at the conference.

2. For a summary of these data, see Sundquist, 1980: 183–208.

3. Several landmark works that emphasize ethical dilemmas in organizations prior to this period include Golembiewski, 1965; Hirshman, 1970; and Weisband and Franck, 1975. The latter report that among top public officials who resigned, the percentage "going public" declined by more than two-thirds in 30 years, a pe-

riod when the New Deal and the Cold War bureaucratized much of public policy. Important reference materials include Nader et al., 1972; Government Accountability Project, 1977; *The Bureaucrat,* 1977; Uris, 1978; and Clark, forthcoming.

4. On these points see Comptroller General, 1980; Caiden and Caiden, 1977; and Etzioni, 1977: 11–17.

5. See Westin and Salisbury, 1980: A recent survey of federal employees revealed that 60 per cent of the respondents say they are willing to blow the whistle. See also U. S. Congress, House, Committee on Post Office and Civil Service, 1980; 196.

6. See U. S. Congress, House, Committee on Post Office and Civil Service, 1980: 196–197. The etymology of the word is discussed in Safire, 1978: 790.

7. On this point also see Boling, 1978: 251–254.

8. Indeed, individuals perceive the organizational environment to be less ethical than their own values and behavior. At least four recent surveys, for example, show that the majority of managers are under pressure to compromise personal standards of conduct to achieve organizational goals. In addition, many respondents feel that their superiors are only interested in results, and not how they are obtained. See Bowman, 1981 and the references cited therein.

In this environment, whistle-blowing may be seen as one means of humanizing organizations, i.e., organizations *are* people. As such, a whistle-blower is a person who acts on behalf of the citizen to blow the whistle on another individual. See Seidman, 1980.

9. For a book-length statement of this thesis see Weinstein, 1979.

10. While the politics-administration dichotomy "may have been abandoned by many scholars, it continues as an ideal role for bureaucracy in democracy and as a symbol against corruption. Its popularity, writes Frederick C. Mosher, remains as a convenient rationale for elected officials, administrators, and political scientists alike to support and justify their current interests. Public leaders take refuge in it in order to transfer blame from themselves to bureaucrats. Practitioners would rather not emphasize that they are influencing policy . . . Scholars prefer not to examine important normative issues since they are not readily observable and easily quantified." See Bowman, forthcoming.

11. For a brief discussion of these see Bowman, 1981.

12. See Blades, 1967 and *Virginia Law Review,* 1971.

13. See U. S. Congress, House, Committee on Post Office and Civil Service, 1980: 33. Also see Badhwar, 1980: 9.

References

Allen, R. F. (1980). "The Ik in the Office." *Organizational Dynamics* 8 (Winter).
Badhwar, I. (1980). "Analyzing the Hoax of Hoaxes." *Federal Times* (August 25): 9.
Blades, L. (1967). "Employment at Will vs Individual Freedom: On Limiting the Abusive Exercise of Employer Power." *Columbia Law Review* 67 (December): 1407.
Bogen, K. T. (1978). "Whistle-blowing by Technical Experts." Unpublished thesis. Princeton, N.J.: Princeton University.

Boling, E. (1978). "Organizational Ethics: Rules, Creativity, and Idealism," pp. 251–254 in J. W. Sutherland (ed.), *Management Handbook for Public Administration*. New York: Van Nostrand Reinhold Co.

Bok, S. (1979). "Whistle-blowing and Professional Responsibility." *New York Education Quarterly* 11.

Bowman, J. S. (1977). "Ethics in the Federal Service: A Post-Watergate View." *Midwest Review of Public Administration* 11 (March): 3–20.

_____. (1981). "The Management of Ethics: Codes of Conduct in Organizations." *Public Personnel Management* 10, 1.

_____. (forthcoming). *Managerial Ethics: Whistle-blowing in Organizations: An Annotated Bibliography and Resource Guide*. New York: Garland Publishing, Inc.

_____. (forthcoming). "Public Administration Without Ethics: The Legacy of the Politics-Administration Dichotomy," in J. Rabin and J. S. Bowman (ed.), *Politics and Administration: The Wilsonian Influence in Public Administration*.

The Bureaucrat (1977). Entire issue.

Caiden, G. E. and N. J. Caiden (1977). "Administrative Corruption." *Public Administration Review* 37 (May/June).

Clark, L. (forthcoming). *Blowing the Whistle: Public Service, Private Agony*. Boston: Beacon Press.

Comptroller General (1980). *Continuing and Widespread Weaknesses in Internal Control Result in Losses Through Fraud, Waste, and Abuse*. Washington, D.C.: General Accounting Office.

Dobel, J. P. (1978). "The Corruption of a State." *American Political Science Review* 72 (September): 958–973.

Etzioni, A. (1977). "American Ethics and the President," pp. 11–17 in Y. Kugel and G. W. Greenberg, *Ethical Perspectives in Business and Society*. Lexington, Mass.: D. C. Heath and Co.

Golembiewski, R. T. (1965). *Man, Management and Morality*. New York: McGraw-Hill.

Government Accountability Project (1977). *A Whistle-blower's Guide to the Federal Bureaucracy*. Washington, D.C.: The Institute for Policy Studies.

Hirshman, A. L. (1970). *Exit, Voice, and Loyalty*. Cambridge: Harvard University Press.

Nader, R. (1972). *Whistle-blowing*. New York: Grossman Publishers.

Raven, P. (1980). "Do's and Don'ts for Whistle-blowers: Planning for Trouble." *Technology Review* 82 (May).

Safire, W. (1978). *Safire's Political Dictionary*. 3rd ed. *New York: Random House*.

Seidman, E. (1980). "Professional Societies and Whistle-blowing: An Ethical Challenge." Paper presented at the Annual Meeting of the American Society for Public Administration. San Francisco, California: San Francisco Hilton. (April 13–15).

Sundquist, J. L. (1980). "The Crisis of Competence in Our National Government." *Political Science Quarterly* 95 (Summer): 183–208.

U. S. Congress, House of Representatives, Committee on Post Office and Civil Service and Comptroller General (1980). *First Year Activities of the Merit Systems*

Retention Board and the Office of Special Counsel. Washington, D.C.: General Accounting Office.

U. S. Congress, House of Representatives, Committee on Post Office and Civil Service (1980). *Civil Service Reform Oversight 1980—Whistleblower.* 96th Congress, 2nd Session.

U. S. Congress, Senate, Committee on Governmental Affairs (1978). *The Whistleblowers: A Report on Federal Employees Who Disclose Acts of Governmental Waste Abuse and Corruption.* Washington, D.C.: Government Printing Office.

U. S. News and World Reports (1979). "Uncle Sam's Fraud Hotline." Volume 87 (August 20).

Uris, A. (1978). *Executive Dissent: How to Say No and Win.* New York: AMACON.

Virginia Law Review (1971). "The Right of Government Employees to Furnish Information to Congress." Volume 57 (June): 885–919.

Walters, K. D. (1975). "Your Employee's Rights to Blow the Whistle." *Harvard Business Review* 53 (July/August): 26–35.

Weinstein, D. (1979). "Opposition to Abuse Within Organizations: Heroism and Legalism." *The ASLA Forum* (Fall): 38.

_____. (1979). *Bureaucratic Oppositions.* New York: Pergamon Press.

Weisband, E. and T. M. Franck (1975). *Resignation in Protest.* New York: Grossman Publishers.

Westin, A. F. and S. Salisbury (1980). "Introduction." *Individual Rights in the Corporation.* New York: Pantheon Books.

19

THE INSPECTOR GENERAL CONCEPT: WHERE IT'S BEEN, WHERE IT'S GOING

Charles L. Dempsey
Director of Government Services,
Alexander Grant Company

The Inspector General (IG) Act was passed on October 12, 1978, establishing Offices of Inspector General in 12 federal departments and agencies (P.L. 95-452). The act created independent and objective units which provide leadership and recommend policy for the promotion of economy, efficiency, and effectiveness and the prevention and detection of fraud and abuse in federal programs and operations. There are now a total of 17 such statutorily created Offices of Inspector General. They have provided a much needed focal point for federal anti-fraud and waste efforts.

Passage of the act resulted in an increased emphasis on the prevention and detection of fraud, waste, and mismanagement in the federal government. Since then, much has been said about the inspector general concept, how it evolved and how we got to where we are today, our impact on the budget process, and where we are headed in the future. This article will highlight some experiences since the act passed seven years ago and suggest future directions.

Events Prompting the Act

It was a series of scandals and abuses within government as well as a renewed emphasis on prevention and detection that led to congressional realization of the need for an IG concept within the federal government and subsequent passage of the act. In May 1977 Representatives Jack Brooks and L. H. Fountain and the House Government Operations Committee began a comprehensive series of hearings concerning proposed IG legislation. Although agency management did not want the legislation and their officials so testified, the committee found that various federal departments and agencies had experienced:

- Lack of a central unit with the overall authority, responsibility, and resources necessary to ensure effective action against fraud and program abuse.
- Lack of affirmative programs to look for possible fraud and abuse.
- Instances where investigators were kept from looking into suspected irregularities.
- Serious shortages of audit and investigative personnel.
- Potential fraud cases which had not been sent to the Department of Justice for prosecution.

The House passed the proposal 388 to 6. In September 1978 Senator Thomas Eagleton introduced the IG Act legislation before the full Senate for approval, stating that:

This legislation responds to the findings that fraud, abuse, and just plain waste in federal programs and operations are reaching epidemic proportions. Undoubtedly the problem is not new: however, increased attention by the press and by government officials has brought to light increasingly disturbing testimony of the magnitude of these problems.

Further emphasizing the need for the IG concept, Senator Eagleton stated:

The Committee on Governmental Affairs and its House counterpart found that a lack of audit and investigative resources has crippled the federal effort to prevent and detect fraud, abuse, and waste in federal expenditures. Audit and investigative efforts also lack independence. Frequently auditors and investigators find themselves reporting to the very officials whose programs they are supposedly reviewing.

The Inspector General concept, which can best be described as the consolidation of auditing and investigative responsibilities under a single high-level official reporting directly to the head of the establishment, responds to the major problems which have been identified in current federal efforts to prevent and detect fraud and waste.[1]

The act passed the Senate unanimously and went into effect on October 12, 1978.

The Inspector General: A Part of, Yet Apart from, the Management Team

One of the act's mandates is that IGs advise agency heads with respect to all matters relating to the promotion of economy, efficiency and effectiveness, and the prevention and detection of fraud and abuse. This is a crystal-clear signal that inspectors general must participate and work with management to ensure program integrity and operating efficiency. The IG community cannot afford to stand back and watch—the job involves rolling up one's sleeves and being willing to get one's hands dirty. At the same time, the act as well as our professional standards clearly require that an IG maintain independence.

An IG's independence is essential to the rendering of fair and impartial conclusions and recommendations on agency activities. It is a state of mind, a quality, that is achieved not by any single action or event, but through the day-to-day conduct of the IG and staff. The IG must constantly assert such independence by challenging any policy that might compromise the office's ability to carry out its statutory mandate or infringe on the rights and authorities assigned the IG by the act. These include: the conduct of whatever investigations and audits are considered necessary or desirable without interference; access to the agency head; the ability to communicate directly with the Congress; access to records, reports and personnel; authority to hire and fire staff, etc.

With this in mind, how does an IG set out to fulfill the intent of the IG Act? How does one strike a balance between auditing and investigating the activities of agency management and at the same time working *with* these same people as a team dedicated to the effective delivery of departmental or agency programs?

In the Office of the Inspector General at the Department of Housing and Urban Development (HUD), this has been done by setting up a separate office of senior experienced professionals to concentrate their efforts on prevention and cooperation with management. The Office of Fraud Control and Management Operations (FCMO) does not perform audits or investigations, since these activities are carried out by the Offices of Audit and Investigation. Instead, the Office of Fraud Control and Management Operations works with management, providing advice and consultation. This concept is nothing new. Public accounting firms have for years had management consulting divisions, yet these same firms still provide audit coverage to their clients. Since early 1979 we have actively worked with management to improve the department's operations and reduce its vulnerability to fraud and abuse. We are listening to each other and working together.

With respect to fraud control, this new office has a wide range of responsibilities, such as:

- Analyzing results of audits and investigations to identify areas sensitive to fraud and abuse.
- Assisting in the evaluation of internal controls for all HUD programs and activities which may be susceptible to fraud.
- Developing and implementing strategies that minimize the opportunities for the occurrence of fraud and waste.
- Providing leadership and participating in a departmental committee dealing with fraud detection and prevention.
- Researching, developing, and testing innovative techniques and systems for the detection of fraud.
- Reviewing the results of audits, investigations, and reviews of headquarters and regional management to determine the effectiveness of fraud prevention measures.
- Developing and implementing methods to educate, instruct, and train appropriate HUD personnel in fraud detection and prevention activities.

A key activity has been providing support to the departmental Committee on Fraud, Waste and Mismanagement, composed of officials from each major component of the department and chaired by the IG. The committee was established as a departmental management initiative to coordinate HUD's efforts to minimize the opportunities for the occurrence of fraud, waste, and mismanagement in its programs and operations. The committee also recommends policies for improving HUD's ability to detect and prevent fraud and program abuse, and advises the secretary on related policy matters. The Office of Fraud Control provides support and assistance to the committee, and also acts as liaison with other governmental agencies for the committee. Since its establishment, the committee has made considerable progress on such issues as: program participant monitoring, a quality control system for tenant eligibility, performance bonding, and public housing management.

In February 1979 a HUD employee telephone hotline was established in FCMO. This hotline is available to all HUD employees and program participants to report allegations of fraud, waste, and mismanagement in the department. The office refers all hotline calls to the proper organization for action, including calls from HUD employees and referrals from the Office of Management and Budget and the General Accounting Office.

Another effort undertaken by the Office of Fraud Control and Management Operations is the issuance of a series of "fraud information bulletins." These bulletins are designed to alert employees to schemes used to defraud HUD programs: vulnerable areas in program or administrative operations; or measures being taken to address fraud and abuse, such as the hotline operations or internal control initiatives.

The office has also worked with the Committee on Fraud, Waste and Mismanagement to assure that adequate attention is given to implementing management controls in new or substantially revised programs or activities. A sound system of management controls can reduce the chances for persons or firms to use HUD program funds improperly. In 1979 HUD implemented the Fraud Vulnerability Assessment System designed to:

- Provide a framework for ensuring that adequate controls are built into new or revised programs or activities.
- Require program officials to take positive steps to ensure that adequate safeguards are incorporated into handbooks, regulations, etc.
- Provide top management with risk decision packages when new or revised programs or activities are to be implemented.

And have these joint ventures with the management side of the house in any way jeopardized the OIG's independence or its ability to scrutinize management actions with a critical eye? The answer is a resounding "no." The inspector general continues to audit and report to Congress, as required by the act. A review of the semiannual reports to Congress shows that responsible management officials who have not taken appropriate action to correct cited deficiencies are identified by name. Working together with management is essential to carrying out the IG mission.

Changing Roles of the Auditor and Investigator

With the advent of the IG Act came a change in the role of auditors and investigators, particularly with regard to their prevention and detection roles. Both disciplines have learned to better appreciate the other's role and are actively supporting each other. Through information exchange, joint activities and other means, they have begun putting the IG concept into practice.

At one time most fraud detection, and follow-through once fraud was discovered, was considered primarily an investigative function. If the auditor had any role in fraud detection, it was perceived as one of initial detection or discovery of the fraudulent act. That is no longer true. The auditor's role has grown to full participation in the ensuing investigation and prosecution, including support of both the investigator and prosecutor. This places the auditor in a rather enviable position in that he or she may be the only person to follow a problem through the full cycle.

During my tenure with HUD, many changes have taken place in the auditing profession. In my opinion, one of the more important changes has been the auditor's new responsibility to seek out fraud. After all, the OIGs are in a stewardship role to protect the public's resources and the integrity of the programs our auditees administer.

At the federal government level, auditors are enjoying the full support of an administration which not only encourages, but demands, the elimination of fraud and waste. The IG community has always believed that this was one of its primary functions. The results of audits and investigations are perfect examples of the commitment to this effort.

At other levels of government, initiatives have been taken by audit managers which have led to an expansion of the audit function to look for fraud and waste. Even though the initiatives taken by government organizations and audit managers are commendable, with the recognition by the American Institute of Certified Public Accountants (AICPA) and the General Accounting Office (GAO) that auditors search for fraud, the days of relying on individual initiatives are over.

The AICPA, in its January 1977 Statement on Auditing Standards No. 16, "The Independent Auditor's Responsibilities for the Detection of Errors or Irregularities," outlines responsibility for detecting errors and irregularities and suggests procedures to follow when evidence indicates their existence. It states in part:

> The auditor should plan and perform his or her examination with an attitude of professional skepticism, recognizing that the application of . . . auditing procedures may produce evidential matter indicating the possibility of errors or irregularities. The scope of the auditor's examination would be affected by . . . consideration of internal accounting control, by the results of . . . substantive tests, and by circumstances that raise questions concerning the integrity of management.[2]

In line with this standard, the GAO *Standards for Audit of Governmental Organizations, Programs, Activities, and Functions* now recognizes fraud detection, once thought of as an investigative function, as one of the evaluation standards for economy and efficiency audits as well as program results audits. This volume states that "Auditors shall: (1) be alert to situations or transactions that could be indicative of fraud, abuse, and illegal acts, and (2) if such evidence exists, extend audit steps and procedures to identify the effect on the entity's operations and programs."[3]

While auditors have been alerted to fraud detection, previously a territory more familiar to the investigator, the investigators have also ventured into the area of prevention. The nature of their discipline offers them a unique opportunity to understand in detail how fraud is perpetrated. The IG community is increasingly taking advantage of the investigator's knowledge to prevent recurrences of fraud and identify "loopholes" or weaknesses in program and administrative operations. At HUD, for example, the OIG set up a systemic implications report program to gather information on irregularities or fraud and to develop suggestions to prevent recurrence. Investigators prepare a report on each case referred for prosecutive consideration, identifying possible internal control weaknesses which surfaced during investigation. These reports are studied for trends and patterns, and recommendations are made to program officials for appropriate program changes. Similar systems are in operation at the Departments of Health and Human Services, Interior, and Commerce. It is likely that this will be a standard IG function in the future.

President's Council on Integrity and Efficiency

Other changes as well have had an impact on the IGs and their efforts to fulfill the IG concept. Since the inception of the concept, inspectors general governmentwide have taken measures and made strides in accomplishing their objectives. One major contribution to the IGs' ability to do their jobs was the creation of the President's Council on Integrity and Efficiency (PCIE). The council was established by executive order in March 1981 as an integral part of a broader plan to attack fraud, waste, and inefficiency in federal programs. The functions of the council include:

1. Developing plans for coordinated governmentwide activities to attack fraud and waste.
2. Developing standards for the management, operation, and conduct of IG-type activities.
3. Developing policies to ensure a corps of well-trained and highly skilled auditors and investigators.
4. Developing interagency audit and investigation programs and projects to deal with fraud and waste.
5. Assuring that all of these efforts are accomplished with consistency so that the federal government speaks with one voice on fraud and waste matters.

This council provides a forum through which IGs can develop innovative approaches to deal with areas ranging from the effectiveness of the IG program to policies and procedures for improving investigation and law enforcement efforts of the IG program to courses of action to meet the training needs of auditors and investigators. As President Reagan phrased it, the council will enable agencies to:

> Focus their total efforts in the places that will do the most good. . . . Bringing together these efforts will permit all agencies to share knowledge of fraudulent and wasteful activities. They will exchange information on the kinds of inves-

FIGURE 19.1   President's Council on Integrity and Efficiency: Total
Monetary Impact

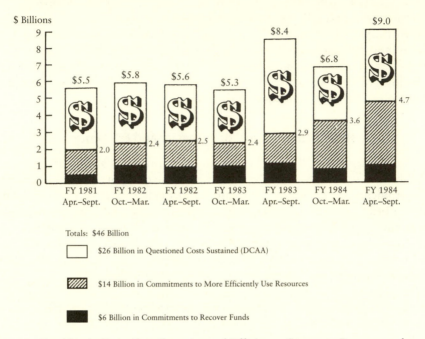

Totals: $46 Billion

☐ $26 Billion in Questioned Costs Sustained (DCAA)

▨ $14 Billion in Commitments to More Efficiently Use Resources

■ $6 Billion in Commitments to Recover Funds

SOURCE: President's Council on Integrity and Efficiency. Summary Reports to the
President, April 1, 1981, through September 30, 1984.

tigations which will provide the most promising results. And they will be
ready to move in quickly with tough and effective criminal prosecutions
where such prosecutions are warranted.[4]

Since its creation in 1981, the council has made significant strides in accomplishing the presidential directive. More than 10,000 successful prosecutions of wrongdoers have occurred. Over $46 billion has been better
used as a result of council activities: $26 billion in questioned costs sus-
tained by contracting officials resulting from audits of the Defense Contract Audit Agency; $14 billion in management commitments to use funds
more efficiently; and $6 billion in commitments to recover funds. The
trends in these areas have steadily risen as Figures 19.1 and 19.2 show.

Through standing committees and interagency task forces, the council
has also undertaken such projects as:

• Performing interagency computer matches that detected hundreds
  of individuals fraudulently obtaining federal subsidies.

FIGURE 19.2 President's Council on Integrity and Efficiency: Successful Prosecutions of Fraud, Waste and Abuse

By Number of Successful Prosecutions and
Dollars Recouped by the Government

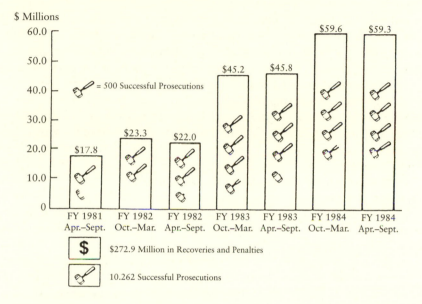

SOURCE: President's Council on Integrity and Efficiency. Summary Reports to the President, April 1, 1981, through September 30, 1984.

- Determining the feasibility of a governmentwide system for debarments and suspensions so that individuals doing business with the government who have performed incompetently or dishonestly at one agency will not be awarded contracts at another agency.
- Studying governmentwide unliquidated obligations for construction-related projects, and recommending policies to monitor project status more effectively.
- Developing a model prevention plan which is now used governmentwide to help agency managers integrate and enhance their prevention strategies.

Currently, proposals for new council work are being evaluated in light of their likely impact on the budget deficit. The council fully supports and hopes to respond to the current public, congressional, and executive demands to reduce the deficit and generally "tighten our belts." The IGs are getting back to basics and seeking out ways to help management cut costs and increase revenues, while still maintaining an acceptable level of program delivery. Such projects would examine government procurement, grant and loan management, property management and disposal, travel, telephone and space expenses, and the like.

But it is important to note that cost recoveries and cost reductions are not the only measures of the IG effectiveness and productivity. Of importance also is the positive influence our audit findings and recommendations have had on the way the agency program participants administer their programs and activities. As a result of audits, improvements have been made in departmental and program participant procedures and systems for implementing programs. While these improvements cannot always be expressed in monetary terms, their beneficial impact is real in view of the improved efficiency and effectiveness of operations that result from such improvements.

Over the past few years, the terms accountability, internal controls, integrity, and responsibility have become "buzz words" not only in the IG community, but in government in general. These are concepts that have been ignored too long, and they are areas in which the IGs have made and can continue to make a difference.

In the past few years, the issuance of OMB Circular A-123, "Internal Control Systems," followed by the passage of the Federal Managers' Financial Integrity Act of 1982, have shown us that the president, the Congress, and the public are demanding greater accountability from the federal manager.

OMB Circular A-123 requires management to review, evaluate the effectiveness of, and identify and correct weaknesses in management controls. It also calls for inspectors general to review, in conjunction with their internal audits, internal control documentation and systems and to determine whether the policies and standards established by this circular are being implemented properly. More importantly, it directs the program managers themselves to assess vulnerability and perform internal control reviews to assure programs are being administered effectively and efficiently. The Federal Managers' Financial Integrity Act of 1982 legislatively required these internal control evaluations and further required the agency head to report the results to both the president and the Congress each year.

In describing the roles of management and the IGs in the internal control evaluation process, OMB said it this way:

> It is imperative that management throughout the agency be heavily involved
> in the evaluative process, since it is management that has primary responsibil-
> ity for the maintenance of a strong system of internal control. But the Inspec-

tor General or equivalent is encouraged to provide technical assistance to further the overall goal of strengthening internal control systems.[5]

I wholeheartedly agree. Inspectors general are charged with this responsibility. The IG Act requires that IGs advise the agency head with respect to all matters relating to the promotion of the economy, efficiency, and effectiveness in the administration of departmental programs and operations, and in the *prevention* and detection of fraud and abuse. The best way for the IGs to do this is to participate and work with management to improve internal controls.

In testifying on the implementation of the Federal Managers' Financial Integrity Act, Charles Bowsher, the comptroller general of the United States, also acknowledged an IG role. He recognized the high degree of cooperation among the agencies. OMB, the IGs, and GAO and went on to say that: "The IGs, by virtue of their experience and expertise, represent a valuable resource that agency management needs to use to a great extent in the future in evaluating their internal control and accounting systems."[6]

Comptroller General Bowsher has made it clear that the inspectors general cannot afford to isolate themselves, coming in only after the fact, and criticizing after all the decisions have been made. Those days are over; things happen too fast today. To have an impact, the IGs must be willing to work closely with management in the area of internal controls and elsewhere.

At HUD, the OIG monitors and evaluates the department's internal control systems on an ongoing basis by:

1. Assessing the department's effectiveness in addressing the OMB circular and statutory requirements and keeping the secretary apprised of HUD compliance. This is being accomplished, in part, through joint reviews with the General Accounting Office on HUD's implementation of OMB Circular A-123 and the Federal Managers' Financial Integrity Act of 1982.
2. Providing technical assistance to HUD's administrators in conducting all phases of the internal control evaluations. This is done through conducting training programs, developing guidelines, responding to questions, providing input based on audit and investigative work performed, and meeting regularly with officials of HUD's Office of Administration to review progress and plans.
3. Auditing internal control systems documentation and compliance.
4. Evaluating the audit follow-up system to ensure that corrective action is taken, and reporting in semiannual reports to Congress where it is not.

5. Coordinating the department's fraud vulnerability assessment system to ensure controls receive adequate front-end attention in implementing new programs or activities.
6. Reviewing legislation, regulations, and handbooks to suggest control measures and comment on other prevention aspects.

As time passes, the IGs' record in helping to establish effective internal controls will speak for itself. Frederic Heim, the coordinator of OMB's Internal Control Task Force, and Harold Steinberg, former associate director for management at OMB and currently a partner at Peat, Marwick, Mitchell & Co., wrote in *The Government Accountants Journal* that:

> The Inspector General (or internal audit where there is no IG) staffs have proven to be extremely valuable in assisting agency internal control officials to establish and improve their internal/management control process. This is due to their training and skill in performing internal control and related reviews as part of the audit function.

*   *   *

> Other important assistance has been provided by the IGs through the performance of audits or other evaluative work in problem areas they have addressed separately, and in the performance of independent assessments of the agencies' evaluation processes and letters to the agency heads on the results of the assessments.[7]

An Inspector General Retrospective

In the seven years since the act passed, the inspector general organizations have gone through the "growing pains" of any new idea or organization, and the IG concept has come of age. This growth can be measured and assessed against three criteria: putting together the right team of people, getting the message out, and producing results.

The first of these criteria initially involved getting the auditors and investigators to work as a team and collaborate under a single leadership. The auditors had to stop seeing the investigators as "gumshoes" and the investigators had to stop seeing the auditors as "beancounters" with green eyeshades. Both sides had to realize that they could benefit from the other's unique knowledge and perspective of program vulnerabilities and operating deficiencies. This has happened in some of the more successful IG operations; however, there is still much work to be done in this area in other IG shops.

Some cross-training between the two disciplines has helped, as well as more training in general. Since 1982 a training committee of the President's

Council on Integrity and Efficiency, under the chairmanship of Frank S. Sato, the Veterans Administration inspector general, has been developing IG-specific educational programs, including executive development workshops attended by senior staff. In addition, a large number of professionals have become proficient in the use of microcomputer technology as a result of training courses developed and implemented by the Council's computer committee under the direction of June G. Brown, inspector general at the National Aeronautics and Space Administration. Over 2,500 IG staff had been trained by January 1, 1985.

The second criterion, that of getting the message out, refers to the IG community's effectiveness in making the act more than an abstract piece of paper in employees' minds. IGs have had to let the federal manager and employee know who they are and what they do, making certain they understand that IGs are independent. IGs had to establish lines of communication, through hotlines and other means, and have been largely successful. There are unlikely to be many of you reading this who have not had some experience with an inspector general operation, directly or indirectly.

Finally, the IGs have proven themselves through concrete results, individually and in the collective efforts of the President's Council. In addition to the monetary impact and prosecutions cited earlier, administrative actions taken against federal employees and against federal contractors and grantees have totaled 6,759 and 2,605, respectively, since the council was established in 1981. The number of hotline allegations received was 66,887 over the same period. Concurrently governmentwide studies were produced in such areas as debt collection, cash management, unliquidated obligations, and use of fraudulent identification to obtain federal benefits.

Outlook for the Future

So where do we go from here? Two legislative proposals supported by the President's Council would expand the basic IG concept outwards. Certain technical amendments to the IG Act of 1978, if passed, would establish inspectors general at the Departments of Justice and the Treasury. Another amendment through the proposed Agency Audit and Investigation Act of 1984 would require agencies in which IGs have not been established by law to comply with certain provisions of the 1978 act. Both attest to a growing confidence in the IG concept in practice.

Another influence on the practice of the inspector general concept is the "New Federalism" which is increasingly transferring program administration from federal to state and local levels. To complement this policy, members of the IG community testified in support of "single audit" legislation. The successful implementation of Public Law 98-502, the Single Audit Act of 1984, passed on October 19, 1984, and OMB's Circular A-102. Attachment P, is vital to ensuring continuing accountability of public programs. With this in mind, the President's Council established a standing committee on single audit issues last year to respond to issues regarding inspector general roles and responsibilities, and provide interpretations of existing authorities.

Lastly, the theme in federal government now is clearly one of cutting back, making do with less, and getting more for our money—in other words, good management and strong accountability. The taxpayers are demanding accountability from federal managers; the budget deficit must be reduced; the public sector has been living beyond its means for too long. The climate in the executive branch and on the Hill is ripe for change, more so than ever before. The inspectors general must do their part in helping managers to carry out these reforms.

Towards this end, OMB for the first time this year used the IGs' semi-annual reports to the Congress as a resource during the budget review process. Staff from the management side of OMB, in consultation with the IGs, identified those recommendations which might result in budgetary savings or improve program operations. This information was then provided to the OMB budget examiners for consideration in making budget reductions, or to formulate questions for agency management during the budget hearings.

The inspectors general must have more of a "bottom line" perspective in audit work; looking for those places where the government can actually reduce its expenditures or increase its revenues. So while the detection and prevention of fraud remains an essential mission, an increased emphasis on economy and efficiency will be the thrust of the next few years. It will take hard work, positive application and proper attitudes, but I believe that together the federal managers and the inspectors general can succeed. There is too much at stake to allow for failure.

Early in his administration. President Reagan addressed the Congress and emphasized the significance he attached to the problems of waste, fraud, and mismanagement in the federal government. The president said: "No administration can promise to immediately stop a trend that has grown in recent years as quickly as government expenditures themselves, but let me say this: waste and fraud in the federal government is exactly what I've called it before—an unrelenting national scandal, a scandal we're bound and determined to do something about."[8]

And in a statement which sums up what is basic and vital to the IG concept and our mission, the president stated: "It's about time the notion that government is the servant, not the master came back into fashion. One of our highest priorities is to restore to the American people a government well managed and responsive to their needs and respectful of their tax dollars. And the greatest nation in the world deserves the best government."[9]

Notes

1. Excerpt from statement of Senator Thomas Eagleton before the United States Senate on September 20, 1978.

2. American Institute of Certified Public Accountants, *Codification of Statements on Auditing Standards*, Section 327, "Errors or Irregularities," pp. 130–131.

3. Comptroller General of the United States, *Standards for Audit of Governmental Organizations, Programs, Activities, and Functions* (Washington, D.C.: GPO, 1981), p. 47.

4. From statement by President Ronald Reagan on establishment of the President's Council on Integrity and Efficiency, March 1981, p. 1.

5. Office of Management and Budget, "Guidelines for the Evaluation and Improvement of and Reporting on Internal Control Systems in the Federal Government," December 1982, p. II–3.

6. Charles A. Bowsher, comptroller general of the United States, in testimony before the House Government Operations Committee on "Implementation of the Federal Managers' Financial Integrity Act of 1982," May 1984, pp. 11–12.

7. Frederic A. Heim, Jr., and Harold Steinberg, "Implementing the Internal Control Evaluation. Improvement and Reporting Process in the Federal Government," *The Government Accountants Journal*, 32 (Winter 1983–1984), p. 8.

8. From address by President Ronald Reagan before a joint session of the Congress on the Program for Economic Recovery, February 1981.

9. From radio address by President Ronald Reagan, July 30, 1983.

Part SIX

Ethics Education

Articles about educating students for ethical public service were a long time coming. Although the first graduate programs in public administration began in the 1930s, no article addressed ethics education in an ASPA journal until 1976, when John Rohr published "The Study of Ethics in the P.A. Curriculum" in *PAR* (Chapter 20 here). In its beginnings, as now, ASPA was a professional organization dedicated to the improvement of professional practice, not to the development of educational endeavors.

The purpose of Rohr's article is to "suggest a method for integrating the study of ethics into a public administration curriculum." This method begins with administrative discretion and offers regime values as the appropriate starting point for ethical reflection by students of public administration, as they are, after all, aspiring to positions in government as it exists. Rohr explains his method for assisting students to systematically reflect on the values of the "present republic." This method asks students to study recent Supreme Court decisions on such values as freedom, property, and equality, to compare and contrast them, and to look for consistencies of interpretations. These consistencies reflect agreement on that issue and provide guidance for the student's own administrative decision making.

Chapter 21 appeared in 1982 in ASPA's *Criminal Justice Review*. Written by William C. Heffernan, "Two Approaches to Police Ethics" describes the two kinds of problems in police ethics and raises the following question: "Should education in police ethics seek to guide students toward specific outcomes, or should it be concerned primarily with analysis of moral dilemmas in policing?" Although Heffernan writes about teaching police ethics, his concerns about what kinds of teaching methods to use is important for the whole discipline of public administration. If the purpose is to develop ethical police officers, the educational method will focus on building the capacity to recognize basic values and the strength of character to act on those values. If the purpose is to enable officers to make difficult decisions, teaching will emphasize applying ethical reasoning to administrative problems. Heffernan discusses the features of applied ethics and notes the educational issues involved, particularly that of finding individuals with the interdisciplinary qualifications to teach a class such as police ethics. Citing the Hastings Report, he suggests that any instructor of applied ethics should have at least the equivalent of one full academic year of training in philosophical or theological ethics.

Also in 1982, the *Southern Review of Public Administration*[1] carried an article about teaching ethics in public administration. Written by Richard T. Mayer and Michael M. Harmon, "Teaching Moral Education in Public Administration" (Chapter 22 here) addresses the complaint made by Mark Lilla that a moral vacuum has been created in curricula of public administration and policy programs. Their emphasis on rational analysis has deterred public administration programs from offering moral education. Lilla's work prompts Mayer and Harmon to ask: "What is our responsibility as teachers of public administration?" They lament that this has become a world where "'to administer' means only to carry out a task" and that much of the infrastructure of government is "in disrepair." Using historical perspective, they call for a return to responsible administration that appreciates generally agreed upon virtues and recognizes that administrators are morally responsible actors.

What the authors of all of these articles on ethics education have in common is the conviction that ethics can and should be taught. Each provides arguments for teaching students in such a fashion that they acquire shared moral convictions about what is good and right, while also developing the analytical skills necessary for informed and careful judgment.

Notes

1. *Southern Review of Public Administration* is now *Public Administration Quarterly.*

20

THE STUDY OF ETHICS IN THE P.A. CURRICULUM

John A. Rohr
Governors State University

The purpose of this article is to suggest a method for integrating the study of ethics into a public administration curriculum. Although the Watergate scandals succeeded in transforming ethics into a growth industry, it might be unwise to put too much stress on Watergate in discussing future curriculum developments. An obvious reason for this caution is that the primary offenders in Watergate were officials who were either elected or politically appointed rather than career bureaucrats.

Secondly, an undue emphasis upon the Nixon scandals would neglect the solid academic foundation for ethical reflection that was laid by the "New PA" before we knew that Watergate was anything more than an elegant apartment complex. Thirdly, there is the prudent counsel of Paul Appleby, whose classic study, *Morality and Administration in Democratic Government*, appeared at the height of the Truman scandals. Despite the headlines of the day, Appleby was able to assert that "crude wrong-doing is not a major, general problem of government" but that "further moral advance turns upon more complicated and elevated concerns."[1] Taking this hint from Appleby, I would suggest that we de-emphasize Watergate and instead take administrative discretion as the starting point of our investigation.[2]

In stressing administrative discretion, a course in ethics can build upon principles that have been well established by political scientists and students of public administration. The demise of the dichotomy of politics and administration raised serious normative issues which, until recently, have received little attention.[3] The reason for this neglect may have been the salience of value-free social science during the years when the dichotomy was becoming increasingly suspect. Whatever the reason for the neglect, however, the well-established recognition of the political role of the bureaucrat has underscored the compelling public interest in addressing the normative questions consequent upon that role. Through the extensive discretion that bureaucrats necessarily enjoy in a modern administrative state, they can be said to share in the governing process. To the extent that bureaucrats govern in a democratic polity, they should somehow reflect the values of the people in whose name they govern. This is an ethical question.[4]

It is not only the abuse of administrative discretion that raises ethical questions but its simple existence as well. The proper exercise of administrative discretion authoritatively allocates values, determines who gets what, promotes the common good, etc. Persons performing these functions govern and should therefore somehow respond to the values of the people. Since a merit system precludes the propriety of subjecting administrative personnel to the discipline of the ballot box, other ways must be found to encourage this responsiveness. Among these ways is an approach to public service education that includes a course in ethics that will encourage reflection upon the values of the American people.[5]

In stressing the values of the American people as the content of a course in bureaucratic ethics. I find myself somewhat at odds with dominant trends in "New PA" literature. At the risk of making an overly broad generalization, I would suggest that the principal academic foundations for ethical reflections in writings associated with the "New PA" come from political philosophy and humanistic psychology.[6] While any public administration curriculum that neglected these disciplines would be impoverished indeed, I do not believe they provide a satisfactory *foundation* for a course in ethics.

As far as political philosophy is concerned, my reason for questioning its propriety as the foundation for the study of ethics is that it is too demanding to be included as *part* of a course in ethics. If it were possible to include one or two courses in political philosophy as a preparation for the study of ethics, I would withdraw my objection. I fear, however, that other demands of the curriculum would make this impossible.

I sympathize with David Hart's call for "a new tradition of administrative philosophy" leading to curriculum revision with new courses that "must reflect the rigor of the philosophic tradition."[7] I am less persuaded, however, by his position that John Rawls' theory of justice should provide the philosophic foundation of such courses. If we are to follow the "rigor of the philosophic tradition," we would have to examine carefully the foundations of Rawls' position. There is, of course, a formidable (and growing) body of literature critical of Rawls. Students would have to be familiarized with this literature before accepting Rawls as a starting point. One might add that to understand Rawls, one must first have read Kant, and that Kant is unintelligible unless one understands Hume's influence upon him.

My point is not to enter a full-scale debate over the merits of Rawls' position, but simply to point out the kind of questions of political philosophy.[8] The "rigor of the philosophic tradition" demands that issues of politics be related to broader issues of linguistics, psychology, metaphysics, and epistemology. This is both the glory and the frustration of philosophy. If a public administration curriculum is to maintain its professional focus, certain valuable intellectual investigations must be sacrificed. We can hope that graduate students in public administration programs have already acquired a rich background in the liberal arts and rejoice when our expectations are fulfilled. But I do not think we can prudently demand extensive philosophical investigations from public administration students after they have started their professional studies. To settle for a smattering of political philosophy as part of a course in ethics would not be fair either to the students or to philosophy itself. For this reason we must look elsewhere for the *foundation* for a course in ethics.[9]

As far as humanistic psychology is concerned, my main criticism is that it necessarily focuses upon the individual as a person rather than upon his chosen career. One cannot ask a psychologist to take seriously the formal distinction between public and private. When Maslow writes about a person who is "self-actualized," it makes no difference if the person is a bureaucrat, a carpenter, a dentist, or a novelist. The same is true of the six stages of moral development in Kohlberg. It is the *individual person* that is important in humanistic psychology—not how he is employed. Since the starting point of our problem is the discretion consequent upon a certain type of employment (public), a normative system based upon the individual person is not suitable for our purposes.

I hasten to add that in criticizing a normative system based on the individual, I am not attempting to dichotomize personal and political morality. All morality is personal in the obvious sense that only persons are morally accountable. A person, however, is morally accountable in *different* ways for different aspects of his life. Familial morality, business morality, sexual morality, political morality, etc., are all matters that concern individual human beings. The same man is father, salesman, husband, and citizen. He might well believe that beating his children, cheating his customers, committing adultery, and failing to pay taxes are all morally reprehensible, but the reasons for condemning each of these forms of behavior might be quite different. Humanistic psychology could be quite helpful in assisting an individual to integrate the various roles he must play, but it is less helpful in raising specific questions pertaining to one of these roles. Since the focus of our inquiry is the ethics of one very specific role, it seems that the moral foundation we are looking for must be tailored to the demands of that limited role rather than expanded to consider the broader question of how to be a well-integrated human being. Obviously, government agencies are no less in need of well-integrated human beings than any other institutions in our society, but if specific questions of ethics for governmental administrators must be postponed until they have first become well-integrated human beings, we may never get on with our work.[10]

Jacques Maritain once used the term "hypermoralism" to describe a moral stance that applied ethical norms suitable for interpersonal relations to political situations.[11] Maritain argued persuasively that "hypermoralism" is as dangerous as "amoralism," for they both lead to moral cynicism. In judging political actions in interpersonal terms, one puts intolerable strains upon the political system for the simple reason that the behavior consequent upon a commitment of civic friendship can never measure up to the rigorous demands of an "I-Thou" relationship. For Maritain, politics is a part of ethics, but unless one distinguishes *in principle* the norms for appropriate behavior in governmental relationships and personal relationships, one will soon be disillusioned with public life and despair of the relevance of *any* moral consideration in government. At times the best is enemy of the good.

As an alternative to political philosophy and humanistic psychology, I would suggest that, since students of public administration aspire to positions of leadership within the bureaucracy of a particular regime, the values of that regime are the most suitable starting point for their ethical reflections.[12]

This is especially true in countries like our own where bureaucrats are expected to take an oath to uphold the Constitution. An oath is an important moral event in the personal history of an individual. Oaths take on added significance in pluralistic societies like the United States where there are myriad philosophical and religious starting points from which people derive their ethical norms. Pluralism of this nature makes it almost impossible to hope for an operational understanding of the public interest derived from some common metaphysical premise. Despite our pluralism, however, I think it is safe to assume that most of us would agree that one should adhere steadfastly to the oaths one has taken.[13] Since the Constitution of the United States is the preeminent symbol of our political values, an oath to uphold the Constitution is a commitment to uphold the values of the regime created by that instrument.

In arguing the normative character of the values of the regime, I am, of course, avoiding the more important question of the fundamental justice of the regime itself.[14] Before one asks oneself "how can I reinforce the values of the regime," one should first ask "is the regime fundamentally just." That is, can I be a good man and a good citizen at the same time? Although this is the more important question, it cannot be the focus of the course in ethics unless this course is simply to collapse into political philosophy. To say the justice of the regime cannot be the focus of the ethics course, however, does not mean the question is simply ignored. An argument might be made that one should not enter a career in government unless one is first convinced that the regime is fundamentally just. Once he is so convinced, the public servant can then investigate the full implications of the values of the regime whose justice he acknowledges.

Unfortunately, however, the moral universe is never this tidy. The very nature of judging the justice of a regime is an ongoing process rooted in contingency. Such a judgment cannot be made once and for all unless, of course, one is willing to acquiesce in the moral abdication symbolized by "my country right or wrong. . . ." Any serious consideration by a bureaucrat of how he might further the regime's values will continually invite higher questions of the moral authenticity of these values and, therefore, of the justice of the regime itself. Nevertheless, the justice of the regime cannot be the *focus* of the course if it is to retain its identity as a course in ethics for bureaucrats. It must, however, remain the backdrop against which the course in ethics examines the less majestic questions of regime values.

The price, then, that the professional study of ethics for bureaucrats exacts from the curriculum is that questions of political philosophy (is the regime just?)[15] must yield to less fundamental questions such as "how can I promote the values of the regime." The method of "regime values" eschews metaphysics and addresses the student in the existential situation in which it finds him—a person who has taken or is about to take an oath to uphold the values of a particular regime. It admonishes him that taking such an oath presupposes an acceptance of the fundamental justice of the regime but does not inquire into how the student arrived at the conclusion that the regime is just.[16]

Law and Values

Thus far the main point in this article has been an argument supporting the study of regime values as the most appropriate method of integrating the study of ethics into a public administration curriculum. The argument is rooted in the obligation of bureaucrats in a democratic polity to use their discretionary (i.e., governing) power in a manner that is consistent with the values of the people in whose name they govern. The remainder of this article will be devoted to explaining how American students of public administration might best go about the task of systematically reflecting on the values of the present republic.

The method of "regime values" involves two tasks. The first is to identify American values and the second is to look for meaningful statements about them. The first of these tasks is much easier than the second, provided one is content to identify just *some* values instead of attempting to provide an exhaustive list. One might find indications of the values of the American people in the writings and speeches of outstanding statesmen, in major Supreme Court opinions, in scholarly interpretations of American history, and even in the rhetoric of standard Fourth of July oratory. For example, it would seem one could safely assert that freedom, property, and equality are values of the American people.[17] I hasten to add that these three are not *the* values of the American people but are simply among our many values. To safeguard their widespread appeal, they must be presented without any gloss on their meaning. The equality affirmed in the Declaration of Independence may be quite different from the equality underlying the equal protection clause of the Fourteenth Amendment, but we shall get ahead of ourselves if we make such distinctions now. For the present it is sufficient to offer freedom, property, and equality as examples of American values. Most Americans would have little trouble in saying they "believe" in such values as long as they were not pressed to say just what these values mean.

Far more difficult than simply *naming* some values of Americans is the task of infusing them with meaning suitable for ethical reflection. One might object that splendid generalities like freedom, property, and equality are universally accepted only because they mean nothing. I do not think such an objection is sound. There is a difference between a word or a symbol that is vague and one that is meaningless. For example, the three symbols of the French Revolution, *liberté, fraternité, égalité,* are vague and indeterminate. They have been invoked by Frenchmen of remarkably diverse political persuasions for nearly two centuries. For many years these symbols appeared on French coins, but during Marshal Pétain's Vichy regime the customary symbols disappeared from the coins and were replaced with *travail, famille, patrie*. These symbols, like the ones they replaced, were vague but they were not meaningless. They said something about the character of the Vichy regime. To be sure, a man could be quite devoted to his work, his family, and his fatherland without being a Nazi sympathizer. Nevertheless, the change in symbols had some significance. It represented an attempt by the Nazis to signal the arrival of a new order in France with a consequent change in traditional French values.

I would, therefore, contend that when Americans invoke symbols such as freedom, property, and equality—both in serious and trivial discourse—there is some minimal content to which these symbols point and that this content embodies some of the values of our society. These values may not be the highest values to which a regime might aspire, but nevertheless they carry some normative weight for American bureaucrats precisely because they are values of the American people.[18]

· The search for meaningful statements about our values is a more difficult task than simply naming them. At this point the consensus which would support certain values in a general, abstract way begins to fall apart. For example, some of those who would agree that equality is a fundamental value of the American people might not agree that this value should govern the relationships between the sexes as well as among the races and economic classes. Or equality might go no further than equality of opportunity for some while others would insist it means equality of income as well. Property might mean "big business" to one person, a modest dwelling to another, and a right to gainful employment to a third. Freedom could mean freedom for a woman to have an abortion on demand or Exxon's freedom from government regulation.

Thus, as the general values of the regime become sufficiently specific to have a practical effect on bureaucratic decision making, the bureaucrat will have to decide which of many interpretations he will take seriously in his efforts to respond to the values of the American people. This is a very difficult undertaking. Eminent scholars after years of research reach very different conclusions on the "meaning of America."[19] This would seem to suggest that there is no one interpretation of the American tradition so compelling as to win the assent of all thoughtful persons. Further, we must recall that we are dealing with students whose professional education demands that serious attention be given to so many other areas of inquiry that it would be quite unrealistic to expect them to undertake a profound study of the American tradition.

In the paragraphs that follow I shall outline a method for encouraging the public administration students to reflect on American values in a disciplined and systematic manner that will invite them to develop their own understanding of what these values mean. This method does not promise "instant wisdom" nor is it offered as a substitute for serious scholarly investigation of the American tradition. It may, however, be a practical teaching device to enable career-oriented students to be more thoughtfully concerned with the values of the people they will serve.

The method involves the study of major Supreme Court decisions on such salient values as freedom, property, and equality. There are four characteristics of Supreme Court decisions that make them particularly suitable for ethical reflection on the values of the American people. Supreme Court decisions are (1) institutional, (2) dialectic, (3) concrete, and (4) pertinent. Let us examine each of these characteristics in detail.

1. Institutional

In studying the values of the American people, the student-bureaucrat must distinguish between stable principles and passing whims. A "value" in the life of a person as well as a nation suggests a pattern of attitudes or behavior that recurs with some frequency. An attitude or a passion or a principle must have a history—either personal or societal—before it becomes a "value." It is this need for historical continuity that makes the opinions of Supreme Court Justices particularly useful as "value-indicators" when compared with the writings and speeches of most prominent statesmen and philosophers. Every individual is, of course somewhat limited by the vision of his/her time in history. This is no less true of Supreme Court Justices than of statesmen and philosophers. But because the Justice is part of an institution, his time-bound reasoning is balanced, nuanced, and therefore enriched by the reasoning of other Justices writing at other times. Thus Chief Justice Taney did not say all there is to say about racial equality in *Dred Scott;* nor did Chief Justice Warren in *Brown* v. *Board of Education.* Somewhere between the opinions of these two men are the majority and dissenting opinions of the Justices who first addressed the problem of separate but equal facilities for blacks and whites as well as the Justices who upheld and those who condemned the Japanese relocation program in World War II. In recent years the Court has manifested its attitude on equality in decisions dealing with public accommodations, poll taxes, and "busing." This network of jurisprudence offers the bureaucrat insights into the values of our society that are always rich and complex, frequently confusing, and occasionally contradictory. It is the bureaucrat who must decide just how the moral values (and non-values) underlying the Court's opinions will affect individual decision making.

The institutional character of the Court's decisions suggests a parallel between the development of a society's public morals and an individual's personal morality that is useful for our purposes. In interpreting such majestic generalities as "due process of law" and "equal protection," the Court must constantly remain in touch with its past. The nature of the judicial process requires that the Court must at least consider the original meaning of the phrases as well as its own precedents. This ensures some kind of continuity with the past. To be sure, the Court has shown remarkable skill in distinguishing precedents, but this is because the focus of the Court is on current problems which cannot always be settled equitably on the basis of precedent alone. The nature of the judicial process involves tension between past and present. Courts frequently solve current issues with a creative interpretation of a familiar principle. This enables a political society to address new problems without sacrificing the stability and continuity that come from invoking familiar principles. In a word, the Court is a contemporary institution in dialogue with the past.

A similar process often characterizes the moral development of individuals. The principles learned in childhood from parents, teachers, and churches may never be abandoned, but they may be constantly reinterpreted to meet changing times and the demands of adulthood. For example, a child who has been taught to love his country may manifest fidelity to that principle by approaching the daily salute to the flag seriously even though his friends may be giggling and playing. As an adult the same person may show his devotion to the maxim "love your country" by participating in a civil rights march. The familiar principle, "love your country," is now being applied in a more sophisticated manner which an earlier generation might neither understand nor approve. The individual, however, has maintained his personal moral continuity along with his integrity by remaining in dialogue with his past. An individual, of course, can do this only for the limited years of a lifetime, but an institution can do this sort of thing for centuries. This is one of several reasons why I suggest that bureaucrats look to Supreme Court decisions for meaningful statements of American values.

2. Dialectic

The presence of concurring and dissenting opinions in Supreme Court decisions makes the work of the Court dialectic. Such opinions offer the prospective bureaucrat the opportunity to follow a public debate in a highly structured and formal context. Since constitutional cases usually turn on the interpretation of such vague phrases as "due process of law," "equal protection," or "commerce among the states," these public debates necessarily point to higher questions on the nature of the common good. When the Court must decide the constitutionality of a minimum wage law, a censorship ordinance, a public accommodations act, or an anti-miscegenation statute, the Justices nearly always include in their arguments some of their own views on the nature of a just American society. Since most Supreme Court Justices have been men of considerable experience and talent, such argumentation can be quite instructive for the bureaucrat seeking enlightenment on the meaning of American values.

Concurring and dissenting opinions offer the bureaucrat alternative ways of looking at the same problem and thereby help him to avoid the danger of accepting dogmatic assertions uncritically.

Chief Justice White once remarked that "the only purpose which an elaborate dissent can accomplish, if any, is to weaken the effect of the opinion of the majority, and thus engender want of confidence in conclusions of courts of last resort."[20] White's opinion is, I believe, very questionable. Dissenting opinions undermine the confidence only of those who look upon courts of last resort as divine oracles. A vigorous dissent can at times force the majority of the Court to provide better reasons for its decision than it would have offered if there had been no challenge. The reasons may not always be altogether compelling, but public confidence should be increased, not diminished, when serious argument replaces bland assertion.

3. Concrete

For our purposes, one of the most useful aspects of Supreme Court decisions is that they are concrete. A Justice may soar to the highest abstractions in discussing such lofty generalities as due process of law, but eventually he must decide whether the confession was admissible, or the book obscene, or the statement libelous. He is disciplined by reality in a way that the philosopher is not. He must *apply* his wisdom immediately to a concrete situation demanding his attention. This aspect of the Court's work should win warm approval from bureaucrats who are constantly called upon to perform similar tasks themselves. Not only do the Court's opinions offer reflection on American values, but they show what these values mean in practice as well. This model of decision making should be most helpful to the bureaucrat. As a practical man, he might be bored by discourse that is purely theoretical, but the Court's opinions provide an excellent illustration of how theory and practice combine to generate public policy.

Another instructive aspect of the concrete element in the Court's decisions is that value-oriented questions are usually not exclusively legal. That is, the Justices seldom decide such questions by mechanically applying a principle learned long ago in law school. Value-oriented questions usually involve the use of considerable discretion by the Court. As Justice Brennan remarked in *Wyman v. James:* "This Court has occasionally pushed beyond established contours to protect the vulnerable and to further basic human values."[21]

Bureaucrats, like judges, enjoy considerable discretion. Take, for example, the familiar practice of plea bargaining in which law enforcement agencies enjoy tremendous power to give or withhold concessions from persons accused of crimes. There are (perhaps unfortunately) few precise rules instructing prosecutors on how they are to conduct themselves in plea bargaining. Here would be an area in which bureaucrats in law enforcement agencies might "occasionally push beyond established contours to protect the vulnerable and to further basic human values." It would be wise, of course, to do this, as Brennan suggests, only "occasionally." Naturally, such a procedure is fraught with danger for all concerned, but a careful reading of Supreme Court decisions might give the bureaucrat some ideas on how to "push beyond established contours" in a responsible manner.

4. Pertinent

Supreme Court opinions are pertinent in the sense that they raise questions that are useful for reflection on fundamental values. So significant has the role of the Court been in this area that one eminent constitutional historian has commented on the "fact that the study of American constitutional law casts its followers, willy-nilly, in the role of political theorists."[22] De Tocqueville remarked long ago on the tendency of Americans to transform major political problems into legal issues. The accuracy of his remark has been generously confirmed by the fact that such crucial issues as slavery in the territories, a federal tax on income, and government regulation of industry have all found their way into the courts. In recent years anti-war activists never tired of initiating litigation in the hope that the courts would find the Vietnam War or the draft unconstitutional. The Watergate scandals offered further confirmation of de Tocqueville's insight. Such questions as whether a President must surrender tapes and documents to a Senate Committee and/or a grand jury, whether he can be indicted before he is impeached, whether he can claim executive privilege against a congressional committee considering his own impeachment, and what is the meaning of high crimes and misdemeanors—all these questions reveal the American tendency de Tocqueville noticed so long ago.

There can be no doubt that the questions raised by the Watergate scandals had a profound relation to the values of the American people. The revelations were literally front page news for two years. Such sustained interest can only be explained by a widespread awareness that serious questions of public morality were at stake—questions that reflect and affect our values as a political society. The fact that nearly all parties involved in the controversy turned almost instinctively to the courts is eloquent testimony to our confidence in the courts as arbiters of values. The fact that Americans have followed this pattern so often in their history is one reason I feel Supreme Court opinions are especially and, perhaps, even uniquely suitable for the bureaucrat seeking enlightenment on the meaning of American values.[23]

Conclusion

In studying Supreme Court opinions, the bureaucrat will be exposed to many conflicting interpretations of American values. Wherever possible, he will look for some consistency in the values of the American people, and the judicial process with its concern for precedent will be of some help. Frequently, however, mutually exclusive values will arise within the tradition and he will have to choose the position he finds most appealing and persuasive. There should be no embarrassment if two bureaucrats choose interpretations of American values that are mutually exclusive. The purpose of "regime values" is not to make all bureaucrats march in lock step. There is no one "authoritative" interpretation of the American experience that all bureaucrats must adopt. What is important is that they accept the moral obligation to put themselves in touch with the values of the American people. Just how those values are interpreted is a decision only the bureaucrat himself can make.

One might object that all this is terribly subjective—that in the final analysis the bureaucrat responds to those values to which he chooses to respond. This is true, but the subjective character of the method I propose is intended to respect the radical responsibility of the bureaucrat to his God, his conscience, his philosophy, or to whatever forms the basis of his moral life as a person. The bureaucrat, like every other human being, must be faithful to his deepest beliefs if he is to preserve his moral integrity. Hopefully, "regime values" will enable the bureaucrat to refine the content of his deepest political beliefs. In upholding the duty of the bureaucrat to "follow his conscience," I am not suggesting that he simply "do his own thing." It is unfortunate that these two phrases have become confused in popular speech. I would hope that my method would provide the bureaucrat with an informed conscience that would lead him into dialogue with the political society he serves and that he would ponder its values seriously. After submitting himself to this discipline, he would be free to follow his conscience.

Notes

1. Paul H. Appleby, *Morality and Administration in Democratic Government* (Baton Rouge: LSU Press, 1952), p. 56.

2. For a persuasive study of the connection between ethics and administrative discretion, see George A. Graham, "Ethical Guidelines for Public Administrators: Observation on Rules of the Game," *Public Administration Review,* Vol. 34, No. 1 (January/February 1974), pp. 90–92. See also my article, "Ethics for Bureaucrats," *America,* Vol. 128 (May 26, 1973), pp. 488–491.

3. H. George Fredrickson has called attention to "Dwight Waldo's contention that the field [of Public Administration] has never satisfactorily accommodated the theoretical implications of involvement in 'politics' and policy-making." See Fredrickson's article, "Toward a New Public Administration," in *Toward a New Public Administration,* Frank Marini (ed.) (Scranton: Chandler, 1971), p. 312.

4. The best recent analysis of administrative discretion is Kenneth C. Davis, *Discretionary Justice: A Preliminary Inquiry* (Baton Rouge: LSU Press, 1969). Davis

suggests several institutional approaches to reducing discretion that pertain to administrative law rather than ethics. Even Davis, however, acknowledges—indeed insists—that there is an irreducible quantum of discretion that cannot be taken away without destroying the integrity of the administrative process. It is this *necessary* discretion beyond the bounds of institutional reform that raises the most interesting ethical questions.

5. In stressing reflection on values, I do not intend to disparage the usefulness of administrative codes of ethics. However, I do question their propriety as part of an *educational* curriculum. It seems safe to say that education should aim more at inviting reflection than giving answers. Also, the strong emphasis in most codes on avoiding conflicts of interest, putting in a full day's work for a full day's pay, etc., offers little guidance on the policy implications of administrative discretion.

6. No attempt will be made here to determine what is and what is not "New PA" literature. It will suffice to refer to the papers included in *Toward a New Public Administration,* as well as the articles in the "Symposium on Social Equity and Public Administration" in *Public Administration Review,* Vol. 34 (January/February 1974), pp. 1–51. See also Fredrick C. Thayer, *An End to Hierarchy! An End to Competition!* (New York: Franklin Watts, 1973).

7. David K. Hart, "Social Equity, Justice, and the Equitable Administration," *Public Administration Review,* Vol. 34 (January/February 1974), p. 10.

8. See William G. Scott and David K. Hart, "The Moral Nature of Man in Organization," *Academy of Management Journal,* Vol. 14 (June 1971), pp. 241–255. The authors suggest certain parallels between the anthropologies of Hobbes and Taylor, Locke and Mayo, and McGregor and Rousseau. While the article is fascinating, I would object that the authors exaggerate the differences between Hobbes and Locke. I would also question their interpretation of Locke's *Second Treatise* on the relation between liberty and property. I am not sure my criticisms are correct, but I think they would have to be investigated before making applications to current administrative problems. Is a PA curriculum the place to undertake such an investigation?

9. This same criticism applies to Wayne A.R. Leys, *Ethics for Policy Decisions: The Art of Asking Deliberative Questions* (New York: Prentice-Hall. 1952). Leys' book is an excellent example of an effort to join the worlds of philosophy and praxis, but I wonder if students would benefit from this book unless they have had a generous background in philosophy.

10. The insights of humanistic psychology would be quite useful for ethical problems that arise within an agency—e.g., enlightened methods of personnel management. Such problems, however, are not peculiar to government agencies. The emphasis on the discretion of public employees gives the ethical analysis in this article a strong policy orientation and attempts to isolate problems that are peculiar to those who work for government agencies.

11. Jacques Maritain, *Man and the State* (Chicago: University of Chicago Press, 1951), pp. 61–62.

12. I am not using the word "regime" in the journalistic sense of the "Nixon regime" or the "Ford regime." The word is offered as the most appropriate translation of what Aristotle meant by "polity."

13. Even Hobbes goes this far. See *De Cive* 111, 3.

14. I must beg the readers' indulgence for continually repeating the word "fundamental." It is very important, however, that we distinguish between a regime that is fundamentally just and one that is perfectly just. To attempt to defend a theory of the meaning of fundamental justice would require nothing less than a recapitulation of the history of political thought. To give the term some content, let me simply assert that the following questions might help one decide whether a particular regime is fundamentally just: (1) What are the professed values of the regime? (2) Are the professed values consistent with my personal values? (3) To what extent does the regime achieve its professed values? (4) To the extent that it falls short of its professed values are there corrective mechanisms that offer some hope of reform?

15. Obviously, there are other questions in political philosophy, but few, if any, are more salient than the character of regimes. The fact that authors as diverse in time and content as Aristotle and Rawls are concerned primarily with the justice of regimes is a sound indication of the perennial importance of this issue.

16. See Abraham Kaplan, *American Ethics and Public Policy* (New York: Oxford University Press, 1963), pp. 8–10 for an argument that in matters of public values a conclusion is more important than the principles on which it is based. See also Maritain's position on Christian and secularist support for the Universal Declaration of Human Rights, *Man and the State,* pp. 77 ff.

17. I do not believe that anyone would contest the presence of freedom and property among American values. Equality might be somewhat controversial. See Willmore Kendall and George W. Carey, *The Basic Symbols of the American Political Tradition* (Baton Rouge: LSU Press, 1970), and Alvin Johnson, "Party and Ideology in America," *Yale Review,* 1948.

18. Once again, let me stress that I am dealing with a regime that is fundamentally just and not with the best possible regime.

19. Take, for example, the differences between men like Turner, Beard, Parrington, and Boorstin.

20. *Pollock v. Farmers' Loan and Trust Company* 158 U.S. 601 (1895).

21. 400 U.S. 309.

22. Thomas Reed Powell, "The Logic and Rhetoric of Constitutional Law," *Journal of Philosophy, Psychology, and Scientific—Method,* Vol. 15 (1918), p. 654.

23. The specific cases the bureaucrat might study for insight into American values are many and varied. Some cases, however, would probably appear on anyone's list—e.g., *Dred Scott v. Sandford,* 19 Howard 393 (1857), and *Brown v. Board of Education,* 347 U.S. 483 (1954), on equality; *Dartmouth College v. Woodward,* 4 Wheat, 518 (1819), and *Home Building and Loan Association v. Blaisdell,* 290 U.S. 398 (1934), on property; and the flag-salute cases of the early 1940s on freedom *[Minersville School District v. Gobitis,* 310 U.S. 586 (1940), and *West Virginia State Board of Education v. Barnette,* 319 U.S. 624 (1943)].* In addition to studying individual cases, the bureaucrat might profit from studying clusters of cases dealing with the same problem—e.g., church-state relations, the conflict between "sit-in" demonstrations and trespass laws, or the recent cases in which the Supreme Court has adopted in part Charles Reich's theory of "new property." See my article "Property Rights and Social Reform" in *America,* Vol. 133 (July 19, 1975), pp. 27–30.

21

TWO APPROACHES TO POLICE ETHICS

William C. Heffernan
John Jay College of Criminal Justice,
The City University of New York

In the 1970s, two separate trends were discernible in police ethics. First, as the extent of police corruption in New York and other cities became clear, many practitioners advocated training in ethics as one step among many that could curb officers' abuses of their roles (Doucet, 1977; Doyle & Olivet, 1972; Olivet, 1976). When conceived in this way, the role of police ethics is frankly practical. Through the educational process police attitudes are to be changed, dispositions shaped, moral evasions banished, and, consequently, performance and service improved.

At the same time, another trend developed independently of the practical approach. In a reaction against what they perceived as the remoteness of much twentieth century ethical theory, scholars began to produce a literature of applied ethics designed to illuminate moral problems of daily life, particularly those confronting professionals.[1] The scholars' goal was, in at least one sense, inconsistent with the practical one underlying the original call for attention to police ethics. Where practitioners had turned to ethics as a means of changing behavior, specialists in applied ethics disclaimed any ambition to influence their students by specific ethical precepts.[2] As long as the movement in applied ethics was confined to professions such as medicine and law (Clouser, 1980; Kelly, 1980), the tension between the two approaches to problems in policing was merely a potential one. Recently though, there has been increasing evidence that criminal justice scholars view police ethics as a discipline which could benefit from the analytic approach used in applied ethics. Textbooks have been produced in the field (Bowie & Elliston, 1982; Elliston & Sherman, 1982); the number of courses employing analytic perspectives has been growing;[3] and the Hastings Center for Ethics and the Life Sciences, one of the chief sponsors of the applied ethics movement, held a conference early in 1981 for scholars and practitioners on the subject of police ethics.[4]

Which approach should prevail? Should education in police ethics seek to guide students toward specific outcomes, or should it be concerned primarily with analysis of moral dilemmas in policing? I argue here that both approaches are needed, though for different kinds of issues in law enforcement. The original interest in police ethics centered around problems of integrity: perjury and illegal force, for instance, as well as corruption. There is little a moral philosopher would say in favor of these practices, and thus they do not require sustained ethical analysis. However, because they pose perennially important challenges for policing, they remain appropriate targets for change via education. The new interest in applied ethics, on the other hand, arises out of moral dilemmas in policing: when deadly force should be legally permitted; when it is proper to use deception in undercover operations; or when if ever, police departments should employ affirmative action programs. In these cases no intuitively obvious solution presents itself for the problems raised. The second approach, employing ethical analysis, is thus needed to clarify the issues contained in each problem and to help in constructing the general principles by which the problems can be resolved.

My purpose in distinguishing between the two approaches is to provide a framework for analyzing the development and potential of education in police ethics. In the latter half of 1980, while preparing for the Hastings conference on police ethics, I conducted a survey of the current state of ethics instruction in both police academies and criminal justice programs.[5] My survey determined that many institutions now have courses in police ethics, but it also revealed a lingering confusion about what education in this emerging discipline should try to achieve. My goal is to help resolve this confusion by defining the essential characteristics of both approaches to police ethics and by suggesting the role each can play in police education. I shall note during the course of my discussion the stage of police education where each is most appropriate.

The First Approach: Developing Police Integrity

When proponents of the first approach ask whether someone is an "ethical police officer," they take for granted the value of honesty and avoidance of corruption and ask instead whether an officer in fact honors these in professional life. Education conducted in this vein would be devoted only incidentally to the justification of moral values; it would be primarily concerned with developing in students both the capacity to recognize basic values and the strength of character to act on this recognition. When moral education is conceived in this way, contemporary philosophers would disclaim any expertise in its teaching and, in all likelihood, would experience a certain unease in endorsing its goals. Yet moral education historically has sought to cultivate integrity (see, for example, Aristotle, 1941, VII, 13–14), and there are at least two reasons why this version of it remains relevant, though in limited form, to police training today.[6]

First, effective law enforcement in a democratic society is possible only when the police honor basic standards of integrity. Our Constitution has created a series of checks on police power via the Fourth and Fifth Amendments, but these provide the courts with opportunities to control the police only when an arrest is made. When the police either decline to arrest or issue commands without invoking the arrest power itself, then court control over the police is of necessity quite limited. Furthermore, administrative authority within departments cannot place significant limits on patrol officers when they engage in activities for which no report is required. The fundamental check on police power in situations such as these, situations which provide the opportunity for corruption as well as for the use of illegal force, is the internal one of conscience. Law enforcement itself risks becoming ineffective unless police officers exercise this internal discipline. While one might consider it presumptuous under other circumstances to give integrity training to adult men and women, there are strong reasons for offering it to state agents who exercise the kind of power delegated to the police.

Second, the special challenges to police integrity encountered in this century indicate why training in that trait must be accorded a high priority. Left to themselves, many recruits would no doubt resist the temptations arising in situations of unchecked authority. Historically though, there has been a pattern of new officers "bending" under pressures placed on them by more experienced personnel who have already established questionable practices of their own. The problem here is seldom a cognitive one; new officers usually are able to identify the basic standards of right and wrong prevailing in their profession. Instead, an attitudinal challenge exists, with temptation particularly difficult to resist because it is grounded in peer pressure rather than the desire for financial gain. It is unlikely that integrity training could influence an officer who readily yields to peer pressure. However, it could set a tone for a department and thus could provide the margin of difference for officers who are wavering in their own decisions about what to do.

There are two ways in which the first approach to police ethics can be applied in police academies: by example and by direct instruction. To speak of teaching by example may appear to be an apology for ignoring ethics in the curriculum, particularly when it is realized, as my survey has shown, that the great majority of academies devote 10% or less of their time to formal instruction in ethics.[7] Upon further reflection, however, it should be clear that role models can play a vital role in achieving the aims of the first approach. The goal here is to help students acquire the disposition to prefer other interests over their immediate ones, and when this is the case, the example of others who live by this preference often can be a more powerful influence than an analysis of moral values. In fact, if police ethics is to be cordoned off to one area of the curriculum but otherwise ignored, then students could conclude that their superiors view it as a matter of public relations rather than an essential part of policing. The importance of integrity must pervade police academy instruction.

How, though, should the 10% or so of academy program time specifically devoted to ethics be organized? The survey revealed that academy instructors prefer to use three teaching methods: lectures, homilies, and small group discussions. These responses came as something of a surprise. I would suggest that, with the possible exception of group discussion, the methods favored are not well suited to the goals of the first approach. The purpose of this approach, it should be remembered, is to help students recognize and act on their recognition of basic moral values. Formal lectures and homilies by priestly instructors are unlikely to succeed at this. They fail to bring home the realities of police practice and they involve frontal assaults when persuasion and empathy are needed instead.

As an alternative to these traditional methods of instruction, I would suggest that academies which have succeeded in setting a good tone in the rest of their curriculum can afford to delay ethics instruction until immediately after graduation, when their students have begun their full-time assignments. Small groups, led by officers with training in group dynamics, could then explore the kinds of temptation encountered in police work. The topics which academies responding to the questionnaire agreed to be centrally important—corruption (64%), perjury (70%), and violations of constitutional rights (78%)—could be brought up via reflection on the realities of practice. In a setting where anonymity could be guaranteed, the moral evasions that officers develop to escape some of the rigors of ethics could be examined just as these tendencies were beginning to take root. Anxieties which accompany policing and frequently set the stage for rule violations also could be mentioned in these discussions, and with the diminution of these anxieties could come a corresponding reduction of the impetus to engage in the violations.

Group exchanges of this kind have little to do with the moral education offered by philosophers. It goes without saying that philosophers can offer justifications for the value of honesty and avoiding bribes, but careful analysis along these lines seems superfluous and in any case would distract students from the motivational purpose underlying the exchanges. Rather than seek philosophers as group leaders, academy directors might be wiser to turn to those who combine an insider's knowledge of policing with special expertise in managing group dynamics. Both characteristics are important for the success of the first approach, the former because outsiders often are rejected when they offer even slight criticism of police practices and the latter because the emotions voiced in group discussions must be guided toward constructive goals. Of course, the guidance must be nonmanipulative. Instructors should make clear at the outset the purpose of the discussions and should provide students with ample opportunity to dissent from positions expressed by the majority. In this way, group leaders could point toward dispositional change while trying to avoid the kind of stampede that threatens individual autonomy. The choice as to standards would remain with students; however, for those who are interested in change or in reaffirming their integrity, the groups could provide a supportive environment.

To this point, the first approach has been considered solely as a teaching device for police academies. Some criminal justice programs, however, also offer courses dealing with police ethics, and one might wonder whether these too should try to exert a direct influence over student conduct. In my survey 50% of the criminal justice instructors responding indicate that influencing students to adopt specific standards of conduct was one of the goals of their courses. This result was quite surprising, and, with an exception to be noted shortly, I must enter a dissent concerning this goal.[8]

There is a special reason why academies are entitled to adopt the first approach. Academies, it should be borne in mind, are charged with the duty of producing public servants of integrity. Thus they not only share the traditional goal of higher education—developing in students a capacity to reason clearly—but also are bound by one created through their governmental role: fostering in students the habit of doing what is right. Thus police academies may legitimately seek to modify the conduct of their students. In fact, their role even requires them to pursue this goal, with due respect for individuality.

A different conclusion, however, must be reached for the majority of criminal justice programs of higher education. In a few jurisdictions, such programs are charged with performing the training function normally accorded to police academies. Where this is true, the justification available to academies for employing the first approach would be available to criminal justice programs as well. However, in the more commonplace situation in which police academies and criminal justice programs exist side by side, the latter lack the special justification for seeking to influence student conduct. This is the case even when they are based on what has been called the professional, as distinguished from the liberal arts, model of instruction. Even on basic issues such as honesty and corruption, the aim of moral education in criminal justice must be to help students develop reasoning powers of their own, rather than to instill in them a habit of acting in a certain way. This is not to say that criminal justice students will frequently conclude that dishonesty, corruption, and the use of illegal force leading to serious injury are morally desirable. The goal of moral instruction in higher education should be to create in students the capacity to determine on their own the desirability of these practices. This goal would be seriously compromised if college teachers were to encourage students to adopt certain standards rather than others.

Having said this, higher education nonetheless can have significant indirect impact on the development of police integrity. In his article on ethics instruction in criminal justice programs, Gerald Lynch (1976) has argued that there are numerous ways in which this indirect effect can occur. Lynch suggests, for instance, that faculty members can set an important example for students simply by honoring their own professional norms of accuracy and confidentiality. He also argues that college education provides officers with an opportunity to view from a critical distance, and perhaps modify, practices they had previously taken for granted (Lynch, 1976, pp. 289–290). In these ways, higher education can offer significant indirect support for the goals of the first approach while adhering to the pedagogical methods essential for the preservation of its own values.

The Second Approach: Applying Ethical Theory

Police ethics involves making hard choices, as well as avoiding violations of basic moral standards. The latter have been relatively easy to specify; in fact, our list included only corruption, perjury, and the use of illegal force resulting in serious injury to suspects. The former are more elusive, however, and thus this section will begin with an inventory (though not an exhaustive one) of the hard choices in policing and then will discuss an analytic approach that could be brought to bear on making them.

Hard choices in policing usually arise within the confines of the law. Thus one distinction between our first and second approaches is that the first always focuses on illegality by state agents whereas the second generally does not. This point is made clear in the following analysis. The first two categories—issues confronted by administrators and individual officers—are confined to legal conduct. The third deals with illegality, but unlike the practices discussed earlier, those considered here will be at least arguably defensible from a moral point of view.

Ethical Problems Confronted Primarily by Police Administrators

Manpower Allocation Decisions.   Police administrators must select from among competing goals in making allocation decisions. Even if an administrator were to conclude that combatting crime is the sole goal to pursue (allocation decisions are made harder since other interests must also be weighed), he still would have to decide whether to seek crime minimization (the maximum possible reduction of crime in his jurisdiction) or crime equalization (the equalization of crime risks for all citizens of the jurisdiction) as the goal (see, for example, Shoup, 1964; Wilson, 1968, pp. 61–62).

The Use of Deceit in Undercover Operations. At least two issues are at stake here: the legitimacy of *any* deceit, and, if its employment is allowed, the extent to which it should be permitted. Both issues, it should be noted, revolve around the legitimacy of government participation in deceit. It is at least arguable that government should be held to a higher standard than private citizens.[9]

The Selection of Targets in Undercover Operations. Even if the question of deceit is resolved, one could still ask whether the targets of an undercover operation have been properly selected. How much evidence of wrongdoing must the government possess before it determines that a person should be subjected to the temptations provided by undercover police agents? This question has most recently arisen in Abscam, but it in fact is relevant to all operations of this kind (see Sherman, 1982).

Privacy Issues in Police Surveillance. The police are legally permitted to employ informants to penetrate dissident groups. Furthermore, they are not legally liable when informants' conduct violates standing orders. Because of this police authority, there has been extensive disagreement as to the kinds of groups which should be penetrated. For instance, should extremist groups that do not advocate violence be subjected to surveillance by informants? There has also been disagreement about the extent of supervision which police should exercise when employing informants. This includes consideration of the extent to which the personal safety of informants should be monitored by supervisors. Important interests must be balanced in these cases: individual privacy versus the public security and informant safety versus lawful activity by state agents.[10]

Use of Deadly Force. There has been no debate over the moral acceptability of administrative directives permitting the use of deadly force to protect either civilians or officers who face a reasonable threat of deadly force from another person. Recently, though, it has been recognized that an important moral question arises when departments permit their officers to use deadly force against fleeing, unarmed felons. For a legislature or administrator to sanction this could increase the protection of the community against criminality in the future, but, it also might violate one of the basic principles of criminal justice that only appropriate punishment should be meted out.[11]

Affirmative Action Programs.   In recent years one of the most widely discussed issues in police ranks has been the use of affirmative action programs to aid women and members of minorities. Affirmative action (itself
a term of multiple meanings) deserves consideration on a wide variety of
grounds: (a) whether, because of past practices, police departments should
offer compensatory justice via affirmative action or perhaps some other
means; (b) whether affirmative action is required as a principle of distribu-
tive justice; and (c) whether affirmative action would be desirable, though
perhaps not obligatory, because of the heterogeneity it could bring to institutions like police departments.[12]

Ethical Problems Confronted by Individual Patrolmen

Problems of Comparative Justice Posed by the Exercise of Police Discretion.
Every police officer, it probably would be agreed, is under a moral obligation to treat like cases alike. Two difficulties accompany this obligation,
however. The first is one of classification. What makes a case similar to
others? The second arises because discretion is exercised individually by
multiple officers. Thus even if Patrolman A believes an arrest is warranted
in a given case, he would still have to ask whether he should refrain from
making one because he knows Patrolmen B, C, D, etc. decline to arrest under similar circumstances.[13]

Loyalty to One's Peers.   Trainees are frequently told, when they join the
force, that they should report to superiors the misconduct of any of their
peers. As noted, many recruits discover that they lack the strength of character to resist the temptations accompanying their role and thus they do
not report the misconduct of others. Assuming that they do confront this
decision, however, arguments can be marshaled for and against turning to
police superiors. Certainly there is a strong public interest in police integrity. However, there is also perhaps a morally protected area of privacy
in which individuals are entitled to discount to a certain extent the public's
need for integrity and to give at least limited consideration to the interests
of their friends. If the latter point does have some merit, would an officer
act in a morally acceptable way if he sought to persuade a friend to termi-
nate his misconduct but did not report him? Would it be morally acceptable if, after three months during which the misconduct persisted, the officer were to turn to a priest rather than to a police administrator?

Illegal Conduct by Individual Police Officers

Violations of the Rules of Search and Seizure.   The literature of policing is
filled with instances of officers' claims that they are morally entitled to vio-

late the Fourth Amendment if their conduct serves a useful purpose such as preserving public safety while involving only minimal inconvenience to those searched. Officers justify this conduct by arguing that many of the current restrictions of search and seizure jeopardize public security while their illegal action serves to buttress it. The entire argument is a controversial one, but it cannot be rejected as patently unacceptable in the way that a defense of corruption or the infliction of serious and illegal harm would be (see Davis, 1975, pp. 16; 20–22; Wilson, 1968, p. 36).

Police Strikes. Officers frequently work in jurisdictions where (a) police strikes are illegal, and (b) the law does not provide for mandatory arbitration when management and labor disagree, thus allowing management to hold out indefinitely on a police union. Under these circumstances, officers certainly have a claim to be entitled to strike that deserves careful consideration.[14]

Discussion

What approach should scholars and practitioners take to hard cases such as these? At first, many might suppose it would be wise to concentrate on expanding the codes of ethics (of the IACP, for instance) which already deal with police problems. Those codes have expressed well the aspirations of law enforcement officials, but there is a good reason why they should not be made the focal point of reflection upon hard cases. Police codes, it should be borne in mind, are, like those of other professions, essentially political documents. They are designed to reflect the broad sentiment of the profession. By the same token, they are not meant to contain detailed analyses of the reasons that could be advanced for or against this sentiment. This is what gives them such force when they comment on problems of basic integrity. In such cases there is already general agreement about what should be done and codes can thus play a useful role in reminding those tempted by misconduct of the shared goals of the profession.

By contrast, codes are insufficient by themselves to shape opinion regarding the hard cases confronting a profession. Admittedly, on polling the police, we might discover widespread consensus on some of the hard choices just discussed. However, even if consensus did exist on one of the hard cases, it would have to be deemed precarious compared to that prevailing on problems of integrity since it had not been preceded by debate and reflection. Without prior debate, consensus on a hard case could easily evaporate, with its resulting behavioral prescription falling into disfavor once reasoned arguments were advanced against it. Since no argument is likely to change officers' minds on problems of integrity, it makes sense to use a code to express the basic ideals of the law enforcement profession.

But when officers' ideals are in doubt, then the wise step would be to investigate the sources of doubt, not to seek a fragile consensus that could evaporate overnight. Code writing thus should be an adjunct to the second approach; it should not, however, be made its centerpiece.

As the experience of law and medicine has made clear, the best strategy for stimulating reflection on hard choices in professional life is to foster the development of an appropriate literature of applied ethics. In medicine, the field where applied ethics has the longest history, moral philosophers and practitioners have been engaged in an ongoing dialogue for more than two decades concerning problems such as abortion, euthanasia, and patients' rights (Clouser, 1980, pp. 76–77). In law, issues such as the moral accountability of advocates, the justifiability of legislative creation of victimless crimes, and the moral dimensions of sentencing discretion have all been clarified by sustained analysis by moral philosophers and lawyers (see Kelly, 1980, pp. 66–69).

In generalizing on the experience of other professions, one might suggest that three values have been realized through the development of a literature of applied ethics. First, books and articles on hard choices encountered in professional life have helped practitioners better understand their own positions as to what constitutes proper conduct. Second, as a result of this, debate among practitioners has been sharpened concerning the rules governing their professional lives. And third, agreement on hard cases has sometimes emerged, thus making possible the formulation of code rules that have a significant chance of enduring.[15] Of course, in many cases practitioners have divided sharply among themselves and have not gone beyond the debating stage. However, even when this has been true, the applied ethics literature has performed an important function in stimulating practitioners to act according to internally consistent principles, though of course the content of these principles has varied throughout their profession. Thus, as far as law enforcement is concerned, books and articles in applied ethics could at the very least lay the groundwork for debate among police practitioners about the principles that should govern their profession. And, on occasion, general agreement might emerge from this debate, thus making possible the creation of code rules which would be likely to endure precisely because they were based on the reasoned assent of police practitioners.

In addition to this, one special feature of a literature of applied ethics should be noted. Because scholars writing on subjects such as police ethics will inevitably take stands on difficult and controversial topics, one must anticipate the related dangers that some practitioners will assent too readily to the arguments presented them while others will resent what they perceive as attacks upon their profession. In a sense, these reactions are attributable to a misperception. Once it is realized that the literature of applied ethics questions no one's disposition to do what is right, but instead assumes the existence of this attitude and then asks what it would be right to do in a given case, then both reactions should become less prevalent. Books and essays on police ethics must of course take stands on dilemmas of law enforcement; that is the only way these can be resolved. But the positions authors take in these cases should not be confused with the strongly directive guidance characteristic of the first approach. As practitioners will come to understand, the arguments presented on the hard cases are meant to provoke thought. They are intended to gain assent only if this can be justified on the basis of rational reflection.

Besides offering practitioners a means of considering the dilemmas of professional life, the second approach can also play an important role in criminal justice education. There are, however, many important pedagogical issues raised by applied ethics in general and police ethics in particular. At least three deserve consideration here: (a) the method by which police ethics should be taught; (b) the means by which students should be introduced to ethical theory; and (c) the qualifications teachers should possess in order to teach an interdisciplinary subject such as police ethics.

The danger just discussed—that practitioners will confuse hard cases with easy ones—is relevant to the issue of teaching method as well. On the one hand, because of this confusion, some students will be inclined to accept unquestioningly whatever position their instructor takes, thus missing the educational value that can be realized by studying hard cases. On the other hand, also because of this confusion, certain students will conclude that their teachers are trying to deliver holy writ on subjects where such an approach is inappropriate. The solution to this is for instructors to emphasize the potential fallibility of judgments of hard cases and then encourage intellectual openness and candor in discussing them. This does not mean that teachers should invariably decline to state their positions on matters under discussion, although as a matter of pedagogical strategy, it is rarely wise to reveal one's position at the outset. The critical point is a different one: Students must be brought by classroom instruction to see that credible solutions in ethics cope with the many-sidedness of problems and offer convincing arguments concerning each of the issues they address. An instructor's method should be keyed to this. Whatever the exact approach, he or she should be patient, show a willingness to consider an issue from numerous perspectives, and insist that students honor the standards of rationality in the course of discussion. In the long run, this general method can have greater value than any substantive point discussed during the course of instruction.

A second educational issue in applied ethics centers around the moment at which students should be introduced to ethical theory. Teachers have two options on this matter: to review theory at the outset or to begin with

concrete cases. My survey showed that a majority of criminal justice instructors (52%) prefer the former approach, no doubt because it allows
them to examine the internal logic of different theories before applying
them to specific cases. Important as this consideration may be, there is a
good reason to delay the introduction of theory. As many instructors have
discovered, students often become impatient with what they perceive to be
the remoteness of theory when it is discussed apart from cases (Hastings
Report, 1980, pp. 70–71). By contrast, once students have not only considered a situation but also have examined their conflicting intuitions as to
how it should be handled, they then welcome theory for the light it casts
on what they have already come to see as a perplexing problem. Of course,
even this strategy can have its drawbacks if a teacher fails to use the awakened interest in theory to remind students of the hazards of using it selec-
tively and inconsistently to support preconceived opinions. However, this
problem can arise with the first strategy as well, and in that case, unlike the
second, an instructor runs the extra risk of creating student skepticism
about the enterprise of theorizing itself.

Third, the qualifications needed to teach an interdisciplinary subject
such as police ethics must also be considered. The authors of the Hastings
Report wisely note that all instructors should have at least the equivalent
of one full academic year's formal training in philosophical or theological
ethics before teaching a course in applied ethics (1980, pp. 62–64). Without this background, a social scientist or police officer would in all likelihood be unable to alert students to the relevance of ethical theory, a challenging subject in its own right, to actual problems of policing. However,
as the Hastings authors add, it is equally important that instructors understand the complexities of the professional practices with which they are
dealing (1980, pp. 64–65). Thus, if a philosopher were to teach police
ethics, he or she should have the equivalent of one full academic year's
training in police studies plus some time spent in the field before offering
instruction to students. In this way, instructors' initial deficiencies can be
remedied and minimal competence in teaching guaranteed. Ideally, instructors should take a research interest in the field, thus going beyond the
threshold standards outlined here.

Finally, one might ask whether the approach to hard cases just discussed
should be offered in police academies as well as in college-level criminal
justice programs. As noted, there are good reasons for not using the first
approach in criminal justice instruction. The converse, however, is not the
case. In fact, it seems clear that trainees and beginning patrol officers could
only benefit from instruction that introduces them to methods of analyzing
the dilemmas of their profession.

Two points should be borne in mind if an academy wishes to adopt this
method of instruction. First, since the directive techniques of the first approach are pedagogically incompatible with the analytic ones of the sec-

ond, the two should not be used together. This poses no real difficulty though, since moral analysis can be applied to problems of integrity as well as more complex dilemmas of professional life, while directive instruction, by contrast, is ill-suited to the consideration of complex dilemmas. Second, the analytic approach is more time consuming than its alternative, a point of some significance since, as was already mentioned, virtually no academy presently devotes more than 10% of its curriculum to ethics.

The second approach should be adopted only if an academy's directors are willing to grant ethics instruction a more central role than it now plays in the training of officers. Clearly, academy directors would have to reconsider instructional goals before approving this, and the restructuring of priorities is not a trivial matter. The possibility of change is not wholly remote, however. In the last few years, for example, some police departments in New England have shown an interest in sustained ethics instruction. They have gone so far as to offer in-service courses on ethical problems in policing taught by a moral philosopher.[16] Furthermore, during the last decade or so, other professions such as law and medicine have increased significantly the amount of instructional time devoted to the hard choices encountered by their practitioners.[17] There is some basis for hope that as law enforcement increases its consciousness of itself as a profession, it will follow suit.

Conclusion

There has been a tendency among police administrators to view police ethics solely in terms of problems of integrity. Moreover, as philosophers have turned to the ethical issues confronting professionals, they have tended to focus on hard choices arising in professional life to the virtual exclusion of challenges to individual integrity. In fact, both kinds of issues are at stake in any profession, a point that is particularly important for policing, given both the temptations and the genuine moral dilemmas that are inescapable features of the police role. This essay has suggested that different educational approaches are appropriate for each kind of problem. It has defined the two approaches, specified the safeguards which must accompany them, and suggested the educational settings in which they should be used. The quality and effectiveness of policing itself will be enhanced when each approach is employed in its proper context.

Notes

1. For a brief summary of the history of the applied ethics movement, see Hastings Report (1980, v–viii).

2. The disclaimer is to be found in the rejection of ethics instruction as a means of indoctrination. See, for instance, Macklin (1980, pp. 81–101). It should be

noted that sponsors of applied ethics instruction have endorsed attempts to exert general influence over student conduct. The Hastings group suggests that students should be encouraged through ethics instruction to develop a general sense of moral obligation and personal responsibility (Hastings Report, 1980, pp. 50–51). However, the Hastings authors reiterate Macklin's objection to using ethics instruction in higher education to influence students to adopt specific precepts in their conduct (Hastings Report, 1980, pp. 55–62).

3. In my survey of criminal justice ethics instruction, described subsequently at Note 5, I identified 94 courses offered in the subject at the undergraduate and graduate levels during the 1980–81 academic year. I also identified 23 police academies which then offered instruction in ethics to trainees, police officers, or both. A further survey of instruction is being undertaken by Frederick Elliston of the Criminal Justice Research Center of Albany, New York, on a grant from the National Endowment for the Humanities.

4. The conference, held on February 27–28, 1981, at the Hastings Center, Hastings-on-Hudson, New York, brought together two police chiefs, an instructor from the FBI Academy, and twelve scholars with a special interest in police ethics.

5. Questionnaires were sent to the 79 police academies listed in the directory *Criminal Justice Agencies,* which was first published by LEAA in 1970 (USDOJ) and has been updated periodically on a regional basis. Responses from 23 academies were received. As for criminal justice programs, the following criteria were employed in selecting institutions listed in the IACP's *Criminal Justice Education Directory 1978–80:* (a) all institutions graduating more than 100 students in 1977; (b) all institutions listing courses whose titles indicated that they were primarily concerned with criminal justice or police ethics; and (c) all institutions offering doctoral degrees in criminal justice. In all, 199 questionnaires were sent. Responses were received from 44 undergraduate and 14 graduate programs.

6. The first approach to moral education has been defined in a working paper of the National Humanities Center (1980).

7. Of the 23 academies responding, only one (Cincinnati) devoted more than 10% of its time to ethics instruction.

8. For a discussion of the distinction between criminal justice education based on the liberal arts model and that which is based on a professional one, see Pearson, Moran, Berger, Laudon, McKenzie, & Bonita (1980).

9. The issues surrounding lying by public officials are discussed in Bok (1978, chaps. 9 & 12).

10. For a case study of the questionable uses that can be made of undercover agents, see Zimroth (1974, pp. 16–17; 48–51; 61–68).

11. For appellate court decisions disagreeing over the constitutionality of statutes permitting police officers to fire at unarmed, fleeing felons, see *Mattis v. Schnarr,* 547 F.2d 1007 (8th Cir., 1976), which invalidated a Missouri statute authorizing this on the ground that it violated due process, and *Wiley v. Memphis Police Department,* 548 F.2nd 1247 (6th Cir., 1977), which upheld the constitutionality of a Tennessee statute authorizing the police to use deadly force if necessary to effect the arrest of a felon.

12. For a general discussion of affirmative action, see Goldman (1979).

13. For a general discussion of the obligation to treat like cases alike, see Feinberg (1973, pp. 98–107).

14. A preventive approach to police strikes has been suggested in Gentel (1979). Surprisingly, an ethical analysis of this widely debated issue has yet to be published.

15. For an illustration of the influence which an applied ethics literature can have on the formulation of new professional rules, see Rule 3.1 of the proposed Model Rules of Professional Conduct of the American Bar Association (1981) which, if adopted, would replace Disciplinary Rule 7–102 of the current Code of Professional Responsibility. The citations following 3.1, which, when compared with 7–102, place significant restrictions on the representations advocates may make to a tribunal, indicate which books and articles influenced the drafters of the new code.

16. The course has been taught by Professor Howard Cohen of the University of Massachusetts, Boston. For the instructor's description of the course see Cohen (1982).

17. The American Bar Association now requires instruction in legal ethics as part of law school curricula (Pipkin, 1979). A 1975 survey indicated that 97 of the 107 medical schools responding offered some form of instruction in medical ethics (Veatch & Sollitto, 1976).

References

American Bar Association, Model rules of professional conduct (Proposed, draft). Chicago: Author, 1981.

Aristotle, *Politics* (B. Jowett, Trans.). New York: Modern Library, 1941.

Bok, S. Whistleblowing and professional responsibilities. In D. Callahan and S. Bok (Eds.), *Ethics teaching in higher education.* New York: Plenum, 1980.

Bok, S. *Lying: Moral choice in public and private life.* New York: Pantheon, 1978.

Bowie, N., & Elliston, F. *Ethics, public policy and criminal justice.* New York: Oelgeschlager, Gunn and Hain, 1982.

Clouser, K.D. *Teaching bioethics: Strategies, problems and resources.* Hastings-on-Hudson, New York: Hastings Center, 1980.

Cohen, H. Working ethics for police officers. *Criminal Justice Ethics,* 1982, *1,* 45–47.

Davis, K.C. *Police discretion.* St. Paul, Minn.: West, 1975.

Doucet, R. Training: A pro-active approach towards corruption and integrity problems. *Police Chief,* 1977, *44*(8), 72–74.

Doyle, E., & Olivet, G. An invitation to understanding: Workshop in law enforcement integrity. *Police Chief,* 1972, *39*(5), 34–44.

Elliston, F., & Sherman, L. *Police ethics.* Englewood Cliffs, N.J.: Prentice-Hall, 1982.

Feinberg, J. *Social philosophy.* Englewood Cliffs, N.J.: Prentice-Hall, 1973.

Gentel, W. *Police strikes: Causes and prevention.* Gaithersburg, Md.: International Association of Chiefs of Police, 1979.

Goldman, A. *Justice and reverse discrimination.* Princeton: Princeton University Press, 1979.

Hastings Report. *The teaching of ethics in higher education.* Hastings-on-Hudson, New York: Hastings Center, 1980.

International Association of Chiefs of Police. *Criminal justice education directory 1978–80.* Gaithersburg, Md.: Author, 1978.

Kelly, M. *Legal ethics and legal education.* Hastings-on-Hudson, New York: Hastings Center, 1980.

Lynch, G. The contribution of higher education to ethical behavior in law enforcement. *Journal of Criminal Justice,* 1976, *4,* 285–290.

Macklin, R. Problems in the teaching of ethics: Pluralism and indoctrination. In D. Callahan and S. Bok (Eds.), *Ethics teaching in higher education.* New York: Plenum, 1980.

Mattis v. Schnarr, 547 F.2d 1007 (8th Cir. 1976).

National Humanities Center. *Ethics and moral education* (Working paper). Research Triangle Park, N.C.: Author, 1980.

Olivet, G. Ethical philosophy in police training. *Police Chief,* 1976, *43*(8), 48–50.

Pearson, R., Moran, T.K., Berger, J.C., Laudon, K.C., McKenzie, J.R., & Bonita, T.J. *Criminal justice education: The end of the beginning.* New York: John Jay Press, 1980.

Pipkin, D. Law school instruction in professional responsibility: A curricular paradox. *American Bar Foundation Research Journal,* 1979, *1979,* 247–262.

Sherman, L.W. Deceptive investigations: The ethics of selecting targets. In W. Heffernan and T. Stroup (Eds.), *Police ethics: Hard choices in law enforcement.* New York: John Jay Press, 1982.

Shoup, C. Standards for the distribution of a free governmental service: Crime prevention. *Public Finance,* 1964, *19,* 383–392.

United States Department of Justice, Law Enforcement Assistance Administration. *Criminal Justice Agencies.* Washington, D.C.: Author, 1970.

Veatch, R., & Sollitto, S. Medical ethics teaching: A report of a national survey. *Journal of the American Medical Association,* 1976, *235,* 1030–1033.

Wiley v. Memphis Police Department, 548 F.2d 1247 (6th Cir. 1977).

Wilson, J.Q. *Varieties of police behavior.* Cambridge, Mass.: Harvard University Press, 1968.

Zimroth, P. *Perversions of justice.* New York: Viking, 1974.

22

TEACHING MORAL EDUCATION IN PUBLIC ADMINISTRATION

Richard T. Mayer and Michael M. Harmon
George Washington University

Introduction

In a recent issue of *The Public Interest*, Mark T. Lilla makes a troubling complaint about public administration and policy programs. A moral vacuum has been created, he argues, by the ascendance of rational analysis techniques in their curricula. These techniques have effectively displaced the democratic ethos that underpinned administration from the time of Woodrow Wilson until the 1960s. The chief attribute of this former ethos, he implies, was its understood trust between the public (personified in the legislatures and the courts) and the administrator: (Lilla, 1981:6)

> No matter how much debate there was over the nature of administrative responsibility in a democracy, there was no question but that democracy in the U.S. was itself legitimate; the only question was how the moral public officials could best serve that democracy when government agencies and programs became large and complex, and administrators found themselves with discretion.

But then came the growth of government, particularly of social programs, in the 1960s. This "not only gave public officials more to do, it also gave them evermore discretion with which to do it." (Lilla, 1981:7) A different kind of public administrator was called for, one well-versed in the latest analytic techniques. The new emphasis on evaluating program and policy efficacy, in its turn, occasioned a transformation of public administration schools into graduate programs in public policy. Lilla (1981:8) does not argue against this shift, per se:

> ... the value of this sort of training for government service is, I think, great. However one may feel about the broad responsibilities given to federal career officials, those officials will certainly be ill-equipped to carry out their duties if they are unable to understand the language of formal analysis.

The central fault, he argues, is that students in such programs learn nothing about democracy: (Lilla, 1981:8)

> ... however inadequate the old public administration was in analytic sophistication, it did not embody an ethos which prepared the student, through an informal moral education, to take his place within a democratic government ... Graduate programs in public policy are simply silent about democracy, and, given the state of undergraduate education, neither can we be certain that entering students assume democratic principles.

The response in the 1970s—with ethical analysis added to the grab bag of analytic tricks—is one which Lilla (1981:11) understandingly deplores:

> Out of all this emerged, in the past five years, the marriage of the new public policy schools and the new moral-political philosophers. Without an ethos to hold onto, and under attack for unethical behavior, schools of public policy decided to buy some ethics.

The goal of the resulting "applied ethics" (itself a sibling of the value clarification and ethical analysis being promoted in some secondary schools) is "to raise the consciousness of students so that they 'recognize ethical issues,' 'develop analytic skills,' and 'become morally responsible.'" (Lilla, 1981:13) The crime, as Lilla sees it, is that while "this may be ethics, it is not moral education. By turning away from the way men live to higher and higher levels of abstract moral reasoning, philosophers and 'ethicists' no longer teach men to be moral, and may make them less so." (Lilla, 1981:13–14) This is so because: (Lilla, 1981:15–16)

> Applied ethics ... threatens to teach future public officials how to justify their actions with high-flown excuses without teaching them what sorts of duties and virtues make up the moral life of someone in a democratic government, and without turning that understanding into habits.

This insightful critique lays bare a number of important questions, not the least of which are the perennial ones of the relationship between policy and administration and the role of public administration as an academic discipline and professional activity. But, more importantly, it forces us to ask of ourselves: what is our responsibility as teachers of public administration? Lilla's answer—that we provide moral education by "preaching, witnessing, setting a good example for the children"—is unsettling at best, particularly when it is coupled with his implicit call for the return of the democratic ethos. (This is an ethos, this author hastens to add, that Lilla himself concedes as insufficient for the contemporary world of administration.)

Many writers, of course, have tackled this question and offered numerous pictures of the good public administration.[1] From Wilson's historic essay through Frank Goodnow's and Paul Appleby's work on to the Friedrich and Finer debates and beyond, there emerges a portrait that is both striking in its constancy and yet evermore blurred in its detail over time.

The common syllogism used to rationalize this increasing unclarity is the one cited by Lilla: government has grown and the duties of the administrator have grown with it, requiring the use of more discretionary responsibility with a corresponding diminishment of clear accountability. Consequently, it has become difficult to separate the role of the public administrator from that of the analyst or the policy-maker. And this logic is particularly persuasive when you add a strong measure of rationalism (our belief that problems are by definition soluble by articulable means); throw in two dashes of instrumentalism (the best distance between here and there is always a straight line); and don't forget a good pinch of optimism (we really do know which way is up): the resulting stew is that in which public administrators now find themselves as, by association, do we teachers of administrators. To try to contain this by fashioning our kettle out of discretion and accountability merely begs the question—responsible and accountable for what?

But what if we view our history slightly differently and, therefore, our options for the future as well? For example, to state that government has grown inexorably over the past fifty years may be to describe the effect rather than the cause we usually presume it to be. The role and place of government have changed not merely because we as a society want government to do more; it has grown because there is simply more to do. This is in part the case because, as a result of technological advances, the world is more complex and inter-related; our notions of public and private have understandingly broken down. But in a way that is unclear to the last generation and unintelligible to the one before that, we have a picture of ourselves that shows the moles and blemishes on our collective face in awesome detail. More people just simply know more about other people, their situations, and their lives, making it near impossible for the usual social structures—the habits of society, so to speak—to operate in a fashion we had come to believe was moral.

When our "fix-it" attitude—a positive and negative legacy from our fantastically successful experience with changing and manipulating our world—combines with this exponentially expanded detail and knowledge, the result is a potent social shove: not only do the rich know more than they ever cared to about the poor but so do the poor, both about themselves and about the rich. The same is true for the other dichotomous groups into which we are so wont to divide ourselves, including the powerful and the weak, the manager and the worker, and so forth. Having measured everything in sight (whether measurement is indeed legitimate or appropriate has clearly been beside the point) and having made this information accessible to everyone, we have then made the judgments which follow from this information both accessible to and required of everyone. The resulting participatory democracy has meant a pluralism of interests that is far deeper and more complex than anything imagined in the usual political science textbook.

As we have organized—and re-organized—ourselves around this bewildering array of "special interests," we have turned increasingly to the only vehicle that has any legitimacy in this society for arbitrating such a contest of interests—the government, be it legislature, the court or the executive. As individuals have come to understand—in the deepest sense of that word—their uniqueness (emphasized to them again and again at every turn), the once-adequate generalized rules and ways of organizing that world have begun to falter. For Lilla this is the crumbling of the democratic ethos.

Why this is happening and where it may lead us (and we, it) are well beyond the authors' scope here. What is relevant, however, is to address what this requires of the teachers of public administrators. For one thing, it entails acknowledging, and then understanding, this altered ethos. In a world where "to administer" means only to carry out a task, the problems are ones of technology; when "to administer" requires some kind of sorting through of interests, accounting for consequences, and justifying actions, the problems facing the administrator are very wicked ones indeed. They are ambiguous, value-laden, political, constantly changing, and not amenable to clear definition, much less "solution" in any sense this word is commonly used. The preponderance of such wicked problems is a defining characteristic of the world of the new ethos.

In apprehending the above, it is necessary to acknowledge that the change in the role of government has been even more of substance than of size. The burgeoning of government has not meant, for example, a burgeoning of its traditional functions, such as construction and maintenance of the infrastructure. Quite the contrary; by most accounts much of the infrastructure is in a serious state of disrepair. Rather, this growth has meant that enormous portions of government activity at all levels deal with the mediation between one part of society and another. While this, in a sense, characterizes all of government's work—the effect of the interstate high-way system on the development of suburb and city is only a case in point—the shift from the tangible to the intangible has been significant.

Affirmative action, for instance, has altered not only the work place in general but workers' perceptions of themselves. It has opened avenues and created opportunities that were once non-existent; at the same time, it has—by making the very weaknesses of society explicit—both raised anxiety and hostility while lowering cohesiveness and, potentially, short-run productivity of the work. Whether this bodes well or ill is irrelevant to the main point: we have altered the role of government from what we once saw it to be and, in doing so, have altered the society from which that government springs. Now, any alteration in any direction will force a concomitant alteration in the social fabric. The significance of this cannot be cloaked in the impersonal language of "secondary and tertiary effects"; while useful analytically, in thinking about them in this way we hide ourselves from the reality we have created.

While Lilla is rightly distressed by the amorality of much of modern policy analysis and applied ethics, given this picture of the world, responsible administration must entail more than simply a resurrection of a bygone conception of moral action. The changed (yet still "democratic") ethos recognizes the administrator's accountability to legitimate political authority. It also appreciates the radically pluralistic context and wicked nature of contemporary administrative problems that often serve to obscure the very nature of political accountability. This means there is not, and cannot be, any predetermined "correct" administrative action; rather, it suggests a moral umbrella under which professional, political, and personal tensions must be worked out. To grasp the significance of this for the teaching of public administration requires recognizing the altered role of the administrator.

To govern requires administration; to administer is therefore to govern—a civic book cliche at first appearance but in truth a very real statement of the issue. The administrator mediates not just between the policy of the government and the governed but also between the interests that make up both sides of that traditional equation. The role of the administrator is to mediate, not merely to judge or to solve problems, but to interpose between two parties as the equal friend of each. Performing this essential role requires that the administrator be responsible in each of three senses: professionally, politically, and personally.

Being professionally responsible is both a state of mind and a morality. It means having sufficient knowledge of the task at hand to appreciate its consequences, yet not allowing that knowledge to dominate the appreciation of the situation. This suggests that being objective is necessary in the sense of the ability to weigh the available evidence both impersonally (without concern for personal gain) and impartially (without concern for where the benefits accrue). In other words (so as not to allow this to appear too high-flown), being professional means making no decision on subjective factors alone and being conscious that is one's professional responsibility.

Being politically responsible in this context means to be cognizant of the dominant societal values as expressed not only through the pronouncements of whichever current regime but also through the law and society's history. It means comprehending that a decision that affects people's lives (both corporate and individual)—and no matter how seemingly technical and value-free—is always in part a political decision because it allocates resources through the mediation of interests.

To be politically responsible is also to be responsibly political. Although the politics/administration dichotomy has long been discredited, both a conceptual and real-world difference between the two remains. Knowing there is and must be a difference that matters prods us to define in explicit, though still general, terms the proper relationship of politics in and to administration. Part of that definition, not surprisingly, was articulated by Wilson when he clearly emphasized that the then-emerging science of administration be adapted to the unique features of the American political system. Within the value consensus of that system, he urged, administrators should be granted broad decision-making discretion in execution of the law.

Subsequent writers have taken a more generous view of what it means for administrators to be responsibly political. In view of the complexity of modern administration, however, it is doubtful that Wilson would vigorously disagree with some of their conclusions. Friedrich's advice, for instance, that administrative discretion should be informed by popular sentiment (as well as by standards of professional conduct) hardly violates the spirit of Wilson's prescription. Nor does Gibson Winter's (1970:352) more contemporary description of the administrator's role as the executor of public policy:

> Policy has to do with man's problems in coping with the future—man's problem as maker of history as well as being made by history. Policy brings to statement what is judged to be possible, desirable, and meaningful for the human enterprise. In this sense, policy is the nexus of fact, value, and ultimate meaning in which scientific, ethical, and theological-philosophical reflections meet.

Certainly there is room for debate about the proper limits of administrative discretion, especially in determining what is "possible, desirable, and meaningful for the human enterprise." It is also certainly clear that such a debate can no longer be couched in absolute terms. The limits are likely to be found—and continually re-found—by examining the tension between political and professional responsibilities.

Being personally responsible is to acknowledge that it is one's actions that are affecting people's lives. Social forces, institutions, parties, and even government itself are chimera; they are ways we have of speaking about, generalizing about, the combined actions of others and they are ways of recording our history. They are real to the extent we stand outside of them and to the extent we allow them to alter and define our lives. But at root they consist of those actions taken by innumerable individuals, each of whom is responsible—that is, can be held accountable by other members of society—for the consequences of the collective action. The utility of framing responsibility in this sense lies not in arousing paroxysms of guilt but rather in reminding each of us who works and teaches in an administrative context that we cannot escape from our actions, we cannot shift the burden of those actions to others (nor to such social constructs as institutions), and we cannot hide our actions under a blanket of rhetoric about orders, requirements or the like.

Lilla is correct in urging that an administrator's moral education requires an appreciation of generally agreed-upon virtues. Moreover, it is also correct that there is general agreement about the content of those virtues, at least in the abstract. However, two classes of important details remain for the moral education of administrators, details that bear on the relevance of virtues to practice.

The first class has to do with how the virtues may be related to the particular and often unique situations that call for judgment and action. Even seemingly unambiguous rules require interpretation and judgment; even more so do moral virtues. The second class of details are those conflicts between virtues that inevitably arise when they are applied to concrete situations. Whatever benefits may be derived from abstract discussions about the priority of particular virtues, such discussions are ultimately sterile without context. Moral education teaches, and if need be preaches, that virtues exist in tension with one another. The danger is not so much that administrators act consciously without or contrary to virtue but that their action will be on balance immoral and socially irresponsible because one virtue is not assessed in relation to others with which the first is competing in particular situations.

Professional, political, and personal responsibility are neither additive nor exclusive notions. Each is meaningful only in relationship to the other two. Each provides a check against those pathologies of the others that would develop were they alone left to define the actions of administrators. Political responsibility, for example, rescues both professionalism from being a narrow instrumentalism and personal responsibility from being either ethical narcissism or moral dogmatism. Professional responsibility, in turn, checks both the tendency of the political to degenerate into opportunism and the personal to lapse into naive impracticality. Finally, personal responsibility helps clarify the difference between political responsibility and unquestioning obedience as well as between professionalism and mindless technicism. This new administrative ethos, then, is one that accommodates and calls for the constant negotiation of the tensions between these three categories of responsible action.

Moral education for public administrators requires the development of an awareness of each and an understanding of their relationship. To emphasize that morality is intrinsic to the human condition helps us rehabilitate the ethical analysis that Lilla rightly deplores. Such ethical analysis is made technical and, in Lilla's sense, immoral precisely because the teaching of it is divorced from any reminder that administrators are personally responsible actors constantly confronted with moral, albeit at times mundane, choices. The regrettable tendency of ethical analysis to be used for post hoc rationalizations results as much from the impersonality with which it is taught as from the absence of an external ethos, democratic or otherwise.

Notes

1. For those interested in pursuing the vigorous debate and discussion that surrounds the entire area of ethics and public administration, one might consider some of the works of Aaron Wildavsky, Christopher Lasch, C. West Churchman or Sir Geoffrey Vickers. Because writers of the past decade have no monopoly on this subject, the sincere student might wish to return to Plato's Republic and the various works of Aristotle.

References

Lilla, Mark T. (1981). "Ethos, 'Ethics,' and Public Service." The Public Interest 63 (spring):3–17.
Winter, Gibson (1970). "Toward a Comprehensive Science of Policy." Journal of Religion 50 (October):352.

Part SEVEN

Professionalism

Ethics in the public service is a reflection of the professionalism of those who work for government. A profession is defined in *Webster's New Universal Unabridged Dictionary* (1983) as "a vocation or occupation requiring advanced training in some liberal art or science, and usually involving mental rather than manual work," while a professional is "engaged in or worthy of the high standards of a profession."

Criteria for a profession in public service appeared as early as the 1936 *Municipal Year Book* (pages 211–212). They include: a well-developed sense of the dignity and worth of public service, a deep feeling of obligation to serve the public honestly and well, and a code of ethical conduct, the violation of which by any member will serve to bar him from the profession. Thus, to talk about ethics is to talk about a professional service.

The four articles reprinted in Part 7 all reflect some dimension of professional public administration. The first appeared in 1983 in *Public Productivity and Management Review.* Written by David S. Brown, "The Managerial Ethic and Productivity Improvement" (Chapter 23 here), views professionalism from the standpoint of practical outcomes. By becoming a manager in the public sector, Brown believes, one becomes obligated to act both morally and productively. He suggests that "ethics" implies "conformity to accepted or approved standards of conduct" and offers, in its place, the concept of "ethos," which is the "distinguishing character, tone or belief of a community or society" that inspires its members to greatness. He ends the article with a powerful notion worth deep reflection by us all. The hallmark of the difference between successful and unsuccessful executives lies in the level of awareness: "The successful executive is critical of his own performance; the unsuccessful, of the performance of others."

Whereas Brown focuses on the ethical obligation to produce, Terry L. Cooper in Chapter 24 argues that "the ethical obligations of the public administrator are to be derived from the obligations of citizenship . . . ." In his 1984 *PAR* article, "Citizenship and Professionalism in Public Administration," Cooper presents the public administrator as a fiduciary, employed by fellow citizens to work on their behalf and to assist with the "covenanting process." He provides both legal and ethical definitions of citizenship and suggests that "technical expertise, rational approaches to problem solving, and specialized knowledge are not to be eschewed, but they must not provide the norms for the professional identity of the public administrator." He calls for a "redefined professionalism" in which we explore what it means to be a "citizen/administrator" and in which we include deliberations about serving one another in the public administration curricula.

Chapter 25, "The Public Service and the Patriotism of Benevolence" by H. George Frederickson and David K. Hart, was published in *PAR* in 1985. Frederickson and Hart continue Cooper's theme, and for all the authors in Part 7, the ideal of American democracy assumes a special relationship between public administrators and citizens. Indeed, Frederickson and Hart find the reduction of citizens to consumers a particularly "baleful effect" of the emphasis on efficiency and product excellence. By contrasting the behavior of Germans and Danes during World War II, Frederickson and Hart show the difference between careerism and the patriotism of benevolence, with a benevolent administrator akin to Cooper's citizen/administrator. They, like Cooper, believe that "public servants must genuinely care for their fellow citizens."

In Chapter 26, John Rohr addresses the theme of professionalism from the standpoint of a "crisis in legitimacy." His 1985 article, "Professionalism, Legitimacy, and the Constitution," published in *Public Administration Quarterly,* is an early development of his work on legitimizing the profession by grounding it in the Constitution and rooting it in regime values. He explains the theoretical foundation of the Constitution pertinent to public administration and relies on the constitutional principle of sovereignty to suggest that public administration is the instrument of the Constitution itself, and, therefore, inherently legitimate.

These classic arguments about what it means to be a professional public administrator have not been resolved. Does professionalism mean commitment to efficiency, technical expertise, and methods for rational analysis of complex problems? Or does professionalism truly mean that public administrators are citizens acting on behalf of other citizens in a covenantal relationship that will ultimately empower the served as well as the server? Today's seduction by technical rationality is as pervasive as it was in the first decade of this century, when scientific management became the model and efficiency became the ideal. Professional public administrators in the twenty-first century must still confront the same issues and ultimately decide what our profession represents.

23

THE MANAGERIAL ETHIC AND PRODUCTIVITY IMPROVEMENT

David S. Brown
George Washington University

There are many reasons why American productivity has failed to continue the growth patterns that characterized the period immediately after World War II and through 1977. Most of these are familiar to those who have explored the problem. . . .

Professionals and Professionalism

Managers, are, of course, professionals. In today's complex and demanding world, it could not be otherwise. They, like others, have earned their positions by education, training, observation, and performance. By the same reasoning, attorneys, accountants, engineers, and economists—those who meet the standards of accepted professions and many others in lines of work which have not yet qualified for this distinction—are managers as well as professionals. Whether or not they hold organizational titles which authorize them to guide or direct the work of others is of little consequence. They are managers all the same.

The passing of a CPA examination, the admission to the bar, the acceptance of membership on a university faculty, the joining of the staff of a corporation, or the appointment to a middle or higher level position in a government agency are merely the *pro forma* requirements of entrance to a sphere of work which demands more than their basic job descriptions prescribe. They carry out organizational tasks. They fulfill responsibilities. They are part of an intricate system in which they influence others and are influenced by them.

By becoming managers, they obligate themselves, as do other managers, to act morally and productively. This is the genesis of professionalism. This is the *ethos* which the professions demand.

Professionalism implies quality of performance. It upholds professional standards. It demands a commitment to excellence. The professional is, *ergo,* committed to being productive. The demands of professionalism, however, go well beyond what the individual does. Large and complex systems cannot function properly without appropriate interpersonal relationships. In the modern organization, one must for a variety of reasons be aware of, and assume some responsibility for, what others do. Whether explicitly stated or not, obligations do exist and our times require that they be met.

The managerial ethic (or *ethos*) which this suggests is more derived than prescribed. It is a cumulation of knowledge, tradition, morality, faith, and good sense. There is little to be gained by looking to codes of ethics for one will rarely find it there. Ethics applies to matters of conduct which suggest the rights and wrongs of behavior. The word "ethical" has come to mean conformity to accepted or approved standards of conduct.

Ethos, on the other hand, holds far deeper meanings. It is the distinguishing character, tone or belief of a community or society. It is the *ethos* which has inspired great religious movements or caused civilizations to be innovative or productive. It is *ethos* which has marked the performance of individuals whose character and work we admire. It is the soul of the individual as well as the group. It is the modern version of the work ethic, the fire in one's belly.

Codes of ethics, of course, do have their importance but they are more likely to treat surface behaviors than the deeper matters of conscience. As one comes to understand how they are developed, one can better understand why this is so. They identify behavioral patterns which are either of dubious morality, if not anti-social in nature, and prescribe against them. They warn practitioners who are subject to peer and client pressures of the limits of professional *mores*. As the product of often-conflicting views, they represent a kind of common denominator of conduct, neither the best nor the worst, but what one writer has called "safe mediocrity."[1]

An examination of professional codes of ethics will bear this out. One should not be misled by the attention they get. They are described, variously, as statements of principles, ethical policy statements and professional standards as well as codes. They come in a variety of forms. Some are terse and general, others detailed and specific. There is an impersonality and a self-righteousness—but also a sterility—about them.[2]

That of the American Medical Association is less than a page in length and consists of only seven items.[3] The Professional Standards of the American Institute of Certified Public Accountants, on the other hand, covers 168 pages and includes interpretations of rulings and an index by topics.[4] (Perhaps doctors feel less need of detailed guidance than accountants.) The American Bar Association made the front pages earlier this year with a debate over attorneys' responsibilities to the public as against the confidentiality of their relationships to clients. The matter was resolved, as might have been expected, in compromise.[5] Most lawyers, alas, will undoubtedly continue to do what they are already doing. Practice is always persuasive.

Most large American corporations have developed ethical policy statements to which those who accept employment with them are expected to subscribe.[6] The American Society of Association Executives estimates that almost three-quarters of the major companies of this country now have written codes of ethics and recommends that the several thousand associations do the same.[7] In style and content, these are not greatly different from those of the professions.

Recently, the American Society for Public Administration produced a new statement of principles. A page in length, it is more a monument to the American ability to reach agreement in an area where substantial differences of opinion exist than it is to the development of deep or abiding rules of conduct. It indulges generalities.

It recognizes the sovereignty of the people for whom public administrators work and emphasizes the importance of service to the public. It speaks also of the "safeguarding of the public trust." It states that "efficient and effective management is basic to public administration" and in this—a commitment in a general way to productivity—is ahead of most such codes. It does not, however, elaborate on what this might be, nor does it attempt to indicate what has made the public service so compelling a calling to millions of Americans who have joined it. It demands of the public servant "sensitivity to the qualities of justice, courage, honesty, equity, competence, and compassion."

In the fashion of similar ethical codes, it speaks out against misuse of influence, waste, fraud or their abuses: "Conflicts of interests, bribes, gifts, or favors which subordinate public positions to private gains are unacceptable." (Earlier drafts contained a greater number of specifics.) One looks in vain, however, to find among the nine principles enunciated there a single one which challenges the individual to do more than what any right-thinker should be expected to do without being reminded.[8]

And yet, if professionalism is to mean anything at all, it must ask for much more than this. Some have met the challenge and they are the greater, and the public service the richer, for it.

The *ethos* which real professionalism requires is to be found (where it is not observed in actual practice) in the writings of those who have understood its importance. Chester I. Barnard, for example, in his masterpiece, *The Functions of the Executive,* makes much of it.[9] He writes:

> *The point is that responsibility is the property of an individual by which whatever morality exists in him becomes effective in conduct.* (Italics his.)

Gardner makes this even more specific:

> Our society cannot achieve greatness unless individuals at many levels of ability accept the need for high standards of performance and strive to achieve those standards within the limits possible for them. . . . We must foster a conception of excellence which may be applied to every degree of ability and to every socially acceptable activity.[10]

Bain writes: "A common characteristic of truly effective leaders is a continual striving for excellence."[11] Leo Cherne, an economist and later a government official, says: "When you get a case of excellence, hang onto it, water and feed it with the best you have, protect it and don't let it die."[12] Drucker writes: "The purpose of an organization is to make common men do uncommon things."[13] Levinson states: "The major difference between the most and least successful executives lies precisely in the latters' lack of awareness. The hallmark of this difference is that the successful executive is critical of his own performance; the unsuccessful, of the performance of others."[14]

There should be no doubt of what professionalism requires by way of the productivity of its members. . . .

Notes

1. Drucker, *Management: Tasks, Responsibilities, Practices* (New York: Harper and Row, 1973), 456.

2. The reader is advised to consult any number of codes of professional ethics. Of particular interest are those of the American Society for Public Administration, the International City Management Association, the American Bar Association, the American Medical Association, and the American Institute for Certified Public Accountants.

3. AMA's Principles of Medical Ethics (New), adopted by the American Medical Association House of Delegates (Washington, DC: July 24, 1980).

4. American Institute of Certified Public Accountants, *Ethics, Bylaws* (Washington, DC: AICPA, June 1, 1982).

5. Jethro K. Lieberman, "When Should Lawyers Squeal on Their Clients?" Outlook Section, *Washington Post* (Jan. 30, 1983), C–1, C–4.

6. For more on this subject, see *A 1980 Study of Corporate Ethical Policy Statements* (Dallas, TX: Foundation of the Southwestern Graduate School of Banking, 1980).

7. "The Status of Codes of Ethics in Associations and Corporations," *Ethic* (American Society of Association Executives), 11–13.

8. "Principles of the American Society for Public Administration," *Applying Professional Standards and Ethics in the Eighties,* edited by Herman Mertins, Jr. and Patrick J. Hennigan (ASPA: 1982).

9. Chester I. Barnard, *The Functions of the Executive* (Cambridge, MA: Harvard University Press, 1938), 267.

10. Gardner, *Excellence,* 267.

11. Bain, *Productivity Prescription,* 83.

12. As quoted by Harry Levinson in *The Exceptional Executive: A Psychological Conception* (Cambridge, MA: Harvard University Press, 1968), 201.

13. Drucker, *Management,* 455.

14. Levinson, 254.

24

CITIZENSHIP AND PROFESSIONALISM IN PUBLIC ADMINISTRATION

Terry L. Cooper
University of Southern California

In searching for the source of legitimacy for the public administrator in a democratic society I conclude that it is to be found in the role of citizen.[1] Public administrators are "professional citizens," or "citizen-administrators"; they are fiduciaries who are employed by the citizenry to work on their behalf. In the words of Walzer, public administrators are to be understood as "citizens in lieu of the rest of us."[2]

With this role definition in mind, I argue that the ethical obligations of the public administrator are to be derived from the obligations of citizenship in a democratic political community. These obligations include responsibility for establishing and maintaining horizontal relationships of authority with one's fellow citizens, seeking "power with" rather than "power over" the citizenry.[3] This attitude on the part of public administrators calls for engaging in activities which amount to an ongoing renewal and reaffirmation of the "social contract."[4] The public administrator is one who, in the language of our Puritan forebears, is responsible for assisting the rest of us in the "covenanting" process.[5] This use of the social contract metaphor and this allusion to the Puritan concept of covenanting are intended to refer to a regular readjustment or reconstruction of the mutual expectations of citizens in a democratic polity.

This "covenanting" or "social contracting" is an ongoing process which is carried out at all levels of government through the exercise of citizenship

344

as the public office of the individual member of a democratic society. This office obligates one to look beyond his or her own particular personal interests in search of the larger common interest.[6]

The public administrator's role as citizen takes priority over less fundamental demands, such as organizational imperatives, pressure from politicians, or blind commitments to worthwhile values, such as efficiency, stability, orderliness, and timeliness.[7] Specific administrative tasks and duties are properly viewed as penultimate responsibilities. They must be carried out, but their modes of conduct should be ones which encourage participation in the political community and help to maintain the horizontal bonds of political authority. Ultimately, a public administrator's actions should reflect respect for the public office of citizenship for which he or she bears an obligation, which is prior to any other associated with public employment.

It is clear that this view of the public administrative role has some rather significant implications for an understanding of professionalism in public administration. Questions emerge, such as: Is this perspective compatible with professionalism? If so, what would professionalism mean? How would public administration education be affected?

These are important questions to which I will attempt some response. Before addressing them, however, it seems appropriate to outline briefly the citizenship role and its functions, and then to consider what is meant by professionalism in public administration. At that point, it should be possible to deal with the questions from some clearly understood points of reference.

Definitions of Citizenship

Since the terms "citizen" and "citizenship" are employed in a variety of ways with a range of meanings, from precise and limited to vague and broad, it is essential to establish some definitional boundaries. We might begin with very broad definitions of "citizenship" and "citizen" such as the following:

> Citizenship is the status and role which defines the authority and obligations of individual members of a community. This status and role may be formally codified in terms of qualifications, rights, and obligations by constitutions, charters, and laws, or informally determined by values, tradition, and consensus. A citizen is one who qualifies for the status of citizenship as prescribed formally, or informally, by a particular community, and is encumbered with the obligations assigned to this role by that community.

This definition is so broad in scope that it requires more detailed distinctions within its boundaries if it is to be useful for our purposes. Recent essays by Richard Flathman and T. J. Lowi provide two dimensions of citizenship which establish more specific definitional reference points. Each of these dimensions can be viewed in terms of its polar extremes, and/or in terms of continua between those poles.

The first of these dimensions has to do with the distribution of authority. Flathman deals with authority in terms of high and low views of citizenship.[8] High definitions of citizenship are those which assume wide distribution of authority and describe citizens as peers who share equally in the exercise of authority. Low citizenship assumes a hierarchical distribution of authority with only a limited claim provided for the individual citizen. Flathman associates the high view with Aristotle and Rousseau, together with current authors such as Walzer, Arendt, Thompson, and Barber who argue from a similar perspective. The low view is identified with Hobbes and those such as Michael Oakeshott who currently share his basic position on authority. Flathman also associates the 20th century "democratic elitists" with this perspective.[9]

Lowi deals with the extent to which the citizenship role is defined by law, on the one hand, or by less formal influences, such as values, norms, traditions, culture, and religion on the other.[10] The terms which he uses to identify the poles of this dimension are "legal citizenship" and "ethical citizenship." "Legal citizenship" is prescribed and defined in terms of qualifications, rights, and obligations by constitutions and statutes. It is related to particular governmental jurisdictions. Citizenship, in this sense, is a purely political status and role.

"Ethical citizenship" involves a much broader definition of the role, which includes the social and economic aspects of life as well as the political. Citizenship, from this perspective, has to do with membership in a community—any community. These communities include, but are not limited to, political communities. Ethical citizenship is a role in neighborhoods and voluntary associations, as well as governmental jurisdictions such as cities and nations. The qualifications, rights, and obligations of citizenship, understood in this way, are defined and prescribed by the values, norms, traditions, and culture of any given community or by consensus among members of the community in specific instances.

Table 24.1 depicts the results of relating the four poles of the two dimensions of citizenship to each other. Four types of citizenship can then be identified: high legal, low legal, high ethical, and low ethical. This simple typology provides us with a useful conceptual chart for clarifying how "citizenship" is used by various authors and what is implied by their particular usage. Flathman, for example, deals primarily with the legal dimension of citizenship. His concern is with the problems of adopting either a high legal or a low legal view of citizenship. He leans toward the high perspective with a shared exercise of political authority and insists that the citizenship role be narrowly confined to the political realm.

TABLE 24.1   Definition of Citizenship

	Legal	Ethical
High	*Membership in a government jurisdiction *Membership status, rights, and obligations legally defined *Obligations limited to governmental arena *Authority shared among members by law *Extensive participation provided by law	*Membership in any community, including, but not limited to, governmental jurisdictions *Membership status, rights, and obligations defined by values, norms, tradition, and culture *Obligations include political, social, and economic arenas *Authority shared among members by custom, tradition, and consensus *Extensive participation provided by custom, tradition, and consensus
Low	*Membership in a governmental jurisdiction *Membership in status, rights, and obligations legally defined *Obligations limited to governmental arena *Authority hierarchically distributed by law *Minimal participation provided by law	*Membership in any community, including, but not limited to, governmental jurisdiction *Membership status, rights, and obligations defined by values, norms, tradition, and culture *Obligations include political, social, and economic arenas *Authority hierarchically distributed by custom, tradition, and consensus *Minimal participation provided by custom, tradition, and consensus

However, the ethical dimension of citizenship becomes the fundamental focus for some other scholarly treatments of the concepts. For example, William Mosher's preface and opening chapter in *Introduction to Responsible Citizenship* assumes a high ethical understanding of citizenship. Mosher explains that the citizenship course at the Maxwell School during the 1930s and 1940s, from which his book evolved, began by defining citizenship "largely with respect to politics and government." However, "in the course of time," according to Mosher, "the citizen was considered to be man in society."[11] In his introductory chapter, Mosher identifies two characteristics of a good citizen which fit this high ethical perspective of citizenship: (1) "Sensitiveness to the Social Rights and Needs of Others" and (2) "Capacity of Independent Thinking and Critical Evaluation." In a summary statement, he argues that "Acceptance of the predominance of human values in all situations and under all circumstances is a primary characteristic of the thoughtful citizen."[12]

And, of course, in the literature there are treatments of citizenship which focus on the interaction or blending of the types. These more complex variations on the four simple types in Table 24.1 indicate, of course, that in reality there are continua among the types with a range of gradations. Although the full development of these continua is not of prime importance for this particular essay, a few illustrative examples may be helpful in suggesting some of the permutations that are possible.

One such perspective is Norton Long's discussion of the relationship between "legal constitutions" and "ethical constitutions."[13] Building upon the Aristotelian assumption that a consensus about the nature of the good life is more fundamental than the legal structures of a polity, Long argues that the legal constitutions of the United States must be "interpreted by the ethical constitution that informs it." Effective citizenship, by his line of argument, is the result of this process of interaction between the ethical and the legal dimensions of citizenship.

Paul Sniderman's research on citizens and the attitudes they hold toward government led him to some conclusions about the nature of citizenship in democratic society which are a complex blending of the types. He assigns primary importance to factors which I have identified with Lowi's ethical dimension, but his exclusive concern is with the governmental arena. He does not view citizenship in the broad fashion associated with the ethical types in Table 24.1, but neither are the legal definitions of citizenship the exclusive considerations in his study.

In treating this hybrid type, which suggests a continuum between the legal and ethical types, Sniderman argues that the existence of a "civil temper," coupled with certain attitudes and values concerning the nature of political authority and allegiance owed to government, are the critical factors in the working out of the citizenship role in the United States. He is concerned with the citizenship role established by laws, but he views these "ethical" components of the role, rather than any legal provisos, as critical in shaping the forms of citizenship in this country.

The two major role types which emerged from Sniderman's field research are the "supportive citizen" and the "committed citizen."[14] The latter tends to be passive, acquiescent, and compliant in the face of hierarchical governmental authority, while the former is far more likely to resist, criticize, question, and insist on sharing the authority of government. In this way, Sniderman's work also suggests the continuum which exists between the high and low types of citizenship in Table 24.1.

Robert Salisbury views citizenship in the broadest sense, consistent with the ethical types in Table 24.1, but does not ignore the legal bases of citizenship.[15] Salisbury's view is similar to Long's in that he views both the ethical and the legal components as essential, but he gives greater weight to the former.

Salisbury argues that citizenship in any community requires at least some minimum degree of formal rules, laws, or agreements to establish peer status among the members. In some communities, such as the U.S. Congress, there are also elaborate systems of rules for distributing specific responsibilities, granting conditional authority, and establishing procedures. However, according to Salisbury, these formal, legal definitions are never sufficient, even when fully elaborated. They merely provide a foundation or framework for "the moral community" with its informal norms and values, such as "civic commitment" and "loyalty." Salisbury's emphasis on equality of status among citizens, and the necessity for active citizenship identify him with the high view. These commitments, coupled with the significance which he attributes to the ethical dimensions, locate him somewhere in the high ethical category. However, Salisbury's view of the formal legal aspects of citizenship as the essential structures within which ethical citizenship emerges, once again, suggests a continuum between the legal and ethical types. It is not possible to determine on the basis of Salisbury's article whether it is a continuum between high ethical and high legal or high ethical and low legal.

This application of the conceptual matrix in Table 24.1 to the works of Flathman, Mosher, Long, Sniderman, and Salisbury has been presented to illustrate its usefulness in clarifying what particular authors intend by the term citizenship. However, beyond that function as an analytical device for dealing with the literature, this matrix should be of value in orienting one's own concerns and commitments. It should help one to specify the dimensions of citizenship one wants to address, the streams of literature which are most relevant, and the critical issues which need to be engaged.

Legal and Ethical Citizenship in the United States

With these broad definitional types before us, I wish to indicate that the primary concern of this essay is with the ethical dimensions of citizenship and that my own commitment lies somewhere in the high ethical category. However, my position also evidences the existence of a more complex continuum than is portrayed in Table 24.1. It is a continuum which extends between the high ethical and low legal types of citizenship. That is, I recognize that the legal constitutional definition of citizenship is one which distributes authority in a limited hierarchical fashion. That was the intent of the framers of the Constitution and their reasons for doing so are set out in the *Federalist Papers*.[16] Their preference for a limited exercise of authority by the citizenry resulted in the structure of our representative government with its limited franchise, indirect election of the Senate and president, and the dependence of local governments upon the states.

Some of these constitutional provisions have been subsequently amended, and statutory action has created more extensive opportunities for citizens to more directly participate in government. Thus, our legal definitions of the status of citizens are not as low as originally stated, but still fall generally into that category.

This relatively low legal framework for citizenship has also provided us with a weak formal tradition of citizenship in the United States, as I argued in the previous paper mentioned at the beginning of this essay.[17] The founders did not distribute authority on an egalitarian fashion, nor did they articulate the functions and obligations of citizenship in much detail. The emphasis of the Constitution is more upon rights than obligations. The *rights* to vote and hold assemblies freely are established, but nothing is said about any *obligations* to participate in the electoral process or to engage in public discussion of issues. While one might argue that obedience to the law is certainly an obligation, that obligation is imposed upon everyone—citizens, resident aliens, and tourists alike. Obedience to the law is not distinctly associated with citizenship.

In spite of this weak formal approach to citizenship there has been a rather lively American tradition of ethical citizenship. From the covenantal tradition of the early Puritan communities with their styles of participatory self-governance, the New England town meetings, the experience of forming voluntary associations, which captured the attention of de Tocqueville,[18] and the cooperative establishment of frontier settlements, there has emerged a set of values, customs, beliefs, principles, and theories which provide the substance for ethical citizenship. In the founding years it was informed by the participatory democratic thought of Jefferson and the egalitarian philosophy which he put forth in the Declaration of Independence. And it has been further inspired by certain strains of the Judeo-Christian tradition which have been expressed politically and economically from time to time in movements such as the "Social Gospel" led by Walter Rauschenbusch.[19] The participatory dimension of ethical citizenship has found expression in the abolitionist movement, the populist movement, the labor union movement, the feminist movement, the civil rights movement, the environmental movement, the neighborhood movement, and the anti-tax movement.

All of these perspectives, ideas, experiences, and activities represent a continuing stream in American history which has functioned as a counterpoint to the formal definition of citizenship. They have tended to encourage more active participation in political, social, and economic affairs. They have motivated citizens to assume greater obligations for collective life, and they have provided experience in the sharing of responsibility. Without this multifaceted tradition of ethical citizenship, the nation would have lacked political and social dynamism. It has been the source of the motivation to collaborate, build, and maintain the common good.

The ethical dimensions of citizenship tradition have regularly given rise to changes in the legal definitions of citizenship. The franchise has been extended to nonwhites and women, slavery has been abolished, civil rights have been expanded, the right to equal employment opportunities has been established, and citizen participation in public policy making has been mandated. These changes, based on law, would never have taken place without the sense of obligation and the insistence upon active participation in governance which has been embodied in the tradition of ethical citizenship. It has been the driving force behind the democratization of the relatively elitist form of government provided in the Constitution and the elitist society of the founding era.

On the other hand, I must acknowledge that while the participatory aspect of our tradition of ethical citizenship has enhanced our legal definition of citizenship it has produced mixed results. The emergence and growth of the very interest groups which demand and generally receive greater participation in the political process has not always been accompanied by a broad sense of obligation for the common good. In an expanding economy, and with the blessing of pluralist theory, unfettered competition for power and resources has been pursued by interest groups and tolerated by the political community. This quest for the satisfaction of particular interests must be balanced with the more cooperative and communal strains of our heritages of ethical citizenship. The exercise of citizenship as the public office of the individual must carry with it an obligation to consider individual and group interests in the context of larger social and community interests.

It is not the legal definitions of citizenship that are of concern here because they are not of major consequence for conduct. It is the ethical dimension of citizenship that warrants our primary attention at this time in public administration. It is the values, norms, and traditions that encourage the sharing of authority and active participation in collective life that are essential. They transcend governmental jurisdictions and extend across political, social, and economic realms. It is essential that public administrators identify with this perspective if democratization is to continue. Public administrators, as key agents in the administrative state, play a critical role. They may actively and intentionally encourage democratic government, or they may subvert it, consciously or otherwise. Their professional identity and self-understanding will be crucial in moving them in one direction or the other.

If citizenship is the appropriate normative basis for the public administrative role,[20] it is the view of citizenship which is characterized above as the high ethical type which should inform and shape the professional identity and role of public administrators.

Professionalism in Public Administration

What are the implications of these proposals for the professionalism of public administrators? That depends on what is meant by the term "professionalism." It is not very fruitful to begin with the construction of an ideal type of professionalism to which we compare ourselves. Rather, it is better to examine first the phenomena which have been associated with professionalism in public administration, and then to consider the values inherent in those phenomena. We then need to ask whether those values are consistent with those associated with citizenship in a democratic society. If not, we need to ask what shape professionalism should assume in order to be consistent with those values.

Beginning in that fashion, if we mean by professionalism something akin to the drive for neutrality, order, efficiency, control, standardization, and quantification which characterized the Progressive era of public administration and much of our history since, then there are serious problems, indeed. While organizations like the Bureau of Municipal Research in New York contributed a great deal to the rationalization of government, their efforts, and others of a similar nature, have also tended to subvert active citizenship.

Although Progressive reforms were typically advanced under the banner of a citizenship movement, with journals such as *The Efficient Citizen*,[21] the long-term result was not one of enhancing the control and participation of the citizenry.[22] It was rather the strengthening of an emerging class of technically-oriented administrators who were committed to the development of a scientific approach to public administration, as suggested by Wilson[23] and others. What those reformers failed to foresee was the impossibility of maintaining the subordination of "expert," "professional" administrators to the politicians in a modern industrial state. The power of technical expertise and specialized knowledge, the complexity of the problems to be faced, and the scale of government have tended to crowd out both the citizenry and their would-be representatives. Single-minded attempts at furthering this kind of professionalism among public administrators cannot but continue to erode the ethical dimensions of citizenship.

Technical expertise, rational approaches to problem solving, and specialized knowledge are not to be eschewed, but they must not provide the norms for the professional identity of the public administrator. Otherwise, we reinforce the role of the politically passive citizen who views government as a provider of public services, on the one hand, and the role of the professional administrator who views the citizen as a consumer, on the other.

It was this "consumer" image of the citizenry, with its deprivation of political responsibility for government, which emerged as one of the central concerns of the bicentennial conference of the Center for the Study of Federalism. In commenting on the deliberations at that conference, Daniel Elazar observed:

> Particularly in a republic and most particularly in a democratic republic, those
> who share in the polity cannot be less than citizens if the polity itself is to sur-

vive in its chosen form. Consumers, at most, pick and choose among goods offered them by others, in whose offering they have no real share. How different such a course is from that of citizens who must share in determining the activities of the government as well as in utilizing its products.[24]

Again, it is not that the expertise of public administrators as providers of public goods and services should be shunned or dismissed. Rather, it is that expertise and the capacity for achieving efficient operations of the bureaucracy must not provide the fundamental norms for the public administrator's relationship to the citizenry. As Norton Long has argued, we must not "substitute a market with consumers for a polity with citizens."[25] This is precisely the risk in identifying professionalism in public administration with technical expertise and efficiency.[26]

Rosenbloom cautions against adopting the traditional goals of professionalized public administration in the United States for similar reasons. He identifies the tradition of professionalism in the late 19th and 20th centuries with values which were derived from Wilson's famous essay, the scientific management school, and the movement for scientific principles of public administration.[27] He argues that these values were efficiency, economy, and effectiveness—"the trinity for the professional bureaucrat." Rosenbloom further maintains that at some point "orthodox public administration" adopted "the greatest good of the greatest number" as its definition of the public interest because this principle was most consistent with its professional values.

However laudable these values and this principle may be when applied conditionally, according to Rosenbloom, when employed unconditionally, they present a threat to the rights of the citizenry. Rosenbloom correctly insists that this perspective is at odds with the values and principles of the U.S. Constitution which "places no premium on efficiency, economy, or even effectiveness in a programmatic sense." Rather the Constitution places limits on majoritarianism and sets a high value on liberty, individual freedom, and "moderately representative government." He concludes that "constitutional values simply do not mesh well with the values of professionalized public administration."

What is the source of this conflict or tension? It is the lack of a normative base for the public administrative role which would properly condition the influence of that trinity of values which Rosenbloom attributes to traditional professionalism in public administration. These are penultimate values for democratic government which must always be measured against the more ultimate values associated with citizenship. Efficiency must never be allowed to displace the right and the obligation of the citizenry to debate the issues and influence the formation of public policy. Effectiveness of particular programs and policies should always be viewed in terms of their positive and negative impacts on the ability of citizens to secure and maintain self-governance. Economy should never be the justification for actions which threaten the common good. The application of "the greatest good of the greatest number" should never be allowed to jeopardize the constitutional guarantees of a minority.

An understanding of professionalism in public administration which is appropriate for a democratic society should be one which is grounded in what is described earlier in this paper as a high ethical view of citizenship. We should identify ourselves first with the citizenry in their sharing of authority and their right and obligation to participate in the affairs of the political community. We should begin to identify the meaning of professionalism in public administration from this normative base. We should not do it for the self-serving instrumental reasons which are so typical of "professional" activities in many fields. I recognize the problems of poor professional image and indiscriminate attacks upon the public services by unscrupulous politicians.[28] However, these are insufficient justifications to move ahead on the subject of professionalism. These are expedient reasons which will be so perceived by the people. These are problems which are only symptomatic of the extent to which we have a deeper problem of the legitimacy of the public administrative role.

Why then should we be concerned with professionalism, and why should we begin from the perspective of citizenship? My answer to the first question is that we should be concerned with that problem of legitimacy. And that means we should be clear about what we "profess," or "avow publicly."[29] We need to be accountable for the core values that guide the exercise of our role. We will achieve that not by measuring ourselves against the plethora of generic definitions of professionalism nor by working our way down the "laundry lists" of professional attributes, but by clarifying the source of our authority, toward what end we exercise that authority, and in what status we do so.

We should begin our redefinition of professionalism from an understanding of citizenship because that is where the clarification of our role in a democratic society leads. The source of our authority is the citizenry. We are employed to exercise that authority on their behalf. We do so as one of them; we can never divest ourselves of our own status as members of the political community with obligations for its well-being. A search for a redefined professionalism in public administration necessarily requires an exploration of what it means to be a citizen/administrator.

Public Administration Education

If this image of the public administrator as a professional citizen is to be pursued, public administration education will have to be a critical component of any strategy for moving in that direction. What we offer as a formal definition of professionalism should be supported by our curricula.

The courses we offer, the requirements we establish, and the allocation of scarce time among competing topics reflect the *de facto* normative definition of professionalism just as surely as a budget reveals the actual mission of an organization.

Under the assumptions that the leading academic programs in the nation represent the dominant educational emphases of the field, I have attempted to review their curriculum outlines in order to assess the current state of affairs in a general fashion. Eight of the top 10 schools in the Morgan and Meier reputational survey of master's degree programs in public administration were selected for this purpose.[30] Their bulletins and catalogs of courses were then reviewed and compared with two lists, one consisting of topics related to technical expertise and the other composed of topics dealing with citizenship in a democracy.[31] The result of this review was so unsurprising that it is not really necessary to belabor the obvious. The great weight of all of the curricula of these programs appears to lie in topics associated with technical expertise. The real question is whether any course-length treatment of citizenship related topics is provided at all.

If public administration is moving toward greater concern for professional gatekeeping (credentials, licensing, accreditation, standards), it is essential that we deal explicitly and overtly with those priorities before we create machinery to implement and enforce them.

David Rosenbloom has maintained that "professionalism requires an understanding of constitutionalism." He insists that "public bureaucrats who interact with people must learn to understand, respect, and protect the constitutional rights of those individuals."[32] This would be only a beginning, albeit a significant one. The value base for professionalism in public administration should include constitutional theory and history, along with other topics listed which are essential in order to "understand, respect, and protect" the rights of the citizenry, but also to be responsive to their preferences and able to work constructively with their conflicting demands.

Technical expertise, competence in specialized fields, and the ability to employ the best available scientific methods are unquestionably also essential for modern public administration. However, they will better serve the purposes of democratic government if employed by men and women who view themselves first as citizens in a political community, who are obligated to wield their expertise on behalf of their fellow citizens and under their sovereignty.

Notes

1. Terry L. Cooper, "Citizenship in an Age of Scarcity: A Normative Essay on Ethics for Public Administrators," in *Politics and Administration: Woodrow Wil-*

son and Contemporary Public Administration, James Bowman and Jack Rabin, eds. (New York: Marcel Dekker, forthcoming).

2. Michael Walzer, *Obligations: Essays on Disobedience, War and Citizenship* (Cambridge, Mass.: Harvard University Press, 1970), p. 216.

3. Mary Parker Follett, *Dynamic Administration: The Collected Papers of Mary Parker Follett,* Henry C. Metcalf and L. Urwick, eds. (New York: Harper and Brothers, 1940), pp. 101–106.

4. The term "social contract" is used metaphorically here and is not intended to suggest a dependence upon social contract theories.

5. Lawrence A. Scaff, "Citizenship in America: Theories of the Founding," in *The Non-Lockean Roots of American Democratic Thought,* J. Chaudhuri, ed. (Tucson: University of Arizona Press, 1977); Michael Walzer, *The Revolution of the Saints: A Study in Origins of Radical Politics* (New York: Atheneum, 1970); John Wise, "A Vindication of the Government of New England Churches," in *Colonial American Writing,* Roy Harvey Pearce, ed. (New York: Rinehart, 1950).

6. Samuel Walker McCall, *The Liberty of Citizenship* (New Haven: Yale University Press, 1915), pp. 17, 19; J.G.A. Pocock, *Politics, Language, and Time* (New York: Atheneum, 1971), pp. 86–87; Robert Pranger, *The Eclipse of Citizenship: Power and Participation in Contemporary Politics* (New York: Holt, Rinehart and Winston, 1968), p. 92; Walzer, *Obligations, op. cit.*

7. Herbert J. Spiro, *Responsibility in Government: Theory and Practice* (New York: Van Nostrand, 1969), p. 101.

8. Richard Flathman, "Citizenship and Authority: A Chastened View of Citizenship," *News for Teachers of Political Science* (Summer 1981).

9. Flathman, *ibid.,* cites Schumpeter, Berelson, and Lipset among others.

10. Theodore J. Lowi, "The Two Cities of Norton Long," in *Cities Without Citizens,* Benjamin R. Schuster, ed. (Philadelphia: Center for the Study of Federalism, 1981).

11. William E. Mosher, ed., *Introduction to Responsible Citizenship* (New York: Henry Holt and Company, 1941), p. v.

12. *Ibid.,* pp. 4–7.

13. Norton E. Long, "Cities Without Citizens," in *Cities Without Citizens,* pp. 7–8.

14. Paul Sniderman, *A Question of Loyalty* (Berkeley: University of California Press, 1981), pp. 1–46.

15. Robert H. Salisbury, "On Cities and Citizens," in *Cities Without Citizens,* pp. 22–29.

16. See especially No. 10.

17. Cooper, "Citizenship in an Age of Scarcity."

18. Alexis de Tocqueville, *Democracy in America* (New York: New American Library, 1956).

19. Walter Rauschenbusch, *A Theology for the Social Gospel* (New York: Abingdon Press, 1945).

20. Cooper, "Citizenship in an Age of Scarcity," see summary at beginning of this essay.

21. Lawrence Joseph O'Toole, *The Concept of Participation in the Literature of American Public Administration: A Study of the Orthodoxy of Reform,* unpublished doctoral dissertation, Syracuse University, 1975, pp. 207–218.

22. Samuel P. Hays, "The Politics of Reform in Municipal Government in the Progressive Era," *Pacific Northwest Quarterly* (October 1964).

23. Woodrow Wilson, "The Study of Administration," *Political Science Quarterly* (June 1887).

24. Daniel J. Elazar, "Is Federalism Compatible with Prefectorial Administration?" *Publius* (Spring 1976), p. 3.

25. Norton Long, "The Three Citizenships," *Publius* (Spring 1976), p. 21.

26. This concern for the consumer image of the citizenry emerged again in *Publius* (Spring 1981). See especially pp. 21, 49, 52–53.

27. David H. Rosenbloom, "Constitutionalism and Public Bureaucrats," *The Bureaucrat* (Fall 1982), p. 54.

28. Jack Rabin, "The Profession of Public Administration," *The Bureaucrat* (Winter 1981–82), p. 11.

29. *Webster's New World Dictionary,* Second College Edition, 1970.

30. David R. Morgan and Kenneth J. Meier, "Reputations and Productivity Among U.S. Public Administration and Public Affairs Programs," *Public Administration Review* (November/December 1981), p. 669.

31. Although they were requested, materials were not received from Georgia and Princeton.

32. Rosenbloom, "Constitutionalism and Public Bureaucrats," p. 55.

25

THE PUBLIC SERVICE AND THE PATRIOTISM OF BENEVOLENCE

H. George Frederickson
Eastern Washington University

David K. Hart
Brigham Young University

> *When one sees one's fellows in danger, one's duty is to go to their aid; strong men do much, the weak little, but being weak is no reason for folding one's arms and refusing one's cooperation.*[1]
>
> —Alexis de Tocqueville

I. The Public Service and the "Special Relationship"

There is warranted concern in public administration circles about the widespread, and largely unjustified, disenchantment with public bureaucracies which has contributed to the decimation of public programs and agencies. As a result, it is increasingly difficult for bureaucrats to meet their professional obligations in a responsible manner. Furthermore, there appears to be a loss of purpose among public service professionals. Summarizing the work of the ASPA Centennial Agenda Committee in 1983, James Carroll and Alfred Zuck wrote that "... American public administration is *acutely alien-*

ated from society, bedeviled by complexity, and *guided by limited knowledge and understanding."*[2] These persistent situations must be rectified.

No small part of the problem is the result of public administration's excessive and uncritical reliance upon the value assumptions of business administration.[3] With some notable exceptions, too much of the literature about the public service[4] makes no significant distinction between the moral entailments of service in the public and the private sectors. The most destructive effect of this "privatization" has been the devaluation of public service to just another arena in which one can achieve essentially private ambitions. "Careerism" has been substituted for idealism.

Careerism, rooted in an egoistic, utilitarian philosophy, is considered to be the primary inducement in almost all American management theory.[5] Thus, the primary inducement for organizationally effective behavior is the advancement—through promotion or security, or both—of one's career. All organizational actions are considered as instrumental to one's career advancement: efficiency, product excellence, and even loyalty are sought *because* they contribute to one's career and not because they are valuable in themselves.

This is particularly destructive in public administration, for it attacks the assumption that a "special relationship" should exist between public servants and citizens in a democracy.[6] A singularly baleful effect has been the reduction of citizens down to "consumers"—simply customers of an agency, existing in "a mercenary exchange of good offices according to an agreed valuation."[7] The public expects something more from the bureaucracy, and rightly so. In truth, public servants expect something more.

The ideal of American democracy assumes that a special relationship should exist between public servants and citizens. Stated briefly, it is the belief that *all* public administration must rest upon, and be guided by, the moral truths embodied in the enabling documents of our national foundation. As Woodrow Wilson wrote: "Liberty cannot live apart from constitutional principle; and no administration, however perfect and liberal its methods, can give men more than a poor counterfeit of liberty if it rests upon illiberal principles of government."[8]

But something more is necessary. Arendt alluded to it in her condemnation of Adolf Eichmann:

> Fundamental to Arendt's political theory is the distinction between the public and the private. . . . *The public realm is the locus of community distinguished by the disposition to care for fellow citizens.* In contrast, the private realm is the domain of instinctual individualism marked by the disposition to advance self-interest. . . . Public life characterized by an excessive and almost exclusive concern for the private self and its interests is a precondition of evil: it is a necessary though not a sufficient condition.[9]

Along with the commitment to correct principles, public servants must genuinely care for their fellow citizens. In this, Eichmann had defaulted on his moral obligation as a public servant. For him, as for most of the Nazi bureaucracy, the public service was simply a place for the achievement of personal ambitions. No special relationship existed.

We contend that the special relationship lies in a conception of political community which is defined by the existence of a pervasive patriotism based upon benevolence. To illustrate, we will contrast the actions of public servants and citizens toward the Jews in Germany and Denmark during World War II, because the conduct of the Danes stands as a paradigmatic example of the patriotism of benevolence.

II. The Bureaucrat: Careerist or Moral Hero?

In order to rid Europe of all Jews, the Nazis concluded—with no pangs of conscience—that the most effective means to that end was "administrative genocide."[10] While it was necessary to enlist many organizations in Germany for the murder of the Jews,[11] the most essential organization was the bureaucracy.[12] Thus, by the time of the creation of the vast killing centers in Eastern Europe, all of the significant bureaucrats knew what was happening to the Jews.[13] Yet, almost without exception, they continued to do their jobs and slaughter went on unabated. As Yahil wrote:

> What is surprising . . . is the number of "veterans" in the ministry—in the main respectable and enlightened persons steeped in tradition and culture— who faithfully served Hitler's interests. This phenomenon was not peculiar to the Foreign Ministry; it was characteristic of the whole political and administrative system and to a great extent of the military in the Third Reich.[14]

After the war, with few exceptions, those same bureaucrats excused their complicity, by claiming that, as bureaucrats, they had no option but to obey their leaders, since the prime duty of the bureaucrat is to be obedient. But "administrative neutrality" is scarcely an acceptable excuse for abetting unmitigated evil. Sensing this, most of them fell back to their next line of defense: self-preservation. But the record does not support their claim. Individuals within that "ubiquitous complicity" were seldom forced to assist in the processes of the Final Solution. They could have resigned, or sought transfers (and some did). The only reprisal would have been the dead-ending of their careers, and that appears to have been the decisive consideration. They were committed above all else to their careers. It would seem that, except for the fanatic Nazis, they were driven by no ideology beyond the desire for career advancement.

By contrast, the Danes gave us a paradigmatic example of bureaucratic moral responsibility. After the German invasion of April 9, 1940, Denmark became a model protectorate, its government intact, and watched over by a minister plenipotentiary from the German Foreign Office. From the outset, Berlin pressured the Danish government to disenfranchise the Danish Jews and to deport the stateless Jews to the concentration camps. To its considerable surprise, the orders were met with immediate and complete refusal from every segment of Danish society: politicians and ministers, business and labor leaders, teachers and ordinary citizens.

The pressure to deport the Jews continued to build, and things came to a head in the late summer and fall of 1943. The Danish armed forces were disbanded, martial law was imposed, and the Danish government was dropped into limbo. Because of this crisis, the constitutional monarch, Christian X, asked the heads of the bureaus to take over.[15] Thus, during the critical events of October of 1943, when the Nazis moved against the Jews, the nation was led by the bureaucracy.

Space is inadequate to describe the nearly unbelievable rescue operation. Suffice it to say, the Danish people, in both their public and private capacities, set new parameters for what people can and should do.[16] Furthermore, the bureaucracy performed with exemplary courage, albeit after a somewhat shaky start. They found finances, guaranteed the sanctity of Jewish homes and properties, protected Jewish funds, and performed innumerable other responsibilities. For the small number of Jews who were captured in the round-up, the Danish government provided oversight. The bureaucracy watched after them in the concentration camp at Theresienstadt, eventually assisting in their release and transfer to Sweden.

While the Danish people as a whole were heroic in their defense of their fellow citizens, we must be especially aware of the moral courage of the bureaucracy. They refused to compromise concerning the rights of the Jews, whether citizens or not. Their professional careers were secondary to their primary professional obligation: the guarantee of the rights of all:

> Above all differences of opinion, however, the people and its leaders were conscious of a number of basic values, which were not merely subscribed to by everyone, but for which every Dane who associated himself with the essentials of the constitution was prepared to fight. These were the basic principles of freedom, equality, law, and justice."[17]

The bureaucracy steered its course by an unwavering commitment to the democratic values of the Danish nation. As Arendt wrote of the entire Danish population, it ". . . was the result of an authentically political sense, and inbred comprehension of the requirements and responsibilities of citizenship and independence. . . ."[18]

As a final note, some might think the example of the Danes and the Nazis is too dramatic. But the drama must be separated from the context of the war. The routine activities of the Nazi bureaucrats was quite similar to their peace-time activities: they did small, routine tasks every day that aided in the realization of state policy. Thus, their example is not dramatic, even though the state policy was hideous beyond comprehension.

There was, however, a real drama in the actions of the Danish bureaucrats. But would there not have been real drama if American local government officials had simply refused to discriminate against black people in the 1950s? And is there not real drama in the moral heroism of Marie Ragghianti in Tennessee?[19] We do not discredit our own examples of bureaucratic heroism, and we must not discredit examples from other nations. If nothing else, they demonstrate that the moral truths and obligations of democracy are not limited by national boundaries.

III. Careerism vs. the Patriotism of Benevolence

Thus we have two radically different examples of the moral responsibilities of the public service. In Denmark, the actions of the bureaucracy were distinguished by moral heroism in the service of democratic values. In Germany, the actions of the bureaucracy were distinguished by an obsession with career success, which abetted monstrous evil. What accounts for the difference? It is not our purpose to discuss the cultural differences between the nations, as important as they are. Rather, we believe the difference can be understood by considering the relationship between patriotism and benevolence.

It is assumed that a significant reason why people enter the public service is some feeling of patriotism. It is further assumed that the bureaucrats in Germany and in Denmark believed in their respective nations and considered themselves patriots. The difference between them lies in contrasting perceptions of the moral obligations of patriotism. In Denmark, the bureaucrats considered their moral obligations to be at the heart of career service, while the bureaucrats in Germany placed governmental careers above their moral obligations to the people.[20] In other words, the Nazi bureaucrats were state careerists, while the Danish bureaucrats were patriots of the people.

For the Nazi bureaucrat, patriotism meant the acceptance of a supreme leader whose will was the foundation of the laws of the nation and participation in the pageantry of nationalism. But their moral responsibilities ended in the charade of uniforms, salutes, and rallies. By terminating the morality of patriotism in display, they were relieved of any necessity for moral thought, or, more important, of any need to love the people within their political areas of responsibility. This allowed them to concentrate all of their efforts upon their careers.

On the other hand, patriotism for the Danes consisted of a profound commitment to the democratic values of their nation, and a genuine love of the people. As Yahil observed:

> What is significant here is that for the Danes *national consciousness and democratic consciousness are one and the same.* Only as a free citizen in a lawful and democratic state can the Dane behold his patriotism. . . . Equality, freedom, the rights assured to every Dane, and the duties incumbent upon him as laid down in the constitution are valid for all citizens without exception, and all citizens constitute a mutual guarantee to one another that these principles will be maintained.[21]

Thus, the Danish bureaucrats coupled ideological commitment with a politically significant love of one another, which was the guarantee of the extension of those democratic rights to all. The Danes were, of course, correct in their understanding of their moral obligations, and that the patriotism of benevolence is the prior and necessary condition for public service in a democracy.[22]

Therefore, we define the primary moral obligation of the public service in this nation as the patriotism of benevolence: *an extensive love of all people within our political boundaries and the imperative that they must be protected in all of the basic rights granted to them by the enabling documents.* If we do not love others, why should we work to guarantee the regime values to them? The "special relationship" that must exist between public servants and citizens in a democracy is founded upon the conscious knowledge about the citizens that they are loved by the bureaucracy.

IV. The Recovery of Benevolence

It is not our purpose here to discuss in detail the concept of benevolence. That will be done in a future essay. But it is our purpose to emphasize the singular importance of the ideal of the patriotism of benevolence for the public service. The essence of political idealism, as envisioned by the Founders, was the embodiment of the ideal in the present. Jefferson typified their idealism:

> Jefferson's political theory is fundamentally a moral—i.e., normative—theory. It is not a theory about how people, or nations, actually behave, but about how they should and can behave. . . . But Jefferson also believed that a moral political order could really be created in the world, and that such an order was approximated by the United States. Thus it is a highly practical morality which is being espoused, for men can so design their political structure as to realize the moral order.[23]

This is the model for the public service—the combination of patriotism (the love of the regime values) with benevolence (the love of others) that is realized in action. That linkage was summarized by Adam Smith:

The love of our country seems, in ordinary cases, to involve in it two different principles; first, a certain respect and reverence for that constitution or form of government which is actually established; and secondly, an earnest desire to render the condition of our fellow-citizens as safe, respectable, and happy as we can. He is not a citizen who is not disposed to respect the laws and to obey the civil magistrate; and he is certainly not a good citizen who does not wish to promote, by every means in his power, the welfare of the whole society of his fellow-citizens.[24]

Since the extension and protection of the regime values to all citizens is the purpose of our government, then benevolence becomes the necessary condition of that purpose. The problem, however, is not as much with the entailments of patriotism as it is with the entailments of benevolence. The 18th century meaning required not only the love of others, but "disinterested" love at that:

From the standpoint of the agent, he acts morally when he seeks to bring about a state of affairs which constitutes the happiness of another and does this not from motives of self-interest nor from any other motive save that of seeking the good of another, the good being understood in terms of his happiness.[25]

In contemporary literature, benevolence is given, at best, a cursory nod as an oddity of intellectual history, but it is seldom suggested that we should take the idea seriously or try to put it into practice. We have almost completely lost the belief that benevolence is essential to democracy.

But for the political philosophers of the 18th century who were influential for the Founders,[26] it was of vital importance for any meaningful democracy. They looked upon benevolence, along with self-love, as one of the two major motivations for action.

There are several affections or feelings which can motivate action, but self-love and benevolence are the most important.[27]

Benevolence, thus, was not just a theoretical concept, it was something to be practiced.[28] In contemporary America, we have reduced that duality to the single motivation of a self-love rooted in a hedonic egoism, summed up in the unpleasant Mandevillean phrase: "private vices, public virtues." No matter that that notion was generally rejected by the most significant of the Founders, it dominates today.

The concept of benevolence is the key to understanding the aspirations of the Founders about how democracy could be achieved in this nation. Certainly they understood human frailty and did not rest everything upon the voluntary benevolence of the individual. James Wilson acknowledged the problem:

According to some writers, man is entirely selfish; according to others, universal benevolence is the highest aim of nature. One founds morality upon sympathy solely: another exclusively upon utility. But the variety of human nature is not so easily comprehended or reached. It is a complicated machine; and is unavoidably so, in order to answer the various and important purposes, for which it is formed and designed.[29]

Certainly, *The Federalist Papers*—while unfortunately one-sided—are evidence of their concern with the creation of a system which would compensate for those human frailties.

But even as they made provisions for human weakness, they also stressed the importance of human strength. They were quite clear about the importance of benevolence, and they included it in their prescriptions for government. Writing about the foundations of Jefferson's moral philosophy, Koch observed: "Jefferson considered . . . benevolence, or active affection for others, as the true expression of our natural, instinctive moral equipment. Any moral system which should attempt to ground morality on self-interest was foredoomed to failure, in Jefferson's eyes."[30] A significant number of the other Founders were of a similar opinion.[31]

For them, the success of the governmental system was (and is) dependent upon the prior acceptance, by both the public servants and the citizens, of the truth of the regime values. But that immediately raised another problem. Even if everyone believed, there was still no reason why they should exert themselves to extend those values to others, especially if it should entail personal loss or inconvenience. In the jargon of today, why not just maximize one's own utility and let the others fend for themselves? Whenever altruism is necessary, it will be predicated upon its utility to self and achieved through bargaining.

This issue was extensively debated by the Founders. They were aware of the problems of self-interest, of course, but they also believed that the necessary element for the realization of a true democracy was (and is) that both citizens and public servants be possessed of an extensive and active love for others—in other words, they possess a sense of benevolence. Without that sense of benevolence, there will remain only a careerist, egoistic motivation to guarantee the regime values to all of the people. That, as our recent history so sadly demonstrates, is insufficient.

V. The Patriotism of Benevolence and the Public Service

How might the patriotism of benevolence be realized in the public service today? The first step in the process must be to rid ourselves of the notion that idealism has no place in the bureaucracy. Conventional wisdom has it that the very nature of bureaucratic organization precludes public servants from any significant moral action on behalf of their citizen clients, unless directed by policy. In an excellent essay, Mainzer argues:

> Does not bureaucracy, embodying obedient, routinized, joint, anonymous action, destroy the possibility of personal responsibility for the deed? Does it not destroy, thereby, the possibility of personal honor? If so, the dominance of bureaucracy in our day may require that old virtues be re-examined or that we reconcile ourselves to the impossibility of living a worthwhile life within a large organization.[32]

It must be noted that the negatives he cites are much more the function of large-scale organization, rather than anything intrinsic to the public service. But, unfortunately, his pessimism reflects a consensus about the public service: that due to the nature of bureaucratic organization, there is scant opportunity for honor and moral heroism.

Nevertheless, it was the intent of the Founders that all public servants should view the processes of government as a moral endeavor. Theirs is not just to administer, but to assist in bringing the ideal into existence. Jefferson set the model, as Parrington wrote about the Declaration:

> The words were far more than a political gesture to draw popular support; they were an embodiment of Jefferson's deepest convictions, and his total life thenceforth was given over to the work of providing such political machinery for America as should guarantee for all the enjoyment of those inalienable rights.[33]

For that reason, public servants must be both moral philosophers and moral activists, which would require: first, an understanding of, and belief in, the American regime values;[34] and, second, a sense of extensive benevolence for the people of the nation. From that, the primary duty of public servants is to be the *guardians* and *guarantors* of the regime values for the American public.

This does not mean public servants should try to usurp the policy responsibilities of elected officials. Those officials must articulate such policies that will, in the light of changing events, be most effective in realizing the regime values for all of the people. The bureaucracy must, of course, administer such policies, as effectively and as efficiently as possible. But we must distinguish between the regime values and public policy. The regime values are the absolute values which all elected officials and public servants are sworn to protect. They are the touchstone. In this area, the public servant can accept no compromise, either in law or in practice.

For example, if a public policy depends upon racial or sexual discrimination, it offends the regime values and is automatically forfeit. Public servants are then bound, by the oath of office implied in their employment, to refuse to implement such policies. This is, of course, what the Danish public servants did and, for instance, what most American public servants failed to do during the years of sanctioned racial discrimination. Obviously, decisions of conscientious refusal must never be taken lightly, nor for simple partisan reasons. But the honorable bureaucrat must be fully capable of conscientious refusal at any point where the regime values are violated.

But why should this be a responsibility of the public servant? Is it not the responsibility of the courts to watch after the regime values? Certainly. But even if corrections of injustice are made by the courts, they can be circumvented. For instance, *Brown* v. *The Board of Education* was decided in 1954, but to this day we have not achieved racial equality in education. Furthermore, racial and sexual discrimination still persists within the governments of the United States, sometimes with official approval and bureaucratic compliance. The honorable bureaucrat cannot, according to the obligations of the patriotism of benevolence, administer such flawed programs.

Others will argue that it is the responsibility of elected officials to watch after the regime values. Certainly they do have that responsibility, but they must also be aware of the flow of political events and the ceaseless movement of public opinion. Also, and this is most important, politicians come and go—bracketed by periodic elections and subject to the whims of their constituencies, their minds must be in other places. The bureaucracy, however, stays forever and has the responsibility for the day to day implementation of public policy. It is precisely because of that permanence that their political obligation to the regime values is greater—for they must superintend the realization of those values in the everyday lives of the citizens of the Republic.

Finally, some will argue that the patriotism of benevolence is too idealistic, as if idealism had no place in the public service. They see the demands of practicality as all-consuming and idealism as a waste of time. But this glorification of practicality cuts at the essential idealism that should guide the public service. While practicality is, of course, essential, our government was also intended to achieve the ideal. To abandon idealism in favor of practicality is to violate a central purpose of our government. Furthermore, an obsession with practicality only will not allow us to meet the challenges we face. Eric Hoffer caught the situation eloquently:

> The tangibility of a pleasant and secure existence is such that it makes other realities, however imminent, seem vague and visionary. Thus it happens that when times become unhinged, it is the practical people who are caught unaware and are made to look like visionaries who cling to things that do not exist.[35]

We are not without contemporary examples of such patriotism, and even moral heroism, in the American public service. In the countless day-to-day processes of administering cities, counties, states, and the national government, public servants weigh issues of justice, equality, fairness, and common human dignity. When they function with honor and benevolence, all citizens are benefitted, and when they do not, citizens are alienated from their government and are hostile to the public service.[36] It is our argument that the demands of the patriotism of benevolence are such that there would never be a question about what the public servant should do in such circumstances.

VI. Conclusion

Some contemporary public administration scholars are reemphasizing the importance of a return to the idealism of our origins—Waldo, Van Riper, Ostrom, Newland, and Rohr, to mention just a few. But at the same time, we must recognize the singular importance of benevolence. Gawthrop has addressed the problem, reminding us both of the importance and the difficulties of benevolence. In the ethics of public administration, the adage of "love thy neighbor" is comparatively easy. The great difficulty is in extending benevolence beyond the family and the neighborhood to include the unseen others of the nation and of the world.[37]

John Rawls has also acknowledged the importance of benevolence, but, unfortunately, he argues that it is a morality of "supererogation," and thus not for ordinary people.[38] This was not the belief of the Founders, however. While the love of proximate others may be reasonably attainable, the love of humankind does require a form of moral heroism, not easily come by, but nonetheless it is achievable if people commit themselves to its attainment.

Therefore, public servants must inculcate the patriotism of benevolence. Idealistic this charge may be, but we are bound, by the covenants of our inception, to both idealism and practicality. It is within the patriotism of benevolence that the ideal and the practical are fused. As Parrington wrote of Jefferson, so should our aspirations be: "That Jefferson was an idealist was singularly fortunate for America; there was need of idealism to leaven the materialistic realism of the times."[39]

Notes

1. Alexis de Tocqueville to Louis de Kergorlay, January 1935, in Roger Boeshce (ed.), *Alexis de Tocqueville: Selected Letters on Politics and Society* (Berkeley: University of California Press, 1985), p. 95.

2. James D. Carroll and Alfred M. Zuck, *The Study of Administration Revisited* (Washington, D.C.: American Society for Public Administration, 1983), as reported

in Chester A. Newland, *Public Administration and Community: Realism in the Practice of Ideals* (McLean, Va.: Public Administration Service, November 1984), p. 6.

3. In a recent review essay, Terry W. Hartle observed: "A central theme of American public administration is that government can and should be run like a business." He notes, however, that there are significant differences between public and private endeavors: "Sisyphus Revisited: Running the Government Like a Business," *Public Administration Review,* vol. 45 (March/April 1985), p. 341.

4. We equate the "public service" with "bureaucracy," meaning those who are employed in the public sector, as opposed to those who are elected or appointed.

5. To illustrate, note the concept of egoistic inducements in the classic works in Chester I. Barnard, *The Functions of the Executive* (Cambridge, Mass.: Harvard University Press, 1938); Herbert A. Simon, *Administrative Behavior,* 2nd ed. (New York: Free Press, 1957); and James G. March and Herbert A. Simon, *Organizations* (New York: Wiley, 1958). See also William G. Scott, "Barnard on the Nature of Elitest Responsibility," *Public Administration Review,* vol. 42 (May/June) 1982, pp. 197–201.

6. H. George Frederickson, "The Recovery of Civism in Public Administration," *Public Administration Review,* vol. 42 (November/December 1982), pp. 501–509; H. George Frederickson and Ralph Clark Chandler (eds.), "Citizenship and Public Administration," *Public Administration Review,* vol. 44 (March 1984), Special Issue, Proceedings of the National Conference on Citizenship and Public Service, April 1983; H. George Frederickson (ed.), "Curriculum Essays on Citizens, Politics and Administration in Urban Neighborhoods," *Public Administration Review,* vol. 32 (October 1972), Special Issue.

7. Adam Smith, *The Theory of Moral Sentiments,* eds. D. D. Raphael and A. L. Macfie (Indianapolis: Liberty Classics, 1759, 1982), p. 86.

8. Woodrow Wilson, "The Study of Administration," *Political Science Quarterly,* vol. 2 (June 1887), p. 212.

9. Shiraz Dossa, "Hannah Arendt on Eichmann: The Public, the Private and Evil," *Review of Politics,* vol. 46 (April 1984), pp. 165–166.

10. For a good overview see Raul Hilberg, *The Destruction of the European Jews,* rev. ed. (Chicago: Quadrangle Books, 1967); and Lucy S. Dawidowicz, *The War Against the Jews: 1933–1945* (New York: Holt, Rinehart and Winston, 1975).

11. Arendt, *Eichmann,* p. 159.

12. "The destruction of the Jews was . . . no accident. When in the early days of 1933 the first civil servant wrote the first definition of a 'non-Aryan' into a civil service ordinance, the fate of European Jewry was sealed." Hilberg, p. 669.

13. We do not contend that "every last *Wachtemeister* and *Brieftrager* knew about the 'Final Solution.'" But the evidence supports the fact that bureaucrats in reasonably significant positions knew something wretched was happening to the Jews. Note, for instance, the materials in Raul Hilberg (ed.), *Documents of Destruction* (Chicago: Quadrangle, 1971); and Chapter X in Hilberg's *Destruction of the European Jews,* pp. 662–669.

14. Leni Yahil, *The Rescue of Danish Jewry,* trans. M. Gradel (Philadelphia: Jewish Publication Society of America, 1969), p. 402.

15. Yahil, pp. 125–126.

16. See Harold Flender, *Rescue in Denmark* (New York: Simon and Schuster, 1963); and Aage Bertelsen, *October '43,* trans. M. Lindholm (New York: Putnam's, 1954).

17. Yahil, p. 33.

18. Arendt, *Eichmann,* p. 179.

19. Peter Maas, *Marie: A True Story* (New York: Random House, 1980).

20. The careerism of the Nazi bureaucrats is discussed by both Arendt and Yahil. See also Albert Speer, *Inside the Third Reich,* trans. R. and C. Winston (New York: MacMillan, 1970).

21. Yahil, pp. 43–44.

22. The Danes were uncomfortable with that claim, however. As Yahil observed: ". . . perhaps the most astonishing phenomenon, and the very element in which greatness lay, was the fact that the Danes regarded their deed as not in the least extraordinary or worthy of praise and admiration. In their opinion they merely did the natural and necessary, and never for a moment considered the possibility of abandoning the Jews to their fate." pp. xi–xii.

23. Elizabeth Flower and Murray G. Murphey, *A History of Philosophy in America* (New York: Putnam's, 1977), vol. I, pp. 337–338.

24. Adam Smith, p. 231.

25. T. A. Roberts, *The Concept of Benevolence: Aspects of Eighteenth Century Moral Philosophy* (London: Macmillan, 1973), p. 7.

26. There is considerable debate over which moral philosophy was most influential upon the Founders. The dominant position is in favor of John Locke. See Carl Becker, *The Declaration of Independence,* rev. ed. (New York: Vintage, 1942). For a darker version through Bernard Mandeville, see Arthur O. Lovejoy, *Reflections on Human Nature* (Baltimore: Johns Hopkins Press, 1961). A most interesting interpretation merges Locke and the Scots through Burlamaqui. See Morton White, *The Philosophy of the American Revolution* (New York: Oxford University Press, 1978). Finally, there are those who argue that the Scottish influence was most decisive. See the controversial book by Garry Wills, *Inventing America* (Garden City, N.Y.: Doubleday, 1978). While we are not in full agreement with Wills, we believe the Scottish influence was very significant. Perhaps the best single volume summarizing the views of the Scots is Gladys Bryson, *Man and Society: The Scottish Inquiry of the Eighteenth Century* (New York: Augustus M. Kelley, 1945, 1968).

27. Roberts, pp. 107–108.

28. Among the Scots, the dominant philosopher of benevolence was Francis Hutcheson. See Henning Jensen, *Motivation and the Moral Sense in Francis Hutcheson's Ethical Theory* (The Hague: Martinus Nijhoff, 1971). David Hume wrote most insightfully about the problems—for a brief reference, see: Bk. III, Pt. III, Sec. III, "Of Goodness and Benevolence," *Treatise of Human Nature* (1739); and "Of Benevolence," Sec. II, *Enquiry Concerning the Principles of Morals* (1751).

29. Robert G. McCloskey (ed.), *The Works of James Wilson* (Cambridge, Mass.: Harvard University Press, 1967), Vol. I, p. 200.

30. Adrienne Koch, *The Philosophy of Thomas Jefferson* (Gloucester, Mass.: Peter Smith, 1943, 1957), p. 30.

31. To illustrate, see John R. Howe, Jr., *The Changing Political Thought of John Adams* (Princeton: Princeton University Press, 1966), especially Chapter Two, "A

Virtuous People." Madison is a bit more problematic, but see Adrienne Koch, *Madison's "Advice to My Country"* (Princeton: Princeton University Press, 1966), especially Chapter One, "Liberty," While Hamilton was beyond the pale, he is more than offset by people like James Wilson and Benjamin Rush.

32. Lewis C. Mainzer, "Honor in the Bureaucratic Life," *Review of Politics,* vol. 26 (January 1964), p. 71.

33. Vernon L. Parrington, *Main Currents in American Thought: The Colonial Mind—1620–1800* (New York: Harcourt, Brace & World, 1927), vol. I, p. 350.

34. David K. Hart, "The Virtuous Citizen, the Honorable Bureaucrat, and Public Administration," *Public Administration Review,* vol. 44 (March 1984), pp. 111–119.

35. Eric Hoffer, *The True Believer* (New York: Harper & Row, 1951), p. 72.

36. H. George Frederickson, *New Public Administration* (University: University of Alabama Press, 1980).

37. Louis C. Gawthrop, *Public Sector Management, Systems and Ethics* (Bloomington: Indiana University Press, 1984), pp. 137–162.

38. John Rawls, *A Theory of Justice* (Cambridge, Mass.: Harvard University Press, 1971), pp. 478–479. For a splendid work about supererogation, see David Heyd, *Supererogation: Its Status in Ethical Theory* (Cambridge: Cambridge University Press, 1982).

39. Parrington, p. 350.

26

PROFESSIONALISM, LEGITIMACY, AND THE CONSTITUTION

John A. Rohr
Virginia Polytechnic Institute

> [T]he world of administration is a pluralistic *rather than a* monistic *world and reposes in great measure on the loyalty and competence of individual bureaucrats, qualities that thrive best in conditions making for independence of judgment and pride in a job well done.*
>
> —Edward S. Corwin

This article approaches the theme of professionalism from the perspective of a "crisis in legitimacy" (Freedman, 1978) in the institution of Public Administration.[1] The cloud of illegitimacy that hangs over administrative activities presents public service professionals with a problem that is serious and challenging. By illegitimacy the author does not mean illegality. Administrative institutions and processes are quite legal, but so are the American Nazi Party, the Flat Earth Society, and *Hustler* magazine. Legitimacy means more than a grudging acceptance of the inevitable. The word suggests at least confidence and respect and at times even warmth and affection—qualities not readily associated with our modern administrative state.

This professional problem is also a constitutional problem because the illegitimacy can be traced to a fundamental conflict between the origins of the theory of American Public Administration and the pre-eminent symbol of legitimacy in American politics, the Constitution of the United States. The tension between Public Administration and the Constitution is an oft-told tale that usually centers on the pressure administrative agencies place upon the traditional principle of separation of powers. (Rosenbloom, 1983) The present article attempts to move beyond this traditional concern by examining the origins of Public Administration theory at the turn of the century and by arguing that this theory was grounded in a commitment to legislative supremacy that is fundamentally at odds with the original theory of the Constitution.

"Origins" are stressed because of the presumption in this article that in politics "foundings" are normative for the subsequent development of regimes that survive and flourish. Political philosophers are fond of making this point. Plato, Machiavelli, and Hannah Arendt come readily to mind as teachers of this doctrine in ancient, medieval, and modern times. This position is put forward as a *presumption* because an extended examination of it would swallow up the remainder of the article. There is abundant literature on the subject. (Plato; Machiavelli; Arendt, 1961; Shumer, 1979; Ball, 1978)[2]

The substance of this article will be presented in two parts: (1) a statement of the political theory of the Constitution and (2) a statement of the constitutional theory of Woodrow Wilson and Frank Goodnow, the two leading architects of classical Public Administration. These statements will be presented in such a way as to highlight the differences between them. The article will conclude with some reflections on an amended theory for Public Administration that is more in line with the principles of the Constitution.

Constitutional Theory

A thorough discussion of the theory of the American Constitution is beyond the scope of this article. Indeed, it is probably beyond the scope of any article for the very good reason that no single theory is equal to the task of explaining the Constitution of the United States. Many, perhaps most, of the framers of the Constitution were men who gave serious attention to the principles of government and the political science of their day. The records of the 1787 convention amply support this judgment. This is not to say, however, that the convention was a seminar and the Constitution the product of applied research. There could be no theory of the Constitution during the convention because no one knew what the final result would be. Certain principles guided the framers' debate, e.g., popular government, individual rights, federalism, separation of powers, republican institutions, bicameralism, and efficient administration. It was only after the document had been completed that the men of "the Federalist Persuasion" could look back on what they had done and try to present a coherent argument in support of their handiwork. The contributions of Madison, Hamilton, and Jay to *The Federalist Papers* are, of course, the best known efforts of this genre. Important statements were also made by James Wilson, Charles Pinckney, John Dickinson, James Iredell, and a host of pseudonymous pamphleteers. (Storing, 1976:215–247)

The post-convention effort to discover a theory in the Constitution was only the beginning of a long and rich tradition. This effort continues to the present day through the scholarship of historians, lawyers, and political scientists. In explaining the theoretical foundation of the Constitution pertinent to Public Administration, the author will rely on *The Federalist Papers*, the post-convention activities of James Wilson of Pennsylvania and the recent scholarship of Gordon Wood (1969) and Herbert Storing (1981).

For our purposes, the central issue is the framers' innovation in constructing a regime that was democratic in principle but was not endowed with a supreme legislature. During the ratification debate of 1787–88, many Anti-Federalist critics of the Constitution found this no innovation at all but simply an impossibility. As Storing (1981:59) observes: "The Anti-Federalists were . . . the conservatives believing that the framers of the Constitution had fallen awkwardly and dangerously between the two stools of simple, responsible government and genuine balanced government."

The Anti-Federalists maintained there were only two ways of designing a government that could legitimately be considered popular. What Storing calls "simple, responsible government" was republican in spirit and featured a unicameral legislature that was directly responsible to the people. The "genuine balanced government" came out of the Whig tradition and attempted to balance the various orders in society—King, Lords, and Commons in the British experience—in the legislature.[3] What both systems had in common was the principle of legislative supremacy. With this principle as a starting point, the Anti-Federalists had considerable difficulty grasping the theoretical foundation of the new Constitution.

Nowhere is this clearer than in the interminable debate over sovereignty which the Anti-Federalists linked to their belief in legislative supremacy. Sovereignty is supreme and undivided power and the legislature, as Blackstone had insisted, is its accustomed place. (McMaster and Stone, 1970, Vol. 2:229) Since the proposed Constitution created a legislature whose acts would be the supreme law of the land, the Anti-Federalists argued that the new government would be sovereign and therefore its nature would be national and consolidated rather than federal. Hence, the rights of the states and perhaps even their very existence were in jeopardy.

The Federalists' reply in defense of the Constitution rested on an appeal to sovereignty in the people with a consequent denial of legislative supremacy. The object of the people's choice was not a supreme legislature that embodied their will, but a constitutional order, an arrangement of offices, a "system" that would provide efficient government and protect individual rights.

James Wilson was perhaps the most articulate spokesman of this Federalist theme during the Ratification debate. Speaking in support of the Constitution at the Pennsylvania Ratifying Convention, Wilson argued that the sovereignty of the states was not destroyed by the new Constitution for the excellent reason that the states had never been sovereign. The people had always been sovereign. At one time they chose to delegate some powers to their state governments and others to Congress under the Articles of Confederation. Now they wished to rearrange this distribution of powers. As Wilson (McMaster and Stone, 1970, Vol. 2:302)[4] put it:

> When the principle is once settled that the people are the source of authority, the consequence is that they may take from the subordinate governments powers with which they have hitherto trusted them, and place these powers in the general government, if it is thought that there they will be productive of more good. They can distribute one portion of power to the more contracted circle called State governments; they can furnish another portion to the government of the United States. Who will undertake to say as a state officer that the people may not give to the general government what powers and for what purposes they please? how comes it, Sir, that these State governments dictate to their superiors?—to the majesty of the people?

Throughout the process of shifting these powers from one level of government to another, it is the people alone who possess that power "from which there is no appeal and which is therefore called absolute, supreme, and uncontrollable." (McMaster and Stone, 1970, Vol. 1:229) Although the principle of popular sovereignty was invoked most frequently in debates over federalism, it is the application of the principle to the structure of the federal government itself that is of interest to students of Public Administration. On the issue of federalism, popular sovereignty nullifies state sovereignty; the states are not supreme because the people are. On the issue of separation of powers within the federal government, the legislature is not supreme because the people are. The object of the choice of the sovereign people is not a group of legislators who will carry out the people's will. What the people have chosen is a constitutional order which balances the powers they have delegated to three equal branches. In describing "the Federalist Persuasion," Gordon Wood (1969:547) notes that because "the Federalists were equating representation with the mere flow of authority, every officer would be in some way a representative of the people."[5]

Every *officer a representative;* interesting language this for students of Public Administration. It is pregnant with a legitimating argument for the non-elected official to participate in rule.

Herbert Storing (1981:230) makes the same point from a different angle. Because it exists as *part* of a constitutional order that the people have chosen, "[t]he legislature is a body of constitutional *officers,* not a microcosm of the sovereign people." (Italics added.) Members of Congress "like other officers of government, derive their authority from the Constitution, not from their election." Elections are "merely a method of choosing, not a method of authorizing."

Although Storing speaks of *officers* and Wood of *representatives,* they are at one in leveling the differences between elected and non-elected government personnel. For Storing, elected officials are officers; for Wood, the non-elected officials are representatives. What both men are affirming is the *irrelevance of election* to ground a special claim to speak for the people. This is an important consideration in any effort to legitimate the administrative state. It provides the beginnings of a principled response to the congressman who would raise doubts about the legitimacy of monetary policy by asking, "Who elected Paul Volcker?"[6]

What unites Storing and Wood is their careful reading of the Federalist argument that pointed to ratification as the decisive act of the Sovereign. Wood notes that the Federalists "were equating representation with the mere flow of authority," whereas Storing describes the Federalist theory of election as "merely a method of choosing, not a method of authorizing." The emphasis is different but the main point is the same. It is the act of ratification that initiates the "flow of authority" for Wood and that is "authorizing" for Storing (1981:62).[7] The authoritative act is the people's ratification of the distribution of various offices in the proposed Constitution. The fact that some offices are filled by election and others by appointment says nothing about the connection between the people and the occupant of a particular office. The Senators and Representatives of Article I; the President, department heads, and inferior officers of Article II; and the judges of Article III are all the objects of a popular choice that determined how each office holder would be selected—some by popular election, some by indirect election, some by appointment. They are all *equally* the object of constitutional choice, though they are quite unequal in the scope and nature of their constitutional duties.

When Wood maintains that the Federalists "were equating representation with the mere flow of authority," he is distinguishing the innovative Federalist position on representation from the traditional understanding that through representation in a legislature the entire society was *re-presented,* i.e., presented a second time on a smaller scale. Storing speaks to the same point when he maintains that for the Federalists "[t]he legislature is . . . not a microcosm of the sovereign people." It was the microcosm view of representation in a legislature that grounded the case for legislative supremacy. That is why Wood refers to the Federalist interpretation of representation as "a *mere* flow of authority." (Italics added.) It is "mere" because it is a purely juridical act that lacks the rich sociological flavor of the legislature as microcosm. If the legislature is a microcosm of society as a whole, then, of course, it should be supreme. There is no principle that would allow an executive or judiciary that is not part of the microcosm to "check" a microcosm of society itself. If the legislature is supreme, the executive and judiciary are inferior to it.[8] This the Federalists denied. The three branches are equal. The only way to justify their position was to consider the Constitution as a whole with its separate and balanced powers as the object of sovereign popular choice.

In putting forth this theory, the Federalists were departing from the traditional idea of a mixed regime. James Madison notes this departure explicitly in *Federalist* 14. The theory of mixed regime was based on the British experience where the various orders in society—King, Lords, and Commons—came together in Parliament. This was balanced government but the balance was struck *in the legislature,* in Parliament, which was sovereign.

In republican America, where there were no "orders" in society, the mixed regime theory continued to flourish because of a belief in a "natural aristocracy" that would have to be represented and balanced in the legislature. John Adams, of course, is the most famous advocate of this position. His celebrated *Defense of the Constitutions of Government of the United States of America* was an elaborate justification of the need for a balanced legislature in a republican society. His adversaries were Turgot in France and Franklin and Paine in America. All three of these men had argued that under republican government there was no need for a bicameral legislature because there was only one order in society—the people themselves. To speak of an "upper" and "lower" house was inconsistent with the genius of government. Where there was only one order in society, there should be a unicameral legislature.

Adams' rejoinder to this argument was that every society had an inevitable tendency toward aristocracy. If the aristocrats are not recognized as a class by law, they will find other ways to assert themselves. They would quickly dominate a unicameral legislature in such a way as to deny the common people any effective voice; and this while paying homage to the principles of republicanism. For Adams, the path of wisdom was to maintain bicameralism as a way of constitutionally confining the natural aristocrats in a legislative chamber of their own which would be part of the legislature as a whole. This would preserve one house for the people and thereby assure a balanced Constitution.

The argument between the unicameral republicans and the advocates of the balanced constitution as an American version of the mixed regime became inextricably entwined in the argument over the ratification of the Constitution. Many Anti-Federalists attacked the Constitution as an expression of Adams' version of the mixed regime. Indeed, Adams himself supported the Constitution because of its similarities to his own position. This similarity, however, was only on the surface. President, Senate, and House in the Constitution were by no means the same as King, Lords, and Commons in Parliament. Nor were they the same as the aristocrats and common people of the American version of the mixed regime.

The Federalists' theory of the Constitution challenged both the unicameral republicans and the advocates of a mixed regime on the issue of legislative supremacy. The unicameral republicans saw the legislature as the supreme institution of government because it was chosen by the one social order in a republic, the people. They hailed Pennsylvania's unicameral legislature as comporting with sound republican doctrine. The advocates of the mixed regime saw Parliament (or the bicameral American state legislatures) as supreme because the various social orders had a voice in Parliament. The constitutional balance was struck in Parliament itself. There and only there all of society was represented and hence Parliament was supreme.

In preferring constitutional supremacy over legislative supremacy, the Federalists bypassed the unicameral-mixed regime argument and broke new ground. Instead of balancing social orders in a legislature, they would balance *interests* in the Constitution itself. Congress, the legislative branch, was not where the balance would be struck; it was itself part of the balance.

Public Administration Theory

The origins of Public Administration theory in the United States can be traced to the civil service reform movement of the final third of the nineteenth century. Like the framers of the Constitution, the Reformers were practical men bent on practical results and, like the framers, they took principles of government seriously. After their first goal was achieved in the Pendleton Act of 1883, certain reformers began to look for ways to ground their merit system triumph in a broad theory of Public Administration. Chief among these theoreticians were Woodrow Wilson (1887) and Frank Goodnow (1967).

The best starting point for examining the constitutional background of Wilson's theory of Public Administration is his position on popular sovereignty. As indicated above, it was the doctrine of popular sovereignty that enabled the Federalists to explain how there could be three equal branches of government without one being superior to the other. Sovereignty, as all admitted, was supreme and indivisible. For the Federalists, the supreme and indivisible power remained with the people. Each of the constitutional branches had specific powers that were carefully limited and therefore, by definition, less than sovereign.

For Wilson, the term popular sovereignty suggested the excesses of Jacksonian democracy and found nothing but withering scorn in his writings.[9] He rejected the term as a product of muddled thinking that confuses the source of authority with authority itself. As Wilson put it, "[T]he springs of practical action are hopelessly confused with governing power." This misleads the people into thinking that they, the governed, are actually the governors. It confuses the act by which the people consent to be governed with the actual activity of governing. (Link, 1970, Vol. VII:352–354)

For Wilson, it is nonsense to speak of sovereignty remaining with the people *after* a government has been formed. Sovereignty must be found in an *institution* of government that is "daily in command of affairs." (Ibid., 333–334)

> The Sovereign Power is the highest originative organ of the State. That free populations themselves elect the sovereign body by the selection of its members does not make those populations that sovereign body. That that sovereign, originative body must prudently regard the state of opinion among those populations does not make them any less sovereign than kings have been who reigned by hereditary right and yet found it needful to please their subjects.

In maintaining that the sovereign power is the highest originative organ of the state, Wilson faithfully restated the 18th century teaching of Blackstone and, also like Blackstone, he identified the legislature as the highest organ. (Blackstone, 1979, Vol. 1:156–161)[10] It was from this pulpit that Wilson preached his famous instrumental view of administration.

An instrumental view of administration fits neatly into a model of government that rests on legislative supremacy. The people elect their representatives who, acting in their sovereign capacity, pass laws which are duly carried out by the Public Administration. Frank Goodnow (1967:9), relying on a thinly veiled Hegelianism, explained this process in terms of the two basic governmental operations that comprise "the action of the state as a political entity": (1) the expression of the will of the state and (2) the execution of the will of the state.

As is well known, the administrative theory of both Wilson and Goodnow is far more subtle and complex than this simple instrumentalism would suggest.[11] Although a full examination of this matter is beyond the constitutional focus of this article, we should note that, somewhat paradoxically, their instrumentalism was intended to strengthen the Public Administration and to free it from politics in its daily operation though not in its overall objectives. What is crucial for our purposes, however, is to note the compatibility between an instrumental view of administration and a regime of legislative supremacy. This is one reason why both Wilson and

Goodnow favored profound changes in American government that would
alter or circumvent the constitutional principle of separation of powers.
Wilson favored a constitutional amendment that would permit members of
the cabinet to hold seats in Congress. (Wilson, 1884:17–33) Clearly he had
the British Parliamentary-Cabinet model in mind. Goodnow, despairing of
a constitutional amendment, looked to renewed and strengthened political
parties to bring together the legislative and executive powers that the Constitution kept apart.

Goodnow's position is particularly interesting because he brings the executive and legislative powers together in order to separate administrative
functions from both of them. When Goodnow designated the two great
operations of government as the expression of the will of the state and its
execution, he did not identify execution with "executive power" in the
constitutional sense of that term. Constitutional executive power is but one
of three ways in which the will of the state is executed. As Goodnow
(1967:17) puts it:

> If we analyze the organization of any concrete government, we shall find that
> there are three kinds of authorities which are engaged in the execution of the
> state will. These are, in the first place, the authorities which apply the law in
> concrete cases where controversies arise owing to the failure of private indi-
> viduals or public authorities to observe the rights of others. Such authorities
> are known as judicial authorities. They are, in the second place, the authori-
> ties which have the general supervision of the execution of the state will, and
> which are commonly referred to as executive authorities. They are, finally, the
> authorities which are attending to the scientific, technical and, so to speak,
> commercial activities of the government, and which are in all countries, where
> such activities have attained prominence, known as administrative authorities.

This threefold way of executing the will of the state is crucial for understanding Goodnow's book. A careless reading of Goodnow might lead one
to equate execution of the will of the state with constitutional executive
power and equate both of these with Public Administration. This would be
a serious error and would tend to distract the reader from the profound
disparity between the origins of Public Administration theory and the Constitution of the United States. When Goodnow calls for vigorous parties to
unite legislative and executive power, he means the constitutional executive—the President and the state governors whose independence from their
respective legislatures he deplores. (Goodnow, 1967:Chapter 11) When he
designates the "administrative authorities" as *different* institutions charged
with the execution of the will of the state, he does so to keep administrators independent of the legislature. This is because the administrative authorities "are attending to the scientific, technical, and so to speak, commercial activities of the government." Throughout his book, Goodnow

offers the independence of the "judicial authorities" as the proper model for the "administrative authorities." (Goodnow, 1967:45, 85–87, 120–121, 131) This model contrasts sharply with the "executive authorities" who are linked to the legislature through vigorous parties to remedy by informal means the constitutional defect that formally separates them.

The reasoning behind Goodnow's plan is quite clear. The "executive authorities" are generalists charged with "the general supervision of the execution of the state will." The administrative and judicial authorities also execute the state will but they rely on technical expertise to do so. The generalist who executes the state's will must be closely linked with the legislature that expresses that will. Otherwise, there will be a "[l]ack of harmony between the law and its execution." (Goodnow, 1967:23) This will lead to "political paralysis." (Ibid.)

Judicial and administrative authorities are subordinate to the legislature because execution is always ultimately subordinate to expression. However, they must also be separated from the legislature to insure that their technical execution is consistent with the expression of the will of the state. There is no inherent contradiction between being ultimately subordinate and institutionally separate, as the British courts have shown. (Ibid., 40–43) If judges and administrators are influenced by politics, there is a danger that their powers will be "discharged not so much with reference to the execution of an already expressed state will as with reference to influencing the future expression of the state will, i.e., in the interest of political party or social class." (Ibid., 38) Thus Goodnow argues that the executive authorities must be joined to the legislative authorities for the same reason that the administrative authorities must be kept separate from both of them—to insure that the expressed will of the state is carried into execution.

Wilson's position on separation of powers, though less well developed than Goodnow's, is no less clear. In his 1885 book, *Congressional Government,* Wilson stated the constitutional underpinnings of his 1887 essay on administration. The fundamental flaw in the American Constitution is the independence of the President from Congress. This independence scandalizes Wilson's belief that sovereignty must rest in one supreme governmental institution and that institution in the United States is Congress. Wilson understood and rejected the traditional theory of the Constitution—"that there is no single or central force in our federal scheme . . . but only a balance of powers and a nice adjustment of interactive checks, as all the books say." (Wilson, 1967:31) This, for Wilson, is the "literary theory" of the Constitution that is doomed in practice because in all governments there must be one center of power, one "self-sufficient authority," i.e., one sovereign body. (Ibid., 30)

Thus Wilson has no trouble stating: "In so far as the President is an executive officer he is the servant of Congress; and the members of the Cabinet, being confined to executive functions, are altogether the servants of Congress." (Ibid., 177) By the qualifying words "in so far as the President is an executive officer," Wilson refers to the president's veto power. Instead of following the traditional constitutional theory that treats the presidential veto as a check on the legislature that preserves the independence of the executive branch (*Federalist* #73), Wilson sees it as making the President "a third branch of the legislature." (Ibid., 177) Since cabinet officers have no veto power, they are "altogether the servants of Congress." (Ibid.)

Indeed, in discussing the merit system, it is only the veto power that dissuades Wilson from considering the President as "the first official of a carefully-graded and impartially regulated civil service system, through whose sure series of merit promotions the youngest clerk might rise to the chief magistracy." (Ibid., 170) Since "his power of veto constitutes him a part of the legislature," the President cannot join the career service; if he were "merely" the chief executive officer of the Republic, he could be part of the civil service.

Statements of legislative supremacy abound in *Congressional Government*. (Wilson, 1967:30, 142, 147, 164, 181–2, 183) Many of these statements are prescriptive. Wilson deplores the tendency of congressional committees to control executive departments. He knows this is not supposed to happen under separation of powers. Rather than adopt the Hamiltonian solution of subordinating the executive departments to the President, Wilson attacks the principle of separation itself. He argues the case for a parliamentary form of government where there is central control and direction of administration in a cabinet which is a part of the legislature and responsible to it as a whole. (Wilson, 1967:147, 181–190)

This is the constitutional vision that supports Wilson's instrumental view of administration. Wilson knew, of course, that such far-reaching constitutional changes were unlikely and therefore considerably modified his instrumental view of administration.[12] Despite his cautious hedging, the clarity of Wilson's instrumentalism carried the day and laid the foundation for the Public Administration orthodoxy that prevails even today at the highest levels of the United States Office of Personnel Management.[13] It is an orthodoxy that is fundamentally at odds with the Constitution of the United States and for this reason had considerably weakened the modern administrative state.

Conclusion

This article has approached the topic of professionalism by the wide avenue of illegitimacy and has attempted to locate the origins of this illegitimacy in certain contrasts between the theory of the Constitution and the original theory of American Public Administration. In highlighting these contrasts, the author does not suggest that Wilson and Goodnow were simply out of touch with American political thought. The men of "the Federalist Persuasion," who successfully argued for the ratification of the Constitution, are not the sole architects of our constitutional heritage. Goodnow's inclusion of judicial authority as part of executive power finds explicit support in John Locke. John Adams would agree with Woodrow Wilson that the veto power of the President makes him part of the legislature. Leading Anti-Federalists championed the principle of legislative supremacy no less than did Wilson and Goodnow. Indeed, when he gets away from the issue of separation of powers, Wilson's views are remarkably similar to the principles of *The Federalist Papers.* (Rohr, 1984:44–45)

It is not enough, however, for a theory of Public Administration to be well integrated into the broad sweep of American political thought if, at the same time, it is fundamentally at odds with that aspect of American thought that forms the principled basis of the Constitution. This is because the Constitution is not only a set of principles but is positive law as well. When American Public Administration moves from theory to practice, it is necessarily and appropriately caught in the perennial crossfire involving a Congress, a President, and courts that are fiercely independent of one another. American Public Administration can never be purely instrumental because there is no way of telling whose instrument it will be. A struggle for control of the Public Administration is part of the wholesome politics of a regime of separation of powers. Constitutional law trumps administrative theory.

If we are to make any progress in legitimating the administrative state, we would do well to swim with the constitutional tide rather than against it.[14] A good starting point might be the constitutional principle of sovereignty in the people that teaches us to think of the Public Administration as the instrument of the Constitution itself rather than of the officers elected according to constitutional prescription. This suggests that administrators become active participants rather than feckless pawns in the continuing constitutional struggle for control of the Public Administration.

Rather than wait to be captured now by Congress, now by Presidents, now by the courts, statesmanlike administrators might ponder delivering their agencies for a time to a constitutional master of their own choosing. Which master the administrators would favor and for how long would depend on the administrators' judgment of which branch of government needs to be strengthened to maintain the correct constitutional balance and to achieve the appointed ends stated so elegantly in the Constitution's Preamble. An administrative theory resting on such principles would have the advantage of preserving a certain professional autonomy within the framework of the Constitution. Without some sort of principled autonomy, professionalism in Public Administration is no profession at all.

Notes

1. An earlier version of this article was presented at the 1983 National Meeting of the American Political Science Association in Chicago.

2. Lest the presumption of this article seem arbitrary, the author would note as a simple example of the "founding as normative" position the perennial American tendency to appeal to the "Founding Fathers" to support a major policy initiative or a momentous effort in foreign or military affairs. Lincoln was perhaps the greatest exemplar of this high rhetoric and it is only fitting that he should be enshrined in the nation's capital as the architect of its "second founding." At a more pedestrian level, appeal to the Founding Fathers can be heard in election campaigns as well as from such diverse groups as the American Civil Liberties Union, the AFL-CIO, the National Rifle Association, and the Moral Majority. This middling rhetoric is important because, however manipulative and opportunistic it might be in the short run, it signals the myths and principles that make the Moral Majority and the ACLU part of the same community and keeps alive the hope and reality of a dialogue—however strident—in some sort of civic friendship.

For western minds the "founding as normative" principle has powerful religious overtones. The promise to Abraham, the theophany at Sinai, and the redemptive death and resurrection of Jesus are for men and women of faith great "founding" events in terms of which they evaluate and order religious experience. It is not by chance that the holy places of American civil religion in Boston, Philadelphia, and Washington are linked to the persons, places, and events readily associated with the founding period of the Republic. This underscores the seriousness of foundings in our culture in general and in particular it underscores the seriousness of the legitimacy problem for Public Administration if the principles of its founding are seriously at odds with the principles of the Constitution itself.

3. A good comparison of the Whig and Republican positions can be found in Wood (1969: Chapters I and II).

4. Wilson's position is interesting (McMaster and Stone, 1970:302). He was among the most democratic members of the 1787 Convention and hence it is not surprising that he should take the lead in developing a popular sovereignty interpretation of the Constitution. During the Convention he held a microcosm view of the legislature but he had abandoned this position by the time the ratification debate in Pennsylvania.

5. See also Wood (1969:532): "Relocating sovereignty in the people by making them 'the fountain of all power' seemed to make sense of the entire system. Once the Federalists perceived 'the great principle of the primary right of power in the people, they could scarcely restrain their enthusiasm in following out its implications. One insight seemed to lead to another, until the Federalists were tumbling over each other in their efforts to introduce the people into the federal government, which they had 'hitherto been shut out of.' 'The people of the United States are now in the possession and exercise of their original rights, said Wilson, 'and while this doctrine is known and operates we shall have a cure for every disease.'"

6. The use of "representative" and "officer" by Wood and Storing is not a twentieth century innovation. They follow eighteenth century usage. For example, see the ratification debate in Pennsylvania (McMaster and Stone, 1970, Vol. 1: 229,

250, 260, 270). See also *Federalist* 27 where Publius refers to "legislative officers" and *Federalist* 46 where all government officials are called representatives.

7. Storing (1981:62) develops this point more fully: "The complex or balanced government provided for in the Constitution is, then, fundamentally a balance of *constitutional* orders or powers, blended with a constitutional differentiation of functions, formed by the makers of the Constitution and requiring only the impulse of popular consent to breathe life into it and the private interests and ambitions of citizens and representatives to keep it in motion. It was on this basis that James Wilson considered it the distinction of the Americans to have invented a mixed government made wholly out of popular elements. 'What is the nature and kind of that government which has been proposed for the United States by the late convention? In its principle, it is purely democratical. But that principle is applied in different forms, in order to obtain the advantages, and exclude the inconveniences, of the simple modes of government.' The differences are not derived from natural or conventional differentiations of society but are constitutional or legal constructs."

8. Even with a supreme legislature, there can still be a separate but inferior executive and judiciary. See discussion of Goodnow (1967) in part 2 of this article.

9. In all likelihood, most of the framers of the Constitution would have sympathized with Woodrow Wilson's dim view of Jacksonian democracy.

10. See Volume I, pp. 156–161 for Blackstone's (1979 reprint) defense of legislative supremacy. When Blackstone defends legislative supremacy, it is of course Parliament that he defends where the executive is part of the legislature. See Stanley N. Katz's introduction to the first volume of Blackstone's *Commentaries*.

11. In the case of Goodnow (1967), one should note that he usually avoids simply identifying the legislature with the body that expresses the will of the state. He prefers to speak of the *function* of expressing that will regardless of the institution that happens to express it in particular circumstances. When he speaks of the United States, however, where the legislature and executive are separated, the supremacy of the legislature is unmistakeably clear. (See p. 79.) It would be inaccurate to impose a legislative supremacy model on Goodnow when he speaks abstractly about government in general. At such a level, it is the expression of the will of the state that is supreme over its execution. (See pp. 21–22.)

12. Wilson abandoned his instrumentalism in the lectures on administration he delivered at Johns Hopkins University from 1888–1897. The 1891 lectures provide a particularly clear statement of a non-instrumental view of Public Administration. See Link (1970, Vol. VII:127ff. These lectures are discussed by John A. Rohr (1984). A thoughtful discussion of non-instrumental aspects of Wilson's administrative thought can be found in Kent A. Kirwan (1977). Also helpful is Kirwan (1981). For the development of the broad outlines of Wilson's constitutional thought, see Christopher Wolfe (1979).

13. See editorial on remarks by Donald Devine (1981).

14. This is not to say the Constitution or its framers are above criticism. The legitimating force of the framers need not become ancestor worship. See Wood (1969:562–564) for a discussion of how the framers' theory of the Constitution has impoverished American political debate; and Storing (1981:63) for a discussion of the inadequate provisions for responsibility to the people in the Constitution. Such criticisms go beyond questions of legitimacy and examine the wisdom

of the Constitution itself. The Public Administration can certainly play a part in healing the defects of the Constitution but such matters are beyond the scope of this article.

References

Arendt, Hannah (1961). "What Is Authority," in *Between Past and Present.* New York: Viking Press.

Ball, Milner S. (1978). *The Promise of American Law: A Theological, Humanistic View of Legal Process.* Athens: University of Georgia Press.

Blackstone, William (1979). *Commentaries on the Laws of England,* 4 Volumes. Chicago: University of Chicago Press. A facsimile of the first edition (1765) of Blackstone's *Commentaries* is provided in this reprint.

Devine, Donald (1981). *Public Administration Review* 41 (May/June):iii–iv.

Federalist. ##27, 46, 73.

Freedman, James O. (1978). *Crisis and Legitimacy: The Administrative Process and American Government.* Cambridge: Cambridge University Press.

Goodnow, Frank J. (1967). *Politics and Administration: A Study of Government.* New York: Russell and Russell. The 1967 edition is a reprint; the book was first published in 1900.

Kirwan, Kent A. (1977). "The Crisis of Identity in the Study of Public Administration: Woodrow Wilson." *Polity* 9 (Spring):321–343.

_____. (1981). "Historicism and Statesmanship in the Reform Argument of Woodrow Wilson." *Interpretation* 9 (Summer):339–351.

Link, Arthur S. (ed.) (1970). *The Papers of Woodrow Wilson,* Volume VII. Princeton: Princeton University Press.

Machiavelli, Niccolo (1981). *The Discourses,* trans. Leslie J. Walker, edited by Bernard Crick. New York: Penguin Books.

McMaster, John B. and Frederick D. Stone (1970). *Pennsylvania and the Federal Constitution 1787–1788,* 2 vols. New York: DaCapo Press. The DaCapo edition is a reprint. The book was originally published in one volume in Philadelphia in 1888.

Plato (1980). *The Laws,* trans. Thomas L. Pangle. New York: Basic Books.

Rohr, John A. (1984). "The Constitutional World of Woodrow Wilson," in James S. Bowman and Jack Rabin (eds.), *Politics and Administration: Woodrow Wilson and American Public Administration.* New York: Dekker.

Rosenbloom, David H. (1983). *Public Administration and Law: Banch v. Bureau in the United States.* New York: Dekker.

Shumer, S.M. (1979). "Machiavelli: Republican Politics and its Corruption." *Political Theory* 7 (February):5–34.

Storing, Herbert J. (1976). "The 'Other' Federalist Papers: A Preliminary Sketch." *Political Science Review* 215–247.

_____. (1981). *What the Anti-Federalists Were For,* Chicago: University of Chicago Press.

Wilson, Woodrow (1884). "Committee or Cabinet Government." *Overland Monthly* 2 (June):197–222.

_____. (1967). *Congressional Government: A Study in American Politics.* New York: Meridian Books. This edition is a reprint of the book that was first published in 1885.

Wolfe, Christopher (1979). "Woodrow Wilson: Interpreting the Constitution." *Review of Politics* 41 (January):124–142.

Wood, Gordon S. (1969). *The Creation of the American Republic, 1776–1787.* Chapel Hill: University of North Carolina Press.

Part EIGHT

Ethics in the Twenty-First Century

Part 8 is included because the classic issues presented here remain relevant, as we embark on the twenty-first century. Basic to all three of the articles reprinted in this part is a theme of discouragement. All, in their own way, mourn the fact that as public administration scholars and practitioners, we have become so enamored with technology that we have lost our sense of a moral underpinning for the profession. We do this at our peril, all three of the authors argue, each from a different perspective.

Todd La Porte begins his 1967 *PAR* article, "Politics and 'Inventing the Future': Perspectives in Science and Government" (Chapter 27 here), with these words: "In the past two decades the tone and character of public affairs have been increasingly influenced by the growing interdependence of science, technology, and the Federal Government." Now, almost forty years later, we can say the same thing. Technology is now, as then, a force to be reckoned with, an instrument of great efficiency, and a power that must be managed. As a society and as a profession, our greatest challenge will be to utilize technology wisely. Our decisions must not be based solely on what we can do. Rather, we must first decide on what we ought to do. This is La Porte's challenge: "Can we adjust our values to act upon the enormous promise opened to us?"

Now, as in 1967, the technological opportunities open before us are magnificent. Technology, however, has developed much more rapidly than has our ability to deal with it. Will there come a time when humankind will begin to work for technology instead of developing ways and reasons for technology to work for us? La Porte says, "The future holds enormous danger." That danger will magnify unless those concerned with values, morals, and administrative ethics provide a countervailing force that enables technology to better our world and the lives of people in it. Since 1967, one can say with confidence, technology has grown exponentially. Our grasp of what it means to live as moral beings in cooperation with others in our country and in our world seems not much changed at all. We fail to engage in moral reflection, at our peril.

Writing in *PAR* in 1973, William G. Scott and David K. Hart reiterate La Porte's concerns. Their article, "Administrative Crisis: The Neglect of Metaphysical Speculation" (Chapter 28 here), begins: "Americans are fascinated by the successful solution of elaborate technological puzzles, yet many sense at the same time that technology may also be a malefactor as well as a benefactor in their lives." Like La Porte, Scott and Hart attempt to raise their readers' consciousness, as they argue "the real crisis created by the exponential growth of technology is administrative."

Scott and Hart believe that reflection on morality and values is discouraged in public administration and that "attention to the pragmatically proximate is rewarded, while little honor and fewer resources accrue to those whose work does not have the instrumental payoff of making the technical and organizational mechanisms of society more efficient." This emphasis on efficiency at the expense of moral reflection is dangerous and has created a crisis in administration. They itemize and discuss the consequences of this crisis so that administrators can become aware of "the critical moral dilemma facing all of us, through the failure of administration to engage in metaphysical speculation."

Administrative ethics has come a long way since the Friedrich-Finer debate, when politicians and ethicists alike sought ways to make administrators accountable. Whether accountability came from tight controls or from hiring moral and conscientious administrators, the underlying assumptions in the first decades of public administration indicate that administrators serve the will of the people through the directives of the political official. La Porte, Scott, and Hart put administrators on a higher plain. No longer is their concern one of getting administrators to do what someone else expects. Rather, administrators are presented as an elite group, making decisions that affect the rest of society. As public administration moves into the future, a greater burden and a greater series of opportunities move with it. Administrators are no longer functionaries but fully involved members of the community and fully engaged contributors to the policy making process.

Chapter 29, the final piece in this volume, emphasizes this evolution of government and its companion, public administration. Louis Gawthrop, in his 1984 *PAR* article, "Civis, Civitas, and Civilitas: A New Focus for the Year 2000," argues, "The lesson of the first 200 years of self-governing experience in the United States is that of a steady, evolutionary, sociopolitical progression through the 19th century from the simple to the complex, and thus far through the 20th century, from the complex to the supra complex." For Gawthrop, this means that a new era in public administration must begin, and it requires the "revitalization of the character of citizenship and the meaning of citizen." This, he believes, will put a heavy burden on the profession of public administration, as well as on individual administrators, for it changes the locus of accountability. No longer are administrators confined to control by political officials. We are one with the citizens, and we are accountable to them.

As Gawthrop puts it, such accountability allows us to ask the question: "To what extent can the craft of management be employed to revitalize the art of government?" Such accountability calls us to begin the twenty-first century with actions that "ensure the vitality of citizenship in an active citizenry fully engaged in the art of government," requiring "a basic redefinition of public administration as a profession."

Having come to the end of this book containing classical thought about administrative ethics, it is interesting, although somewhat discouraging, to note that "the more things change, the more they remain the same." Not a single article included in this book is irrelevant. A cursory look at news headlines or casual attention to late night news broadcasts lets us know that we need to still be concerned about administrative responsibility, professional conduct, preventing corruption, constructing codes of ethics, enforcing ethical behavior, and educating individuals for responsible public service. We still do not know whether we can hire moral and good people of integrity to conduct the public business or whether we must, somehow, get enough rules and restrictions in place to ensure against immoral and illegal conduct. Our moral reflection has not kept pace with our technological sophistication. The issues with which the profession began and those that emerged in its first forty-five years remain the thorny issues of today.

Confirming Gawthrop's prediction that the field will become more and more complex, the decades after the 1980s have added other areas to which administrative ethicists must also devote their thought and offer their counsel. Gender-based decision making and the ethics of affirmative action are being addressed. So are virtue ethics, citizenship ethics, and ethics necessary for participating in global interconnectedness. New thought about administrative evil is taking place. Spirituality and morality are entering the public administration ethical arena, as are arguments about the relevancy and rightness of religion in the public-sector workplace. Not everyone is concerned about every dimension of administrative ethics; but many people are engaged in learning about and talking about the diversity of subjects that now make up the field.

As we look back over the ethical thought represented in this book, it is rewarding to see how thorough we have been in identifying concerns and disappointing to see how inadequate we have been in addressing them. Remembering that there were frequently long lapses between articles about administrative ethics, it is gratifying to see the increased emphasis on ethics in ASPA publications of today.

27

POLITICS AND "INVENTING THE FUTURE": PERSPECTIVES IN SCIENCE AND GOVERNMENT

Todd R. La Porte
University of California, Berkeley

In the past two decades the tone and character of public affairs have been increasingly influenced by the growing interdependence of science, technology, and the Federal Government. The net effect of this interdependence is an expanding capacity of our government for what Dennis Gabor has called, "inventing the future."[1] Coupling the enormous organizational energy of governmental, industrial, and university complexes with rapid developments in the natural and social sciences has made possible the harnessing of the nation's resources in shaping the future. The undeniable importance of these developments demands a much more vigorous effort than is now evident from the universities and government agencies to understand the interdependence and its implications for democratic political systems.[2]

This paper attempts to frame a perspective for study to stimulate new information and new alternatives for public policy. The empirical and normative considerations important in understanding the reciprocal impact of science-technology and governmental affairs are the writer's principal concerns. The major underlying assumption is that the enterprises of science and their associated technologies, as they act through economic and governmental institutions, are primary determinants of change in our culture and certainly in contemporary politics.[3]

A Point of Departure and Central Questions

The processes of science and technology and the governmental processes are often viewed as separate enterprises, each having a distinct set of institutions and values, and each carried forward by identifiably different groups of people. Until recently, this has been the position of most students of politics and of the sociology of science. It is clear, however, that while many activities in each enterprise are distinct, there are crucial intersections as the processes of science, technology, and the political system become increasingly entwined.

Once the intersections of science-technology and government have been posited, several sets of central questions follow, all stimulated by the increasingly close interdependence of the scientific community and government: (1) In what ways do science-technology and democratic systems reinforce and/or modify each other? (2) What relationships between science-technology and government will reconcile the demands for public accountability and scientific freedom as government stimulates and supports scientific activities? (3) How is scientific knowledge translated into means of achieving public and economic objectives—as technology develops, can it be controlled to serve human values?

As the enterprises of science and government become more interdependent, we see a meshing, however uneasy, of goals and values, on one hand, and organizational processes, or institutions, on the other.[4] The structure and processes of government may be divided into the familiar legislative and administrative processes, each with a characteristic set of values or goals and with related, identifiable organization. Science-technology may also be divided into the research process of science and the engineering process of technology. The shortening links between scientific and technological activities have so often mixed the distinctive features and requirements of each that these distinctions are difficult to observe.[5] However, without losing sight of the close relationship between science and technology, a distinction can be made regarding the characteristic set of objectives and attendant organization for carrying on each enterprise.

The values of scientists and engineers, while often similar as to the essential worth of science and technology, differ in the priorities they personally assign to the intrinsic value of understanding natural phenomena and the use of that understanding for the control of the physical environment. Scientists most often place efforts to explore and understand the relationships that explain the physical world well ahead of utilizing scientific knowledge for solutions to problems of environmental control. This prompts them to place a much higher value on freedom of action in following unexpected developments in their research. They also resist working on problems defined by nonscientists, or even by their peers in other disciplines. Organizationally, they seek a minimum of restraint and actively resist measures of political or administrative control over scientific activities. They generally insist that the managers of scientific programs be scientists, whether or not their duties require work "at the bench."

Engineers, on the other hand, seek a more "pragmatic" solution to technical problems which are generally more capable of solution than those faced in scientific research. They attempt to develop machines and systems that will satisfy requirements, often set by others, rather than optimize a solution in the theoretical sense. The emphasis is upon what Herbert Simon has called "satisficing" rather than optimizing a solution in the strictly scientific sense. As members of complex administrative organizations, engineers are generally familiar with the requirements of *organizational* roles and with the need for coordination and scheduling, the influence of cost on technical choices, the needs for administrative controls, and other tools designed to increase efficiency and effectiveness. This familiarity and the relative importance of organizational goals for engineers, tend to make them more likely than scientists to accept directive controls. A number of major research and development organizations reflect these differences in internal structure, patterns of authority relationships, etc., of engineering groups as contrasted with basic research oriented groups.

When the values and organizational processes of scientific research and engineering, then, are brought together with the more publicly defined values made explicit in the legislative processes and the consequent requirements of governmental administration, they may complement each other, stimulate conflict, or simply be irrelevant. It is to the points of conflict or tension that the most visible attention has been devoted. Developments in scientific technologies often make manifest, even intensify, differences in the values underlying political choices and the conduct of public business.

As changes in technological capabilities occur, the patterns of public organization also change. Thus far, the relationships between government and science, as each attempts to cope with the altered conditions between them, is not clear, nor has there been sufficient experience to expect a stable relationship between them. Yet there is an urgent need to understand likely changes in government in consequence of stimulating and supporting scientific technologies. This is heightened by the need for decisions in the immediate future which will of necessity be based on scant information about effects in the more distant future. Making decisions *now* about the allocation of monies to technical programs limits alternatives for *future* development. It is clear also that the importance of science-technology for the political system is only part of an equation of exchange. As the scope and unity of science increases, both conceptually and in organizational size, the actions of government are much more relevant to the internal structure and strength of science. Many decisions concerning the posture of administration toward scientific organization, for example, harbor potentially damaging effects upon the integrity of science.[6]

Thus, the scope and integration of scientific and technical operations within and for government raise a number of concerns about the capabilities of existing political and administrative institutions to adapt to technology and the consequent "cost of adaptation." It is increasingly crucial that both the universities and government busy themselves in greater efforts to understand the nature of the legislative and administrative responses to the needs *for* science-technology in meeting national objectives and the needs *of* science in maintaining its integrity.

Moving beyond the intersections, it is appropriate to discuss four areas of concern. The first two, the social and economic changes stimulated by technology, and the effects technological changes have upon political and social values, both radically alter the setting of public affairs and radically challenge governmental administration. The remaining two, the effects of scientific and technical development on administrative organization, and the processes and limitations of policy formation in scientific areas, focus on organizational and policy responses to these changes and are discussed at greater length. In each case, these areas flow out of the meshing of government and science and are worthy of sustained research efforts.

Technology and Social Change

Currently, the area which has been given widest attention is the extent and pace of social and economic change stimulated by technological advances. While there have been myriad benefits from these developments, they have also generated a range of important political and governmental problems that are quite likely to be continuing sources of demands upon government for solution. Only brief treatment will be given to these problems, for they are broadly recognized and have been the object of extended comment by others.

Perhaps the most widely acknowledged problems are those associated with widespread adoption of automation and the effects of "cybernation."[7] Introduction of man-machine systems which are largely self-regulating has changed employment patterns and the relations between labor and industry. The extent to which automation has induced "structural unemployment," that is, increasing numbers of unemployables in today's technical industrial environment, is still unknown.[8] In whatever degree this does occur, as in the case of some racial minorities, governmental jurisdictions will continue to be confronted with breeding grounds for juvenile and young adult crime and social unrest. The greater the spread of "structural unemployment," the greater the need for government regulation and remedial programs.

Another aspect of the "cybernation revolution" is the probability of greatly improved production with a decreasing number of "productively" employed people. Since fewer workers are required, this can alter severely the patterns of income distribution through organizations of production and distribution as the usual channels of income flow become relatively restricted.

High production with limited buying power through traditional channels requires government involvement in welfare programs, extended educational opportunities and other efforts to develop alternative channels of income distribution. This will be a considerable challenge to both normative ideals and operational practices in a political system still wedded to a modified market system.

Finally, new alternatives for public policy made possible by scientific and technical advances in the uses of nuclear power, conversion of sea water, weather control, development of underseas resources, etc., are only dimly outlined. The consequences of a new type of policy alternative are discussed more fully later.

Science-Technology and Political Values

The effect of scientific and technical changes on public political values has not been charted, although there are strong prospects that traditional political and social values will undergo continual modification. For example, the efficacy of a "full-day's labor" as a value of considerable moral worth is likely to become eroded for people who suffer sustained conditions of unemployment due to technical obsolescence. Furthermore, deprived portions of a population who see an economy that *can* provide them with more than existing institutions distribute to them, lose confidence in those institutions, political or economic. In sum, as technology is used to change social and economic conditions, the political and social values re-enforced by prior conditions have less and less relevance to individual experience, and are likely to be displaced.[9]

Limited progress toward realizing the nation's technological potential has already forced a vague recognition that, while the means for solving many of man's problems seem tantalizingly near, established social and political values often leave us ill-prepared to act on this potential. Values functional for a frontier culture seem somehow inadequate, and growing disenchantment with traditional mores is evident in all quarters. Fixation on the political desirability of strong, local self-rule often creates in State and metropolitan government a kind of "trained incapacity," a political paralysis, to mobilize the wider geographical support required to implement many technological developments. It seems clear that local governments are often unwilling to cooperate with adjacent communities in mobilizing the necessary political and constituency support to take advantage of technical solutions for problems of rapid transit, resource conservation, etc. More deeply, economic abundance and the apparent certainty of its continuance drastically reduces the compelling quality of narrow definitions of self-interest, and results in an increasing rejection of the profit motive as a major source of normative commitment. This is particularly the case when this commitment appears to create conditions which denigrate the humanity of large numbers of people. At perhaps the most basic level, advances in the biological sciences dramatically alter the efficacy of traditional mores related to sex, ranging from abortion and contraceptive clinics to patterns of marriage.

In the drive to incorporate science through technology into the nation's capabilities for meeting public goals, whether it is pell-mell movement toward automated abundance, vastly improved medical refinements, or increased reality of leisure time, familiar institutions and the values they represent become blurred. The delineation between public and private, politics and business, government and the university are no longer sharp and clear.[10] Thus far, attempts to understand the pressures which warp notions of politics, commerce, etc., have been most meager, even though it is increasingly clear that the context of public affairs is swiftly changing as the problems confronting government come from unfamiliar sources requiring new skills and insight.

We shall turn now to the other areas in the discussion and examine more fully some of the questions raised for the organization of government and policy formation in response to the challenges of science and technology.

Science-Technology and Administrative Organization

The next area is much closer to the ongoing life of government and stems from its deep involvement in stimulating research and development both within and outside the Executive Departments. Experience thus far in administering and managing science and technology has led to a growing recognition that too little is known about organizing technical work, particularly within traditional government and industrial bureaucracies. Scant attention has been paid to testing the appropriateness of traditional notions of bureaucratic formal organization, control, etc., in conducting scientific research. Introducing substantial numbers of technical professionals into large complex organizations, as the support of science seems to require, alters considerably the utility of many familiar administrative precepts and adds immeasurably to the dilemmas of public control and accountability.

Bureaucratic administrative processes, which are typically hierarchical and directive as to type of work, interpersonal relationships, and modes of operation, are proving inadequate.[11] This is clearly evident in the literature of research administration and government operations concerning R & D. Controversy about the "proper" form of organization for scientific activities ranges from insistence on "functional" or disciplinary organization to calls for "projectization" of all scientific and technical ventures. The variations in form stem from differences in the requirements of technical or engineering work and basic research work. In the former, more operational control apparently is reasonable. In the latter case, basic research as a social activity seems to defy rigid structure or close control.

Patterns of authority relationships between the managers who are held legally responsible for the organization's mission and those upon whom they depend for technical skills have undergone a startling shift. Dominance of the superior over subordinate activities has been moved toward a "collegial" relationship in which both manager and researcher have a good deal to say about what will be done, and how.[12] As the skills of the technical professional move well beyond the competence of managers, old patterns of evaluation and accountability prove useless. Managers no longer can judge the quality of performance of their professional subordinates, nor do they have the skills to make decisions independent of advice from those professionals. Furthermore, research suggests that there is a kind of grudging de-bureaucratizing pressure in technical organizations, especially as the basic research end of the spectrum is approached. This occurs with increasing frequency as the range, complexity and interdependence of information required to operate are expanded, either from a technical or administrative point of view.

Whether the issues have to deal with the "proper" form of structure, the changing character of authority relationships in technical organizations, or other problems of organizing for research and development, there is now a modest history of attempts to face these problems in industry and government laboratories. Certainly many laboratories have arrived at a "local" solution. Rigorous study of "trial and error" answers to these problems would add greatly to both practical and conceptual improvements in understanding.

On another level, the Federal administration and organization of science and technology rely heavily upon the ingenious social invention of the grant and contract system.[13] This has enabled the government to move around its own internal operational and political limitations and purchase the technical and managerial skills in sectors outside the Federal agencies. This process, which has greatly expanded the scope of informal government control and dispersed more than three quarters of the public work in science and technology throughout industry and the universities,[14] has wrought a basic change in the traditional relationships between the major "estates" of our political system, i.e., government, the universities and private industry. No longer is there a relatively clean separation of activities among these three. Their increasing interdependence, prompted by the way in which grants and contracts are allocated and the needs they stimulate, has a deep effect in the internal processes of each and relationships between them. Policy regarding the scope, research direction, and administration of public monies can bring far-reaching changes in the character and context of the scientific enterprise.[15]

Finally, stimulating scientific and technical developments has resulted in a greatly expanded demand for trained scientists and engineers.[16] As numbers and demand have grown, so has the proliferation of new specialities, in response to often radically induced development of particular areas, e.g., space sciences. This requires encouraging the training of specialists, and, as technical areas develop, often retraining specialists. Along with the grant and contract system this requirement for stimulating training and recruitment into scientific fields further blurs the traditional distinctions between government and the universities. It adds greatly to the problems of maintaining a balanced program within universities which strive to keep a relatively equal emphasis across academic fields whether or not they garner Federal support.

Science-Technology and the Policy Process

The problems associated with the processes and limitations of public policy regarding science and technology have also drawn considerable attention, and some of the issues are familiar ones. This is particularly true in matters affecting the machinery and internal processes of scientific advice and the access of scientists-engineers to policy decisions which require technical evaluation, on one hand, and those that could affect the conduct of science, on the other.[17]

The recruitment of science advisers who are acquainted with the dilemmas of politics poses a substantial problem. It is clear that the skills of science do not necessarily equip a man for the peculiar rigors of politics or policy formation, i.e., finding the viable political and/or administrative solution for competing values. Skills required for good scientific work may in fact be detrimental. Furthermore, experience concerning the forms of scientific representation in the power structure, on one hand, and the responsiveness of scientists to the needs of government, on the other, while receiving some attention, has been too recent to have demonstrated what may be the optimum arrangement. Perhaps more important in the long run are the opportunities and risks in policy making made possible by rapid developments in science technology.

There are at least two major risks in approaching the problems of science policy; the first concerns the question of technological inflexibility;

the other, the implications for public policy of the limit-breaking advances in technology. Both are of the utmost importance to this country as we continue to "invent the future."

The first major risk is the danger of developing a relatively few, highly sophisticated technological alternatives or means for achieving public policy, limited both in available knowledge and human resources. Government support of science and technology, at its present level, results in the radical stimulation or development of specific and limited sectors within science and technologies to the relative deemphasis of other sectors. For example, in the past decade space research and nuclear energy have been emphasized, to the detriment of botany and physical anthropology, for whatever the reasons. Both the rate and selectivity of support increase the political and organizational inertia to continue in the directions already plotted. This could limit the nation's capacity to encourage and utilize unexpected or unforeseen developments in the natural or social sciences. Furthermore, due to the increased lead time required to build a national capacity in a new scientific or technical field, the manner in which finite resources of government are allocated, in the present, has the effect of putting restricting or determining strictures on future technological capabilities available for accomplishing national policy.

The other risk—potentially much greater—is found in the nature of the new technologies available or foreseen as we continue to harness technology in search of solutions to immediate or longer range problems. For the first time in history, we see a qualitatively different policy-making situation. Radically new policy alternatives exist that never before have been reasonable. In many cases they suggest that the primal assumptions of temporarily finite resources can be pushed far into the future, so far that they will not be nearly so relevant as they are at present. Some of the most captivating of these new technological capabilities make it necessary to re-examine the basic premises about what might be politically and economically feasible. An attack on many of man's most troublesome problems seems enough within reason to warrant serious consideration. For example, a radical reduction of world and/or national poverty through technological advances, providing almost unlimited amounts of energy through cheap nuclear power, limiting world populations or restructuring man's genetic composition all have passed from the region of the impossible to the realm of the probable. These possibilities strike to the center of many of our continuing themes in the dialogue of human suffering. The promise is tantalizing; a *Great Society* indeed seems to be this side of utopia. Yet, before the vision is grasped, a hard look at the consequences of attainment is required.

Political and economic institutions which have been developed during the past two centuries to deal with these problems are largely based on assumptions that the final solution is an ultimate impossibility. Problems of poverty have classically been founded on the assumption of absolute scarcity of resources, labor and a limited capacity for all to share at a relatively high minimum level. Only within the past few years has overpopulation been discussed in terms other than ameliorating the suffering it causes or pessimistic forecasts of disaster. Only recently has an emphasis been placed on limiting population growth rates in any systematic way. These once viable assumptions are the basis for our primary values of economic achievement, the values of a day's work, status and power based on economic wealth, etc., that hold a high place in our social and political hierarchy of precepts. Our economic institutions, for example, are still largely based upon theories which assume scarcity and do not include the condition of abundance. The impossibility of long-range solutions also undergirds many of the social, political and religious organizations of our culture. Possibilities of changing genetic structure, limiting births, improving the social conditions of the poor, all have strong implications for many of the important values of these institutions. In short, contemporary institutions and the values upon which they rest were fashioned during eras when radical solutions were not available, technologies had not been developed or projected, nor had science provided any alternatives to existing forms.

Our present public policy in the support of scientific programs, then, harbors this important probability: that the continued support of rapidly changing technologies will quite probably continue to apply strong pressures upon our familiar institutions. It is entirely possible that our political, economic, and social institutions may be modified past recognition in the future.[18] At present almost all of the official science policy studies under way seem to rest on the assumption that we can continue to develop the nation's scientific technological capabilities and still keep the familiar patterns of political federalism, regulated market economy, and a work-oriented social system. Politically uncomfortable as it may be, this is neither theoretically nor empirically justifiable. Support of technology probably means that we will be required to seek different institutional paths to values we choose to pursue. It may mean that we will have to modify or radically alter our premises about economic organizations and democratic forms. Though it may be tempting to assume implicitly that the support of science and its "naturalistic" translation into industrial and political power is, by and large, a process of continual improvement of our human condition, it would be risky in the extreme to ignore the potentially disastrous long range effects of technologically spawned social change.

The spreading web of dependence that we as a nation have upon science and technology requires that the institutions and values of these enterprises be more thoroughly understood, that the larger impact of changed social conditions upon politically relevant values be monitored, and that alternatives for public policy and their meaning be sought. It is against this background of needed information and insight that the final part of this paper is set.

Science, Government, and the Study of the Future

It is abundantly clear that as a nation we will continue to require innovative capacities in maintaining both political and economic strength into the foreseeable future. If the problems and promise discussed above, arising out of a growing capacity to choose the national path, have any reality in fact, then there is also a demand for devices and programs that can increase understanding of the present and sensing of the future. We *must* turn more of our attention toward establishing university and governmental mechanisms for sensing the present and anticipating and preparing for future social and political problems triggered by science and technology.

In this country, as far as I have been able to determine, there has been very little systematic governmental attempt to examine these problems. Furthermore, only a few university groups are concerned in serious and sustained ways with emerging problems or trends extrapolated beyond the immediate future, say the next five years.[19] Little or no official government attention has been paid to developing ongoing groups considering these problems.[20] We have already developed a small core of what has been called "scientific strategists" for defense matters.[21] In the face of the magnificent and staggering alternatives which science-technology appears to be offering, do we not need to develop strategy sciences for social change as well as for defense?

The pace of change underscores the importance of addressing the central questions outlined earlier. So little is known, however, that the processes of research, study, and policy implementation must go forward hand in hand. Most attempts to improve relationships between government and science-technology, and hence society, have meant simply making the current style or form somehow more "effective," assuming that the current directions ought to be pursued. But this is not a certain assumption. We must pause and ask if, indeed, the effects of scientific progress meet our expectations. Do evident changes represent advance and progress, or do they result in unanticipated and undesired consequence? Clearly this requires a level of examination by scholars and support from government that is not now present.

If there is to be a significant increase in understanding, a "mixed strategy" is probably required. Action must be taken, without waiting upon academic research to give answers to policy questions. Parallel efforts focusing on both the means of implementing present policies and, *at the same time,* carrying out rigorous examination of the effects of current trends, their underlying dynamics, etc., certainly should be pursued both by universities and by government. Ideally, the play between molding day-to-day policy and implementation would encompass research dealing with the effects of past policy and continuous evaluation of the ends to which that policy is tied.

It is quite probable that this process of policy blending with research would require a separation of effort in the social sciences much as we see in the physical sciences, that is, basic research activities carried on by groups and individuals within universities and small sections of other institutions apart from the implementation of engineers doing essentially applied research or advanced development. What is lacking now is a concept of social research linked to questions of public policy but carried out by rather different kinds of organizations than are generally associated with policy-making bodies. Many of the peace research groups seem to be harbingers of what could be done more generally across many of the social sciences.

It is evident that studies of policy effects or the underlying nature of technological impact on our social and political system are not enough. There must also be intensified efforts to peer into the future and engage in "responsible conjecture," attempting to garner insights into what we are doing by stimulating technology. The difficulties of future-oriented studies stem from several sources: the unavailability of data that are in the future, the limited theoretical or conceptual tools to deal with other than the distant or near past, and the professional hazards of slipping into "science-fiction." All these mount a challenge of substantial proportions. Being more precise about future developments may in fact turn out to be impossible, but this assumption has not been tested. Projections by scientists about what is likely to happen in scientific developments are both fascinating and awesome in their implications for changes in social systems.[22] The character of that change we can only dimly sense, but there is no doubt that intuitively we can foresee some likely directions.[23]

Our present level of theory building in the social sciences, however, throws up a barrier to much more than intuitive and very hesitant future-oriented thinking. Strong efforts are required to search out that portion of theory which is most readily factorable in terms which allow for conceptualizing the effects of technological development, not industrialization only, upon political and social systems. We need a treatment of both political and behavioral theory and certainly a theory of technological complexity which have common denominators so that their linkages may be exposed. Whether we decide to promote social change vigorously or simply rise to meet its consequences, mechanisms to anticipate the directions and impact of our scientific activities seem to be quite in order.

Conclusion

The recent history of science and technology and of its linkage to the institutions of government gives ample evidence of the remarkable increase in man's potential to mobilize nature in satisfying human desires. As progress in attaining the goal of release from dominating economic effort is made, the question must be asked: What now is possible in the political and social evolution of man? Whether explicitly asked or not, the question is being answered. It is as much a decision to keep on the present track heedlessly as it would be to reexamine aspirations and hit upon a new or modified azimuth. It is clear that conditions which will result in substantial change are being introduced. Better ideas of the consequences and the relation between the promises of scientific technology and the aspirations of men are essential.

The future holds enormous danger. It is possible that the implicit program for policy outlined above is moot—moot in the shadow of those weapons devised during the Second World War. But that awful prospect is paralleled by another perhaps more awesome—the danger of promise unfulfilled, or turned to ashes through misuse. That man need no longer go as a captive of history and of overwhelming economic effort, projects a danger which is to the spirit. As we move closer to a leisure society, there is the haunting thought that perhaps man cannot bear it. Can we adjust our values to act upon the enormous promise opened to us? Is it possible for our generation and those following to shift from traditional structures and values, ethical and moral, social and political, to new ones that do not end in hopeless awe before the machine, or ennui and anomie as we confront too many choices and changes with which we can neither cope nor understand? What can man become when he no longer must squander his energies upon the elemental activities of garnering subsistence from a stubborn environment?

Notes

1. Taken from the title of Dennis Gabor's distant look into the future, *Inventing the Future* (New York: Alfred Knopf, 1964).

2. Most attempts to deal with this area have been primarily based upon the personal experiences of the scientists who were instrumental in acting out the relationships between science and government (see note 4 below). Only a few scholars have addressed the problem in conceptual terms. Perhaps the best known is Don K. Price in his two books, *Government and Science* (New York: New York University Press, 1954; published in paperback, Oxford University Press, 1962), and *The Scientific Estate* (Cambridge: Belknap Press of Harvard University Press, 1965). See also Norman Kaplan, ed., *Science and Society* (Chicago: Rand McNally, 1965), Robert Gilpin and Christopher Wright, eds., *Science and National Policy-Making* (New York: Columbia University Press, 1964), J. Stefan Dupre and Sanford A. Lakoff, *Science and the Nation: Policy and Politics* (Englewood Cliffs: Prentice-Hall, 1962), Sanford A. Lakoff, ed., *Knowledge and Power: Essays on Science and Government* (New York: Free Press, 1966), and H. L. Nieburg, *In the Name of Science* (Chicago: Quadrangle Press, 1966). For examples of the historical approach to this subject see, A. Hunter Dupree, *Science in the Federal Government: A History of*

Policies and Activities to 1940 (Cambridge: Belknap Press of Haward University Press, 1957), and his "Central Scientific Organization in the United States Government," *Minerva,* I (Summer 1963), 453–469; James L. Penick, Carroll W. Pursell, Jr., Morgan B. Sherwood, and Donald C. Swain, eds., *The Politics of American Science: 1939 to the Present* (Chicago: Rand McNally, 1965); and Carroll W. Pursell, Jr., "Science and Government Agencies," in David D. Van Tassel and Michael G. Hall, eds., *Science and Society in the United States* (Homewood: Dorsey Press, 1966), pp. 223–250.

3. The approach outlined below is explicitly within the American context for reasons of economy. There is no intrinsic reason why these notions would not be readily applicable in cross-national studies, or with appropriate modifications for international studies as well.

4. Examples of scientist-engineers' views of these intersections can be found in C. P. Snow, *Science and Government* (London: Oxford University Press, 1960); Jerome Weisner, *Where Science and Politics Meet* (New York: McGraw-Hill, 1965); Lord Halsham, *Science and Politics* (London: Faber and Faber, 1963); Deal Wolfle, *Science and Public Policy* (Lincoln: University of Nebraska Press, 1959); Ralph E. Lapp, *The New Priesthood: The Scientific Elite and the Uses of Power* (New York: Harper and Row, 1965); and Alan T. Waterman, "Science and Government," in B. Baumrin, ed., *Philosophy of Science: The Delaware Seminar* (New York: John Wiley, 1961–1962), 309–324.

5. See Hendrick W. Bode, "Reflections on the Relation Between Science and Technology," in National Academy of Science, *Basic Research and National Goals* (Washington, D.C.: Report to the Committee on Science and Astronautics, U.S. House of Representatives, 1965), pp. 41–76; Aaron W. Warner, Dean Morse and Alfred S. Eishner, eds., *The Impact of Science on Technology* (New York: Columbia University Press, 1965); Sir Watson-Watt, "Technology in the Modern World," in Carl F. Stover, ed., *The Technological Order* (Detroit: Wayne State University Press, 1964), pp. 1–9; Derek J. De Solla Price, "Is Technology Historically Independent of Science? A Study in Statistical Histography," *Technology and Culture,* III (Fall 1925), 553–568; William O. Baker, "The Dynamism of Science and Technology," in Eli Ginzberg, ed., *Technology and Social Change* (New York: Columbia University Press, 1964), pp. 82–107.

6. *Note:* For the best statement from the scientific community regarding the problems of maintaining its integrity see, "The Integrity of Science," A Report for the American Association for the Advancement of Science Committee on Science in the Promotion of Human Affairs, in Gerald Holton, ed., *Science and Culture* (Boston: Houghton Mifflin and the American Academy of Science, 1965), pp. 291–332.

7. Coined by Donald N. Michael, *Cybernation: The Silent Conquest* (Santa Barbara: Center for the Study of Democratic Institutions, 1962), as a variation on the term "cybernetics" introduced by Norbert Weiner.

8. On one side of the issue are those often associated with the Ad Hoc Committee on the Triple Revolution who raise the fears of rapid, unthinking spread of automation. See Donald N. Michael, *Cybernation: The Silent Conquest,* ibid., and *The Next Generation* (New York: Random House, 1965); the initial statement of the Committee on the Triple Revolution, "The Triple Revolution," *Liberation*

(April 1964), and the *Correspondent* (March-April 1964), pp. 24–30; and Robert Theobald, *Free Man and Free Markets* (New York: C. N. Potter, 1963). Writers who have taken issue with the fears expressed by the group above include Bernard Asbell, *The New Improved American* (New York: McGraw-Hill, 1965); George Terborgh, *The Automation Hysteria* (New York: Machinery and Allied Products, Inc., 1964); and Daniel Bell, "The Bogey of Automation," *The New York Review of Books,* V (August 26, 1965), 23–25, who reviews the current material in this area and attacks the argument of the fearful. See also Stanley Lebergott, ed., *Men Without Work: The Economics of Unemployment* (Englewood Cliffs: Prentice-Hall, 1962); Morris Philipson, ed., *Automation: Implications for the Future* (New York: Random House, 1962); Charles C. Killingsworth, ed., "Automation," *The Annals,* CCCXL (March 1962), for selections covering both sides. Most recent discussions can be found in Lester B. Lave, *Technological Change: Its Conception & Measurement* (Englewood Cliffs: Prentice-Hall, 1966), especially chapter 13; and National Commission on Technology Automation and Economic Progress *Technology and the American Economy* (GPO: Washington, D.C., 1966).

9. A more illusive example is the carry-over of the scientific notion that all "truths" in science are liable to future disproof and are expected to be displaced. Should this frame of reference become generalized to social and political values, there is likely to be further disagreement about the priorities and values of our traditional hierarchy of political precepts. In the future a rather different hierarchy of political values is quite possible which could bring severe pressure to bear on our familiar patterns of political and economic institutions.

10. Price, *The Scientific Estate, op. cit.,* chapters 1, 2, and 6.

11. See for example, Paula Brown, "Bureaucracy in a Government Laboratory," *Social Forces,* XXXII (March 1954), 259–268; Alfred de Grazia, "A Concept of Scientists and Their Organization," *The American Behavioral Scientist,* VI (December 1962), 30–34; Gerald Gordon *et al.,* "Freedom and Control in Four Types of Scientific Settings," *ibid.,* pp. 39–42; Todd R. La Porte, "Conditions of Strain and Accommodation in Industrial Research Organizations," *Administrative Science Quarterly* X (June 1965), 21–38; William Kornhauser, *Scientists in Industry! Conflict and Accommodation* (Berkeley: University of California Press, 1962); Simon Marcson, *The Scientist in American Industry* (Princeton: Princeton University Press, Industrial Relations Section 1960); Norman Kaplan, "The Role of the Research Administration," *Administrative Science Quarterly,* IV (June 1959), 20–42; and the more general treatment of the generic problem by Victor A. Thompson, *Modern Organizations* (New York: Alfred Knopf, 1961) and "Bureaucracy and Innovation," *Administrative Science Quarterly* (June 1965), 1–20.

12. See particularly, Marcson, *op. cit.* and Kornhauser, *op. cit.,* William Evan, "Superior-Subordinate Conflict in Research Organizations," *Administrative Science Quarterly,* X (June 1965), 52–64; Ralph Hower, and Charles D. Orth, 3rd, *Managers and Scientists: Some Human Problems in Industrial Research Organizations* (Boston: Division of Research, Graduate School of Business Administration, Harvard University, 1963); Charles, D. Orth, 3rd *et al., Administering Research and Development* (Homewood: Dorsey Press, 1964); and Fremond E. Kast, and James E. Rosenzweig, eds., *Science-Technology and Management* (New York: McGraw-Hill, 1963), "Summary and Implications for the Future," pp. 320–333. See

also Warren O. Hagstrom, *The Scientific Community* (New York: Basic Books, 1965), Chapter 3; and, Gerald Gordon *et al.*, "Freedom and Control in Four Types of Scientific Settings," *American Behavioral Scientist* VI (December 1962), 39–43.

13. See Price, *Government and Science, op. cit.*, Chapter 3; Price, *The Scientific Estate, op. cit.*, Chapters 2 and 3; Dupré and Lakoff, *op. cit.*, Chapters 2 and 3, J. Stefan Dupré and W. E. Gustasson, "Contracting for Defense: Private Firms and the Public Interest," *Political Science Quarterly*, XII (June 1962), 161–177; V. A. Fulmer, "Federal Sponsorship of University Research," in the *American Assembly: The Federal Government and Higher Education* (Englewood Cliffs: Prentice-Hall, 1960); and V. K. Heymen, "Government by Contract: Boon or Bust," *Public Administration Review*, XXI (Spring 1961), 59–64.

14. For a most recent summary of the statistics of government research and development funding see, *Basic Research and National Goals, op. cit.*, Appendix A, pp. 305–324.

15. For an extended discussion of the character and effects of this interdependence, see Price, *The Scientific Estate, op. cit.*

16. For material from the National Science Foundation, see *American Science Manpower, 1962* (NSF 64–16, 1964); *Scientific and Technical Manpower Resources* (NSF 64–28, 1964), especially Chapter VI; *Scientists, Engineers and Technicians in the 1960's—Requirements and Supply* (NSF 63–64, 1964); and *The Long-Range Demands for Scientific and Technical Personnel—A Methodological Study* (NSF 61–65, 1961). See also, Engineers Joint Council, Engineering Manpower Committee, *Demand for Engineers, Physical Scientists, and Technicians—1964* (New York: by the Council, July 1964); and V. Berkner Lloyd, *The Scientific Age: The Impact of Science on Society* (New Haven: Yale University Press, 1964), especially Chapter 2.

17. For a summary analysis of the problems of science policy, see Avery Leiserson, "Scientists and the Policy Process," *American Political Science Review*, LIX (June 1965), 408–416. See also Price, *op. cit.*; Dupré and Lakoff, *op. cit.*; Weisner, *op. cit.*; Wolfle, *op. cit.*; National Academy of Sciences, *Basic Research and National Goals, op. cit.*; Norman W. Storer, "Some Sociological Aspects of Federal Science Policy," *American Behavioral Scientist*, VI (December 1962), 27–29; Kaplan, *Science and Society, op. cit.*, Part V, "Science and Policy," (collection of articles); Amitai Etzioni, "On the National Guidance of Science," *Administrative Science Quarterly*, X (March 1966), 466–488.

18. See for example the fascinating discussion in Robert L. Heilbroner, "The Future of Capitalism," *Commentary* (April 1966), pp. 23–25.

19. The notable exceptions to this are the programs already established at Massachusetts Institute of Technology, the Program on Technology and Society at Harvard University, the Institute for the Study of Science in Human Affairs at Columbia University, the Seminar on Science and Public Policy at Indiana University, the Science, Technology, and Public Affairs program at Case Institute of Technology, and the program for Policy Studies in Science and Technology at George Washington University. All but the first two of these programs are quite new. Purdue University is also initiating a similar program.

20. For an extended discussion concerning the problem of policy making and academic research, see Todd R. La Porte, "Discontinuities and Diffusion in Science,

Technology and Public Affairs: A Search in the Field," *American Behavioral Scientist,* special issue on Science and Social Policy, forthcoming. The extent that Congress has gone in examining some of these issues can be seen, in part, in *An Inventory of Congressional Concern With Research and Development,* issues for the Subcommittee on Government Operation, United States Senate, December, 1966. This is a one hundred page listing of publications from Congressional Committee reports, etc.

21. Bernard Brodie, "The Scientific Strategists," in Gilpin and Wright, *op. cit.,* pp. 240–256.

22. Several members of the RAND Corporation have issued reports in this regard; see T. J. Gordon and Olaf Helmer, *Report on a Long Range Forecasting Study* (Santa Monica: RAND Corporation, September 1964), and Olaf Helmer, *Social Technology* (Santa Monica; RAND Corporation, February 1965). The American Academy of Arts and Science has recently designated a Commission on the Year 2000, headed by Daniel Bell. See his "Twelve Modes of Prediction—A Preliminary Sorting of the Approaches in the Social Sciences," *Daedalus,* Vol. 93, No. 3 (Summer 1964), 845–880, and "The Study of the Future," *The Public Interest,* I (Fall 1965), 119–130. See also Bertrand de Jouvenel, *The Art of Conjecture* (New York: Basic Books, 1967). There are several smaller groups on the West Coast also engaged in beginning discussions focusing on the future at the California Institute of Technology and the University of California at Berkeley. The Institute of Policy Studies in Washington, D.C., is also focusing broadly on some of these problems.

23. Recent examples of these "forecasts" include, Gabor, *Inventing the Future, op. cit.;* René Dubos, *Man Adapting* (New Haven: Yale University Press, 1965); John R. Platt, *The Step to Man* (New York: Wiley, 1966); and Gordon Wolstenholme, ed., *Man and His Future* (Boston: Little, Brown, 1963).

28

ADMINISTRATIVE CRISIS: THE NEGLECT OF METAPHYSICAL SPECULATION

William G. Scott and David K. Hart
University of Washington

> *It was a world half convinced of the future death of our species yet half aroused by the apocalyptic notion that an exceptional future still lay before us. So it was a century which moved with the most magnificent display of power into directions it could not comprehend. The itch was to accelerate— the metaphysical direction unknown.*
>
> —Norman Mailer, *Of a Fire on the Moon*[1]

Some of the magnificence and the malaise in America is captured by the headnote quotation from Norman Mailer. Americans are fascinated by the successful solution of elaborate technological puzzles, yet many sense at the same time that technology may also be a malefactor as well as a bene-factor in their lives. Deeper still beneath this ambiguity lies the uneasiness that technology is detaching the nation from the traditional values which gave it strength and purpose in earlier decades.

These concerns, of course, are not exclusively American. They are artic-ulated by the French philosopher Jacques Ellul, who fears technology *not* because of its assault upon man's person nor his environment. Rather, he

410

argues that technology's greatest menace lies in its potential to warp the human spirit.[2] As technologically based affluence increases in advanced societies, for some mysterious reason the sense of goallessness, drift, and insecurity also increases.

Recent social criticism has reflected this particular malaise, sounding themes of crisis and urgency. This literature is dominated by fears of nuclear and ecological catastrophe, born from a dehumanized and ungoverned technology. However, the symbolism of a willful technology trapping man and shaping him to its own design is dangerously misleading. Technology is the creation of men and is managed by them. Technology and administration are inseparable both in practice and in theory. Therefore the deleterious effects of technology are the responsibility of those who control and administer the complex organizations within which it is embedded. For this reason we believe that the conditions of the contemporary malaise have not been adequately identified, and that the fundamental crisis of advanced societies remains obscure. That the real crisis created by the exponential growth of technology is administrative is the thesis of this article.

Some authors, recognizing the administrative crisis, have treated it as if it were just another technical problem to be solved. For instance, John Platt lists "administrative management" third on a list of American crises surpassed only by (1) total nuclear annihilation, and (2) great destruction short of human annihilation. Platt argues that unless we become better at administration, within five years our nation will face unbearable tensions arising from the stagnation of social institutions. Platt believes, however, that such tensions will yield to enlightened management practices. In his opinion, the administrative crisis has resulted from insufficient support for the discovery of better administrative processes. Thus he observes: "The cure for bad management designs is better management designs."[3]

Platt's argument should gain nods of assent within the administrative fraternity. However, like many others, Platt has fallen for the deceptively simple belief that good processes automatically guarantee good results. To suppose that our society's integrity and progress will be secured by spending more to improve our efficiency of administration requires a mighty leap of faith.

Ellul's assertion that technology has assaulted the traditional notions of man in ways unparalleled in human history is probably correct. In our opinion, this assault does not stem directly from science, engineering, or other forms of technology, but mounts instead from the administrative policy decisions that support both technological development and application. Therefore the unique element in the technological revolution concerns the values of the administrative elite that direct its course.

While part of the present administrative crisis may be of a technical nature, it is not the important part. We maintain that the values of the administrators are the most basic aspect of this criterion. This assertion is made on the grounds that: (1) an administrative elite performs the functions of leadership in advanced societies, and (2) this elite subscribes to a metaphysic that influences its decisions and its behavior in the management of technology in complex organizations, but (3) this administrative metaphysic is unarticulated, and, therefore, is unexamined. Thus, the crisis in administration is the neglect of metaphysical speculation.

Where such speculation has occurred in other disciplines (such as political science) it has focused upon two indispensable ingredients of moral discourse: (1) a vision of the innate moral nature of man, and (2) the value criteria used for judging the morality of behavior. We contend that these ingredients exist in the contemporary administrative metaphysic, but they are not the subjects of intellectual discourse. It is because of the absence of this sort of moral discourse that Mailer concludes, "our metaphysical direction [is] unknown."

Organizational Sources of the Administrative Crisis

Organizations are so familiar that their presence among us is either accepted uncritically, ignored, or mindlessly despised. Nonetheless, complex organizations continue. Therefore, to begin to understand why administrative scholars and practitioners have neglected metaphysical speculation, it is necessary to note certain features of the organizations they study and serve.

Contemporary life in advanced societies is dominated by complex organizations, because they support the technology essential to development, affluence, and world power. However, these organizations do more than provide a technological superstructure. They create a way of life that subsumes nearly all peoples in overlapping interdependencies. They significantly color, through their administrative elite, the values that people hold.[4] Therefore, they must be considered among the most important socializing agencies in modern society. For this reason, the administrators who control these organizations will continue to have an increasingly influential role in determining all human values.

The reverberations of the various decisions made by administrators in strategic organizations are felt throughout society. Yet the appraisal of these decisions, and of the administrators who make them, is distorted by the material largesse created in the way of jobs, products, and services. The difficulty of appraisal is the result of peculiar attributes of complex organizations which require administrators: (1) to devote themselves to matters of expediency, but (2) to shield them at the same time from evaluation by any criteria other than those derived from the paradigms of technical and economic rationality. We have entitled these conditions the "method of the pragmatically proximate" and the "shield of elitist invisibility," thus suggesting that they grow directly from the logic of complex organizations and that they are refined by the administrators of these organizations.

The Method of the Pragmatically Proximate

Administrative theory appeared in the early 20th century, when the methods of natural science were well advanced and when there was nearly universal optimism about the efficacy of those methods for social progress. One of the most basic features of the paradigm of natural science was the logical separation of fact and value. This accelerated scientific progress, since it allowed scientists to avoid the troublesome value questions and concentrate on the empirical world. Scientists confined their inquiries to the puzzles presented by the natural order and they developed, concomitantly, techniques that enabled them to predict (and often to control) the events which occur in this empirical universe. Natural science limited itself to a world capable of being known and, thus, acquired research goals that could be realized and an endless number of paradigmatic puzzles for scientists to solve.[5]

The success of the methods of natural science was not lost on administration. Theorists and practitioners presumed that their discipline could obtain similar results by utilizing the paradigm of natural science for the study and management of resources in organizations. Administrative theory began with the transposition of that paradigm as the guide for its own research methods.[6]

Some of the research results justified bootlegging the paradigm of natural science, because impressive quantities of information, along with certain low-order predictive models, were added to the knowledge inventory of administration. Unfortunately, the methodological single-mindedness with which administration embraced the paradigm of science in part resulted in normative sterility.

While failing to attend to values is dangerous for "applied behavioral science," it is, nevertheless, consistent with the ambient conditions that influence administration. Clearly the value poverty of administration is not the fault of the scientific paradigm. This indigence is the result of a combination of circumstances that elaborated the paradigm of science into a paradigm peculiar to an applied discipline like administration. The combination of the paradigm of science *and* the need to solve the immediate problems of complex organizations brought about a mutant paradigm for administration in which the method of the pragmatically proximate is rooted.

To illustrate, administration is an exercise in puzzle solving. The rational imperative of technology, the coordinative requirements of task specialization, and the productivity expectations of society at large demand that administration direct its energies and talents to finding solutions for practical, materialistic problems in the immediate time frame of the complex organization. So the urgency for pragmatically proximate puzzle solving has overridden whatever propensity for moral discourse that might exist in administration.

Administration has *not* reluctantly turned away from moral discourse. The truth is that the materialistic promise of administrative puzzle solving is so inherently compelling, the metaphysical speculation is condemned as a wasteful excursion into mysticism. Attention to the pragmatically proximate is rewarded, while little honor and fewer resources accrue to those whose work does not have the instrumental payoff of making the technical and organizational mechanisms of society more efficient. Thus:

> A technologically oriented organization has its rationalized purposes geared to the world of empirical fact rather than to transcendental value: Absolutistic beliefs, unquestioning loyalty, and the excommunication of heretics just do not fit into a value system of pragmatic operationalism. . . . The technological system creates experts who are heavily task oriented, who fly no flags, and who are completely bored by ideological considerations.[7]

So policies in complex organizations become oriented toward the expedient, under the direction of experts who are bored by value questions. The practitioners and theoreticians who commit themselves to the methods of science and to the existential problems of organizations enter into an orderly, purposeful, and fascinating world of puzzles, "that only their own lack of ingenuity should keep them from solving."[8] That world offers security and status for administration so long as the paradigm remains intact. Since metaphysical speculation is a major threat to the paradigm, there should be little wonder that it is neglected.

The Shield of Elitist Invisibility

Another aspect of organizational predominance is the tendency for the administrative elite to be hidden within the thickets of complex organizations. Two reasons for this are particularly important. The first is the persistent tendency to reify the organization. How familiar are the phrases: organizations "do" this or "decide" that, and that organizations "behave" with or without a "conscience." What consummate nonsense this is! Yet we continue to write and speak about organizations as if they were persons. The reification of organizations obscures the simple fact that people, called administrators, make moral judgments within organizations. To reify the organization masks these people from view, and depersonalizes the human value judgments they are required to make.

A second reason for the invisibility of the administrative elite (and one that aggravates the first) is that their performance is evaluated in terms of the functional criteria of efficiency. Because advanced societies are so intent upon the analysis and performance of organizational systems, they hold administrators functionally accountable for their actions. In other words, their "morality" is estimated from their contributions to the "health" of their organizations, using the criteria of rational efficiency as the measure of that morality.

The wall of organizational reification, reinforced by a nearly total acceptance of functional morality, effectively shields administrators and their acts both from view and accountability. This shield has the further effect of relieving administrators and, of course, administrative theorists, from the burdens of moral discourse and metaphysical speculation. This shield must be removed in order to illuminate the ultimate metaphysical premises upon which modern administration is based, and in order to suggest a manner by which moral discourse might proceed. Both these subjects are treated next.

The Unspoken Metaphysic of Administration

We suggest it would be useful for administrative theorists to begin such moral discourse by using political philosophy as an example.[9] On the one hand, a vision of a moral nature innate to man is antecedent to all political philosophies. Every important political philosopher made some *a priori* assumptions about human nature that were fundamental to his formulation of a political system, whether real or ideal. Of equal importance was the recognition of the absolute human need for order. So, again, no political philosopher of any consequence has advocated a society without at least a minimal system of order. It can be argued that political philosophy arises in the tension (or lack of it) between some vision of innate human nature and the pervasive human need for order. This tension intrudes into the world of applied politics and is therefore basic to an understanding of any political system.

On the other hand, administrative theory has not made any appreciable analysis of the relationship between order and innate human nature. Since its inception, administrative theory by necessity has concentrated upon the subject of order, variously treated as structure, consensus, coordination, or integration. The idea of order in administrative theory evolved to embrace all the structural and managerial leadership modes that are necessary to offset the fragmenting effects of the specialization of task and labor.

Without order, organization is unthinkable. So consistent with the method of the pragmatically proximate, administrative theorists have made powerful statements about order. However, it is rare to find them making similarly forceful statements about the moral nature of man. *Nevertheless, administrative theorists have an image of man's moral nature.* Imbedded in their writings are implicit moral assumptions which are seldom recognized by them as the foundations of theory and practice.

Very few new ideas about man's nature have been developed, even of late. Rather, familiar ideas are examined from unfamiliar positions and familiar questions are restated in unfamiliar ways. By this method new combinations and permutations of ideas are brought to light. We attempted to demonstrate all of this in a recent comparative essay, wherein some of the traditional visions of man in administrative theory were rephrased by casting them in the context of political philosophy.[10]

We found in our study certain remarkable parallels when the writings of Thomas Hobbes were compared with Frederick W. Taylor, Elton Mayo with John Locke, and Douglas McGregor with Jean-Jacques Rousseau. One of the reasons for the comparisons was to make explicit some implicit assumptions about innate human nature held by administrative theorists. We observed:

> Taylor and Hobbes believed in the need for maximum control to beat back *predatory* man. McGregor and Rousseau, in opposition, agreed to a minimization of the institutions of control to allow man's *innate compassion* to be released.... Mayo and Locke occupied somewhat the center ground where man, being *basically indeterminate,* had to be *formed* through education to develop his own rational controls.[11]

The conclusion we drew was that the view of human nature held by administrative theorists influences every one of his prescriptions for organizational design, managerial leadership style, and social goals. A Taylor would prescribe differently from a McGregor! This particular point is so obvious in administrative theory that the systems proposed by Taylor and McGregor are often exemplified as the polar alternatives of organizational governance: e.g., autocracy and democracy, respectively.

Administrative theorists have been compulsive about this polarity, discussing the utilities of autocracy vs. democracy since the 1920s. Few, with the possible exception of McGregor himself, seemed to realize that they were really arguing about the nature of man: *For if man is good and compassionate by nature then his institutions should be designed to free him, but if he is evil and predatory by nature, then his institutions should be designed to contain him.* Otherwise, order will not prevail in society.

Theoretical fashions do change, however, and the old good-evil, democracy-autocracy polarities implicit in administrative models of man are fading. Younger theorists are rejecting the operational usefulness of the polar concepts.[12] Currently in favor is the "contingency approach," which holds that there are no "right" management styles or organizational designs.

Rather, proper theory must reflect the fact that what administrators do (and what theorists think) is contingent upon environment and technology. Concepts and practices that are not framed as relative to these forces are condemned as being reductionist and determinist.

The contingency approach attributes a marvelous plasticity to administrators for adapting themselves and their organizations to technological change and environmental turbulence, whatever might be required and as often as it occurs. We contend that this conviction about the adaptive potential of administrators (and man in general) has grown out of the contemporary image of human nature in administration. This image is predicated on the belief that man is by nature *neither* good nor evil, but is by nature nothing. If man is nothing, he has the potential to be made into anything. *Therefore, man's institutions must be designed to build him,* since there is nothing in principle about man's nature that prevents his adaptation to the various exigencies that the environment presents. To us, it appears that the contemporary image of man in the eyes of administration is nihilistic.

Modern administrative nihilism dates back to Elton Mayo in the 1930s, although he would probably be appalled by the extent to which it has been carried: Man was assigned an indeterminate nature at best and it may be that man's nature is plastic or interminate or contingent.[13] The point is that this position is one of the implicit metaphysical foundations of contemporary administrative theory. This assumption has profound administrative consequences that are barely understood in our technological society.

The Metaphysic of Administrative Nihilism

In our judgment the predominant value paradigm that instructs the theory and practice of administration assumes the following form: What is desirable or undesirable in our society is measured by the degree to which a cluster of norms, an act, or an event contributes to or obstructs the progress of scientific and technical rationality applied to all planes of human existence. Ellul, among others, believes that contemporary technological culture is a historically unique event. It is neither a linear extension of the industrial revolution, nor a simple evolutionary change in a paradigm of rationality. The technological culture is a mutation, having certain historical roots, but in itself quite new.

Perhaps the most disquieting aspect of this mutation is its impact upon values. One of the distinctive features of our society is its apparent goallessness. More than one observer of western culture has noted the ceaseless busyness of its people, questing for better and better means to achieve instrumental ends. The creation, production, and consumption of goods and services require so much energy and talent, and are so interesting and satisfying, that few pause to inquire as to the purpose of all this frenetic activity.

It is assumed that ultimate ends will take care of themselves, and they tend to be taken for granted. Presumably it is sufficient for technological society to be governed by the principles of science, engineering, and economics, since in their refinement lies the surest course to social improvement. Thus, we are without a metaphysical direction because we are culturally prepared to accept the premise that beneficial ends will emerge automatically from increased technological development.

This is a foolish assumption, but it has been fully embodied in administrative philosophy. Administrative activity has been impelled along two avenues: (1) administration does not admit for serious consideration the force of chiliastic ends; consequently (2) it gravitates toward the existential reality of the organization in its proximate environment. Hence the discourse of administration is about the present; but with little consideration of the forces of the past or future, the present must be interpreted as contingent and capricious. Is it any wonder, therefore, that administration puts such a high premium on man's adaptative potential? And, if man's destiny is accepted as contingent, what can be said about the image of his nature upon which administrative policy decisions are predicated?

Thirty-five years ago, Mayo presented us with a vision of man with an indeterminate nature. That vision was a presagement of the requisite man for the technological age. It meant simply that man need not get in the way of rational administrative responses to technological and organizational requirements, since nothing in man can cause him to move *necessarily* in different directions. Given this metaphysical base, administrative strategy is clear: with the scientific discovery of appropriate techniques, man can be shaped or, given a shift of contingencies, reshaped to be "good members" of the organizations that compose the technological society. Men need not impede administrative process. The problems of "how-to-do-it" are reduced to puzzle solving within the dominant paradigm of scientific and administrative rationality.

A New Technology for Administrative Puzzle Solving

Abroad in the land of contemporary administration is a bastardized variant of the Mayo-Locke image of man. It is a vision of men who are innately malleable, vulnerable to techniques of control, and shapeable through the modification of the environment and of the mind. The vision of malleable human nature, implicit in and necessary to the strategy of administrative nihilism, is a metaphysical position far beyond either Locke or Mayo. This vision is a mutation, much as the technological society is itself a mutation. To fulfill this vision the only element missing is for man himself to *accept* his malleableness.[14]

Men have always been socialized, trained, and organized, to some extent, without necessarily being harmed. The difference now is that science is developing the capacity to intervene directly to alter man's mental and social processes. Scientists are rapidly perfecting methods for drastically changing human personality. There is not space in this article to present an inventory;[15] suffice it to say that we are experiencing a bio-medical and behavioral revolution, stemming from science, which will permit the human mind, and thus human relationships, to be altered to produce behavior that scientists and administrators deem desired or required.[16]

Dr. Jose Delgado, one of the pioneers in the bio-medical revolution, classifies available techniques into two main categories:

(1) Use of chemical and physical agents to induce modifications in neurophysiological activity. This category includes psychoactive drugs and direct electrical manipulation of the brain. (2) Use of positive or negative social reinforcements, based on the sensory relations between the subject and his environment, mainly other human beings who are the suppliers of stimuli.[17]

While most of these techniques are crude at present, their refinement is only a *scientific* puzzle to be solved.

The puzzle that confronts administrators is different, since it involves the selection of appropriate behavioral and medical technology that will induce optimum human adaptation to changing organizational and technological circumstances. The selection of techniques requires two distinct administrative decisions: (1) the support of research that seems to have the greatest promise for administrative and organizational application, (2) the translation of scientific research findings to use in administrative practice. What is important to note about these decisions is that they are technical in nature. The moral commitment to their use is already present in administrative metaphysics.

Mayo was correct when he identified administrators as the elite of advanced societies. They have the most effective access to the technological system, and they can use the techniques of the system to write "programs" for mankind. Perhaps Mayo was even correct in his supposition that man's nature is basically malleable, capable of formation into an almost limitless number of patterns. Certainly, given resources and reasons, the scientific potential for human modification is practically beyond comprehension.

Some Proportions of the Administrative Crisis

The combination of administration and technology has promise and danger. In our view, the danger to man from this combination is heightened out of proportion to its promise because of the unwillingness in administration to reflect on the moral direction of policy. A crisis exists because those responsible for administrative concepts, policies, and programs have not systematically introspected, rationally deduced, and consciously expli-

TABLE 28.1   Problems and Consequences of the Neglect of
Metaphysical Speculation

Problems	*Consequences*
1. Administration holds images of innate human nature. However, these images are implicit and unarticulated. The failure to deal consciously with the question of the innate nature of man has produced a moral diffuseness in administration.	1. These unexamined images are the ephemeral grounds for theory building and policy making and they are as likely to be misleading as useful to administrative leadership. So the aimlessness of the theoretician is matched by the practitioner. Neither can offer more than platitudes and metaphors regarding the purpose of man in organizations nor the *raison d'etre* of organizations. Hence we suffer from the absence of "metaphysical direction."
2. Administration is the handmaiden of technology. It addresses mainly the problems of the pragmatically proximate, using the criteria of technical rationality and efficiency to judge the "functionality" of administrative theory and practice.	2. Technological puzzle solving is not sufficient to set a sense of metaphysical direction in administration, unless we are willing to say that it is the purpose of administration. If we accept these kinds of standards as the criteria for judging the behavior of administrative leadership, then the moral bankruptcy of administration is complete in terms of the inadmission of other ethical criteria, e.g. humanistic, theological, political.
3. The surge of technology in the pharmacological, neurological, biological, and behavioral sciences, coupled with continuing developments in the now commonplace engineer technologies (e.g., information systems) have accelerated the reality of control by an administrative elite over the instruments of science and technology.	3. This kind of control might lead to totalitarianism in the fullest sense. The potential of this consequence is clearly present, and without moral discourse and metaphysical speculation, its realization is a virtual certainty.

cated the metaphysical premises from which they operate. Unless these basic exercises of metaphysical speculation are done, there is little chance of predicting the consequences of administrative techniques and theories; much less is there a chance to discover a basis for evaluating these consequences and to question the value paradigms in which they are located. The fact that moral discourse has not evolved along with the technical capabilities of administration creates urgent contemporary metaphysical problems that cannot be ignored, unless one believes our present condition is acceptable. Our concern has led us to the conclusion that most of the problems emanate from a crisis in administration, the elements of which are summarized in Table 28.1.

However, some readers might ask: Why blame administrative theorists and practitioners for not addressing themselves to ultimate metaphysical questions? Are not their responsibilities to the pragmatically proximate organizational reality, and not to "blue-sky" speculation? Why insist that they should perform philosophical tasks any more than scientists, teachers, wage earners, physicians, or engineers?

The answers are implied throughout this essay. Those who do administration and those who think about administration are the human intermediaries of technologically based organizations. Administrators, supported by theorists, as one: (1) seek the rational expression of technology within complex organizations, (2) provide a bridge from such abstractions as rationality, technology, and organizations to the mass of mankind through the concrete manifestations of goods and services, (3) marshall and control the vast amounts of technical expertise and material resources necessary for the continuous technological development of advanced societies, (4) occupy the focal points of communication networks both within and without organizational boundaries that gives them considerable influence leverage, and (5) possess and use a singular theoretical knowledge and expertise that is quite apart from the conventional forms of scientific learning and engineering applications associated with pure technology.

This role of administration is new, and its presence among us—although announced—has not been given attention commensurate with its importance. Nevertheless, the direction of social change and the structure of social priorities are being determined increasingly by administrative policy, informed by administrative theory. Therefore, to call administrators the *elite of advanced societies* is hardly unreasonable. They are the elite because they alone have the expertise to do the significant jobs which give them access to the technological apparatus.[18] The control of these jobs permits the elite to direct the course of policy; the control of the technologies inherent in these jobs makes whatever course chosen a self-fulfilling prophecy. Given the awesome power acquired by doing the significant jobs, why should it not be appropriate to expect administrators to have a heightened awareness of the implications of their metaphysical premises?

Our purpose in this essay has not been to formulate solutions, but to depict the critical moral dilemma facing all of us, through the failure of administration to engage in metaphysical speculation. By realizing that now all things are possible in a technical, and thus in an administrative sense, the debate about man's moral nature and about the criteria used to judge his behavior can be rendered nonrelevant. The advance of technology and the ascendency of the administrative elite could actually eliminate the transcendent nature of man's conception of himself.

Notes

1. The book is Mailer's personal appraisal of the Apollo 11 moon mission (Boston: Little, Brown, 1970), pp. 51–52.

2. Jacques Ellul, *The Technological Society,* John Wilkinson (trans.) (New York: Knopf, 1954, 1964).

3. John Platt, "What We Must Do," *Science,* Vol. XXVIII (November 1969), p. 1117.

4. This issue is of considerable importance and will be the subject of a future essay.

5. See Thomas S. Kuhn, *The Structure of Scientific Revolutions* (2nd ed.) (Chicago: University of Chicago Press, 1970).

6. It is suggestive on this point to mention that the first major movement in administrative theory was "scientific management," later on, two key fields of study and practice emerged called management science and operations research, and presently two of the most respected professional journals are *Administrative Science Quarterly* and *Management Science.*

7. Daniel Katz and Robert L. Kahn, *The Social Psychology of Organizations* (New York: John Wiley & Sons, 1966), p. 55.

8. Kuhn, *op cit.* p. 37.

9. This notion is presented in more detail in William G. Scott and David K. Hart, "The Moral Nature of Man in Organizations: A Comparative Analysis," *Academy of Management Journal,* Vol. XIV (June 1971), pp. 241–255.

10. *Ibid.*

11. *Ibid.,* p. 255, emphasis added.

12. See, for example, Don Hellrigel, "The Moral Nature of Man in Organizations: A Comparative Analysis: Comment," *Academy of Management Journal,* Vol. XIV (December 1971), pp. 533–537.

13. Elton Mayo, *The Human Problems of an Industrial Civilization* (Boston: Harvard University, Graduate School of Business Administration, 1933), esp. pp. 150–151.

14. This point is of the utmost importance. Not only must all men believe their nature to be malleable, they must accept it as a positive benefit. At that time they make themselves completely susceptible to the values and behaviors demanded by (administrative) leadership.

15. For examples, see John Taylor, *The Shape of Minds to Come* (New York: Weybright and Talley, 1970), and Gordon Rattray Taylor, *The Biological Time Bomb* (New York: New American Library, 1968).

16. Scientists justify this type of research either in terms of the value-free pursuit of truth or in terms of therapy. See Jose M.R. Delgado, *Physical Control of the Mind* (New York: Harper and Row, 1969), esp. Part IV. However, when it comes to recommendations for application of these techniques, which must inevitably involve an administrative policy decision, they lead to circumscribing freedom of

choice. The moral premise is that "goodness" artificially induced is better than "evil" freely chosen. This is precisely the point of Kenneth Clark's 1971 presidential address to the American Psychological Association on the efficacy of the use of drugs to end violence, cruelty, and war. See *Intellectual Digest*, February 1972, pp. 50–52.

17. Delgado, *op. cit.*, p. 249.

18. The concept of the "significant job" is most important, and we will deal with it at greater length in a future article.

29

CIVIS, CIVITAS, AND CIVILITAS: A NEW FOCUS FOR THE YEAR 2000

Louis C. Gawthrop
Indiana University

Whatever else may be said of the Middle Ages, they did present the Western world with a preface to modern democratic theory. For example, the notion of citizenship—as we generally define it today—is a derivative of the emergence of the nation-state which, in turn, was a direct outgrowth of the medieval period. To be sure, citizenship was a meaningful concept in the Greco-Roman period, but from roughly the 5th to the 16th centuries— "... from the fall of the Roman Empire in the West to the fall of the Roman Empire in the East; from the triumph of Christianity over classical paganism to the revolt of Protestantism against Catholic Christianity"[1]—the notion of citizenship evolved into that which clearly resembled a transcendent ethics of noble civility. In ideal form, this notion of citizenship, and its attendant ethics of civility, was portrayed in a theological motif: Rights and privileges were balanced by obligations and responsibilities, and bound together by such values as honor, loyalty, courage, and forthrightness—all directed and dedicated to the service of God's mankind. In this context, the noble civility of an individual's secular existence was but a prologue to the eternal timelessness of a divinely ordained harmony where all true citizens of the world would be united. In an age when the notion of citizen was defined by the character of citizenship, the ethics of noble civility represented the hallmark of virtue. "The Middle Ages were not dark, but were illuminated by a light which enabled those who walked by it to attain heights of holiness rarely reached by men either before or since."[2] Unfortunately, this exalted or ideal notion of citizenship, or *civitas,* applied to relatively few; for most citizens of the medieval Christian world, life was—to quote from Hobbes—solitary, poor, nasty, brutish, and short.

In round figures, the medieval period ended around 1500 and the elements of the nation-state system began to emerge around 1600. Thus, roughly 200 years transpired between the embryonic development of the nation-state and the emergence of the American Republic. The significant sociopolitical developments of this two-century period need not be repeated here. However, one important characteristic of this period needs to be highlighted if the twin notions of *civis* and *civitas*—citizen and citizenship—are to be kept in proper perspective as we prepare to enter the 21st century.

Reason of State

The notions of *civis, civitas, civilitas* (the art of government), were not unique to the development of Western civilization. In both the ancient Egyptian and Chinese civilizations similar concepts prevailed. Indeed, social anthropologists would advise us that rudimentary characteristics of these traits may be found in virtually all levels of communal life. Equally basic to all social groupings—if not preeminently central—have been the notions of security, stability, and survival. From the beginning of group life to the emergence of the nation-state, the most vexatious intellectual dilemma has focused on the survival of the individual *versus* the survival of the group. Which should prevail when a choice must be made? To ask the question is to answer it; the course of history through the Middle Ages is writ large with the sacrifice of the individual to the collective body, however that body may have been defined.[3]

The emergence of the nation-state did nothing to alter either the dilemma or its manner of resolution other than to formalize the solution in the name of sovereignty and to fortify the concept of sovereignty with the doctrine of *ratio status, Staatsräson,* or, quite simply, reason of state. As Carl J. Friedrich noted, "... if the political order [proved by the nation-state] is assumed to be an essential condition of a free existence [for the individual], the survival of this order becomes crucial ... reason of state is nothing but the doctrine that whatever is required to ensure the survival of the state must be done by the individuals responsible for it, no matter how repugnant such an act may be to them in their private capacity as decent and moral men."[4] The logic of the doctrine of reason of state is incontrovertible if the notion of national sovereignty is recognized as an absolute. "The dogma of sovereignty," Hans Kelsen wrote, "leads to a negation of an international law as a legal order above the states."[5]

The most direct result of this formalized logical sequence of thought was: (1) the subtle (and, in many instances, the not-too-subtle) shift of emphasis of the notion of *civilitas* from the art of government as conducted by citizens to the craft of government as conducted by professionals, and (2) the consequent shift of the notion of citizen *(civis)* as defined by the character of citizenship *(civitas)*, to the notion of citizenship becoming a function of *civilitas*. Thus, with the emergence of the nation-state, the exalted notions of citizen and citizenship were lowered to the realm of the positive legal order which was ultimately defined and justified on the basis of national sovereignty, reason of state, and the craft of government. Similarly, of course, the transcendent ethics of a noble civility were transformed into a juridical ethics of positive law and, subsequently, into a procedural ethics. The effects of these shifts in emphasis were reflected throughout the royal absolution of Europe from the 16th through the 18th centuries with increasing harshness. For many individuals, life became intolerable. The American colonies and the subsequent Republic offered the prospect of relief from the tyranny of the craft of government and the hope of a renewed veneration of *civis* and *civitas*. The perception of democracy based on a transcendent ethics of noble civility, however distant the journey or slim the success, was infinitely preferable to an ethics of officious disdain or benign neglect.

The First Two Hundred Years

Recently, Robert Biller, currently vice president and vice provost of the University of Southern California, conducted a series of thought-provoking exercises in which participants were asked to answer the following questions: What should we have learned from our 200 years of experience with the experiment of self-government in the United States? and, What should we have learned from our 100 years of experience as a profession of public administration? Viewed as discrete queries, a wide range of answers can be imagined. However, if viewed in relation to each other, these two questions suggest an inverse relationship: To the extent that government of, by, and for the individual self does, in fact, prevail, the need for public administration as a profession declines, which is to say that where *civilitas* (the art of government) is a function of the citizen *(civis)*, the character of *civitas*, or citizenship, is essentially self-derived and the professional purposefulness of public administration is narrowly defined. Conversely, however, it may be argued that wherever the notion of citizen becomes a function of the craft of government, the essential character of citizenship is externally imposed, and the purpose of a professionalized public administration becomes broadly defined even to the extent that the most elementary, despotic government needs an administrative apparatus to impose its force. In actual fact, of course, the history of the United States amply documents a professed faith to follow both directions simultaneously, although, in truth, the lesson should be clear—Walden Pond is our vision, but *carpe diem* is our motto.

The doctrine of reason of state would have it no other way. In the United States, the fundamental question of national sovereignty was definitively answered in *McCulloch vs. Maryland*. From that point on, given the subsequent development of the Republic, the notion of citizen became a function of the craft of government, and the purpose of public administration was inevitably set in slowly accelerating but steadily expansive motion. If nothing else, after 200 years' experience in democracy and 100 years' experience in professionalized public administration, we should have learned that broad geographic expanse, plus progressive population growth, plus enormous natural wealth, plus sound intellectual development inevitably yield sociopolitical complexities of major magnitude that need to be managed by professionals if the amateurs are not to be mangled.

Unfortunately, the key lesson of the developmental history of the United States that seems to be lost on many today is that once a certain level of capacity is attained in any social system, systemic complexity can be energized by autochthonous forces that can only be managed but never controlled in any literal sense of the word. Thus, to assume that a reduction in the number of professionals or even, for that matter, a reduction in the number of public policy programs will yield a reduction in the level of systemic complexity and, hence, also yield a resurgence of the art of government as a function of the individual citizen is, indeed, to miss the forest for the trees.

The lesson of the first 200 years of self-governing experience in the United States is that of a steady, evolutionary, sociopolitical progression through the 19th century from the simple to the complex, and thus far through the 20th century, from the complex to the supra complex. Thus, despite a deeply ingrained democratic ethos which places the art of government in the easy reach of every ordinary citizen, government today—and especially the administrative implementation of public policy, i.e., the craft of public administration—has become an enormously complex undertaking.

Of course, no age has a monopoly on complexity. Like change, complexity is a relative and relational term. Complexity, however, does reveal a directional constancy of progression toward increasing gradations of variety. As the composition and interacting pathways of any system, biological or social, become more varied, the system becomes more complex. Moreover, and perhaps inevitably, the significance of the most basic components of our sociopolitical system (i.e., individual human beings) tends to be lost, or taken for granted, or even ignored in favor of larger clusterings of social groups. One way to attempt to control complexity is to aggregate similar elements into separate clusters, and then to generalize about the resulting aggregations. Furthermore, the process of aggregation is, itself, an open-ended process since it is purely a function of the degree of complexity existent within any system. Thus, within any system there can be multiple levels of aggregation.

What this means in terms of the notion of citizen and the character of citizenship in the United States political system after 200 years of operation should be obvious: the idealized notions of *civis, civitas,* and *civilitas*—encircled by an ethics of noble civility—are totally unattainable in high variety, rapidly changing, complex systems. The pragmatic administrative expediencies that have been imposed to control variety in the name of national sovereignty, or reason of state, or the Public Interest, or the Common Good have, it may be argued, contributed significantly to the material development and well-being of the commonwealth. However, if the premises are accepted that: (1) complexity is irreversible, and (2) the level of complexity currently evidenced in our society can only be managed but not controlled, then a new era must begin in the domain of public management whereby the primary purpose of the craft of management is the revitalization of the character of citizenship and the meaning of citizen.

The Next Twenty Years

As noted above, the idealized notions of citizen, citizenship, and the art of government are virtually devoid of practical significance in today's world of nanosecond complexity and change. In terms of the proposition stated above, the basic question to be examined is how the craft of public management can be directed to revitalize the character of citizenship and the meaning of the concept of citizen. One beginning step that is certainly suggested is the need to redefine and revitalize the professional mission of public service and public management. To raise this point, however, is simply to confront a series of corollary questions: What is the ultimate purpose of public service in America? What is its ultimate responsibility? What should the craft of management contribute to the commonweal?

To run the risk of advancing a tautology, public management is public service, or service to the public. Hence, if the concept of democracy is to have any meaning at all, public managers are the servants of the public where the primacy of the body politic is explicitly recognized as the linchpin of our democratic ethos. Therefore, to argue that the primary mission of public management is to serve the public, while not particularly novel or unique, is, nonetheless, somewhat of a radical departure from the notions of aggregate groupings that have constituted a phantom public in the minds of many professional public administrators.

The question of who is the public that public servants are supposed to serve can, should, and has been discussed on numerous occasions in our history. Most recently, the issue was raised explicitly by the New Public Administration,[6] that "the public" was to be viewed in terms of one's neighbor. The thrust of the New Public Administration was to gear public service delivery systems down to the street corner level where administrators could interact effectively with service delivery recipients on a face-to-face basis. Thus, identifiable faces of "brothers," "sisters," "neighbors," or "friends" would replace the faceless aggregates of phantom publics, and public administrators would be supposedly infused with a clearly defined sense of humanistic purpose.

There is a paradoxical dilemma, however, in attempting to relate public managers to clients as neighbors. It is very easy to satisfy professional and personal responsibilities by satisfying a carefully selected subset of clients who can clearly be identified as "friends," "neighbors," or "brothers and sisters." It is easy to serve those whose gratitude for one's "service" is expressed most openly, whose confirmation of one's "responsiveness" is lauded most vocally, and whose allegiance to one's "directives" is demonstrated most clearly. The real challenge—or the nature of the paradoxical dilemma—is presented by Nietzsche as cited in an interesting passage by Dietrich Bonhoeffer.

> Nietzsche, without knowing it, was speaking in the spirit of the New Testament when he attacked the legalistic and Philistine misinterpretation of the commandment which bids us love our neighbor. He wrote: "You are assiduous in your attention to your neighbor and you find beautiful words to describe your assiduity. But I tell you that your love for your neighbor is a worthless love for yourself. You go to your neighbor to seek refuge from your self and then you try to make a virtue of it; but I see through your 'unselfishness.' . . . Do I advise you to love your neighbor? I advise you rather to shun your neighbor and to love whoever is furthest from you!" If beyond his neighbor a man does not know this one who is furthest from him as his neighbor, then he does not serve his neighbor but himself; he takes refuge from the free open space of responsibility in the comforting confinement of the fulfillment of duty.[7]

Before government of, by, and for the self can be realized, public managers must step out from behind the "comforting confinement of the fulfillment of duty" to ensure that government is made available, made open, and

made interesting to whomever is "furthest away." To revive the character
of citizenship and the notion of citizen, public administrators must be prepared to end the isolation, to expand the alternatives, and to revitalize the
nature of authentic choice of the lost "neighbors" of the body politic.

This, of course, not only places a heavy ethical/moral burden of responsibility on public administration as a profession, in a collective sense, and
on each public manager, in an individual sense, but it also moves on a col-
lision course with the deeply ingrained democratic tradition most articu-
lately advanced by such distinguished scholars as Charles Hyneman and
Herman Finer—namely, the ultimate subordination of all public administrators to the legislative branch of government. As Finer quotes from a
1934 British government report,

> . . . good government is not an acceptable substitute for self-government, . . .
> the only form of self-government worthy of the name is government through
> ministers responsible to an elected legislature.[8]

Thus, viewed in this context, the sense of conscience, responsibility, obligation, and accountability of public managers is directed solely to elected legislators who are seen as the direct representatives of the body politic. But
the underlying question remains: Do public managers have no obligations
or responsibilities to the citizenry of the nation? An old American political
dictum reminds us that "where annual election ends, tyranny begins," but
it was Norton Long who suggested,

> If one rejects the view that election is the *sine qua non* of representation, the
> bureaucracy now has a very real claim to be considered much more represen-
> tative of the American people in its composition than the Congress.[9]

This important issue as best exemplified by the now-classic Friedrich-Finer
exchange[10] is inevitably presented in terms of an either/or choice, but the
notion of superior-subordinate relationships in this instance, as in all other
instances where it is made to apply, obscures the essential fact articulated
by Mary Parker Follett that reality is in the relating.

That elected legislative officials relate to the body politic by making their
constituents' wants and needs visible in the legislative process is a reality
that exists in the relating. It is equally apparent, however, that the reality of
career public servants is derived from the relating of public policy programs to their respective constituents in a manner that makes government
available, open, and interesting to the public. Through the transfer of government services and resources by executive agencies, the public policy
process is made available to designated clientele groups and recipients.
Through the direct, proactive involvement and interaction of career admin-

istrators with the body politic, the public policy process is made open. But how is government—i.e., the public policy process—to be made interesting, especially to the neighbor who is furthest away? The seed germ of this idea was planted many years ago in the writings of Herbert Croly.

In a democracy the people may and will necessarily be asked to submit to discipline, but not to discipline for its own sake. The mass of people will need to have the discipline made interesting to them. They will rightly demand the same motive for submitting to discipline that their conquerors have had. A man can reasonably be asked to impose self-restraint upon himself whenever self-restraint is necessary as a part of a positive and desirable individual or social activity; but he cannot fairly be asked to accept a life of which self-restraint is the preponderant character. That, in substance, is what the social conservators are asking the democracy to accept. The democracy is not listening to them and is quite right in its inattention.[11]

The parallel between the two periods of time—when Croly wrote and now—is striking. At the present time the democracy is not listening to the social conservators who are offering nothing except self-denial, self-restraint, and self-discipline as ends in themselves. Moreover, until government can be made interesting, such pleas by the social conservators will be ignored and the democracy—now, just as before—is quite right in its inattention.

Making government interesting involves something more than simply the mechanistic delivery by public managers of services and resources authorized by the legislative process. It involves even more than the direct solicitation and involvement of the public in the policy process by boundary spanning change agents of public executive branch agencies and bureaus. To make government interesting it must be recognized that the *art* of government is, in fact, a function of the individual citizen while the *craft* of government or management is a function of a professional cadre of public administrators or managers. In other words, to make government interesting, the value of an actively engaged citizenry in the essential characteristics of citizenship becomes a primary—if not *the* primary—responsibility of professional public servants. Specifically, this is to suggest that a basic responsibility and ethical obligation of public administrators and managers is to infuse the individual citizen with the character of citizenship and to provide the citizen with an ethical sense of purpose in the system of democratic governance.

The full import of the proposition being advanced needs to be made quite explicit. What is being suggested is that the art of government, if it is to have any meaning at all as we enter the 21st century, is solely a function of the craft of management which, in turn, must be infused by an ethic

aimed at sustaining a higher order ethic of citizenship. Thus, to make government interesting to the people, the character of citizenship must be
made available, open, and interesting to the individual citizen. To be sure,
the established electoral process provides one avenue for the expression of
citizenship; but, on an ongoing, day-to-day basis involving the intricacies
of the public policy process, the art of government must be and can only be
revitalized by the craft of management.

On the basis of the past 200 years' experience with democratic self-government it is painfully obvious that the diminution of citizenship is inevitable if its preservation and protection are seen as vesting solely in an
elected legislature and an independent judiciary. Such protections as are
provided by these two branches of government are essential but not sufficient to ensure the active involvement of the citizenry in the art of government. To the legislative and judicial mandates of democracy must be added
the role of public management and its primary responsibility to end the
isolation of the individual citizen from the essential character of citizenship. If the craft of management may be seen as amplifying the art of government for the individual citizen, then the character of citizenship may become the energizing force for a new focus of democracy.

This, of course, would depend significantly on the development of a new
definition of publicness. If any serious effort to end the isolation of the individual from a direct, participatory involvement in the democratic
processes of governance is to be considered, a new definition of publicness
must be established. Any such effort, however, is inextricably linked to the
manner in which the notion of the public interest is defined and applied,
for it is the doctrine of the public interest that democracies have utilized effectively for centuries to disguise the harsh pragmatics of the absolutist
doctrine of reason of state.

The Public Interest

Much has been written about the transcendent, subjective, and organic nature of the public interest. In its most extreme form it is manifested in the
manner of Rousseau who could argue with absolute conviction that "the
people" could be unwise but they could never be wrong. This organic view
of the public interest was reflected 200 years ago in the temper of such individuals as Jefferson and Paine. It was subsequently embraced by Emerson, Thoreau, and others in the Transcendentalist movement; by such individuals as Herbert Croly in the later Progressive movement; and by the
international idealists such as Woodrow Wilson and Wendell Willkie. In
short, the past 200 years have taught us that every age, every generation,
gives rise to a renewed effort to implant the organic essence of the public
interest squarely in the objective consciousness of the body politic. Seen in

this context, the essence of the public interest is the lifeblood of democratic civilization; it is the interweaving threat—the life chain—that links together the notions of *civis, civitas,* and *civilitas.*

Needless to say, this notion of the public interest, while persistent, has never been all-persuasive in our commonwealth. The pristine purity of Jefferson was offset by the prudent pragmatism of Madison, and although the humanism of Jefferson persists, the pragmatism of Madison prevails. In the framework of our pluralist-bargaining-incremental system that has evolved from the start of the Republic, that which works is the right and that which is the right is the good. In shaping the doctrine of the public interest in a pluralist context, quantity becomes the benchmark of quality, and that which is desired is readily seen as that which is desirable. The public interest in its organic splendor is a persistent theme in our political rhetoric and is an essential component of our democratic ethos. In the objective world of practical, pragmatic politics, however, it is purely a mechanistic contrivance designed to justify the outcomes of balance of power coalition building and decision making. What should have been learned over the past 200 years of experience with a mechanistically applied doctrine of the public interest is how it has contributed to the degeneration and atrophy of the notions of citizen, citizenship, and the art of government. Thus, if these later notions are seen as a function of the doctrine of the public interest, and the public interest, in turn, is seen as a product of the interacting components of the public policy process, then to revive and refocus the notions of *civis, civitas,* and *civilitas* means to revive and refocus the doctrine of the public interest as well as the public policy process. This is a bold experiment and, as has already been suggested, the logical starting point is with the fourth branch of government, the professional career service. In the next 20 years only the craft of management will be capable of providing the energizing force to revive and refocus the doctrine of the public interest, and in this respect the experiment is venturesome, indeed.

The Nature of Civic Responsibility

We must believe, Walter Lippmann wrote nearly 30 years ago, that,

> Living adults share . . . the same public interest. For them, however, the public interest is mixed with, and is often at odds with, their private and special interests. Put this way, I suggest that the public interest may be presumed to be what men would choose if they saw clearly, thought rationally, acted disinterestedly and benevolently.[12]

The central thesis of pluralist democracy relates directly to Lippmann's basic premise; namely, given the multiple and often conflicting demands made on the adult population of the body politic, civic responsibilities are assigned a low-order priority in importance. Especially in terms of the dimensions of citizenship and the extent of involvement in the art of self-government, the democratic pluralists have made a strong case demonstrating the wide-ranging predominance of a popular attitude of noninvolvement in the public policy process. The choice not to choose, like the decision not to decide, can be said to represent a truer expression of the public interest than that which the civic virtue model so frequently espouses.

The essence of this central thesis of pluralist democracy is imbued with the notion of simplicity. That is to say, its logic is persuasive if: (1) a high degree of stability, continuity, and predictability characterizes the body politic, and (2) there is a steadily expanding (even if only incrementally) national resource base. The absence of the latter can obviously lead to the diminution of the former, but the primary lesson which we most surely should have learned over the past 100 years is that an expanding national resource base can, in fact, generate systemic forces among the body politic which create destabilizing, discontinuous, and unpredictable consequences, complexities, and variety. Thus, as we approach the end of the 20th century, a basic question that needs to be asked is: has the concept of self-government been abrogated because of the boredom associated with its routinized simplicity, or because of the incomprehensibility associated with its ever-increasing complexity and variety? Is it possible to say, with Lippmann, yes, the public interest may be presumed to be what men would choose if they saw clearly, thought rationally, acted disinterestedly and benevolently, except for the fact that the history of our national development for the past 50, if not 100 years may be characterized by the steadily increasing inability of the individual citizen to see clearly, think rationally, or act intelligently—i.e., to understand the intricate complexities of the public policy process.

If complexity rather than simplicity can be argued as a primary cause for the loss of a sense of *civitas* and *civilitas,* can it then be argued that it is therefore incumbent upon the formal components of our governmental system to revive and restore a sense of civic responsibility and citizen involvement?

Chief executives at all levels of government may rightly claim this as their historic function, but the evidence is clear that it is a function dispatched more with oratorical rhetoric than positive operational effects. Moreover, given the nature of representative democracy, legislatures at all levels of government are the historical embodiments of compromise, consensus, and cohesion, although, inevitably, these concepts are applied in a Madisonian matrix involving a multiplicity of fragmented, cross-cutting interest groups. Similarly, our court system, at all levels of government, has proved to be the most articulate explicator of an organic and a transcendent public interest doctrine, but history tells us that the courts are generally reluctant to assume this function as a permanent, ongoing responsibility. This leaves the fourth branch of government—the permanent career service—and the question to be posed at this point is: can the profession of public administration [*text missing in the original*] must include a new and explicit function added to the individual citizen's ability to see clearly, to think rationally, and to act objectively and benevolently on the complexities of the public policy process? Specifically, to what extent can and should public administrators and managers attempt to end the isolation of individual citizens by regenerating a public interest in and comprehension of citizenship and the art of government? For example, Emmette Redford contends that disinterested and benevolent thought can arise only from a feeling of kinship and a capacity for empathy among fellow human beings.[13] Thus, the question can be asked: To what extent can the craft of management be employed to revitalize the art of government, and, even more importantly, to what extent can the character of citizenship be directed to revive the character of kinship as an essential basis for a transcendent and viable concept of the public interest?

Of course, there are many arguments that can be advanced to counter the proposition that public sector administrators and managers should be assigned this responsibility, but if the complexities of the public policy process that confront us at the present (and which certainly give no indication of diminishing in the foreseeable future) can and should be presented to individual citizens for clear and rational thought and for objective, intelligent, and benevolent assessment, this responsibility can only be effectively discharged by permanent, career public servants.

One basic element needed to assume this responsibility is an historical memory stemming from a body of cumulative experience which can be used to explain the complexities of the present in terms of the historical patterns of the past, as well as the projections of the future. Such a perspective is only derived from a professional tenure extending over time. To be sure, such tenure may be found in the legislative and judicial branches of our governments, but the tenure acquired by legislators, for example, results from periodic renewals and is dependent on partisan political skills. Consequently, it is neither uncomplimentary nor inaccurate to say that legislators, with only occasional exceptions, live solely in the present with little regard for the past and even less regard for a future extending beyond the bounds of electoral terms.

Members of the judiciary, in many state and local courts, are subject to the same political vicissitudes as legislators, and, hence, of necessity they must be attuned to the present. Nevertheless, the American legal system is grounded on the concept of *stare decisis* which is a presumptive acknowledgment that, with only rare exceptions, the present is determined by the past. Thus, while the legislative perspective is almost immutably fixed to an eternal present, the judicial perspective is fixed to relating the present to the past. Viewed in this context, it is the professional career service alone that is able to combine past, present, and future into an integrated system which can be made comprehensible to the citizenry. It is the professional managers who are capable of tracing backward the derivations of policy complexities and forward the purposeful nature of policy intentions. It is the professional managers who can best grasp what is being done that should not be done, and what is not being done that should be done. Acting as both transfer agents and change agents, it is the professional managers who have the day-to-day opportunities to end the isolation of the individual citizens, to increase their sense of publicness, and, hence, to expand their sense of freedom.

This is not to argue for a new administrative cadre of 21st century technoscientific centurions. The "new" professional managers being suggested here do have a vital responsibility and function but it is not in the direction of increasing the privateness of power in the hands of a new elite. Rather, it is to make the participatory power of the body politic once again real and meaningful. It is to make government interesting once again to the citizenry. It is to enhance and guard the holistic virtues of any democracy worthy of its name—*civis, civitas, civilitas.*

The new focus for the year 2000 should be clear. It must include a new and explicit function added to the constitutional mandates of the executive branch. In addition to ensuring that the laws are faithfully executed, it must also become the primary responsibility of the permanent career service, at all levels of government, to ensure the vitality of citizenship in an active citizenry fully engaged in the art of government—in short, it must ensure a dynamic revitalization of the concepts of *civis, civitas,* and *civilitas.*

But for what purpose, it may legitimately be asked? And one can only respond that as a result of 200 years experience with the experiment of self-government, it should be clear that the most basic need of any democratic polity is the need for constructive self-criticism. The legislature may make the laws, the judiciary may interpret the laws, and the executive may ensure that the laws are faithfully executed, but only the polity—the citizens, the people—are in the expert position of being able to assess the impact of the public policy process with an astute sense of critical judgment—unless, of course, this most basic of all inalienable rights is deliberately denied by the complexities of the process.

The coming irony of the 21st century is already apparent. The quintessence of the public interest in any democracy is a common interest in the art of self-government which, as is increasingly apparent, can only be attained through a redirection of the craft of management. This necessitates a basic redefinition of public administration as a profession and, as such, it represents a bold departure from the past. Is it the proper function of government to elevate the quality of *civitas* in our society? Is it the proper function of public administration to enhance the character of *civilitas* in our polity? The answers to these questions will determine how we begin the year 2000.

Notes

1. F.J.C. Hearnshaw, ed., *Medieval Contributions to Modern Civilisation* (London: George G. Harrap & Co., Ltd., 1981), p. 19.

2. *Ibid.*, 15.

3. It could be argued that medieval Christianity, with its primary focus on the salvation of *individual* souls, attempted to develop a corporatist notion of the collectivity—e.g., the church as the corporate body of Christ. While the theological validity of this distinction may be recognized, the operational distinction when the church is viewed as a socio-political organization is modest, at best.

4. Carl J. Friedrich, *Constitutional Reason of State* (Providence: Brown University Press, 1957), 6, 4–5.

5. Hans Kelsen, "Absolutism and Relativism in Philosophy and Politics," *The American Political Science Review*, XLII (October 1948), p. 910.

6. The literature on The New Public Administration and by the "new public administrationists" is widely scattered in texts, monographs, and journal articles. George Frederickson's most recent book, *New Public Administration* (University of Alabama Press, 1980), is the most convenient starting point for an inquiry in this area.

7. Dietrich Bonhoeffer, *Ethics* (New York: Macmillan Publishing Co., 1955), 259.

8. Herman Finer, "Administrative Responsibility in Democratic Government," *Public Administration Review*, 1 (Summer 1941), 337.

9. Norton Long, *The Polity* (Chicago: Rand McNally & Co., 1962), pp. 71–72.

10. This refers to the Finer article cited supra that was written in response to the argument advanced by Carl J. Friedrich that administrative responsibility is essentially a matter of individual self-responsibility in accord with professional standards. See Friedrich, "Public Policy and the Nature of Administrative Responsibility," *Public Policy* (Cambridge: Harvard University Press, 1940), pp. 3–24.

11. Herbert Croly, *Progressive Democracy* (New York: Macmillan Publishing Co., 1914), pp. 414–415.

12. Walter Lippmann, *Essays in the Public Philosophy* (Boston: Little, Brown & Co., 1955), p. 42.

13. Emmette S. Redford, ed., "The Never-Ending Search for the Public Interest," *Ideals and Practice in Public Administration* (University of Alabama Press, 1958), p. 114.

INDEX